Domesday Studies

The Norman Conquest and its effects on the economy: 1066–86

By the same author

The Domesday Inquest and the Making of Domesday Book
An Introduction to Domesday Book
Domesday Studies: The *Liber Exoniensis*
Domesday Studies: The Eastern Counties

Domesday Studies

The Norman Conquest and its effects on the economy: 1066–86

R. Welldon Finn, M.A.

Sometime Scholar of Peterhouse, Cambridge

Archon Books
1971

Published throughout the world, except the United States,
by Longman Group Ltd.

© R. Welldon Finn 1970

First published in the United States by Archon Books, 1971

ISBN 0 208 01154 4
Printed in Great Britain

Almae matri,
apud quam illam et corporis et mentis
disciplinam Rossalliensam hausi,
hunc per libellum non immeritas solvo

Contents

Preface	xi
List of maps	xiii

Part I
The contribution and limitations of Domesday Book

1	The England of the Norman Conquest	3
2	The information of Domesday Book	6
3	The course and character of the invasion of 1066	19
4	Further factors affecting a study of the economy	23
	Waste	
	Ploughlands and plough-teams	
5	Domesday cartography	32

Part II
The details of Domesday Book

1	The South-East	39
	Kent	41
	Surrey	51
	Sussex	56
	Hampshire	64
	The New Forest	71
	The Isle of Wight	74
	Berkshire	78
2	The South Midlands	84
	Buckinghamshire	85
	Bedfordshire	91
	Cambridgeshire	96
	Hertfordshire	103
	Middlesex	107

CONTENTS

3 The West Midlands — 115
  Oxfordshire — 117
  Warwickshire — 122
  Worcestershire — 127
  Gloucestershire — 133

4 The March Counties — 140
  Herefordshire — 142
  Shropshire — 152
  Cheshire — 168

5 The North Midlands — 176
  Staffordshire — 177
  Derbyshire — 181
  Nottinghamshire — 186

6 The Northern Counties — 193
  Yorkshire: West Riding — 199
  Yorkshire: East Riding — 203
  Yorkshire: North Riding — 207
  Craven — 210
  North Lancashire, Westmorland, and Cumberland — 210
  South Lancashire — 211
  Lincolnshire — 211

7 The East Midlands — 221
  Huntingdonshire — 222
  Leicestershire — 227
  Northamptonshire — 233
  Rutland — 240

8 The Eastern Counties — 242
  Essex — 249
  Suffolk — 259
  Norfolk — 268

9 The South-West — 276
  Wiltshire — 277
  Dorset — 282
  Somerset — 286
  Devonshire — 294
  Cornwall — 299

Bibliography — 306

Index — 313

Abbreviations frequently used in the text

DB	Domesday Book
DBB	F. W. Maitland: *Domesday Book and Beyond*
Dom. Geog.	H. C. Darby et al.: *The Domesday Geography of England*
EHR	*English Historical Review*
ICC	*Inquisitio Comitatus Cantabrigiensis*
IE	*Inquisitio Eliensis*
VCH	The *Victoria County Histories*

Page references for the texts of William of Poitiers and of Orderic Vitalis are to the editions of Foreville and Chibnall as detailed in the bibliography.

Preface

Any study concerned chiefly with the economic and social effects of the Norman Conquest must be dependent for its material largely on the text of Domesday Book, and especially on that portion which deals with manorial valuations and rents, and with statistics of population and ploughlands and the oxen who drag the plough. The values attributed to property, and payments for the use of land generally, have in the past received somewhat scant attention, which in view of the difficulties involved is perhaps intelligible. If this study poses as many problems as it endeavours to solve, and frequently offers only tentative conclusions, it is none the less an honest attempt at tackling problems which in many books are only lightly indicated or are dismissed within the space of an occasional paragraph. Since it is admittedly pioneer work, it is to be hoped that it may someday furnish the basis for an entirely satisfactory study of the subject. As John Milton said: 'where there is much desire to learn, there of necessity will be much arguing ... many opinions; for opinion ... is but knowledge in the making'.

It would be perfectly possible for two people to study and sum the statistics of Domesday Book and arrive at markedly different results. Disagreement could arise over the inclusion or omission of a potentially 'duplicate' entry, or as regards the interpretation of the material, especially where a manor includes sub-tenancies the figures of which may or may not be covered by those of the main entry. One man might see from fifty to a hundred plough-teams in a large county where another would see none, or would omit some quantities where to an alternative student the figures would appear to be orthodox. No slaves are recorded in the Huntingdonshire text, yet the *Inquisitio Eliensis* suggests that there might have been about the same proportion as in neighbouring shires. We could still be quite seriously in error about some of the conclusions drawn from the Inquest documents if we misinterpret the condensed formulae and statements and feel that more than we suspect is missing from them.

The boroughs of Anglo-Norman England have been largely excluded,

PREFACE

except where their rural attributes seem to be germane to this study. The payments made both from and for burghal property, to the king and his lieutenants, are so heterogeneous that they prevent any comparison of the liabilities of one borough with another, even as regards towns of similar status and size. The occasional creation of 'new boroughs' adjacent to the former territory of a town, and the destruction of property where fortification had been constructed or extended, also militate against comparison of 1066 with 1086.

I have to thank the Leverhulme Trustees for a Research Award which enabled me to undertake this study over an extended period, and for many courtesies during its tenure. My debt to Professor Darby and his team for their *Domesday Geography of England* will be obvious. If we seem to be in occasional disagreement, that is because the geographer and the historian do not always interpret in the same way. I am most grateful to Mr G. R. Versey of the Department of Geography, Cambridge University, not only for re-drawing my draft maps, but also for the time he has spent in considering their original form and his valuable suggestions regarding them, though their scope and form should not be regarded as his responsibility. To all those scholars who over the last thirty years have debated Domesday problems with me I also offer my sincere thanks.

Frinton-on-Sea   R.W.F.
Feast of St Thomas Aquinas, 1969

List of Maps

Fig.		Page
1	The Tendring Hundred and district Fall, 1066–86, in (a) value, (b) teams, (c) villeins, (d) recorded population	15
2	Central Hertfordshire (a) Fall in value *tunc–post*, (b) fall in value *tunc–modo*, (c) team deficiency 1086, (d) holdings showing increase or no change in value *tunc–modo*	16
3	Suggested routes used by invading forces Nov.–Dec., 1066	21
4	Kent and East Surrey Fall in value *tunc–post*	44
5	Sussex and south-east Hampshire Fall in value *tunc–post*	59
6	The Winchester campaign Fall in value *tunc–post*	65
7	The move from Winchester to Wallingford Fall in value *tunc–post*	66
8	The move from Winchester to Wallingford Fall in value *tunc–modo*	67
9	The move from Winchester to Wallingford Team deficiency, 1086	80
10	The South Midlands: western section Fall in value *tunc–post*	86
11	The South Midlands: western section Team deficiency, 1086	87
12	The South Midlands: eastern section Fall in value *tunc–post*	92
13	The South Midlands: eastern section Team deficiency, 1086	93
14	The masking of London on the south and west: western section Fall in value *tunc–post*	108

LIST OF MAPS

15	The masking of London on the south and west: eastern section	
	Fall in value *tunc–post*	109
16	The West Midlands: Warwick area	
	Fall in value *tunc–post* and *tunc–modo*	123
17	The Northern Cotswolds	
	Fall in value 1066–86	135
18	The March Shires: southern section	
	Fall in value *tunc–post*	154
19	The March Shires: southern section	
	Fall in value 1066–86	155
20	The Severn–Wye area	
	Increase in value *post–modo* and waste in 1086	159
21	Cheshire with north Shropshire and Staffordshire	
	Fall in value *tunc–post*	166
22	Cheshire with north Shropshire and Staffordshire	
	Fall in value 1066–86	167
23	The North Midlands: western section	
	Fall in value 1066–86	182
24	The North Midlands: eastern section	
	Fall in value 1066–86	187
25	South Yorkshire	
	Fall in value 1066–86	201
26	Lincolnshire and east Nottinghamshire	
	Fall in value 1066–86	213
27	Domesday Leicestershire	
	valuit as percentage of *valet*	230
28	Domesday Northamptonshire and Rutland	
	valuit as percentage of *valet*	234
29	Domesday Leicestershire, Northamptonshire, and Rutland	
	Fall in value 1066–86, and waste	236
30	Domesday Essex	
	Fall in value 1066–86	250
31	East Anglia	
	Holdings with fall in value 1066–86	262
32	Section of Domesday Somerset	
	Holdings with fall in value *olim–modo*	289
33	East Cornwall and West Devon	
	Holdings with fall in value *olim–modo*	301

The contribution and limitations of Domesday Book

Part I

'The scholar who wishes to organise a mass of details into a comprehensive unity is faced by the prospect that it will evoke less assent than dispute. There is certain to be in it a subjective element, due to his own predilections, or the incompleteness of the evidence.'

C. M. Bowra: *Memories*, p. 260

apparent for a few years only, or for several decades. That the Norman Conquest formidably affected the people of England, of whatever degree, both socially and economically, can hardly be denied. But its deleterious effect on the general well-being and economy of the realm has been widely assumed to have been of only short duration. One historian has suggested that 'the apparent drop in the value of land did not amount to much', taking the country as a whole, and another has written of 'the sudden and enormous increase in value'.[1]

Taken at their face value, the figures of Domesday Book show considerable apparent increase in the value of manors over much of England south of the Trent, even in some shires which Duke William's ruthless invading army had traversed. The figures, more often than not, show us a *valet* higher than a *valuit*, frequently very much higher, and not rarely a willingness, implying that full potential had not yet been reached, to rent a property for a sum higher than that of the value set on it. We might so easily say that here is an England which has recovered from the storms of the Conquest and often from the punitive measures imposed upon rebels, which on the whole is more prosperous than it had been in the more tranquil days of the Confessor and possessing latent capabilities yet to be developed.

But from the Englishman's point of view, the Norman Conquest was a catastrophe. Whatever Domesday Book may seem to say, the author of the *Dialogus* thought so, and so did that judicious lawyer Bracton. The chroniclers leave us in no doubt as to the immediate effects of the foreign influx.[2] They comment on the conduct of the king's lieutenants, Odo of Bayeux and William fitzOsbern, and of their followers. The newcomers 'distressed the wretched folk, and always after that it grew much worse'. Orderic deplored the miseries which Normans and English alike inflicted upon England at the time of the rebellions, and the pitiful fate of non-combatants. The English of Yorkshire and Lincolnshire seem deliberately to have received scant protection from Danish raids, and the welfare of monastic tenants and peasants must have suffered when 'King William had all the monasteries plundered'. His obituary stresses his forcible extraction of vast sums from his people 'mostly unjustly and for little need', and Bishop Robert of Hereford noted 'the many calamities which vexed the land through the collection of the royal money'. Meagre though

---

[1] H. R. Loyn: *Anglo-Saxon England*, p. 319; P. Vinogradoff: *English Society in the 11th Century*, p. 382. The latter claimed also that 'the increase in value . . . is so striking that there must have been a considerable addition to the quantity of labour performed for the lord' (*op. cit.*, p. 315).
[2] We must, of course, allow for an anti-Norman bias in some chroniclers, especially Orderic, and in the *Liber Eliensis*.

the information of Domesday Book (hereinafter DB) regarding the boroughs is, it suggests that many English townsmen could have added their complaints to those of the Shrewsbury burgesses (252ai). Nor do weather conditions seem to have made for prosperity. Famine is mentioned as occurring in 1070 and 1082, and the *Anglo-Saxon Chronicle* notes with details 1086 as having been 'a very severe year'. The destruction of much of London by fire in 1077 must have affected both internal and external trade and the market for rural produce.

The Conquest and subsequent rebellions directly affected a minimum of twenty-five counties, and except for the south-west DB enables us to see how steeply land-values dropped as a result of its immediate effects. Some pregnant statements were made by Fowler, and though he was referring to the invasion of 1066, they apply to subsequent campaigns also. 'There was no commissariat', he wrote, 'and the army had to find its daily food in the seed-corn and plough-oxen of the nearest vill. Nor could it move in a compact body, for that would mean starvation; it must break into columns with a common rendezvous.'[1] Thus local damage would be both intensive and extensive. The Conqueror's treatment of the northern shires is apparent fifteen years after the first fury of his vengeance, and the havoc the newcomers and their adversaries had caused was then still largely unrepaired. But in the shires immediately north and west of London, though a score of years had passed since these had experienced major military operations, a general failure to recover the prosperity of King Edward's day is apparent, while the March shires had by no means attained the standards they had enjoyed before the advent of the Norman and the Mercian rebellions. The *Anglo-Saxon Chronicle* tells us that after the descent of the rebel Northumbrians in 1065 'Northamptonshire and the neighbouring shires were for many winters the worse'. Much of England must have been far more grievously stricken in 1066–71 than Northamptonshire had been by a movement of limited scope. It seems unlikely that the disturbed reign of the Conqueror's second son would encourage general recovery from the Conquest's effects.

Invasion, conquest, and rebellion inevitably brought in their train the burning of farm buildings and implements and produce, the requisitioning and slaughter of livestock, and some diminution of the population. Though all were comparatively readily replaceable, lack of capital and lowered resistance to disease would decelerate recovery. Probably labour services and rents and obligations were increased by the newcomers wherever possible, and while these might swell a baron's income, they

[1] G. H. Fowler: 'The devastation of Bedfordshire and the neighbouring counties in 1065 and 1066' (*Archaeologia*, lxxii, 1922, pp. 41–50).

could only decrease a people's material standards. The *minores populi*, the *Liber Eliensis* (II.101) tells us, were inhumanly treated by King William and his followers, and economic desperation as well as Norman greed and harshness must have been as great a governing factor in the inspiration of native revolt as were patriotism and love of freedom.

The value of a manor was not necessarily increased because it was now more efficiently administered and its potential was being more adequately realised. It rose, often enough, because conquered men formerly free had been compelled to perform the labour services which were the burden of the unfree; because there was little to prevent the lord, through his officials, from demanding increased services from those who had always owed them; because, following the royal example of 'letting his land as dearly as he could', landowners were demanding excessive rents and leasing properties at sums much above their fair value. To recoup his outlay the lessee could only extract higher rents and more onerous services from his peasantry and try to work the estate more efficiently. A diminution in the number of slaves does not imply Norman concern for their miseries; it implies rather that much which was formerly slave-labour was now being performed by men who were not classed as slaves. The wealth of England may not have been so vastly different in 1086 from what it had been in 1066. But, like the land on which it depended, it had been redistributed, and those natives who profited thereby were an infinitesimal minority.

2
The information of Domesday Book

So far as the temporary effects are concerned, we are dependent largely on such information as DB provides. It is common ground that some of this is not to be trusted, and that much which should have been included therein is absent from the text. But it would be folly to regard its figures as of only doubtful value. They are so comprehensive that errors induced by their use must be proportionately of only slight account. 'Domesday geographers' have been encouraged to 'face the question of the validity of their statistics', which suggests that either these must be accepted or the text altogether rejected as a source.[1] No middle course presents itself.

The three principal features of DB which can afford some idea of regional and local prosperity and changes therein during the reign of William I are the values of holdings, the extent to which agricultural capacity was being exploited, and the social and economic standing of small tenants and villagers.

The values of holdings as given in DB present so many problems that it is hardly surprising that the subject has been treated somewhat cursorily by most commentators. The information is frequently altogether frustrating and sometimes unintelligible, many figures we need are absent from the record, and for far too many entries we have no means of comparing the pre-Conquest level with that of the Inquest.

At first sight there might seem to be singularly little of a logical character about the sums at which holdings are valued. Manors with equal values in 1086 display wide variation in the figures for ploughlands, plough-teams, recorded inhabitants, and manorial appurtenances. But really this is only to be expected. Soil-differences would largely govern the number of oxen required for tillage. The labour that ten men might be expected to provide on one manor might be shared between twenty elsewhere. Even the average age of the inhabitants might here be a factor influencing prosperity. Certainly the proportions of the varied classes of the population would affect the amount of labour-service, of rents and dues, and the whole character of the economy. Few holdings could operate without the existence of local woodland, pasture, and meadow, but it is altogether impossible to estimate the total or relative contribution of these to the value of a manor. Sometimes the amount a portion of one of these adjuncts was producing in rent or dues is given, but as a rule nothing is said which might indicate either that this formed a supplement to the value set upon the manor or was included therein.

The initial problem is to try to determine the implication of the amounts set down, and of this we must often be uncertain. Maitland considered that those responsible for them asked themselves 'what will this estate bring in, peopled as it is and stocked as it is', and that they are the answers to the question 'what rent would a *firmarius* pay for this

[1] V. H. Galbraith: *The Making of Domesday Book*, p. 222.

estate stocked as it is?'[1] The clerks, especially those of the Exeter Domesday, seem to have regarded *reddit* and *valet* as interchangeable terms.[2] But a lord's steward may have had a conception of value very different from that of a Hundred-jury or of villar representatives. One man might wish to put it high, hoping to obtain the full sum of his valuation for a lease of it; another might think that the lower it was pitched, the less chance of his burdens being increased by reason of his apparent prosperity. Disagreement about the equity of fair valuation is not infrequently noted in the text.[3]

Then, while some of the amounts include odd shillings and pence, suggesting that often they are the sum of actual rents and dues, while others represent conventional conversions of a day's maintenance of lord and household in terms of money, the great majority are in integral numbers of pounds, and so may seem to be arbitrary approximations. When we consider also values *tunc* or *post* or *olim* or *quando* (*cum*) *recepit*, we cannot escape the horrible suspicion that often the responsible parties either knew nothing about past conditions, or did not trouble to discover or estimate them, and so tendered either an arbitrary figure or one which was that of the current valuation or near to it. Within fols. 24a2–5ai, for example, there are 25 consecutive entries giving triple valuations of which 16 show no change at any time, which seems as improbable as it does that none of the four Goring estates (24b2, 25ai) should have altered in value at any time.

Complex manors furnish another problem. Only comparatively rarely are we given the values of their components, and thus it may be that while the manor as a whole was worth more in 1086 than it had been previously, some of its subordinate vills and hamlets had, possibly for varying reasons, in fact fallen in value. It is only occasionally that we are told of the values of the constituent portions of a manor; e.g. the vill of Whitchurch (41ai) had appreciated, while Freefolk, Witnal, and two unnamed places, components of the manor, had become worth less. Nor, when the value of a manor church is given separately, do we know whether this was sometimes included in the manorial valuation or not. Combined values for a manor with its single distant berewick are of frequent occurrence (e.g. Bocking with Mersea, II.8).

---

[1] F. W. Maitland: *Domesday Book and Beyond*, pp. 413, note 3 (478, note 1), and 444, note 2 (511, note 2); he characteristically added 'but there are many difficulties'. Initial references to this book are to the original edition published by the Cambridge University Press, those in parentheses to the Fontana edition issued by Collins.
[2] e.g. the *reddit* of fol. *337* of the Exeter text is *valet* on Exchequer 114ai. It refers to a villein's obligation at Lank Combe.
[3] Particular examples of generalisations such as this in this section are given in the sections dealing with individual shires.

Some figures are obviously erroneous, and others suggestive of clerical lapses. Cookham (56b2) is said to have been worth only 50*s.* after the Conquest, but since it had been worth £50 in 1066 and was still worth £36 in 1086, and was rated at 20 hides, 50*s.* should probably have been £50. We can perhaps envisage Bramshill (48ai) as falling in value from £2 to 2*s.* 1*d.*, though the 25*d.* could be a mistake for 25*s.*, especially as the value *post* had been 20*s.* 5*d.*, the mill was worth 25*d.*, and the holding had been absorbed in the royal manor of Swallowfield in the neighbouring county. But what could make the modern Newbury (*Ulvritone*, 62b2) appreciate from £9 to £24 if the extent of the manor or its burdens had remained unaltered?

A possible explanation of some of the more spectacular increases in value is that the given figures may not all refer to the same moment in time. The text rarely gives us a hint of this, but it does frequently indicate that many a manor had been enlarged since 1066 by the incorporation therein of holdings which had then not been part of it, and had themselves often enjoyed the status of manors. If the 1066 value is that of the manor as it had been, but that of the Inquest a figure appropriate to its enlarged content, many apparently spectacular rises in value are intelligible. So are some depreciated values. The 33-hide royal manor of Wargrave (57a2) had been worth £31 in 1066, but a priest had somehow transferred a hide, perhaps the church land, and 'put it in a manor of his lord', Geoffrey de Manneville. By 1086 the manor had lost £3 13*s.* 4*d.* of its former value. It is perhaps suggestive that Geoffrey's manor of Streatley (62ai) was not very far from the *caput* of what was probably a complex and dispersed royal manor, and that at Streatley a priest had a hide worth £2 10*s.*, while the manor had gone up in value from £20 to £24. Thus some apparent increases in value are probably misleading, and so it might be that manorial components were worth less than before in many instances where we would seem to see appreciation.

It is often difficult to decide whether occasional items mentioned in the text should be added to a valuation or considered to be already reckoned in it. This is of frequent occurrence where the value of the church is given separately, since often a church is mentioned but its value is not given. Fortunately, with large manors where much of the land was leased to tenants, we are usually told that the 1066 value is that of the manor as a whole, and then for 1086 we are given the value of the demesne, the unleased portion, and separately the values of the tenancies, individually or as a whole. The 'whole manor' of Micheldever (42b) had been worth £60 in 1066, but after the Conquest its value was £20 less. The demesne of the abbot was in 1086 worth £57, but there were also seven tenancies for each of which the 1086 value is given, and which were worth a further £37. We are even told that 'in another place' Ælfsige had acquired a hide of the demesne land, for which four villeins paid 7s. It is unlikely that we should in most cases be wrong in treating the values of tenancies as not included in any valuation given earlier in the text. There were three tenants at Midgham (61b2), and we are told that the value given is for the whole manor. On the other hand, it is not impossible that the appreciation at, e.g., Uffington (59a2), first from £15 to £21 and then to £26, was in part because the six hides out of fourteen which Gilbert held were not reckoned in the 1066 value. Large increases in value in the Berkshire Downs are extremely uncommon. It may, too, seem strange that between 1066 and the time described as *post* the huge manor of Cumnor (58bi) should go up in value from £30 to £50, one of only eight Berkshire manors to show appreciation, when one of its components, Seacourt, fell from 100s. to 70s., though both were worth more in 1086, while two more fell by $33\frac{1}{3}$ per cent and 50 per cent respectively between 1066 and 1086.

The formulae used invite varying interpretations. In the shires in which we are frequently given triple valuations, *tunc*, *post* or *quando recepit*, and *modo*, we also find intermittently *valet et valuit*, or *val. semper*. The last might be thought to imply that the value had throughout remained unchanged, but it could well be that no attempt was made to estimate previous values, especially if it was known that they had not changed much. Longworth (*Orda*, 59a2) is said 'always' to have been and to be worth £15. But for about half the abbey of Abingdon's other Berkshire holdings we are given only two values, and some of these display no alteration between 1066 and 1086, and others only a slight one. Thus *valet et valuit* could at least at times imply that the witnesses did not know, or did not care, what the real value in 1066 or later might have been. On the other hand, e.g. on fol. 60ai, where this phrase recurs, a number of holdings are said to have equal values *tunc et modo*, or a change in value is reported. *Valuit semper* may to some have covered only 1066 and 1086. Professor Darlington has pointed out that the *valuit* of Sutton Veny (72ai) is shown by the Exeter Domesday (*47*) to imply *quando recepit* (*VCH*: Wiltshire, i, p. 44). Indeed, collation shows that the *valuit* or *olim* of the Exchequer text is usually *quando recepit* in the Exeter version.

The indefiniteness of *post*, *olim*, *quando recepit*, adds to the difficulties. The first would seem to imply a time not greatly distant from 1066, but there might well have been appreciable difference between the value of a holding ravaged in October, 1066, and that of four or five years later. There is one slender hint that to one clerk *post* implied a moment earlier than that described as *quando recepit*. In the entry for Sutton (23b2) *post*

THE INFORMATION OF DOMESDAY BOOK

has been deleted and *cum recepit* interlined. Probably *olim* refers to the date when the holder at the Inquest received the manor, or perhaps when it was let to a sub-tenant, but, like *quando recepit*, the term must cover a variety of dates. We have small idea as to when the various tenants-in-chief may have received their estates. There may have been appreciable difference between the dates of direct grant to Robert of Mortain and of his acquisition of the manors of Brian of Penthièvre, or of his obtaining holdings to which he was not legally entitled. A pre-Inquest valuation of Church property may refer to the date when a bishop or abbot took office. We cannot be certain how to punctuate a phrase such as *T.R.E. valebat c solidos et post et modo lx solidos*. Probably the value was 60s. *post et modo*, but it might be that a comma should be inserted after *post*.

Another difficulty is presented by parallel entries. These are not always recognisable, nor, when land had been added to or taken away from a manor, is it always possible to discover a further passage in a different *breve* which describes it. This may sometimes cause the use of figures which are higher than they should be. Littleton (66a2) was worth £7, and this was the bishop of Coutances's holding said to be worth the same sum which had been part of Glastonbury Abbey's manor of Grittleton (66bi). These entries and some others are readily discernible as referring to a single property, but there must be very many duplicates which it is impossible to identify. Sometimes slight changes in the circumstances or extent of the holding produce sums not necessarily identical. Thus while we must avoid counting the Littleton holding twice, we cannot be certain about Urso's $4\frac{1}{2}$ hides of the manor of Grittleton. Elsewhere he was Arnulf of Hesdin's tenant (*Chenebuild*, 70ai; Hill Deverill, 70a2; Heytesbury geld account, *ib*, *8*, *14*), so these might be part of Arnulf's manor of Easton Piercy (70a2) close to Grittleton. Equally Richard Poingiant's $7\frac{1}{2}$ hides worth £7 at Trow Farm (73a2) must not be reckoned as well as his holding in the manor of Chalke (68ai), for though one entry records four teams and the other five, they refer to the same place.

There remain a few more points for discussion. Frequently the values of mills, fisheries, and other manorial attributes are provided. It is, I think, unlikely that these were normally included in the amount stated to be the value of the manor. For frequently the phrase *de censu* is tacked on to the sum said to be the worth of such an adjunct, or it is said that a mill is *sine censu*, or that it 'serves the hall'. Such property could be put out to rent where the lord did not wish to have it operated as part of the manorial economy, so that any sum quoted is presumably that at which it would be rented or was in fact being rented. We are told, for example, that the payment for 50 acres of pasture at Whitestaunton (*265b*) was four blooms of iron, for wood and pasture at Guiting (167b2) forty hens, and for pasture at King's Somborne (39bi) 17s. But so many entries do not mention such equipment in places where we should expect to find it (e.g. no salt-pans are recorded in Somerset), that it would be unsafe to assume that absence from the text implies that there was none. Often its worth may have been included in the value ascribed to the manor.

For there is much which DB does not mention yet which must have been in existence. A warren, we may think, would normally be of profit only to the lord, yet though there must have been many, only one is recorded (Gelston, 347b2). There must have been many more markets than are noted, but it is only in some towns and large villages that we hear of them and of the dues payable to the man who had the power to grant market-rights and to extract tolls. It is most unlikely that there was no market at Leicester or Bedford or Colchester, but none is mentioned in DB.

It is indeed somewhat doubtful if valuations were always, or even generally, a matter for the lord or his bailiff. On a few occasions it is said that no return for the property was furnished. Sometimes the Hundred-jury was called upon to give its view of a fair valuation. Occasionally disagreement about this between different panels of assessors is recorded, but the Inquest officials do not seem to have pronounced judgment as to which estimate was the more equitable one. This is of such infrequent occurrence that either it was commonly thought to be not worth while to challenge valuations, or agreement regarding fair value had already been reached.

We do indeed sometimes find contrast expressed between what is said to be the value and what the owner was actually receiving, and the difference between the amounts is often an appreciable one. It is sometimes so great that it is hard to see how anyone could have been induced to rent a manor at a price so much above the stated value, unless he intended to exploit it far more thoroughly than the owner had been doing. But equally in some instances it may be that the lord was in fact already wringing the higher sum from his dependants and peasantry. For we are told in some such entries that the manor 'could not bear' the sum imposed, or that those who leased it were ruined by doing so. Sometimes the 1086 value is a figure lower than a previous return, as though an attempt to extract an unreasonable sum had failed.

The effect of assessment on valuations needs to be taken into account. Maitland described the geld as 'a momentous force capable of depressing and displacing whole classes of men'.[1] Here he was undoubtedly right, and

[1] *DBB*, p. 25 (49).

the heavy gelds of King William's reign must have left the surviving thegns and peasant-farmers and villeins much poorer than they would have been if there had been no Conquest. But the capacity and resilience of England is perhaps shown by the fact that frequent heavy gelds could be collected.

But this is not the only factor to be considered. In counties which were heavily over-rated, such as Wiltshire and Leicestershire, valuations may be found to be below the norm, and surely the amount of geld a man would have to find would be a factor in his decision whether to rent and farm a manor or not, and at what price. Then there is the effect of beneficial hidation. If much of the geld had been excused, a manor would be likely to be more valuable than one equally assessed but which enjoyed no exemption. With this must be coupled the amount of fiscal demesne, about which we know little, outside the south-western circuit, but which, since it was arbitrary in quantity, must also have affected value. The fact that a landholder may have extracted geld from his dependants irrespective of immunity nullifies what may seem to be apparent exemptions. We can hardly compare hidage with *valet* and stress the differences in one against equalities in the other, for too many factors, including the actual amount of geld due, affect the comparison.

Sometimes we may think we can see just how crippling the geld could be. Sbern's virgate at Frustfield (74a2) was worth only fifteenpence, yet the geld of a virgate, on the occasion for which we have geld accounts, was threepence more. What gross income would Sbern need to be able to find such a tax without being financially ruined? We cannot suppose that he had much surplus produce to sell. A Great Somerford holding (73b2) was worth 40*d.*; its geld-liability was 3*s*. The geld accounts frequently show us the *villani regis* as not paying geld, and if this implies, even only occasionally, that they were exempt, such immunity might add considerably to the value of royal manors.

A factor in Domesday valuations which has been somewhat neglected by commentators is the frequency with which they are based on the *ora* of sixteenpence, the Danish unit of accountancy. Even cursory consideration of Domesday quantities has for long shown how frequently it appears as the basis of the valuations or rents of mills, fisheries, and saltpans. Well over one-third of the values of Lincolnshire mills or parts thereof rented at less than £1 are of from one to thirteen *orae*; many of the remainder, e.g. those of 8*d*., 2*s*., probably were based on the half-*ora*. High values also work out at exact multiples, e.g. 21*s*. 4*d*., 25*s*. 4*d*., 26*s*. 8*d*., 37*s*. 4*d*., and we find also 24*s*., 32*s*.[1] But the *ora* enters also into manorial values and

[1] Quarrington (346bi), Kirkby Green with Scopwick (361a2), Ganthorpe (366b2), Houghton (368ai), Winteringham (354bi).

land-rents to a somewhat surprising extent, and while we are accustomed to its regular appearance in Anglo-Danish shires, its use is far more widespread than might be expected. It is, for example, extremely prevalent in the shires bordering Wales, but many Welsh statistics derive from a factor of eight. In the northernmost three, integral multiples of this unit occur in nearly one-third of the sums under £1, and fractional multiples in almost a further quarter. Coupled with the fact that almost all the remaining small values are multiples of twenty pence, suspicion is created that the system of demanding in counted coin this sum for each *ora* due, to compensate or over-compensate for light or worn coins, was not confined to payments from royal manors. These last have recently been considered in detail and the implications of the phrase *de xx in ora*, etc., shown to be a royal device to avoid possible loss of revenue.[1]

In view of all these uncertainties, we may well wonder whether the figures of DB may be used with profit to deduce changes between the Conquest and the Inquest, or whether they could be too deceptive. Long study of them convinces me that over the vast range of statistics serious misapprehension is unlikely. The results obtained, of course, almost certainly vary considerably from those which full information would produce. I very much doubt, however, where they suggest, for example, a fall in values for a shire after the Conquest of 25 per cent, that we should then discover that it should be as little as 15 per cent or as much as 35 per cent. For when the results for the various categories of information are compared, and more especially translated into the form of maps, they induce, for any shire, results which are by no means incompatible with the ideas which would have been forced on us even if DB had never been compiled, and which within obvious limitations tell a consistent tale. For where the ploughland figures suggest approximation to reality, the proportion of teams at work to ploughlands presents a picture not dissimilar to that furnished by falls in value, and it is on the whole those shires which suffered in 1066 which had failed to recover the standards of King Edward's day by the time of the Inquest.

A vivid illustration of the manner in which the valuation, teams, and population figures of DB harmonise is provided by Tendring Hundred in north-east Essex and the country nearby. It was a district in which both values and recorded population fell slightly after the Conquest, in contrast to the increase over the bulk of the county, and teams appreciably. It is certainly suggestive that out of 52 entries furnishing usable information 25 per cent show a decline in all three of these items, and 61½ per cent in two of them.

[1] S. Harvey: 'Royal Revenue and Domesday Terminology' (*Econ. Hist. Rev.*, 2nd. ser., xx, no. 2, 1967).

THE INFORMATION OF DOMESDAY BOOK

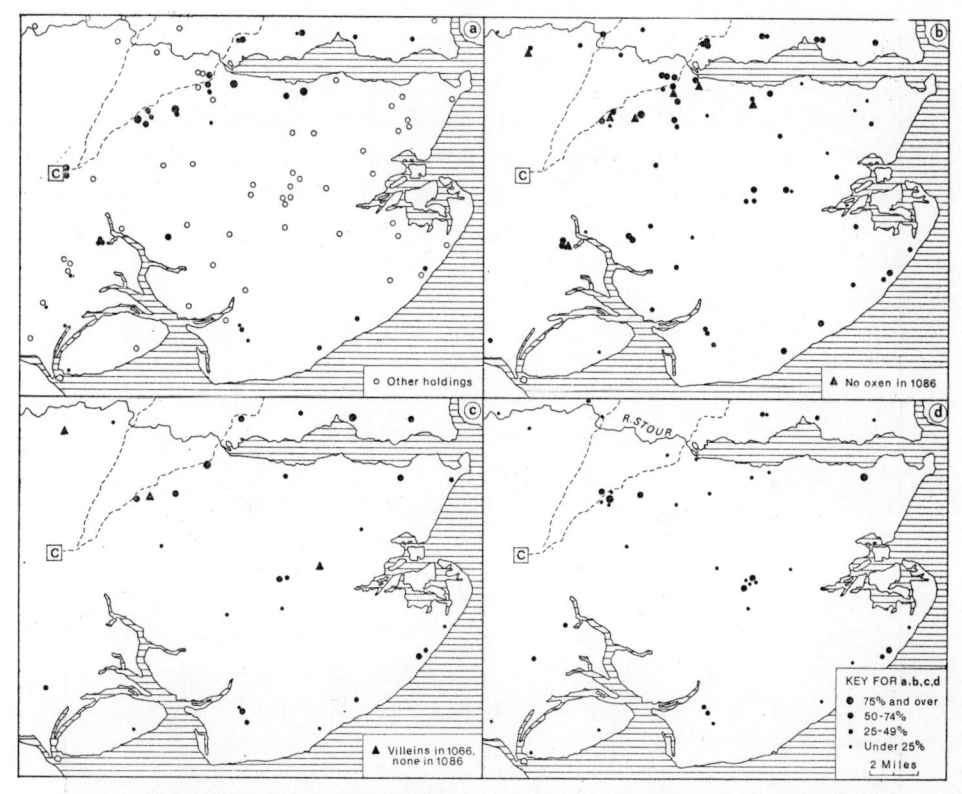

Fig. 1 The Tendring Hundred and district
Fall, 1066–86, in (a) value, (b) teams, (c) villeins, (d) recorded population
C—Colchester   – – – Colchester – Ipswich roads

Fig. 1 shows, moreover, that the distribution-pattern is largely constant for all four categories, supplementing the above with the fall in the number of villeins. The two areas in which decline is most frequent are the coastal district and the line of the Colchester—Ipswich road as this approaches the crossing of the Stour, while it is slightly less marked along the Stour estuary. We might guess that the first and last could have been caused in part by seaborne raiders or were the result of the royal order to devastate the coastal holdings to deny sustenance to the potential invaders of 1085, and the second to some military emergency, possibly that of 1075.

There is a minor concentration of symbols for fewer teams and inhabitants in the neighbourhood of Tendring itself, but which is absent from the map of falls in value. For the six holdings concerned, the increase in value was comparatively small, and may reflect increased demands rather than a real improvement in prosperity. Since on the whole Essex

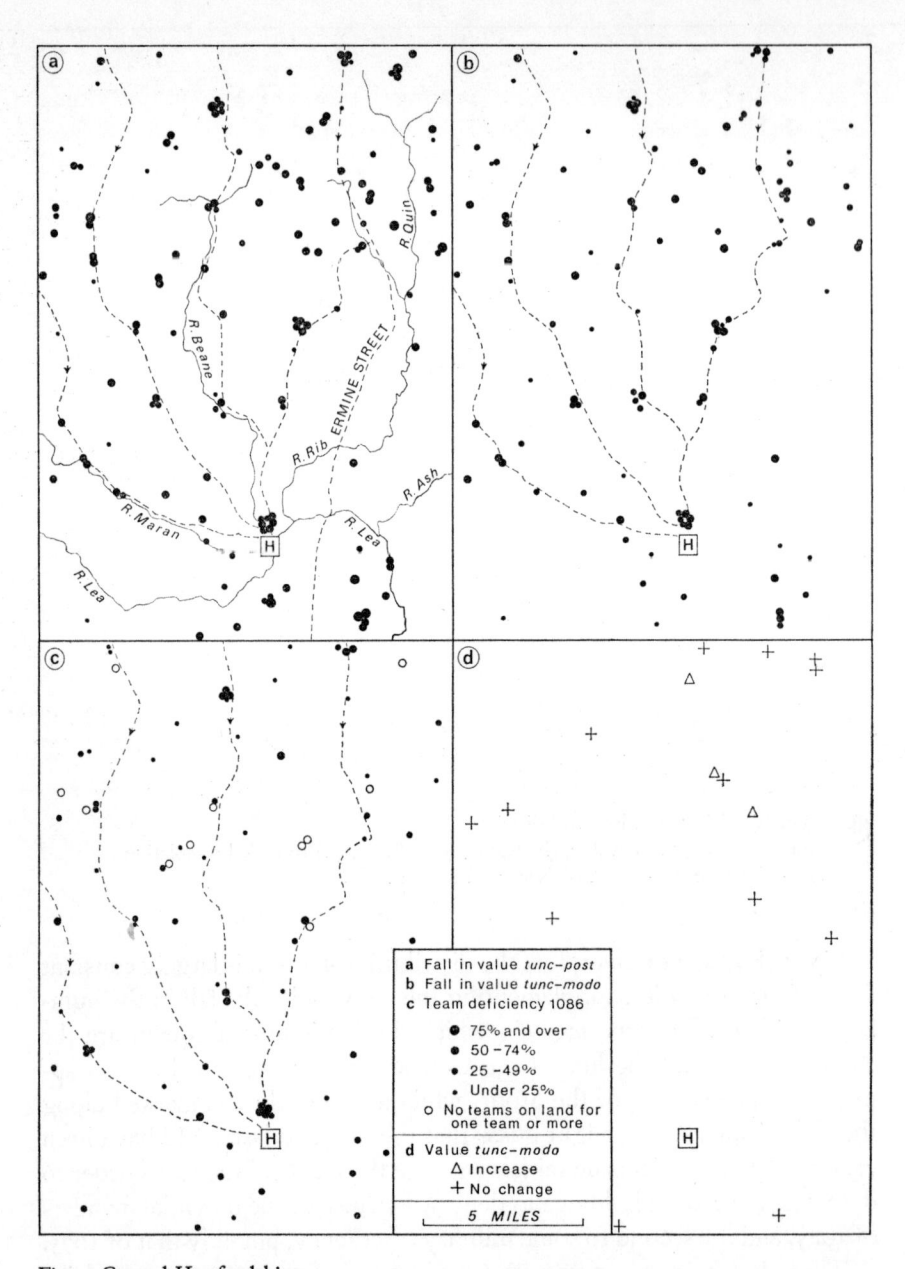

THE CONTRIBUTION AND LIMITATIONS OF DOMESDAY BOOK

Fig. 2 Central Hertfordshire
    (a) Fall in value *tunc–post*, (b) fall in value *tunc–modo*, (c) team deficiency 1086, (d) holdings showing increase or no change in value *tunc–modo*
    Holdings worth less than £1 or with less than one team not plotted
    H—Hertford   – – – Suggested routes of Norman forces

16

THE INFORMATION OF DOMESDAY BOOK

values rose appreciably, it is a matter of degree rather than of an anomalous situation.

As the following figures show, if value increased considerably, teams were not greatly fewer than before, and the recorded population was usually more numerous. But if there was a substantial decline in value, teams and inhabitants were far fewer than before.

		\multicolumn{6}{c}{percentage change in}
fol.		value		teams		population	
		+	−	+	−	+	−
77b	Bentley	66⅔	−	−	22	25	−
77b	Dovercourt	50	−	0	0	20	−
48	Foulton	50	−	0	0	0	0
32b	Tendring	50	−	−	33⅓	0	0
32b	Birch Hall	45½	−	−	33⅓	12½	−
67b	Oakley	28½	−	−	7½	9½	−
89	Bradfield	−	83	−	100	−	100
83b	Bradfield Manston	−	75	−	66⅔	−	16½
81b	Derleigh	−	66⅔	−	75	−	66⅔
67b	Ardleigh	−	62½	−	100	−	75
83b	Bradfield	−	57	−	44	−	15½
59b	Frinton	−	42½	−	37½	−	42½

Or consider the easterly portion of central Hertfordshire, in which holdings are numerous, 194 in all, of which 14 have so far not been identified and so are not plotted (Fig. 2). Many were quite small properties; in 1066 51 were worth less than £1.[1] At the time of the Inquest almost 60 per cent had fewer teams than ploughlands, resulting in an overall disparity of 20 per cent. After the Conquest over three-quarters of these holdings fell in value, from £864 5s. 1d. to £548 9s. 2d., or by about 36½ per cent. By 1086 their value had gone up to only £662 17s. 10d., so that even then they were worth 23½ per cent less than in King Edward's day. West of this area, the fall in value *tunc–post* was 22 per cent, nearly 20 per cent less than that in an area through which we may suppose Duke William's forces to have passed. Such figures do not suggest that the end of the campaign came at Great Berkhamsted west of Watling Street, but rather at Little Berkhamsted south of Hertford.

When the figures of DB are plotted, the maps of Fig. 2 all seem to tell the same tale. The general impression is of a decline in values and a

[1] Holdings worth less than £1, or with less than a full team, have not been plotted; except on map A. The change in value of many of these was naturally small, while for many no alteration is reported, and their inclusion would inevitably falsify the picture.

17

deficiency of plough-oxen stretching southwards to the neighbourhood of Hertford, and it looks as if it was caused initially by the invading force of 1066 moving in several columns towards London from Bedfordshire and west Cambridgeshire. If so, they seem to have kept largely to the drier ground above the courses of the rivers, and to have aimed at concentrating at Hertford. It is plain that retention or recovery of the values of 1066 was infrequent and without concentration in any district. Failure to recover from the consequences of the Conquest seems indeed to have been general. The absence of plough-oxen is naturally on the smaller properties; 41 had no oxen, and 11 less than one team. The deficiency on these, of land for one team or less, was 40 per cent.

But detailed study of Domesday statistics formidably displays their frequent eccentricities. In one Warwickshire Hundred, for example, the hides are about half as numerous as the ploughlands, yet Newnham Paddox (243b2), with eight ploughlands, was assessed at a single hide. Manorial values often seem to bear no relation to the figures of either. A Churchover holding (239bi) was rated at $2\frac{1}{2}$ hides and had three ploughlands; in 1086 its value was given as only 64*d*., and that was fourpence more than it had earlier been worth. A Harborough manor (244b2) had doubled its pre-Conquest value of 10*s*., but even so its four ploughlands and four hides were each worth only 5*s*., which is a low figure for either. Yet at Marston Jabbett (240a2) the solitary hide of assessment was worth £3, and its ploughlands averaged 15*s*. apiece. In addition to economic and agrarian factors, we must often assume the effects of beneficial hidation. Wibtoft with Willey (240a2) had four ploughlands, and a value of 30*s*. But it was assessed at a mere half-hide.

NOTE: There must be instances in which manorial attributes *were* taken into account when stating the value of a manor. Eaton by Chester (263b2) was worth £10 in both 1066 and 1086, and fell only to £8 after the Conquest. But it was assessed at only $1\frac{1}{2}$ hides, and there were but two *bovarii* and two villeins with a plough-team, six fishermen, and an acre of meadow there. The profits of the fishery, which had to supply 1,000 salmon, must surely have been reckoned in the valuation, even if we assume a deliberately low assessment.

3
The course and character of the invasion of 1066

The figures of DB have been employed by several commentators to deduce the routes followed by invading Norman forces. Serious objections to Baring's contention that falls in value to some extent indicate the movements of the invaders in 1066 have never been adduced.[1] We cannot, of course, conclude that all the lessened values in appropriate areas which DB discloses were caused by the events of that year. Fowler, applying Baring's deductions to shires north of the Thames, listed other possible causes, e.g. mortality among English manorial lords and their peasantry, infection of man and beast, poor harvests and bad weather.[2]

The latest intensive development of Baring's hypothesis is that of Lemmon.[3] He classifies the figures according to the amount of spoliation they suffered, e.g. those which fell by an amount of £8 to £11, or of £18 to £22, allots each group a letter, plots the letters, and deduces that clusters of these represent the halting-place of a force, falls of from £4–7 'the stay of a normal unit of the Norman army for a minimum period', and of from £2–3 the work of patrols. It is possible that the percentage falls in value to the values of 1066 may give us a clearer picture, for a fall of, say, £5 may sometimes represent a very small proportion of total value, while in other instances it is a major part thereof. It is noticeable that holdings with small values, whose resources and powers of recovery would be slight, often produce figures in which the fall in value *tunc–post* is high in proportion to the 1066 value.

[1] F. H. Baring: 'The Conqueror's Footprints in Domesday' (*Eng. Hist. Rev.*, xiii, 1898), pp. 17–25; reprinted with some additions and alterations in *Domesday Tables* (London, 1909), pp. 207–16.
[2] G. H. Fowler: 'The devastation of Bedfordshire and the neighbouring counties in 1065 and 1066' (*Archaeologia*, lxxii, 1922), pp. 41–50.
[3] In D. Whitelock *et al.*: *The Norman Conquest* (London, 1966), pp. 116–22. The routes are also discussed in D. Butler: *1066 : The Story of a Year* (London, 1966), pp. 258–77.

The chroniclers unfortunately give us only fragmentary information about the movements of the invading army and its reinforcements. The additional suggestions furnished by DB regarding these will be considered in some detail in the sections concerned with the relevant counties and illustrated by means of maps, but a general conspectus is not out of place here.

There can be no doubt that after Hastings fight the Duke moved to secure Dover and to occupy Canterbury, and thence on London. But before he himself approached the line of the Thames, intelligence from an advance party sent against Southwark, or from friendly sources, advised him that London was not prepared to surrender. It looks as if he felt that direct assault would be unwise until he had received reinforcements. Winchester apparently was willing to offer no resistance, and he turned from mid-Kent in that direction to link with the additional troops he had sent for.

It is improbable that his subsequent meeting with Stigand at Wallingford was not prearranged, and he must have hoped that the archbishop would bring him news that there would be no further serious resistance in southern England. Presumably London showed no sign of acquiescence in his advent, so that to turn eastwards from Winchester would be useless. Already, it seems, he had detached small bands of men which had traversed the country between him and the capital. The alternative solution was to encircle London, while never moving too far from it, in case the moment for descent upon it arrived. He was apparently a believer in the principle to be emphasised by von Moltke: 'march divided, fight united'. Only so could he sustain his troops.

At this stage he may not have been altogether happy about the situation. There was the possibility that the northern earls could muster and lead an army to oppose him, and about this threat he could hardly hope for reliable or early information. There cannot indeed have been many whom he could trust who could give him adequate information about the districts which lay ahead. While interpreters or bilinguists must to a limited extent have been available, he and his followers were in a foreign and an unfriendly land. Possibly intelligence had to be limited to the immediate future: the routes available, the extent to which supplies might be obtained, the temper of the inhabitants. A campaign lasting into late November and December was probably not in his original calculations.

It is unfortunate that the chroniclers mention no places to which the Duke penetrated after leaving Kent except Winchester, Wallingford, and 'Berkhamsted'. Historians have disagreed whether this last was Great Berkhamsted south-east of the Chilterns or Little Berkhamsted slightly south-west of Hertford. The fact that only 71 days elapsed between

THE COURSE AND CHARACTER OF THE INVASION OF 1066

Hastings fight and William's coronation in London may suggest the former. But some doubt must be felt whether the Duke would risk a march through the narrow passages of the Chilterns when England was

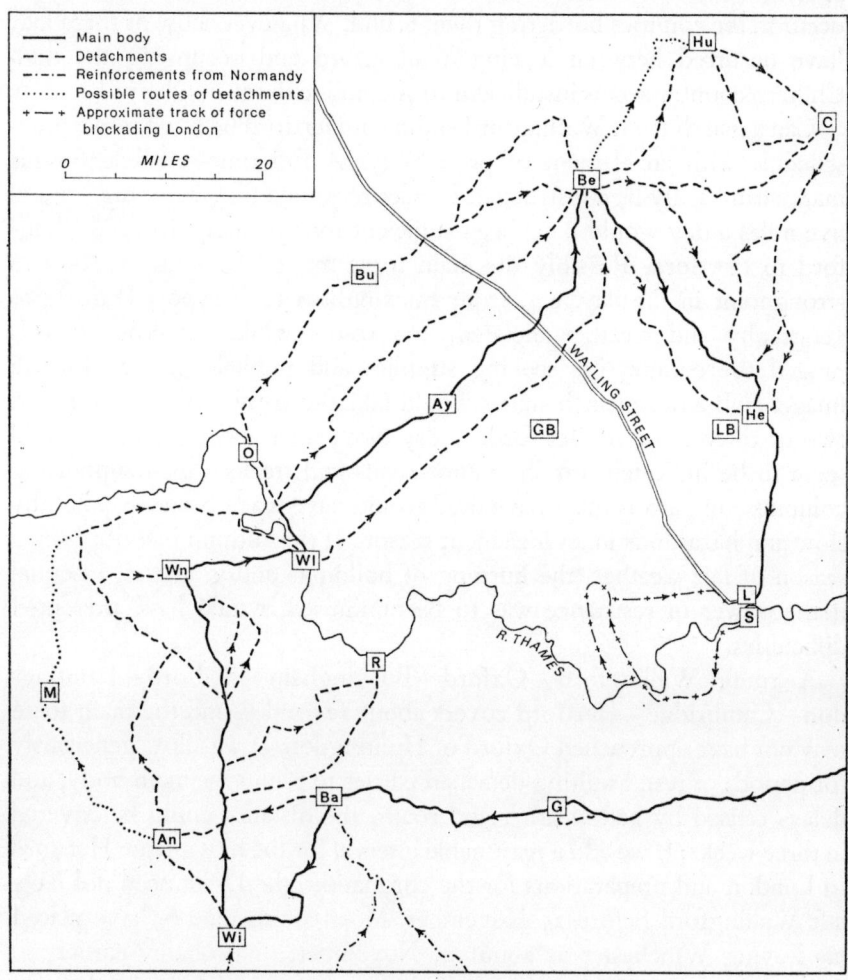

Fig. 3 Suggested routes used by invading forces Nov.–Dec., 1066
An—Andover Ay—Aylesbury Ba—Basingstoke Be—Bedford
Bu—Buckingham C—Cambridge G—Guildford GB—Great Berkhamsted
He—Hertford L—London LB—Little Berkhamsted M—Marlborough
O—Oxford R—Reading S—Southwark Wi—Winchester
Wl—Wallingford Wn—Wantage
——— Main body   --- Detachments   -·-· Reinforcements from Normandy
··· Possible routes of detachments
+++ Approximate tracks of forces blockading London on the south and west
It is not possible to suggest other possible routes in Oxfordshire, and Northamptonshire, owing to the absence of information

still largely unsubdued, or allow potential Mercian forces an unobstructed passage along Watling Street. Also, the heavy falls in value in shires north of London, proportionately heavier than elsewhere, must then be attributed to events unconnected with 1066, and a reason why they do not occur in the counties bordering them found. Whatever show of force may have occurred between leaving Wallingford and occupying the mid-Chiltern country seems insufficient to encourage the surrender of London.

Can a march from Wallingford ending at Hertford be fitted into a time-schedule with an element of probability? A full time-schedule for his march can hardly be constructed. Fowler reckoned that an *average* rate of five miles a day would have been sufficient for the march from Wallingford to Hertford. Possibly the main force moved from strongpoint to strongpoint in the day, e.g. from Buckingham to Newport Pagnell, as geography and weather dictated, and rested while numerous patrols ranged the countryside seeking supplies and publicising the Norman image. Half a dozen such stages would take the army to Cambridge, and two or three more to Hertford. A dry November and December would seem to be indicated, for the minor roads and tracks which supporting columns and patrols must have used would have made progress painfully slow and hazardous in an inclement season. If the autumn had not been a season of fair weather, the burning of buildings and granaries, essential if the power of resistance was to be minimised, would have presented difficulties.

A route Wallingford—Oxford—Buckingham—Bedford—Huntingdon—Cambridge—Hertford covers about 125 miles, and the main force may not have approached Oxford or Huntingdon. If we allow generously for periods of rest, awaiting detached parties to rejoin the main body, and delays caused by bad weather and roads, the distance could be covered in three weeks. If we add a reasonable interval for the move from Hertford to London and preparations for the coronation, the Duke need not have left Wallingford before 25 November. Most commentators have placed his leaving Winchester as about 21 November, or probably earlier, so there is here no major discrepancy. Canterbury had submitted 29/30 October, so that if the march from here to Winchester via Rochester took a fortnight for the 120-odd miles (judging by the track and extent of damage it would be taken more quickly than that from Wallingford), we can allow a week for the delay caused by the illness suffered by William and his troops, but not the month of one chronicler.

Fig. 3 shows the approximate routes followed by the main force and the flank guards. It does not, of course, pretend to reproduce the actualities, and in particular it cannot display what must have occurred throughout the journey, the despatch of small bands who diverged from the direct course with two objectives, the raiding of villages for supplies, and the discouragement of resistance.

In his encircling march the Duke's tactics seem to have been to head directly for strongpoints, especially the boroughs and the larger vills, especially royal vills, which he may have regarded as now rightfully his. This would have the dual advantage of acquiring defensive positions in the event of trouble, and also the maximum of supplies of every kind, not of provisions alone. Always he seems to have kept, judging by the damage it apparently caused, a sizeable force between his main body and the potential threat from the north. Figs. 7–15 show a curious suggestion of halts near county boundaries, as though he hoped to find the local sheriff surrendering the district into his hands.

4
Further factors affecting a study of the economy

The holding of the Inquest of 1086 by means of circuits comprising several adjacent shires, but with each county forming a self-contained unit, inevitable though this was, results in a major difficulty in studying any aspect of DB. Inconsistency of treatment affects every aspect of the text, and where for some shires we have elaborate information, elsewhere we find ourselves without it. Consequently every county necessitates a separate study, which has to be based on the Domesday and not the modern shire. The composition of the circuits is often both geographically and politically illogical; we could wish that Oxfordshire had been taken with Berkshire, and Huntingdonshire not brigaded with Yorkshire and Lincolnshire. Thus the order in which the shires may be dealt with must be a matter of individual choice.

There is hardly a Domesday shire in which it is not essential, for any kind of study, to separate *Terra Regis* from the rest of the land. The valuations given to royal manors, whether they had been King Edward's or had belonged to the houses of Earls Godwine or Leofric or other magnates, are largely based on inconsistencies. We have ample evidence, too, that the composition of many of them in 1086 was not as it had been a score of years earlier. Some of the largest and most complex were valued in terms of the conversion of one or more night's provisions, the *firma unius noctis*, into a sum of money. The proceeds of others, especially comital manors, derived from artificial systems of estimating their worth. Many were let to farm, and the sums paid by the lessees, often stated as a round figure, would usually be smaller than those they hoped in fact to obtain from them. Rents, too, had been set at levels totally incompatible with a manor's true worth. In many a manor the somewhat arbitrary basis on which its render had earlier been based must have been altogether inappropriate to the number of inhabitants at the time of the Inquest, for this must have been subject to frequent fluctuations. What does emerge from a welter of heterogeneous and often detailed information is that a king who was greedy for gold was obtaining far more from the bulk of his property than his predecessors had done, and those who farmed royal manors were usually profiting from them also.

How much of the sums mentioned in DB King William actually received is problematical. It has been shown that he was not obtaining the huge totals for the demesne manors, or all the casual profits, such as payments by the boroughs and the moneyers, for hawks and the maintenance of hounds, that DB would suggest.[1] The sheriffs, who farmed most of the counties, were paying a *firma* usually very much less than the revenue apparently attributed to the king would suggest.

Geld-liability furnishes an additional reason for separating royal manors from the others, especially where these were unhidated and a *feorm* had to be found, whether commuted or not. The *feorm* covered other matters besides the geld, but must have been calculated in a manner which implied that the sum geld would have produced was included. The farm of a night was frequently £100 or thereabouts, which is the equivalent of a value of £1 per hide, which seems to have been the norm, for many of the relevant manors.

---

[1] R. W. Southern: 'The Place of Henry I in English history' (Brit. Acad. Raleigh Lecture, 1962), pp. 158–60, 164–6. This article displays the potentialities of royal property; by 1130 Geoffrey de Clinton paid Henry I £80 for the manor of Wargrave, which in 1086 was valued at £27 6s. 8d. (p. 137), and £70 for Hughenden, £60 more than its Inquest value (p. 138).

Waste

In the accounts of very few counties do we hear nothing of land which is said to be waste. Often the record of a shire suggests that there must have been far more waste than that actually mentioned. Sometimes we are told why the holding lay waste; it had been wasted by the king's army, or had been devastated by Irish pirates, turned into pasture-land, or taken into the royal Forest. Often we are altogether unable to determine whether the over-brief formulae of DB relate to 1066, 1086, or some indeterminate time. We cannot think that we are given the complete picture in 1086, for it seems strange, especially when we compare the record for other counties, that the invasion of 1066 should have left no places waste a score of years after in Surrey or Berkshire or Hertfordshire. We might indeed think that some minor settlements had become waste and in consequence found no place in DB.

In the *Domesday Geography of England* 1,333 places are said to have been waste in 1086, of which 1,076 come from the five northern counties with Lincolnshire. But this figure can hardly give a faithful picture of total waste. Many a vill had consisted of more than one manor, and many a manor must have been represented by two or more physically separated settlements. A large complex manor may have been partially unaffected, especially as regards the *caput*, while some of its components had been wasted. Preston on Wye (181bi), for example, is said to have been waste in King Edward's day, and presumably was waste, like many another March vill, in the early days of King William. In 1086 it was worth £5, but one of its $2\frac{1}{2}$ hides was still waste. When waste has to be considered, it is the individual holding and not, often enough, the vill, which needs to be studied. Of the 53 hides at which Lydbury North (252a2) was assessed, $32\frac{1}{2}$ hides were waste, and land for 31 teams out of that for 40 at Cause (*Alretune*, 253bi). In such cases, a number of distinct holdings must have been affected.

Not only were holdings described as being 'waste' for a variety of reasons, but there were degrees of waste also. Quite commonly we are told that a manor is waste 'for the greater part', or is 'almost waste'. Sometimes we are informed how many of its hides of assessment, or of its ploughlands, lie waste. In some counties what virtually amounts to partial waste may be inferred from the intermittent statements that there could be more plough-oxen employed than there were actually at work. Quite often the holding is said to be waste, but is none the less producing some revenue for its owner, for the payment of rent is mentioned. Sometimes a valuation set on waste is probably the rent to be demanded of anyone who will agree to re-stock and farm it.

We are, however, very rarely given a reason for devastation, or clues to the time or times at which a holding lay waste which might assist us to determine the cause. Moreover, *vasta* or *vastata* obviously has no single meaning. It can, and often does, imply total destruction: the inhabitants and teams are nil, and we may suppose that buildings and implements had largely been destroyed, and livestock appropriated or slaughtered. It is significant that the Domesday names of many such holdings have never been identified and that no trace of the settlement to-day exists. These can have had no power of recovery, and were insufficiently rewarding to be re-colonised. Partial wasting is frequently mentioned, but for a manor to be only partially ruined suggests that in many instances only some of its components or the outlying hamlets and farms suffered. A plain *vasta*, too, may not necessarily imply total ruin. If it did, we should have to assume, we shall see, that under Norman management an enormous number of people were moved in many parts of the country to empty villages and huge quantities of plough-oxen somehow obtained for their support. Such holdings may indeed have suffered severely in the twenty or thirty years before the Inquest, but it seems improbable that they were always totally abandoned. If they were, then 766 adult males and 1,862 plough-oxen were introduced into those of Cheshire, and these furnished almost half of the county totals for 1086.

Some districts may even have been classed as 'waste' simply because earlier they had not been under English or Norman control. This applies especially to the Welsh Marches. For while most of the land now within Wales is said to have been waste both in 1066 and when its new lords received it, it is also often said to have almost as many plough-teams as it has ploughlands. Unless we are to suppose recent colonisation to a most formidable degree, the vills were probably active throughout, but peopled by Welshmen.

Land is quite frequently said to be 'waste' because it is in the royal Forest, or, occasionally, within Forest-land held privately. Such land, which is sometimes said to be only a portion of the manor described, would be classed as 'waste' because inclusion in the king's Forest deprived the owner of the manor of a portion of his potential revenue. Here, as a rule, he and his villagers could not pasture their beasts or take the timber which was so valuable an asset and required for so many different purposes. We are indeed told that Earl Hugh had all the woods of 20 hides of *Atiscros* Hundred in his Forest, 'whereby the values of the manors are much depreciated' (268b2), and the value of Chilworth (47b2) fell because the owner had no power to use the woodland. In a sense, too, land was waste because inclusion in the Forest freed it from its liability to geld, or at least to contribute to the county's geld which the sheriff had to produce. In addition, expressions such as 'the woodland renders nothing' may in fact imply that it did so because the land was really 'in the Forest'.

The cause of waste, other than inclusion in the Forest, is rarely given. We are, however, told that a number of manors on the Welsh border had been devastated before 1066 in Welsh raids. The Conqueror's march from Sussex to Middlesex naturally caused damage to numerous manors. Others must have been affected by the revolts of 1069–75, especially in the west midlands, Cambridgeshire, and Lincolnshire, and by further Welsh irruptions. Pirates wasted some manors by the coast, and may have caused more frequent damage than the solitary mention of this given in DB. But the greatest volume of wasting, as DB clearly displays, must have resulted from the deliberate harrying of the northern counties after the Northumbrian and Mercian revolts as a punitive measure and to discourage further rebellion. A good many holdings described as waste probably indeed received no visit from rebels or royal troops, but, it is thought, were deserted by their occupants because of their marginal character in favour of more fertile settlements which had been depopulated, or were purposely emptied by their new lords because of their economic unimportance and because to transfer men and stock to less unrewarding sites was economically profitable. This theory was in part advanced to explain why, on the evidence of DB, apparently parts only of the Yorkshire plain were devastated, while the uplands were almost completely wasted. It is suggested that 'many places shown as uninhabited in the survey were not devastated in 1069 and 1070, but abandoned between 1070 and 1086, and some of the inhabitants and their equipment moved elsewhere'.[1] Such a movement was probably not confined to Yorkshire, but was in some degree encouraged in many other devasted areas, or those which could yield only the least satisfactory of returns. Only six years after the Inquest, on the authority of the *Anglo-Saxon Chronicle*, 'many peasant people were sent with their wives and cattle to live and cultivate the land' in an underpopulated area about Carlisle.

A possible deliberate population-shift may well have had its effect upon the figures of DB. Where a lord possessed a lowland settlement which was plainly less thoroughly developed than it could be, the temptation to move men and their belongings from hamlets and farms perilously close to a mere subsistence level must have been acute. Possibly such transferences

[1] T. A. M. Bishop: 'The Norman Settlement of Yorkshire', in *Studies in Medieval History presented to Frederick Maurice Powicke*, ed. by R. W. Hunt, W. A. Pantin, and F. W. Southern (Oxford, 1948), pp. 1–14; reprinted in *Essays in Economic History*, ii (London, 1965), pp. 1–11.

were not invariably total. One object would surely be that of enlarging the amount of arable and the draining of marshland. But if the decision to develop was a fairly recent one, in 1086 the extension may not have begun to be exploited. In some districts, and in occasional entries, this might account for an apparent excess of teams over ploughlands. It might, moreover, account in part for the large differences in equipment of manors apparently of equal worth.

Ploughlands and plough-teams

The difficulties adduced by DB's statements about the number of ploughlands and teams vary with the circuit, and while it is obvious that in some areas the first is unrealistic, it is elsewhere often difficult to determine which statements may reproduce actual agricultural conditions and which do not. Many ploughland figures in round decimal numbers can be no more than approximations to the truth. Duodecimal quantities may often represent assessments to the geld, etc., of an earlier date. Judging by a formula sometimes used by the Exchequer clerk, 'there is land for n teams, however there are $n+$ teams', he expected, though receiving copious contrary information, that normally there should be as many teams as there were ploughlands. Sometimes the clerk seems to have arrived at the number of ploughlands by adding up the plough-teams reported. Those responsible would not all furnish information on an identical basis. Some obviously gave the ploughlands for the demesne of the manor, but not those belonging to the sub-tenancies. Some may deliberately have given a quantity appreciably less than the truth. Others may have included land which not only was not being tilled but which had not for some time been tilled, or which, though potentially arable, had never been cultivated. Some may have reckoned land which, though suitable for cultivation, was not regularly so employed. Where resources were adequate and vills thinly spaced, but the soil poor, it must have been necessary to allow land to recover after crop-bearing. Thus we may find a manor with a large number of ploughlands, only a portion of which would be cultivated in any given year. Judging by the number of entries in which no information about ploughlands is given, some made no attempt to furnish an answer to a question which, according to the preface to the *Inquisitio Eliensis*, they had not been asked.[1]

---

[1] The virtual absence of information about ploughlands in some circuits may indicate the local authorities' failure to demand that it should be supplied. Yet all could see that such information was desirable, if not vital, so long as an uniform system was everywhere employed.

Thus while several possible reasons for an apparent deficiency of teams can readily be adduced—the effects of military operations, of mortality among the beasts (recorded in the initial folios of the Essex text) and those who must control them, of insufficient working capital, or of a partial shift from an agricultural to a pastoral economy—it is less easy to suggest why there should comparatively frequently be a substantial excess. There could be no point whatever in maintaining teams for which there could be no employment. There may have been some hiring of teams to men less fortunately situated. Certainly the teams of some manors were used in places where their owner maintained no oxen, e.g. at Barley (139ai), Uffington and Belmesthorpe (346a2, 366b2), Houghton (370bi). On the smaller holdings many a team of eight oxen could only be mustered by co-operative effort, for on a number of small properties the holder possessed only one or two oxen. In one sense it is unfair to class such holdings as among those deficient in teams. So long as the land is cultivated, it does not greatly matter how it is done, provided the cost is not excessive. But an inadequacy of oxen does rather argue sub-standard economic wealth.

It has been suggested also that the creation of demesne land where before there had been none would result in disparity between teams and ploughlands. But a new home farm would usually be situated on the ancient arable, and would not necessarily enlarge the gap between ploughlands available and teams employed. That there must, when capital was available, have been some extension of the cultivated area, is occasionally disclosed by DB. Assarts, reclamation from the woodland, appear in the Herefordshire text. Pasture at Patrixbourne (9a2) and Swyre (80b2) had been converted into arable. Probably there were many more such instances than the few which found their way into DB. Those carucates of land which we find in some south-western counties, and which had never been divided into hides and had never paid geld, may represent enlargements of the manors' original arable. In a number of other counties we hear of demesne land for *n* teams in addition to that covered by the hides of assessment, and which might be of the same order as the carucates which had never gelded, though equally they may represent exempt demesne. Another reason for disparity might be the consolidation of several small former manors into single holdings, or the inclusion in a manor of the previously independent property of free men and sokemen. Both are apparent on almost every folio of Domesday Book. Fewer teams would be required where either change occurred, as Maitland pointed out.[1] This might account for some of the alterations in the number of teams where we have figures for *tunc*, *post*, and *modo*. It should be remembered,

[1] *DBB*, pp. 428–9 (494).

too, that, as with values, we may not infrequently be given one figure for a manor as it had been, another as it was composed in 1086, with the earlier figure relating to an area since enlarged by incorporating within it formerly independent holdings.

Thus to arrive at a satisfactory relationship between ploughlands and teams is often impossible. The form and the implications of the entries differ so widely in character that we can reach acceptable conclusions only by interpreting those which lie outside a straightforward pattern in the manner which seems to be most reasonable. We may feel fairly certain that in complex entries such as that for Micheldever (42b) we should add the teams of the sub-tenancies to those of the demesne and the peasantry, and reckon 60, not 34, teams for 72 ploughlands. We cannot, on the other hand, be sure that the four tenants' teams at Romsey (43b2) should be added to the other 18 to give 22 teams for 18 ploughlands. We have to bear in mind, too, that an apparent surplus of teams does not necessarily imply an inefficient economy. Adequately to till the soil in some places may require more oxen to the ploughland than in more fortunate manors where the land is more easily worked and puts less burdens on men and on the beasts of the plough. Finally, we must be content with approximations. Collation of the Exeter and Exchequer texts displays that 'one team' is not invariably the same thing as 'eight oxen'. The clerks often rounded off their fractions, and to them it was all one to say 'half a team' whether the owner had three or five oxen.

Cursory consideration of DB might suggest that the numbers of oxen owned by villeins and other categories of population should furnish a clue to the extent of local prosperity or the reverse. But this argument cannot be pushed too far. The quantity of entries in which we are told of the teams of villeins only, or of some other class of villager or peasant-farmer, is for every shire comparatively small. In the majority of entries we are merely told that there are so many teams between villeins, bordars, and other categories of the population. We can never be certain that inhabitants of status other than that with which we are momentarily concerned have not on occasion been omitted from the text. The phraseology is often such that we may well feel that 'he has a villein with one team' should be punctuated '... a villein, with one team', and that the team was the lord's and not the villein's. Obviously to arrive at meaningful figures we must take into account those very numerous occasions on which villeins or bordars are without oxen, but again we cannot be sure that always they here had no teams, for omissions are sometimes obvious where there is general balance between ploughlands and teams. Sometimes we are given a single quantity for the teams which probably covers both those of the lord and of the villeins. It is generally assumed that slaves, and perhaps *bovarii*, possessed no oxen, but this may not have been of universal application.

Nor is it safe to say that a high number of oxen per villein necessarily argues prosperity; it may indeed imply the reverse. It may merely mean that the local soil requires a number of oxen above the county's average to till it. These have to be fed and looked after, which might often spell the reverse of prosperity. It might also mean that the oxen, though credited to one vill, are required to help till the land in a neighbouring vill or holding in which oxen are few or absent.

In any case, 'villein' is an undefinable term: it is as imprecise as is the modern 'salesman'. Some villeins were obviously better equipped than certain free men and sokemen; they might indeed be former free men, even minor thegns, who had suffered a decline in their social position, but not always in their economic standard. This applies to other classes also. The prosperity of bordars varied greatly, while *homo* is a most elastic term.

Moreover, the clerks' approximations could produce deceptive results. Both three and five oxen were probably set down as a half-team on many more occasions than we can detect, and this could consequently make a quite substantial difference to averages. Such figures, then, as are given here are to be treated with reservations. So, perhaps, are those of Lennard.[1] But with all their imperfections, they may do something towards evaluating local prosperity.

I have at times found myself in disagreement with some of Lennard's figures. This is only to be expected, since varying interpretations of many a Domesday entry are possible. Moreover, it is often difficult to pronounce judgment as to whether a passage implies an absence of plough-oxen or not. For example, on p. 161 I suggest that in Shropshire the average equipment of a bordar may have been as much as a couple of plough-oxen. I might equally well have taken into account some thirty passages where I feel the bordars had no beasts of the plough, and reduced my figure to $1\frac{1}{2}$. But the difference is not really important, and would invoke further consideration only if varying interpretations gave enormous differences in a single social class, or figures improbable for the district from which they are drawn.

[1] R. Lennard: 'The economic position of the Domesday *villani*', 'The economic position of the Domesday sokemen', and 'The economic position of the bordars and cottars of Domesday Book' (*Econ. Journ.*, lvi, 1946, pp. 244–64; lvii, 1947, pp. 179–95; lxi, 1951, pp. 341–71).

5
Domesday cartography

The principal flaw in the exhibition of changes in manorial values or a team/ploughland relationship by cartographic representation is that induced by the complex manor. Even when plotting is by holdings and not by vills, in far too many instances this involves the appearance of a single symbol where there should be many, probably of widely differing grades. Information not included in DB results in a consequent absence of symbols which could mislead us into thinking that a substantial area was altogether unaffected by changes. What, too, should possibly be a concentration of symbols may display only a few because where there should be others the sites are those of unidentified or anonymous holdings. This occurs, for example, in the neighbourhood of Dover and Eastbourne, though it is not really serious because so many local manors are indeed depicted. A deceptive impression may be induced for areas in which settlements were few, e.g. north-east Cheshire. They may look, quite wrongly, as if they had experienced but little trouble and no diminution of population.

Deductions may be partly falsified, too, because often settlements follow well-marked lines, e.g. in river-valleys or at the edges of escarpments or along spring-lines. In consequence the symbols will follow these lines, and may wrongly make us think that they indicate the track of an armed force bent on spoliation, or of the course of spreading disease. It is, however, unlikely that misconceptions from this cause would be frequent.

Again, lack of information could falsify the picture. It does happen that for some small fiefs we have little or no details for conditions at a date between 1066 and 1086. The lands of some of the smaller ecclesiastical foundations lay in restricted areas, and this could result in a local absence of symbols which might in fact be misleading. The same thing could happen also where the information was omitted for an administrative area.

It is impossible, unfortunately, adequately to weight the symbols. A large fall in value in a small manor, say from 60–80 per cent of its value in 1066, is apt to loom larger than it should. Viewed over an area of some substance, it is not in itself of great importance; it is only when we find frequent heavy falls in manors of every degree of former prosperity that we can say with confidence that such an area had been seriously affected. Where a vill included several manors, and the smaller ones fell steeply in value, whereas the larger holdings were proportionately less badly hit, some distortion inevitably results. But it is noticeable that if the small estates are omitted from the map the general picture is not seriously changed.

In the maps included here, the minimum number of symbols has been used. Numerous experiments show that little is gained by using additional grades of solid circles, or by always differentiating between 'waste' and 'partly waste', since some waste land is implied by the latter. The maps are intended to encourage the reader to form his own conclusions as to the implications of the figures of Domesday Book, which, it has already been stressed, cannot give the complete picture.

The ideal map should show not only falls in value but also the manors which display no change and those which appreciated in worth. But this is apt to overcrowd the map with symbols, and, as has been suggested earlier, indication of no reported change in value could often well be misleading. Again, where there were several manors in a vill, we do not as a rule know even the approximate situations of those which altered in value, any more than we do those of components of manorial complexes. We know that Fulham probably included Acton, Brentford, Ealing, and Hammersmith, but cannot attribute any of the numerous Fulham entries to a definite site.[1] Indeed, to place the holdings with any degree of accuracy is often impossible. The modern Libury, so unimportant that it is not named on the $\frac{1}{4}$-inch map, included twelve Domesday holdings.[2] Was there a single cluster of dwellings, or were some of the holdings at, e.g., the modern Hantwick or Green End or Levens Green within the two modern Munden parishes? Clothall (134bi, 137ai, 138b2, 141bi) could in 1086 have consisted of the modern village of that name, plus Clothallbury, and even a settlement near Baldock, a post-Domesday name, on the Icknield Way, on the outskirts of which is Clothall Common. The nine holdings all styled Bengeo were not necessarily within a mile of the borough of

[1] C. J. Feret: *Fulham Old and New* (Fulham, 1930), p. 13.
[2] *Stotles, Stuterehale;* fols. 133a2, 134a2 *bis*, 134bi *bis*, 139ai *bis*, 141ai *ter*, 142a2 *bis*. Six were very small, and one lay in the manor of Watton, 3½ miles to the south-west; it may have been at Whempstead.

Hertford.[1] Bromyard (182bi) was a 30-hide manor. Three hides were waste, while the woodland 'rendered nothing'. It is probable that some or all of the waste hides were woodland, and 'waste' and paying no geld because they had been taken into a Forest. They may thus have been some miles from the modern town.

We can represent only what we are given, be cautious about improbable quantities, and omit some of the smallest holdings for fear that they should blur or distort the picture worse than do the imperfections of Domesday Book. It is perhaps comforting that the maps here reproduced, which represent only a small selection of all those plotted, do not seriously conflict with what we must suspect were the facts.

Finally, there is the problem of delineating the coastline, which in the eleventh century was often very different from what it is to-day. Here it does not greatly affect the picture except in Kent and Sussex and the eastern counties, but it must be remembered that many places which now appear to be well inland were then on tidal waters.

---

[1] Fols. 137a2, 138b2, 139bi, 140bi *quin.*, 141a2. These were small holdings and possibly represent isolated farms. Was the modern parish of Stapleford north of Hertford entirely empty? No place-name within it appears in Domesday Book.

The following results are obtained from such figures as enable a comparison of values, omitting *Terra Regis*, at different dates to be obtained. Those in parentheses are based on inadequate information.

	Fall 1066–post %	Fall 1066-86 %	Rise 1066-86 %
Kent	15	–	29
Surrey	35½	–	5¾
Sussex	40	11	–
Hampshire (excluding the New Forest)	20½	–	8
Isle of Wight	16	–	9
Berkshire	17	–	½
Buckinghamshire	24	8	–
Bedfordshire	33	23½	–
Cambridgeshire	21½	13¾	–
Hertfordshire	30	20	–
Middlesex	40	18	–
Oxfordshire	(¾)	–	22
Warwickshire	(10½)	–	25½
Worcestershire	(25)	7¾	–
Gloucestershire	–	5	–
Herefordshire	–	–	6¾
Shropshire	(73)	–	9
Cheshire	(86)	34½	–
Staffordshire	–	?	–
Derbyshire	–	35½	–
Nottinghamshire	–	19	–
Yorkshire: West Riding	–	51	–
East Riding	–	74	–
North Riding	–	78	–
Lincolnshire	–	–	3¼
Huntingdonshire	–	–	3¾
Essex	–	–	20
Suffolk	–	–	20½
Norfolk	–	–	38

The statements for Leicestershire and Northamptonshire do not admit of comparisons, while in the south-west figures for 1066 are rarely given. The frequent use of *semper* makes a comparison of *tunc* and *post* in the eastern counties over-speculative.

35

The details of Domesday Book

Part II

1
The South-East

Domesday Book opens with the five counties which first experienced the advent of the invaders from across the English Channel, and which formed one of the circuits of the Inquest of 1086. The Kentish text, however, suggests that in this county the Inquest was not conducted, nor its results inscribed, in altogether the same fashion as is evident in the other four.

But all five have one useful feature in common. In the majority of entries we are given values for three dates. While, as has already been said, the second of these would seem to be a variable, at times applicable probably to 1067, at times to a period appreciably later, the probability is that in the majority of instances it refers to a time not greatly distant from the Norman invasion, and if we normally treat it as such we shall probably not be committing repeated or major errors. Thus many of the frequent falls in value in the south-east have for long been attributed by commentators to the passage of Norman troops and their allies, to deliberate devastation and to the commandeering of supplies. But, as has been suggested above, this was not the sole reason for the decline in value of a holding.

The use made of this information by others, and now to be developed, to attempt to trace the movements of Duke William's forces, has also been discussed above. It is interesting that in this circuit the relationship between the valuations of 1066 and of 1086, when plotted, often displays a pattern similar to that between those of *tunc* and *post*, as though there were many holdings which in twenty years had failed to recover from the effects of the Conquest. So does the relationship between ploughlands and ploughteams, though the frequent absence here of figures for the former, and the existence of obviously arbitrary figures, is inclined to blur the picture.

But at the end we are compelled to think that there are many gaps in the canvas, especially for Kent. Recovery here from the passage of invading forces may have been more rapid and complete than on the Hampshire and Berkshire Downs or on the fringe of the Forest and woodland. Certainly the number and calibre of the falls in value soon after the Conquest is each smaller than we should expect them to be. We are everywhere grievously handicapped, too, by the large number of enormous complex manors with unnamed and dispersed components.

For obvious reasons the Isle of Wight and the New Forest area have been accorded separate treatment.

Any figures for a ploughland–team relationship in this Inquest circuit must be given with extreme diffidence. The number of the ploughlands is absent from a large number of entries, and the statistics of DB are such as to induce a suspicion that the basis for determining the land for n teams is often, though certainly not invariably, an artificial one. The results for Surrey may conveniently preface what will be said about these for each county in this section.

	instances	ploughlands	teams
Ploughlands not given	49	–	$198\frac{1}{4}$
Blank after *terra est*	20	–	$43\frac{1}{4}$
Teams more than ploughlands	57	368	$499\frac{5}{8}$
Parity	30	205	205
Teams less than ploughlands	54	450	313
	210	1,023	$1,017\frac{5}{8}$

These figures include the sub-entries. It is probable that only 18 of the 49 instances in which the ploughlands formula does not appear imply omission; the remainder were most likely parts of manors for which the entire quantity was given in the main entry, or which had no arable land. Thirty ploughland figures are of five or a multiple thereof, and 35 of 4, 6, 8, or 12, with four of 16 and one of 32.

The figures for slaves also invite suspicion, for there seems to be no obvious reason why the recorded population of Sussex included less than 5 per cent who were servile when the proportion for the remaining counties ranged from about 10 to 18 per cent. Nor does it seem altogether probable that such a high number of manors in which there were demesne teams should apparently have included no slaves. There are over sixty such in Surrey, though it is true that almost all had only two demesne teams or less. In Berkshire nearly 35 per cent record no slaves, while on some ten manors there were slaves but no demesne teams. But for some of these, e.g. Buckland (58bi), where there were seven slaves, demesne teams may have been missed. For Kent and Hampshire the figures are 46 per cent and 28 per cent.

Kent

The extremely detailed text for this county could of itself furnish a thoroughly useful introduction to the material provided by Domesday Book as a whole. Not the least of the advantages thence to be derived would be illustration of many of the difficulties, uncertainties, and frustrations latent in the record as a whole. Indeed, it might cause the student to wonder how far the text of Domesday Book is trustworthy, and to what extent deductions therefrom can have validity. But, for many parts of England, Domesday Book is virtually all we have to help us, and if we are constantly conscious of its deficiencies, its scale is so immense that these need not seriously affect our judgments.

Three documents add considerably to our knowledge of Domesday Kent. One, known as the *Excerpta*, is concerned chiefly with the lands of St Augustine's, Canterbury. A second, the *Domesday Monachorum* (hereinafter *Dom. Mon.*), deals with the properties of the archbishop of Canterbury, the bishop of Rochester, and others; the third, the *Textus Roffensis*, is a Rochester production. The originals of all are of such date as to imply that places mentioned therein were inhabited in 1086, and each records a number of villages which do not appear in DB, though often it is only the existence of a church in these which is noted. Allowing for those places which may possibly be recorded in DB, though not by name, these documents add about 150 villages to those of DB. It is unfortunate that nearly forty Kentish place-names have not so far been identified.

Kent was a highly manorialised county, and many a Domesday entry indicates how complex many of the large composite manors were. The canons of St Martin's, Dover, had a number of properties which apparently were parts of St Margaret's at Cliffe (1bi,2). The frequent use of *ibidem* suggests that those so prefaced were physically in that vill, but when we find a joint value for two holdings, one of which was in Bewsborough and the other in Cornilo Hundred, we may wonder if the latter was not really in some other place. Sub-tenancies are often prefaced *de hoc (eodem, ipso) manerio, de terra hujus manerii, de hac terra, de istis solinis, ad hoc manerium pertinet*, and it is only rarely that we are told where the components were.[1] To the situation of a number of holdings we are given no clue; sometimes no place-name is given, but merely *i manerium, iii denae, dimidia*

---

[1] e.g. one sulung of the manor of Northbourne (12bi) is said to be 'at the place called Bewsfield', and some of the land of the manor of Aldington (4ai) was at Lympne. But for Dean Court (10b2) we are merely told that the land was 'dispersed over three places'.

solin, in eodem hundredo. The early folios (1a2,b1) include information about royal rights and mention places for which we have no detailed account and are not otherwise mentioned.

But some of the holdings anonymous in DB can be identified from other sources. For example, some land belonging to the manor of Peckham (4b2) is shown by *Dom. Mon.* (9) to be Stockbury, and some of that of Ickham (5a1) was at Ruckinge (7).

Many or all of these villages and hamlets for which a church is recorded and which do not appear in DB may have been components of manors described therein. But it is disquieting that so many should be in the Weald, where very few settlements are noted in DB. For all we know we should have independent record of them; on the other hand, some may represent denes or swine-pastures far distant from their parent manors, while their population and other statistics may have been included in those of the manor to which they belonged. The number of place-names in the Weald ending in *-den* is large, and Marden certainly belonged to Milton Regis near Sittingbourne not far from Thanet and Tenterden to Minster near Ramsgate, thirty miles and more from Tenterden. We can only hope that this is yet another instance of our ignorance of the composition of manors. Folkestone (9bi) had eight churches, Hoo (8bi) six; the land of these and other manors must have been widely dispersed for them to have had so many. *Dom. Mon.* fol. 2 gives us the customary payments due to be received at Easter from a quantity of churches and priests. Here ten churches contribute to Folkestone, and the place-names recorded include a number which are not found elsewhere, e.g. Lydden and Wolverton. The number of Kentish settlements in 1086 is obviously incalculable.

For the majority of the entries we are given valuations for three periods of time, 336 in all. That described as *modo* must be that of the Inquest; *tunc* that of King Edward's day, while sometimes *tempore regis Edwardi* is indeed mentioned. A great many intermediate values are said to be *quando recepit*, and a few *post* or *olim*, and obviously it is not possible to specify the exact date referred to. It may be that the occasion was the succession of an ecclesiastic to his office; it is probable that not all the tenants-in-chief and sub-tenants recorded in Domesday Book received their grants over even a short space of time. It is, however, unlikely that most of these passages refer to a date appreciably distant from 1066. Odo of Bayeux would have expected and received a prompt reward for his past services and future duties as earl of a county liable to see invasion from the Continent.[1] Lanfranc would obtain the estates of the archbishopric of

[1] The Kentishmen's support of Count Eustace of Boulogne's rising during the king's absence from England in 1067 probably placed much rebel property at Odo's disposal.

THE SOUTH-EAST: KENT

Canterbury on Stigand's deposition in 1070, and the bishopric of Rochester twice changed hands between 1075 and 1077.

The Kent text gives 17 holdings as rising in value between *tunc* and *post*, and 161 as falling. It is doubtful if all the last were due to the activities of 1066, and it is equally doubtful if there was indeed no change in value in the 158 holdings in which DB shows none.

Since the fall in values was about 15 per cent, from £3,482 6s. 10¾d. to £2,954 7s. 2¾d., it may seem surprising that some manors rose in value, but only about 5 per cent of those for which we have comparable figures. Very few of these fall within the area which first experienced the Norman advent. The large appreciation at Wye (11b2) is probably due to the fact that it was a manor of the newly-founded Abbey of the Battle; *quando recepit* here implies a date by which this huge estate would have had ample time for recovery. It may also seem strange that the difference in number between manors showing a fall in value and those with a constant value is only three. But such figures could well be deceptive. Some manors may have been but little affected by the events of 1066; others may have recovered from initial damage by the time of their transference to new owners, or a rentable value may have been set on them which was unfairly high. Witnesses may have had small idea of post-Conquest values, and have casually submitted the same value as that given for King Edward's day.[1] The valuations for 1066 may have been exceptionally low, for the need to guard the English coast may have made it impossible to maintain normal standards.

Yet it is difficult to believe that none of the manors of the bishopric of Rochester altered in value in the years of the Conquest, and figures such as that for Westwell (5a2), £17 11s. 4d. for both *tunc* and *quando recepit*, are obviously open to suspicion. It might be argued that Duke William was careful to avoid damage to the Church lands or those of potential supporters. But it is highly doubtful if such a policy could have been executed in the October of 1066, though it is true that of the holdings which fell in value only 7½ per cent were ecclesiastical property. It cannot safely be presumed that all the manors which show no early change in value had been altogether unaffected by the Conquest, and a map of them could be totally misleading. Too many of them lie in the path of invading forces who were desperately in need of provisions and supplies. An additional complication is that we have no intermediate values for the lands of the canons of St Martin's, or, amongst others, for the manors of Bishop Odo on fols. 6ai,2. Sixty entries, indeed, give us figures for 1066

[1] Boughton under Blean (3b2) is given the same value, £15 16s. 3½d., for both dates. But *Dom. Mon.* (5) says the value in 1066 was £10.

43

and 1086 only. It is noticeable that holdings with small values, whose resources and powers of recovery would be slight, often produce figures in which the fall *tunc–post* is high in proportion to the 1066 value. Court-at-Street (13bi) fell from 10s. to 4s., Hartanger (11a2) from £2 to 10s. Some of these may never have seen the main Norman force of marauding raiders, but suffered in a general decline.

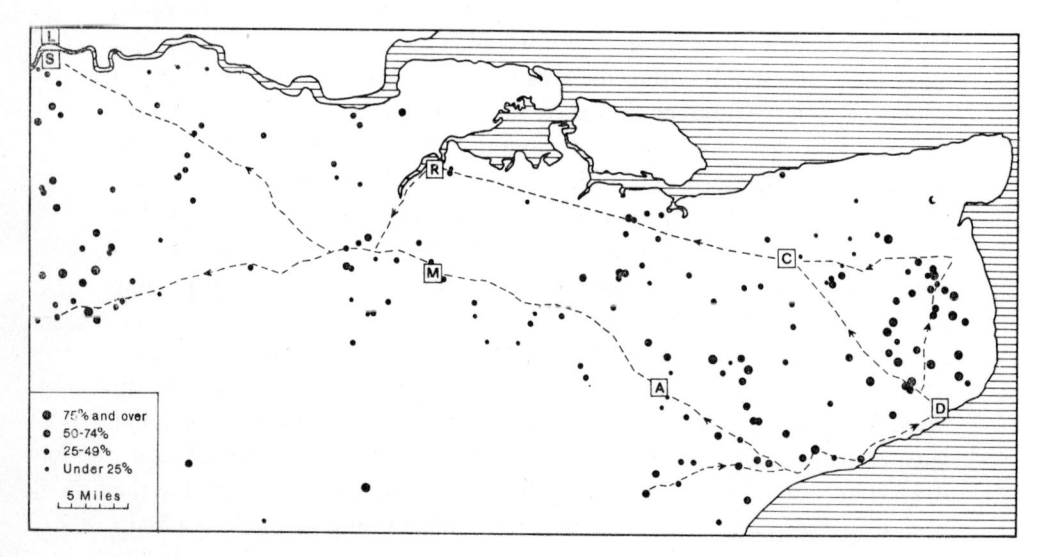

Fig. 4 Kent and East Surrey
Fall in value *tunc–post*
A—Ashford C—Canterbury
D—Dover   L—London
M—Maidstone R—Rochester S—Southwark
– – – Suggested routes of invading forces, 1066

Fig. 4 shows percentage falls in value *tunc–post*. A number of anonymous or unidentified holdings cannot be plotted. It suggests that the invaders entered the county in the Isle of Oxney and proceeded to Lympne and thence to Folkestone, which Lemmon suggests they reached on 22 October. They would naturally skirt Romney Marsh, but a detachment may have carried out a reprisal on Romney and other vills for the slaughter of the occupants of a strayed Norman ship.[1] It is doubtful whether at this moment King William would risk splitting his forces. In Lemmon's opinion he had less than 2,000 cavalry and 4,000 infantry at his disposal after Hastings fight. He may have been able to mount some of his in-

[1] William of Poitiers: II.27, p. 210.

fantry, or at least replace lost horses, by appropriations from the districts through which he passed. But would he dare risk leaving his left flank and rear unprotected? The Weald could conceal the mustering of a body of Englishmen who could have proved a distinct hindrance to his march, though no further major battle was to be expected immediately. Whether he could afford to leave Sussex undisturbed must be considered in dealing with that county. He may however have left a body of men at Lympne who at the appropriate moments moved, some by Stone Street (**12**) on Canterbury, others to Ashford (**131**).[1] The prime objectives at this point would be Dover and Sandwich, and the extensive damage in the neighbourhood probably represents in part the investing of the boroughs and the blocking of the Canterbury road (**1a**) against a potential relieving force. Dover (**1ai**) was burnt, DB informs us, to an extent which made it impossible to ascertain its value when Odo of Bayeux received it. During the following week Canterbury not unnaturally submitted, and the fit portion of an army which William of Poitiers says had been stricken by illness moved there.

The next major objective could only be London, but London showed no signs of submission. One section of the army proceeded to Rochester, doing a good deal of damage around Faversham, either on account of local resistance or from a need for re-provisioning.[2] It looks as if there was now a concentration west of Maidstone by a detachment despatched from Rochester and by troops from the Ashford neighbourhood and perhaps by some of those left behind to garrison Canterbury and by the sick who had recovered.

What in the north-west of the county might suggest only slight damage may be delusive. Recovery may have been easier in the district where the first ferocity of the Conquest was not felt. None the less, the force which proceeded to Southwark and its neighbourhood must have caused considerable havoc. Meanwhile William led the remainder of his army westwards, poised to receive London's surrender or to attack the city, or, in the event of the latter being temporarily unprofitable, to proceed to Winchester. He may have felt that he had insufficient troops for an assault on London, and his intention, once its surrender was not conveyed to him while he was still in East Kent, was probably to strengthen the force at his disposal. Hence reinforcements were sent for from across the

[1] Bold figures indicate the numbers given by I. D. Margary in *Roman Roads in Britain* (revised edn., London, 1967) to the Roman roads, many of which must still have been in use. Where these were grossly decayed, travel seems to have followed their course, but slightly to one side of them.
[2] Some damage on or near the coast may have been caused by the Danish fleet in the summer of 1069.

Channel, and he turned westwards with the dual purpose of effecting a junction with these and of occupying Winchester and eastern Wessex.[1]

But we can now form only the roughest idea of the actual movements of the invaders. The anonymous and unidentified holdings, the so-frequent absence of information regarding values *post* or *quando recepit*, or to what date these refer, and inability to allot manorial statistics to the components, give only a blurred and damaged picture. We can, if we will, as Lemmon does, estimate the numbers and character of troops concerned in the different movements; on the other hand, we can have no idea to what extent garrisons may have had to be left to combat an attack from the rear.

By the time of the Inquest the situation regarding manorial values had entirely changed. What had been valued at £3,792 13s. 0¾d. in 1066 was now said to be worth £4,908 6s. 6¾d., an increase of 29 per cent. None the less, over one-quarter of the holdings show no appreciation on 1066, and for one-sixth a decline in value is recorded, chiefly in those Hundreds of Eastry, Bewsborough, and Cornilo which, already gravely damaged in 1066, may most have felt the effects of Count Eustace's irruption in 1067, or the trouble with Bishop Odo in 1082.

Some of the increases since 1066 are remarkably high ones. Southfleet (5bi) went up from £11 to £21, Northfleet (3a2) from £10 to £27, Cliffe (4b2) from £6 to £16, Boughton Aluph (14ai) and Monkton (4b2) from £20 to £40. A most striking instance is that of Bilsington (10b2), which had appreciated first from £10 to £30 and later to £50, and which in 1086 was actually producing a *firma* of £70. Solton (11ai), worth £15 in 1066, was valued at only 30s. for both post-Conquest entries; an Ewell manor on the same folio declined from £12 to £1 and was worth only £2 in 1086.[2]

But this is by no means the full tale. In over sixty entries we are told that while a manor was valued in 1086 at a certain sum, it was in fact bringing in more.[3] The instances occur in five fiefs only, frequently with the formula *valet ... tamen reddit*. At Newenden (4ai) it was the reeve who was producing the sum, at Dartford (2bi) *praepositus francigenus qui tenet ad firmam*. Those farming the manors of the Canterbury *milites*, of St Augustine, and of Odo of Bayeux are often named, and the fact that the manors are being farmed is stated.

The sums are often grotesquely in excess of the estimated value. Char-

---

[1] It is doubtful if, as William of Poitiers says, the Duke was himself immobilised by illness for a month. For the assault on Southwark, see p. 115.
[2] Totals would be quite seriously affected if the clerks' errors were numerous. The 50s. value given for Sturry (12ai) should surely have been £50.
[3] These do not include the Dover, Canterbury, Sandwich and Rochester entries (1ai, 2ai, 3ai, 5b2), for boroughs should not be compared with manors.

ing (3b2) is said to be worth £34 but paying £60; for Chatham (8bi) the figures are £15 and £35, for Hoo (8bi) £60 and £113, for Barham (9b2) £40 and £100. In all, rents in these entries exceed values by almost 50 per cent.

Nor are these the only manors being farmed; there are at least a dozen further instances where manors were held *ad firmam* or the render was *de firma*; e.g. Teston (8b2), the Newington demesne (14bi), High Hardres (9a2). Luddenham (10bi) had been worth £10 in 1066, fell to £6 'when received', and was worth the latter sum in 1086, but Bishop Odo had 'put it to farm' for £10. The king seems to have taken a hand with at least some of his half-brother's manors after Odo's imprisonment, for that large-scale farmer of manors Robert *latinarius* held two Tottington manors (7a2) *ad firmam de rege*.[1] The farming of manors was hardly a Norman innovation, for Archbishop Stigand had held Barham (9b2) 'of the royal demesne farm of King Edward'. The Wadholt entry (*Platenovt*, 12bi) is suggestive: worth £1 throughout, it was valued at £2 in 1086 'because it could be put to farm'. So is that for Hawley (2bi), a royal manor abstracted from that of Dartford. It seems to have been in the *firma* of Osward when he was sheriff, but he had lost his office, and Hugh de Port, Odo of Bayeux's creature, had the estate. The sheriffs and *ministri regis* we not unnaturally frequently find as the farmers of royal property throughout the country.

Additional payments sometimes appear. An ounce of gold had been added to the renders exceeding the values of Southfleet and Stone (5bi), and a *gersuma* of £5, which might or might not be a premium for a lease, at Adisham (5a2), and one of 10s. at Newenden (4ai).[2]

The picture needs to be supplemented by information furnished by *Dom. Mon.*, which is far more detailed than DB about sub-tenancies and their values. Here, where DB says *reddit*, this text often points out that it is a farm-rent which is recorded: it is not impossible that throughout DB *reddit* implies this. Moreover, it sometimes tells us, where DB does not, that a manor was actually at farm, and for a sum higher than the valuation given there, or that payments additional to the sum stated were in fact due.

There are numerous discrepancies regarding the values and farm-rents; e.g. Sandridge (3ai) is said in DB to pay £23, in *Dom. Mon.* £24 (fol. 6), but none is particularly serious. *Dom. Mon.*, too, records land held by Richard fitzGilbert 'in his castle' or 'in the lowy of Tonbridge' more frequently than DB does, e.g. for Darenth (6) and Frindsbury (10).

[1] For Robert's activities, see Lennard: *Rural England*, pp. 114, 150.
[2] This information regarding Newenden comes from *Dom. Mon.* fol. 8. It is not in DB.

Appledore (5a2) is in DB said to have a value of £16 17s. 6d. But *Dom. Mon.* (8) gives the value as £12, and adds that Robert of Romney has it at farm for DB's sum. Also, it says that Sandwich (7) should 'this year' pay £70, whereas DB (3ai) states that it was at farm for £50 'in the year in which this description was made'. It gives a value of £50 to Teynham (5), for which manor DB has no entry. In its account of the lands of the bishopric of Rochester (10) it adds that the holders pay £11 13s. 3d. and £13 1s. 8d. for Borstal and Stoke respectively, where DB merely gives each a value of £8.

The sums of money are often so curious that many must have been arrived at by adding up dues and rents. Reculver (3bi) has a Domesday value of £25, and 'the archbishop receives £7 7s. above that'; in *Dom. Mon.* (5) this is given as £42 4s. 11¾d. Boughton under Blean (3b2) is in DB valued at £30 16s. 3½d.; four items in *Dom. Mon.* (5) add up to £31 1s. 6d., but here the *firma* is £25 against a value of £20. Saltwood (4bi) was valued at £29 6s. 4d.; Eastry (5a2) at £33 10s. 4½d. in DB, £37 10s. 3d. in *Dom. Mon.* (7).[1]

On fol. 11 of *Dom. Mon.* is a schedule of archiepiscopal demesne manors which gives for each from two to four items of revenue. These are the farm-rent, *gafol*, customary dues and, but rarely, oddments such as swine-rents and fishery-dues. The sums are not in correspondence with those of fol. 5–9; e.g. the farm of East Malling is on fol. 6 said to be £15, but on fol. 11 we hear of a *firma* of £16 13s. 4d. and a payment of £1 to the archbishop (a *gersuma*?), a *gablum* of 24s., and customary dues of 17s., £19 14s. 4d. in all. But it must be remembered that this section is probably to be dated slightly after 1090. Wingham (3bi) has a value in DB of £100, but *Dom. Mon.* states that it was at farm for £100, and also was responsible for a *gablum* of £29 10s. and customary dues of more than £3. But for Bexley, on fol. 6 at farm for £30 8s., we have on fol. 11 £26 *de firma*, a payment of £1 to the archbishop, £3 3s. *de gablo*, and alms of 5s., also totalling £30 8s. Lennard did not think that the figures implied that there were differences in the terms on which the manors were farmed, some payments, e.g. *gablum*, 'being included in the farm-rent and in others paid directly to the lord'.[2] The discrepancies may reflect a small difference in the times at which the relevant documents were drawn up, or of treatment by the Domesday and Canterbury scribes. But, as Lennard stressed, *Dom. Mon.* fol. 11 shows us far more Canterbury property as being farmed than

[1] Perhaps the 8s. 4d. and 16s. 4d. which appear at Little Chart (5ai) and Adisham (5a2; *Dom. Mon.* 7) represent one hundred pence and an error for 16s. 8d., or £⅚. A rent of fifty pence occurs quite frequently, e.g. at Macknade (10a2) and the manor of Northbourne (12bi). Could some of these sums be the result of a payment of twenty pence for every sixteen due?   [2] Lennard: *op. cit.*, p. 120.

DB would suggest. It must make us think that elsewhere also DB does not tell us of such arrangements; in its text for the Canterbury lands farm-rents in excess of values are comparatively rare.

Nor are these all the instances of payment of a rent. A certain Thurstan had a small portion of the manor of Ospringe (10ai), and paid 5s. for it. Ralf de Vaubadon had one yoke of Northbourne (12bi), and 'rendered thence' 50d. Here and at Little Mongeham Wadard, Odo of Bayeux's man, 'rendered no service except 30s.' to St Augustine, and in each case he was renting what had been villeins' land. In King Edward's day some estates had been held by villeins, renting them from St Augustine. One had held Bodsham (12b2), assessed at a whole sulung, which had been worth £4. Thirty had held Kennington (12b2), which had lain in the manor of Burmarsh and had been worth £10.[1] Small properties were being rented by villeins, bordars, and cottars. Eight of the last-named rendered 4s. 6d. at Swalecliffe (10ai), a bordar paid 1s. at Swetton (14ai), and a villein 6s. at Buckland (10bi). What proportion of the assessment their holdings represented we are not told.

In a score of entries we are given the rents of villeins, bordars, and cottars. Three villeins were holding an estate assessed at one yoke at Oare (10a2) *ad firmam*, and paying £1 for it, though they are not said to have possessed any oxen. The sums paid naturally vary appreciably; land was of unequal value. A Shelling villein (9b2) was paying only 2s., two bordars at Hastingleigh (14ai) 4s., and one at Perry (10a2) only 5d. A widow in Aloesbridge Hundred (11ai) paid 1s. 10d., but 'a very poor woman' at Barfreston (9b2) only $3\frac{1}{2}d$.[2] We have enough to show us that the peasantry could rent land, but whether they could comfortably afford the prices asked we are not told.

In addition, we hear of sums paid by priests, perhaps for their benefices (e.g. Minster, 12ai; Wickhambreux, 9a2); the rents and acreages of a few named men (Hawley, 6ai; *Leveberge* or Lynborough, 11ai); and in *Dom. Mon.* small payments by tenants 'for the altar' (Little Chart, Bearsted, fols. 8, 9).

In some counties for which the ploughlands recorded seem to approximate to agricultural reality there is something to be learned from the relation of teams to these. But for Kent the frequency with which the ploughlands were omitted makes deduction hazardous. They are never given for the lands of the canons of St Martin's, Dover (1bi,2; 2a2). A blank where the number of ploughlands should have come was left in 92 entries, and for 65 others no figure was recorded. Some figures seem to be

[1] At Lewisham (12b2) the mills were valued *cum gablo rusticorum*.
[2] See also Stone Street, Bircholt, and Brensett (2a2).

approximations; there are 22 instances where the figures are 120, 100, 60, 50, 40, 30, 20, 15.[1] Moreover, it is highly probable that in a number of entries the quantity of ploughlands on the demesne and villeins' land is given, but not those in the sub-tenancies. Otford (3ai) is said to have 42 ploughlands. There were six demesne teams and 45 between villeins and bordars, plus seven on what had been the land of three thegns.[2] There might well be an element of artificiality about some of these figures, for Dartford (2bi) possessed 55 teams for only 40 ploughlands, and, among numerous other instances, Northwood/Whitstable (3bi) $66\frac{1}{2}$ for 26—here there might be a clerical error—East Farleigh (4b2) 39 for 26. South Ashford (13ai) had only half a ploughland, but the clerks noted that nevertheless (*tamen*) there was a demesne team besides that of the villeins. For what they are worth, the DB figures give $2,294\frac{1}{2}$ teams for $2,191\frac{1}{4}$ ploughlands, but the frequent omissions make real comparison impossible.

An attempt to discover, as a clue to local prosperity, the number of oxen possessed by the different grades of peasantry is handicapped by the existence of the large number of entries in which both villeins and bordars/cottars are recorded. Moreover, there are something like fifty entries where the peasantry are not credited with any teams. In 62 entries where only villeins are mentioned 581 had 136, which gives the average villein less than two oxen.[3] In the only eleven entries in which bordars are isolatable 164 had 15 teams only, which is about one ox for every two bordars. But the deductions which might be drawn from such figures could be altogether incorrect. To say that in Kent, obviously a far from poor county, the peasantry were highly impoverished would be distinctly speculative. There are, however, not infrequent suggestions that *terra villanorum* had been filched, e.g. at Minster (12ai) and Northbourne (12bi), and had become a sub-tenancy. To deduce that the number of plough-oxen had been substantially reduced by the Conquest, and teams not built up again in a score of years, or that under a new and more efficient economy less teams were required, is equally dangerous. For there are plenty of manors in which, if we allow the bordars the not ungenerous quota of a pair of oxen per head, the villeins would average seven (Charing, 3b2) or five (East Barming, 14a2). But the fact remains that we have insufficient information to be comfortable about conclusions regarding the economic status of the peasantry. An apparent small number of plough-oxen a head might indeed imply that the soil of much of Kent was easy to work and necessitated the employment of far fewer beasts than elsewhere.

[1] e.g. Aldington, Lyminge (4ai), Bishopsbourne, Charing (3b2).
[2] See also, e.g., Wrotham, Maidstone (3a2), Westgate (3bi), Lyminge (4ai).
[3] Often no villeins' teams are mentioned where a rent is recorded; e.g. at Oare (10a2), Buckland (10bi), and Solton (11ai).

Surrey

As with the other counties of the circuit, we have to deal with large complex manors, anonymous holdings, and properties attached to one Hundred which were valued in another. Two hides of the royal manor of Merton in Brixton Hundred (30ai) lay in another, but unspecified, Hundred. Burgh in Banstead in Copthorne Hundred (32ai) was valued in Wallington Hundred, probably with the manor of Banstead. Two hides in Copthorne Hundred noted in the *breve* of Richard fitzGilbert (35bi) were Westminster Abbey's, and valued in another Hundred, but the Westminster account does not record them. A hide in Wotton Hundred lay in Earl Roger's Sussex manor of Compton (34a2). But the difficulties produced by the text are comparatively slight, and we have a wealth of exotic and illuminating information, though lacking in consistency of formula and subject, which adds considerably to the interest.

Out of 165 entries giving values in 1066 we have 117, 71 per cent, which furnish also the value *post* or *quando* (*cum*) *recepit*. Only seven entries make use of *semper*. Unfortunately we have comparable information for only five of the 31 holdings of Chertsey Abbey (perhaps because Wulfwold, its abbot, had died as recently as April, 1084), and very rarely for those of the surviving thegns. Excluding *Terra Regis*, land previously worth £866 1s. had declined in value to £559 4s. 4d., a fall of 35½ per cent. No change is recorded for 31 holdings, and only three show an increase.[1]

Some of the losses are heavy ones. Mortlake (30b2) fell from £32 to £10, Farnham (31ai) from £55 to £30, and Battersea (32a2) from £80 to £30. It is not only the large and dispersed manors which suffered. An anonymous manor, perhaps Caterham (31bi), became worth only one-quarter of its pre-Conquest value, £4, as did Woldingham (34b2) and Carshalton (36a2), while Tooting Bec (34b2) declined from £5 by 80 per cent and Balham (36a2) lost five-sixths of its pre-Conquest worth of £6.

Much of the decline in value seems to have been due to the passage of invading Norman forces. The effects of the march which culminated in the surrender of Winchester are clearly apparent in the triangle Tandridge—Farleigh—Reigate, with the next halting-place in the Guildford neighbourhood, and then through Farnham towards Basingstoke in Hampshire (Figs. 14–15). So is the destruction caused by the force which had approached London, part of which had turned away south-westwards and which was to harass the English in west Middlesex and eastern Berkshire and interpose itself between the south midlands and William's encircling march. Possible connecting links between these bodies, one running

[1] Tatsfield (31bi), Sanderstead (32a2), and Streatham (34b2).

through Sutton, and a slighter one through the Dorking gap, are also visible. An unexpected feature is that the fall is heavier (almost 50 per cent) on the score of holdings for which the text says *cum recepit* than on those for which *post* is used. Perhaps a decline begun by the invasion was intensified by its effects and by Norman activities in the early years of the Conquest.

But the decline in values after the Conquest seems largely to have been only a temporary one. We have values for both 1066 and 1086 for 165 of the holdings, which means that for one-fifth of the total we have no information or only a single figure. The total appreciation is indeed small, from £1,142 9s. 10d. to £1,201 10s. 6d., or 5¾ per cent. A few manors may have been affected by extension of the Forests. Three hides at Pyrford (32a2) were in the king's Forest, but the manor was worth half as much again as it had been in 1066, perhaps because only eight of its 27 hides were now liable for geld. The improvement by 1086 since the times described as *post* or *quando recepit* is 68 per cent. We must not, however, think of this as entirely appreciation in value; some of the figures may represent demands made beyond a manor's true worth.

The royal property for which we have comparable values fell in value only from £186 to £161 (13½ per cent), and by 1086 what had been worth £234 3s. was valued at £258 10s., an improvement of no more than 10½ per cent. No pre-Inquest figure is given for Reigate (30a2). Two manors were worth, or rendered, sums equivalent to their value, but 'by weight', and one the same but 'by weight and assay', which might well add 25 per cent to the receipts.[1] In four instances the sheriff's receipts are mentioned; the sums might represent his profit from farming the manors.[2] But Reigate (30a2) was apparently rendering what it was worth, £40, while we are not told the Inquest value of Kingston (30b1). Queen Edith's three former manors furnished him with £7.

But a number of manors were bringing in more than they were adjudged to be worth. In at least fifteen entries, including that for the borough of Guildford and the land about it (30ai), we are told that though a manor is worth so much, it is in fact rendering more. Six of the manors are royal ones; the remainder are all in different fiefs save for two of Richard fitzGilbert's. Thus there may have been many other manors where the rents paid exceeded true values. Never, as elsewhere, are we told of disagreement among witnesses as to fair valuation. The formulae vary. Only once are we told that the increase is because the manor is *ad firmam*

[1] Woking, Stoke next Guildford (30ai,2), and Guildford (30b2).
[2] Woking (30ai), Stoke, and Bermondsey (30a2); 25s., 25s., and 20s. on values of £15 for each manor; from Wallington (30a2) 10s. on a manor worth £10.

(Long Ditton, 35ai), though Ewell (30bi) was either at farm or had been part of King Edward's *firma*, which had included Woking (30ai), Stoke by Guildford (30a2), and Kingston on Thames (30bi). But some royal manors, notably Reigate (30a2) and Dorking (30bi), are not said to produce more than their value. In four entries it is not said that the farmer is paying more than the value, but this is implied by the fact that thrice the manors are said to be worth so much *ad numerum*, but pay the same sum *ad pensum*.[1] This might add up to one-quarter to the face value. But though Wallingstead (34a2) is said to be worth £20, it rendered £28 *ad pensum*, and thus it looks as if the actual payment may have been about £29 17s. 4d. We are not told the value of Countess Ida of Boulogne's manor of Nutfield (34a2), but it was paying *de xx in ora*, so presumably it was worth only £12, 20s. less than its 1066 value, since 'for every 16d. due, 20d. was collected'.[2]

Some of the excesses over value were considerable. That for Long Ditton (35ai) was 60 per cent, for Gomshall (30bi) and Morden (32a2) 50 per cent. Bramley (31a2), for which the *firma* is mentioned, and in which the former manors of Rodsell and Farnham (31bi) and two hides of Chertsey Abbey's Clandon land (34a2) had been placed, was worth £60 but was rendering £79 16s. 8d. Where there are no complications induced by the manner of payment, the manors were producing about one-third more than the valuations, in some instances 50 per cent more. Never are we told who was farming the properties, but three times it is mentioned that the sheriff was receiving money from them (p. 52). But the Gomshall villeins (30bi) were 'free of the sheriff's requirements'. Chipstead (33a) had been at farm for 40s. in the time of William de Watteville, but it is not said what Chertsey Abbey obtained from it in 1086.

Two Canterbury manors in Surrey appear on *Dom. Mon.* fol. 11, where Mortlake is coupled with Hayes in Middlesex. The archbishop's share of Croydon (30b2) is in DB worth £27, and that of his *homines* £10 10s. In *Dom. Mon.* the manor produces a *firma* of £30, plus 20s. to the archbishop, 34s. 7d. for gafol, and 20s. from a thegn. In DB, too, two tenants have seven hides, from which they have £7 8s. *de gablo*. Once the sum is given as a 'mark of silver', the pre-Conquest value of a Barking Abbey holding (34ai), and Odo of Bayeux was claiming two marks of gold or two falcons 'for the king's use' from Picket's Hole in Effingham (36b2).

An abstract of the figures for ploughlands and teams was given on p. 40. Where comparative figures are available, they would seem to argue

---

[1] Woking (30ai), Stoke (30a2), Godalming (30b2), each a royal manor. The Godalming phrase is *ad pensum et arsuram*. See S. Harvey: 'Royal revenue and Domesday terminology' (*Econ. Hist. Rev.*, xx, 1967), p. 222.   [2] S. Harvey: *op. cit.*, p. 223.

THE DETAILS OF DOMESDAY BOOK

that there was only a very slight deficiency of teams, but obviously we cannot trust the ploughland figures where these exceed the number of teams.[1] Some of the excesses are staggering.

	ploughlands	teams	
Woking (30ai)	6	21	(the 6 might be clerical error)
Croydon (30b2)	20	38	
East Horsley (31ai)	5	8½	
Limpsfield (34ai)	12	19	
Nutfield (34a2)	12	16	
Loseley (34bi)	2	4	
Shalford (35bi)	6	11½	
Hambledon (36a2)	4	7	

Elsewhere the difference is sometimes accounted for by the presence of sub-tenancies for which the ploughlands are unrecorded, but here this might be true only of Croydon. Some of the deficiencies are equally striking:

	ploughlands	teams
Egham (32b2)	40	12
Lambeth (34ai)	12	6
East Betchworth (35b2)	7	4

Occasionally the deficiency may in part be explicable. Pyrford (32a2) had only seven teams for its 13 ploughlands, but here three hides were in the king's Forest.

The general correspondence might suggest that the surplus teams of one manor ploughed the holdings where there was a deficiency, were it not that parity is displayed by neither Hundred nor fief. Woking Hundred had 121½ teams where there were 90½ ploughlands, but Godley only 34 teams for 67 ploughlands. Westminster Abbey had only 9½ teams for 16½ ploughlands, but Edward of Salisbury 18½ teams for his 15 ploughlands. Mapping the deficiencies is less satisfactory than it is elsewhere, for the surplus teams are not concentrated in definable areas. However, there are considerable deficiencies immediately south of London, and in a marked degree along the line of the road joining Portsmouth and London, with lesser falls in the neighbourhood of Stane Street. These do rather suggest the action of military forces living off the country, in some respect dating from the early days of the Conquest.

[1] For all we know some ploughland figures do not represent ploughlands at all, and some may relate to manors which had changed appreciably in composition.

The high percentage of villeins, 58 per cent, argues a reasonable degree of prosperity, even though some of these may well represent the free men and sokemen of 1066. We find a villein holding half a hide at Apps Court (35a2) and paying Richard fitzGilbert's 'men' 30*d. de gablo*. Clandon (34ai) had been worth £4 in 1066, but at the Inquest the six villeins who were renting it from Chertsey Abbey paid £6. It is a stiff rent, though presumably the dozen bordars contributed to it. The Gomshall villeins (30bi) were 'free from all liability to the sheriff', but as the manor was rendering £30, double its pre-Conquest value, though it was worth only £20, they may not have benefited much from this immunity.[1] Some villeins' land seems to have been lost to them. Two hides *de terra villanorum* had been converted to a sub-tenancy at Chobham (32b2), and 10½ at Send (36b2), where the manor had fallen in value from £20 to £15 10*s*. Villeins had held Chessington (36bi), which had lain in the manor of Beddington, but in 1086 there was some demesne land.

Few Surrey thegns had managed to retain their lands. Oswold, with four holdings rated at 21½ hides and worth £17, is the only one holding in chief in 1086.[2] Ketel and Wulfwig, who end the text, were huntsmen who still had the land they or their fathers had in 1066, a mere matter of three hides worth £3 10*s*. Probably they were not displaced because their experience made them invaluable to the newcomers.[3] Small sub-tenancies were held by Englishmen at Cuddington (31b2), Weybridge (32bi—held by the same man in 1066), in Kingston Hundred (32b2), and in seven other entries. A royal smith at Carshalton (36ai) seems also to have survived.

We hear also of natives commending themselves to the newcomers after the Conquest. A man in Wallington Hundred (36ai) 'placed himself for his defence in Walter of Douai's hands', and a Coombe woman (36bi) put herself and her land 'in the queen's hand'.[4]

In 18 entries only villeins are recorded. These, numbering 100, possessed 39 teams between them, averaging over three oxen per man. In no instance does it look as if they can have had many more, though at Tooting (33a) the solitary villein had half a team. The only clue to the potentiality of bordars is that at Southwark (32a2) there was a bordar, attached

[1] This may imply that they made no additional contribution to the sheriff's farm. Possibly they did so elsewhere; at Stoke (30a2) the render was £15 by weight and the sheriff had a presumably additional 25*s*.
[2] Perhaps a former sheriff, said to have refused to assist King Harold at Hastings. The three men whose lands follow him under the heading of 'other thegns' seem to be foreigners holding in sergeancy.
[3] But Almær the huntsman had lost Titing (31a2). Coleman *venator* (Betchworth, 35bi) might still have been a sub-sub-tenant in 1086. A forester had a hide at Walton-on-Thames (36a2).
[4] Probably Matilda, not Edith, for Humfrey, Matilda's chamberlain, had the manor.

to the manor of Battersea, 'of twelve pence'. But here and elsewhere the suspicion must remain that *bord.* is a mistake for *burg.*, and the 'bordar', who perhaps elsewhere would have been styled *censarius*, connected with a borough.

Sussex

The chief difficulty presented by the Domesday text, apart from the existence of many complex manors, and a large number of anonymous holdings, is the fact that frequently substantial portions of these complexities were transferred to other manors because these detached components lay in a Rape other than that in which the *caput manerii* was situated. Thus William of Warenne is said to have ten of the thirty-two hides of William de Braiose's manor of Beeding (28ai), and $7\frac{1}{2}$ of these ten were in 1086 in the Warenne manor of Aldrington (26b2) and indeed are said to have lain in the manor of Beeding in King Edward's time. Frequently, however, we are given no clue as to where the transferred portions of a manor lay, except that the Hundred to which they were attached is named. Sometimes, however, deduction as to their situation is possible. Thus eight hides which had been part of the Warenne manor of Iford (26ai) had been allotted to Robert of Mortain's Pevensey Rape, and these were probably eight of the hides at which Frog Firle (21bi) was assessed.

This makes consideration of changes in manorial values exceptionally difficult. Iford had been worth £50 in 1066, but only £35 in 1086. But had the value really fallen by £15, or should we deduct from the £50 at least the £4 which Frog Firle had been worth in 1066 in order to arrive at a truer comparison?

Or consider the vill of Goring. A certain Gilbert held *terra iii carucis* of William de Braiose (28a2); they had lain in Goring, which was in Earl Roger's Rape of Arundel, but was 'outside the Rape and the reckoning of its hides'. It looks as if it may have been land which had been colonised after the most recent hidation of the county. Three-and-a-half hides of the land of William's manor of Sompting (28b2, 29ai) were 'in Goring and other places'. Yet the four holdings of Goring (24b2, 25ai), one of which was a berewick of Steyning, at no time changed in value. We can only hope that most alterations of value caused by transference of land from one Rape to another are reflected in the valuations set down by the clerks.

Because of these transfers, some of the amount by which a manor fell in value must often be attributed, not to military operations or other upheaval caused by the newcomers, but to the loss of a portion of its land. This makes a map of fallen values somewhat deceptive. Hurstpierpoint

(27ai) lost 22½ of its 41 hides, and first fell in value from £36 to £9, and then recovered only to £12. Probably the manor *did* suffer damage during the Conquest, but something like half the loss of value may well be the amount which the detached portions were worth.

A second difficulty is that in the three Wealden Hundreds of Hawksborough, Henhurst, and Shoyswell there were a number of often unnamed holdings which seem to have been detached portions of manors in the Rape of Pevensey, e.g. Alciston (17b2). In such instances, as with all complex manors, we have no means of determining the value of even the principal settlement. Since these Wealden holdings were probably late colonisations, perhaps with no more than half a century's existence, they were most likely quite small, and their values would not seriously lower those accorded to the parent manors.[1]

A further source of dissatisfaction is an appreciable lack of the required information. We have 465 entries and sub-entries giving the values of manors and holdings in 1066. But for only about two-thirds of these, 327 in all, is the value given for dates which cannot have been greatly distant from 1066, for it is improbable that the new king would not have placed most of Sussex in his supporters' hands as soon as possible. It has been shown that Roger of Montgomery was established at Arundel in or soon after December, 1067, Robert of Eu at Hastings by May, 1070, and Robert of Mortain at Pevensey and William of Warenne at Lewes in the same year.[2] The need to guard communications with Normandy was from the first of paramount importance.

Nine holdings, rather unexpectedly, had risen in value, according to the text.[3] About one-third show no change in value, but it is highly possible that portions of these had in fact suffered damage in the early days of the Conquest. Sixteen, almost all in the Rape of Hastings, are said to have become waste, and in all 63 per cent fell in value. Many of the depreciations attained 60–80 per cent of the 1066 values. A holding in Netherfield Hundred (18b2) fell in value from £5 to £1, Ninfield (18ai) from £6 to £1, while Filsham and Crowhurst (17b2), which had been worth £14 and £8 in 1066, were waste. Willingdon's value of £60 (21ai) was apparently halved, but 14½ of its 50½ hides were transferred to Hastings Rape, though not necessarily before the time of the intermediate valuation.

Values *post* may not always refer to 1067 or to the early days of Norman ascendancy. They, and those said to be *quando recepit* also, could be for the

---

[1] See *VCH*: i, pp. 257–8, and L. F. Salzman: 'The Rapes of Sussex' (*Sussex Archaeol. Collns.*, lxxii, Cambridge, 1931), pp. 20–39.
[2] J. F. A. Mason: 'The Rapes of Sussex and the Norman Conquest' (*Sussex Archaeol. Collns.*, cii, 1964), pp. 75–86.   [3] There might be clerical errors about some of these.

moments when the tenants-in-chief sub-infeudated their land. If so, this might in part account for the fact that 107 holdings had the same values *tunc* and *post*; time for recovery had elapsed.

But it seems highly improbable that Sussex was left wholly undisturbed until its new lords were given their lands. Transference might indeed have been made before the dates given above, though the need to cope with the revolts and invasions north of the Thames in 1069–70 implies that full-scale occupation could not have occurred before the end of 1070. Yet could William of Normandy, on beginning his Kentish campaign, leave an unsubdued Sussex in his rear, even though its efficient fighting strength must have been greatly reduced? He could hardly summon immediate large reinforcements from Normandy, nor can there then have been unlimited men in the Duchy from whom to draw reserves, though some are said to have arrived soon after Hastings fight. On the other hand, in the state to which southern England must have been reduced in 1066, quite small bodies of determined invaders should have been sufficient to negative a threat to his rear.

If a detachment was sent to subdue Sussex, it would naturally be expected to secure the boroughs, which alone might provide centres of resistance. If the post-Conquest falls in value are a guide, this is what it did. The Hastings and Pevensey area had already been dealt with, and perhaps Rye also. The first objective would be Lewes, and heavy falls in value are to be seen in the neighbourhood of Eastbourne, and then south of the present Eastbourne—Lewes road. Lines of decline in value from Newhaven and Cuckmere running north to this track are most likely to have been caused by foraging parties than by a force from the sea: reinforcements would hardly arrive so early. From Lewes to Steyning, then a port of considerable activity, the fallen values suggest a progress through Plumpton, Keymer, Hurstpierpoint, and Henfield, continuing through Findon and Patching to Arundel. A line of progress westwards separates into two about Eastergate and passes to north and south of Chichester. Of the bishop of Selsey's manors only Wittering shows no diminution of value: in all they fell from £126 to £84 in value. The most remarkable figure is that for Bosham (1742). The manor was in the hands of Osbern, later the Norman bishop of Exeter, but still it is said to have fallen in value from £300 to £50, though apparently the manor of that name which had been Earl Godwine's retained its 1066 value of £40. Osbern's manor must have occupied a considerable area, and the Bosham holdings may have been harshly treated to ensure that they should not be used as landing-places for seaborne resistance. It must be remembered, however, that the manor had lost 47 of its former 112 hides.

THE SOUTH-EAST: SUSSEX

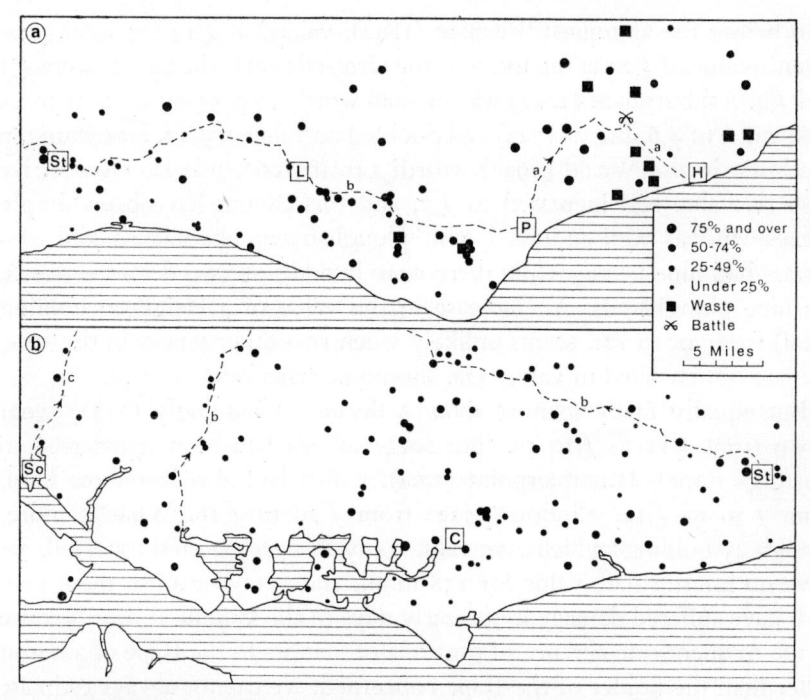

Fig. 5 (a) Eastern Sussex (b) Western Sussex and South-East Hampshire
Fall in value *tunc–post*
C—Chichester H—Hastings L—Lewes P—Pevensey
So—Southampton St—Steyning
– – – Suggested routes of principal Norman detachments
(a) before Hastings fight, (b) reinforcements, concentrating at Alton,
(c) ditto, moving on Winchester

Of the 327 holdings with comparable figures for the period, about 10 per cent give no place-name or that of the manor of which they were part. A map showing falls in value can obviously be only a highly imperfect one.

On the figures Domesday gives us, land worth £3,038 9s. 10d. in 1066 fell in value after the Conquest to £1,825 8s. 6d., a decline of almost 40 per cent. We cannot, because we do not know when the composition of manors was altered, estimate the effect on the individual district, but certainly it seems that the areas which first saw the invaders, the Rapes of Hastings and Pevensey, had suffered most. As these were composed in 1086, Robert of Eu's estates had fallen by 68 per cent, and those of Robert of Mortain by nearly 50 per cent.

The county shows by its 1086 values its powers of recovery. But it does not seem as a whole to have attained even the value of 1066. The total is about 8¼ per cent less than this, although manors which had at some time become completely waste were occasionally worth more than they had

59

been before the Conquest. Filsham (18a2), valued at £14 for 1066, was given a value of £22 at the Inquest; for Drigsell (19bi) the figures were £3 and £4. Ashburnham (18a2) was in 1086 worth 50 per cent more than its 1066 value of £6, Bury (17a2) had doubled its value of £12. Hazelhurst in Ticehurst in the Weald (19a2), worth 14s. in 1066, was later waste. By 1086 its value had increased to £7, and this cannot have been simply because it was well-endowed with plough-oxen; ten villeins and two cottars had nine teams, while there were in addition two demesne teams, for nine ploughlands. An increase in the value of a Heighton holding (20ai) from 2s. to 12s. seems unlikely when two other estates in the same vill had not changed in value; 12s. should perhaps have been 2s.

But equally many manors show a decline. Chiddingly (22a2) went down from £15 to £10 5s. (but some of this had been transferred to Hastings Rape), Hurstpierpoint (27ai), which had also lost some land, from £36 to £12, Slindon (25a2) from £20 to £16. What is more, though 45 holdings which give values only *tunc* and *modo* show a fall, we have no intermediate value for 138 in all, and many or all of these may well have suffered damage in the early days of the Conquest. But because of the frequent transference of portions of manors to the Rape of a baron other than the holder of the Rape concerned, we cannot always estimate just which holdings had been affected. But we are told that £1 had been deducted from the 1086 value of Sherrington (20b2) because half a hide of its five hides (the most profitable part of the former manor, since the residue was worth £2) had been transferred to another Rape.

Fifteen holdings only declined in value between *post* and *modo*, and nearly 70 per cent display recovery. A 1066 value of £3,302 9s. 11d. had become one of £3,028 3s. 2d., and since there are but 35 entries where only a 1086 value is given, the figures are fairly comprehensive.[1] Three small holdings are indeed said to have been waste in 1086 (Hollington, 17b2; West Firle, 21ai; Wilting, 17b2). For none are we given a former value. At Beech Farm (18b2) there was nothing, *nichil*; in 1066 it had been worth only 2s. Of a holding in Hankham (22a2) it is said, *inde nullum responsum*. Yet someone (the Hundredmen?) could value it at 9s. No teams or inhabitants are recorded.[2] Of a Mid Lavant estate (23ai) *nichil est*, 'nothing is there', was recorded. Again no teams or inhabitants are mentioned, and when the clerk added *tamen valet xx solidos*, he must have been giving this former manor, assessed at one hide, its potential value.

[1] If certain doubtful entries are ignored, the county in 1086 was worth 89 per cent of its 1066 value.
[2] The entry for another holding in Hankham immediately preceding it is fairly comprehensive.

THE SOUTH-EAST: SUSSEX

From our calculations, too, we are obliged to omit the manors which in King Edward's day had been liable for a night's farm. Beeding (28ai), which had had this responsibility, had then been valued at £95 5s. 6d.; by 1086 it was worth only £40, but it had lost ten of its 32 hides. Beddingham (20bi) had been only slightly diminished in size, but was worth only £30, plus two sub-tenancies valued at £6. Eastbourne (20bi) too had lost a little land, but with the sub-tenancies was worth but £43 7s. Presumably the night's farm at these two manors of 52½ and 46 hides respectively had been worth not much less than £100.

But despite the evils which had befallen the men of Sussex, the farmers and reeves of over a score of manors and holdings were having to pay, or had paid, more than they were worth. Four times we are told that the manors could not cope with the inflated charges.[1] That on Patching is said to be too heavy, and twice a manor is said to have been at farm (*fuit ad firmam*), with the implication that by 1086 it had been found impossible to extract the sum demanded.[2] What was said to be worth £753 4s. had been or was being expected to produce £1,020 13s. Unless some manors had been greatly enlarged, the demands were indeed formidable:

17a2 Steyning	worth £100,	at farm for £121 18s.[3]
28ai Washington	„	£52 16s., had been farmed for £100
16a2 Rotherfield	„	£12, rendering £30
16bi Pagham	„	£60, „ £80

Only eight fiefs are represented, yet it seems most improbable that none of the manors of Robert of Mortain, William of Warenne, and Robert of Eu was at farm for more than its true value. The only other mention of a farm is a ten-shilling holding in Hartfield Hundred (21b2), and the statement that the other Steyning manor (28a2) had been in King Edward's *firma*. But when the value of Playden (19b2) is given as 112s., but Robert of Eu is said to have 143s. thence (*inde*), it may be that the higher sum is the rent actually received, for five tenants shared the manor.

The *Domesday Monachorum* does not, except on fol. 11, include the Canterbury manors in Sussex. South Malling is here said to have a *firma* of £100, not £90, and to produce in addition 30s. for the archbishop, £10 10s. of *gafol*, and £4 14s. in customary dues. Both Stanmer and Patching, which we are told had been unable to bear their increased burdens, are unmentioned (perhaps these had been withdrawn), but the sums for Pagham and Tangmere, where according to DB the reeve had 20s.

[1] Stanmer, Patching (16bi), Preston (17ai), Shoreham (28ai).
[2] Henfield (16b2), Washington (28ai).   [3] Steyning counted also as a borough.

from the manor, are higher than in DB. In addition to a farm of £10 against a value of £6, Tangmere had to find an ounce of gold, perhaps as a premium for the lease; both Singleton and Harting with Trotting (23ai,2) were liable for a gold mark payable to Earl Roger. *Dom. Mon.* fol. 11 says also that West Tarring and East Lavant were at farm, which DB does not, but the sums mentioned do not vary greatly from the DB values. But it must be remembered that the figures of fol. 11 are post-Domesday.

By no means all the valuations are in round figures, and some may represent the sum of rents. We find such quantities as £89, £80 5s. 6d., £7 3s., £5 14s., £2 18s., 13s., 2s. 1d., with remarkable frequency.[1] Where we find £8 6s., it is not impossible that the 6s. was the value of the $1\frac{1}{2}$ virgates held by two *francigenae*, or their rent (Tillington, 23bi). There are several similar instances.

Of rents paid by the peasantry we learn singularly little. At Ratton (21a2) three cottars paid 2s. and at Willingdon one paid 1s. (19a2). There are, however, a few instances in which the holdings presumably rented by villeins are mentioned. Villeins had held the land of two of the three *alodiarii* who held $6\frac{1}{4}$ hides at Brighton, and the four hides of Balmer; at an anonymous holding in the same neighbourhood a villein also belonging to the manor of Falmer had held a hide worth 6s. Villeins belonging to Keymer had held Bevendean, some of those of Beeding the portion transferred to Aldrington, and villeins had held at Hurstpierpoint and Westmeston.[2] A villein had held and still held a virgate at Lancing (29ai). But in some manors villeins seem to have been robbed of their land. Nine newcomers at Hooe (18ai) had tenancies which had been *de terra villanorum*. Villeins had held Falmer (22bi), but we are not told whether in 1086 they were still renting this part of an unnamed manor.

Stray phrases give some indication that recovery was far from complete. At Tilton (21ai), which had been worth £3 10s., there was in 1086 nothing but two villeins and four acres of meadow, yet it is said to be worth £1, perhaps a potential rentable value. In the following entry, for the same place, no inhabitants are recorded, nor teams for the four ploughlands, yet this is given a value of 15s., only 3s. less than it had been in 1066. Though 'no one lives' at Wootton (27bi), it is said to be worth 12s., and where there was nothing but ten acres of meadow (Woolfly, 28bi), a value of 5s. was set on it. Of a Chancton holding (28bi) it was said *nichil ibi est*, yet it was worth 11s. But that there was also new ground being broken is

---

[1] Singleton (23ai), Ditchling (26a2), Duncton (23bi), Hazelhurst (19a2), Hollington (18bi), in the manor of Loughton (19ai), The Horns (22ai), *Pengest* (21bi).
[2] Fols. 26bi,2; 27ai,2—all in the Warenne fief.

shown by the fact that what had been pasture-land in the manor of Storrington (29a2), was 'newly cultivated' (*hospitata*).

To determine how far the profits of manorial appurtenances were included in the valuations is impossible. Wootton (*Lodintone*, 22ai), is said to be worth £6 11s. 8d., and to possess a mill worth 20s., pasture of the same amount, and five salt-pans worth 41s. 8d. The 1s. 8d. rather suggests that the £6 11s. 8d. includes the salt-pans, and that the arable land was worth 50s. against a pre-Conquest value of 30s. But in the next entry, for Hailsham, the value of the salt-pans exceeds the value given to the manor. We simply do not know whether swine- or money-rents for pasture, eel- or money-rents for fisheries, the renders from salt-pans and quarries, of grain and eels and money for mills, were included in a *valet* or not. Perhaps they were usually excluded; they could be let independently of the arable and meadowland.

Forest land is only once mentioned in the Sussex text; half a hide at Dallington (18b2) worth 5s. Perhaps King William, having bestowed the greater part of the shire on five men, did not wish to antagonise these essential supporters by taking land into the Forest.[1] But the king had a park in his manor of Rotherfield (16a2), and both Robert of Eu and Earl Roger had parks (18bi, 25ai,2 *bis*, 25b2).

In sixteen entries a blank space was left for the quantity of ploughlands, and in over one hundred others they are not given. The latter feature is particularly apparent on fols. 19ai–b2, which are concerned with those Wealden Hundreds attached to manors in Pevensey Rape. Most of the holdings have teams, and where we are not given the ploughlands, it is probable that these were reckoned among those of the parent manors. This might account for a not infrequent excess of teams over ploughlands in the larger manors. Bexhill (18b2) had 37 teams for only 26 ploughlands, Wartling (18ai) 29 for 16. South Malling (16a2,bi) had 94 teams but only the round figure of 50 ploughlands; the latter may have been ignored for the sub-tenancies which had 16 teams, and this was certainly a complex manor. Steyning (17a2) is said to have 55 teams for 41 ploughlands, but some of the manor was in Bramber and some in Arundel Rape (28a2), where there were 20 teams and 21 ploughlands, and some of the latter was in Earl Roger's Rape at Goring (24b2), which had seven of each. Out of 357 entries, 96 show more teams than ploughlands, and 144 less. Where there are demesne teams, 73 per cent of the entries record no slaves, but then on the DB figures, which here may not be accurate, less than 5 per cent of the recorded Sussex population were slaves. Also from the DB

[1] There might have been land 'in the Forest' before the Conquest unmentioned in DB. Much of northern Sussex, virtually without recorded settlements, was wild woodland.

figures, where comparison is possible, there were 2,806 teams for 2,768 ploughlands. To produce a useful relationship between teams and ploughlands is obviously impossible.

Nor can we be altogether happy about calculations as to the number of oxen possessed by the peasantry. In 99 entries 605 villeins had 308⅛ teams, giving an average of half a team a head. There are plenty of instances of villeins with apparently whole teams, e.g. at Filsham (17b2) or Bellhurst (20a2), but there is always the fear latent that in some of the entries where only villeins are recorded the clerk may have accidentally omitted bordars or cottars, and such an omission would vitiate the calculations. There is always the suspicion, too, that some teams apparently those of villeins may not be so. 'A team in demesne, with one villein' (19b1), is clear enough, but 'the earl has two villeins with a team' (19a2) may not imply that the villeins owned the team. Even after the Conquest we can imagine a Sussex villein with half a team, and if an appreciable number possessed so many oxen, the figure of less than two for Kent seems even more improbable. But there is no difficulty about finding teamless villeins. None is recorded for the eight at Frankwell (18a2), nor for the three at Burghleigh (22bi). The two villeins and five bordars at Erringham (28ai) are said to be *nil habentes*. Bordars' teams are isolatable in only ten entries, and in these 48 have 7½ teams, or 1¼ oxen per bordar. But in Sedlescombe (20a2) two bordars had a team; in contrast, a Cudnor bordar (22ai) had a single ox. Over and over again, where there were only bordars or cottars, only demesne teams seem to be mentioned. Thirteen in the manor of Bishopstone (16b2) are not said to have any oxen, nor six at Marden (24ai). Five cottars at Ballington (18a2) may have had two teams, but probably the twenty burgesses who presumably were attached to Hastings had the major share in them. As bordars and cottars never appear together in any entry, the clerks presumably saw small distinction between them.

Hampshire[1]

In this county an enormous proportion of its total wealth was in the hands of the king or the Church, and the Church was more than twice as wealthy as the king. While this results in a detailed and helpful Domesday text, it has the disadvantage of possibly falsifying the picture. King and Church had resources considerably greater than those of the average baron with land in Hampshire, many of whom were relatively unimportant men, or, though of the calibre of Arnulf de Hesdin or Eudes fitzHubert, had only a

[1] The holdings in the New Forest have been excluded from this section.

THE SOUTH-EAST: HAMPSHIRE

single manor, or very few, in the county. Recovery from post-Conquest damage, then, may have been minimal on many lay estates, but spectacular elsewhere.

If the four royal manors with somewhat artificial figures for their *firma* are omitted, we find a fall of 20½ per cent in post-Conquest values, from £2,066 0s. 4d. to £1,644 8s. 11d.[1] Yet of the 265 holdings for which we have comparative values, only 18 are said to have appreciated in value, but 137 to have retained their pre-Conquest values. A holding which had not experienced the passage of troops would find it easier to maintain its standards, or add to its resources, than one which had been impoverished. Only Bishops Sutton (44bi) shows a large appreciation, from £50 to £60, and if Headley was not part of the manor in 1066, as it was in 1086, this

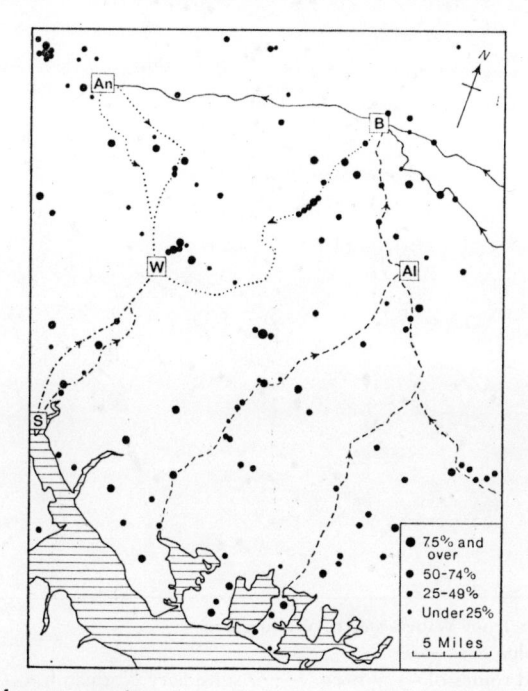

Fig. 6 The Winchester campaign
      Fall in value *tunc–post*
      Al—Alton   An—Andover   B—Basingstoke   S—Southampton
      W—Winchester
      ———— Suggested route of main force and detachment moving to Andover
       –·–· & ···· Forces concentrating at Winchester   – – – Reinforcements

---

[1] The royal manors of Neatham (38ai) and Broughton (38bi) each paid £76 16s. 8d., twice the sum produced by Barton Stacey (38bi) and Eling (38b2). But the resources of the first two, so far as can be determined from the text, were very different. For some large royal manors, e.g. Andover (39a2) and King's Somborne (39bi), we are given no values.

65

might account for the increase.[1] On the royal and ecclesiastical manors the decline in value is only about 17½ per cent.

The invading force whose aim was to clinch the surrender of Winchester seems to have concentrated in the neighbourhood of Basingstoke. Here it

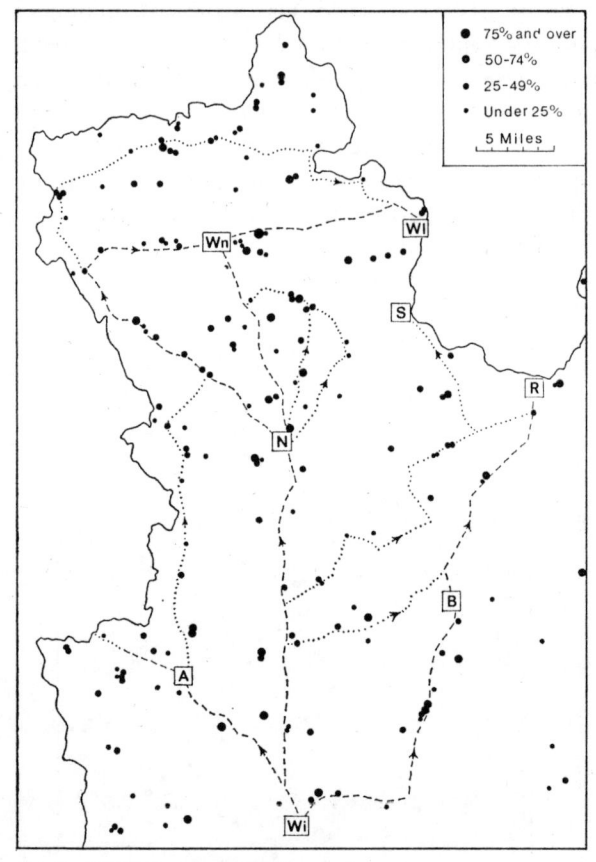

Fig. 7 The move from Winchester to Wallingford
Fall in value *tunc–post*
Suggested routes of – – – main · · · · subsidiary Norman forces
A—Andover B—Basingstoke N Newbury R—Reading S—Streatley
Wi—Winchester Wl—Wallingford Wn—Wantage

was joined by reinforcements from Normandy, who are said to have landed at Fareham. Their movement up the Meon valley is plainly marked. It is noticeable, as in Sussex, that there is a good deal of damage around inlets in the Portsmouth harbour–Hayling Island area. It looks as if reinforcements may also have landed here and in west Sussex, and together

[1] Bishops Sutton is said to have been held by Earl Harold, Headley by his father.

THE SOUTH-EAST: HAMPSHIRE

with a force moving north-westwards from Steyning concentrated at Alton before joining the main body at Basingstoke. It is possible that a further detachment landed at Southampton, perhaps rather later, and advanced on Winchester by the lower Itchen valley. The Duke must have

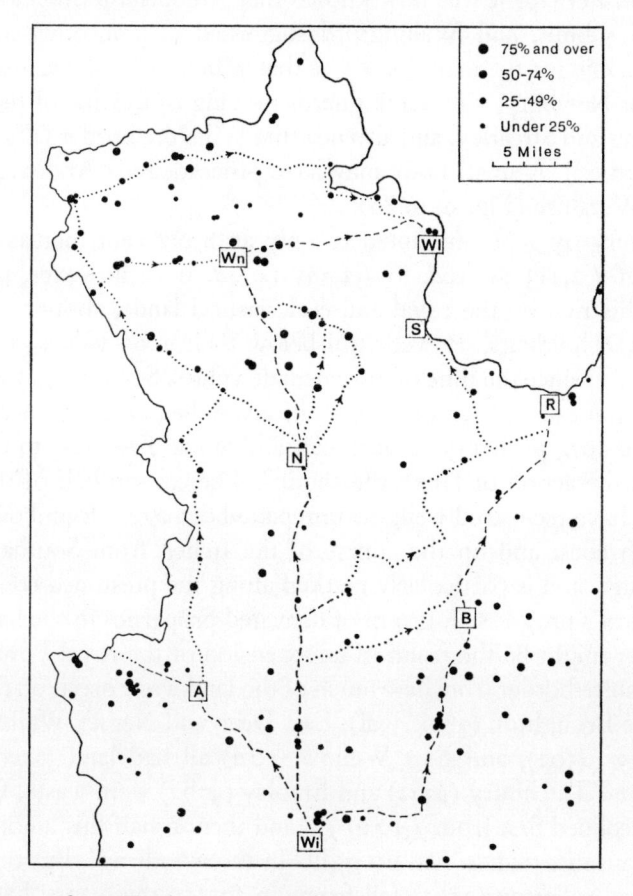

Fig. 8 The move from Winchester to Wallingford
    Fall in value *tunc–modo*
    Suggested routes and places as in Fig. 7

sent a proportion of his ships back to Normandy with orders for the raising of additional troops to strengthen his position.

He seems to have followed his usual procedure by sending a body of men to occupy the Andover district, thus interposing a strong force between Winchester and possible aid to the city from the north and west. Their movement would presumably be swift, first because it was vital to block the roads from Wiltshire, and secondly because the terrain through which they had to pass offered scant opportunity for supplies or plunder. When Winchester offered surrender we do not know, but Queen Edith's city seems to have appreciated the uselessness of resistance.

The invaders then concentrated at Winchester, preparatory to reducing Berkshire. Perhaps it was now known that Archbishop Stigand was prepared to submit, and Wallingford suggested as a meeting-place. The obvious route for the main force was that which led to the crossing of the Kennet at Newbury, with flank guards moving to the line of the Thames at Reading and Streatley, and also near the Wiltshire border (Figs. 7 and 8, pp. 66 and 67). A small body may have proceeded via Andover through eastern Wiltshire (Fig. 9, p. 80).

Recovery by 1086 amounted to only an 8 per cent increase on 1066 values, of £2,213 8s. 10d. to £2,385 1s. 4d. It is, however, more than double this rate on the royal and ecclesiastical lands, about 18 per cent. Out of 326 holdings, 97 were still below their 1066 values, and 22 had indeed fallen since the time of intermediate values. Some falls in value were certainly not caused by military operations. Ashe (47a2) fell in value from £7 to £6 10s., probably because half a hide had been lost to the manor 'through the action of Hugh the sheriff'. The eastern half of the county seems to have recovered well; the unrepaired damage is found on and near the south coast and up the course of the Itchen from Southampton to Winchester, and is particularly marked along the presumed course of the flank guard's progress. A group of damaged properties in the basin of the Test river might be the result of an extension of the royal Forests. Over the Wiltshire border from here much of the land was Forest; on the Hampshire side Broughton (38bi, 39ai), East Dean and Nether Wallop (38b2), Lockerley (45b2), and East Wellow (50ai) all had land taken into the Forest, and Tatchbury (43a2) and Embley (47b2) were waste. Chilworth (47b2) declined first from £10 to £8 and then to half this amount, probably because its owner 'had no rights in the woodland'. But though one holding at Soberton (48b2) fell from £3 to £2, the manor having been diminished in value by the inclusion of half a hide in Earl Roger of Shrewsbury's park, another (49ai), where a virgate had been similarly extracted, fell in value soon after the Conquest only. By 1086 it was worth twice what it had been in 1066.

But whatever the state of the county in 1086, the newcomers were trying to obtain the most from it. At least 44 properties were having to produce more than the values set on them. In several instances it was noted that they could not manage to produce the sums demanded.[1] Already, it seems, the attempt to secure exorbitant rents had had to be abandoned.

[1] East Meon (38a2), worth £60, but paying £100 by weight, Fareham (40bi), Exton (41bi).

The churches of the manor of Alresford (40ai) were worth £4; they had been paying £6 a year, 'but they could not bear it'. West Meon (40bi), worth £30, was farmed for £40, 'but it cannot bear it for long'. Polhampton (47a2) had sunk in value from £12 to £8, but it had been farmed (*fuit ad firmam*) for £9. It looks as if the attempt to secure the extra rent had failed.

Nearly half the instances come from the king's lands and those of the bishop of Winchester and his monks, though fourteen other landholders furnish examples of such demands. These seem at times to be fantastic. Hannington (41b2), with a recorded population of only 28, had been worth £5 in 1066, £6 later, and was valued at £8 in 1086. But it was at farm for £15. East Hoe (45a2), held by the sheriff's tenant, was worth £3, but was at farm for as much as £14, though the recorded population was only nine and there was little wood and only an acre of meadow. We might well wonder whether, when the value of a manor is very high compared with that of 1066, the sum given was in fact a farm-rent. Dean (48bi) was occupied by two bordars who indeed had half a plough-team; it had always been worth 7s., but was at farm for 15s.[1]

The demands made on the royal manors which had furnished a night's or half a night's farm seem to be entirely arbitrary. Barton Stacey (38bi) and Eling (38b2), each worth £38 8s. 4d. in 1066, was each paying £52 6s. 1d., though valued at £33 and £20 respectively. Broughton (38bi) and Neatham (38ai), each worth £76 16s. 8d. in 1066, were finding £104 12s. 2d. and £118 12s. 9d., though Broughton was worth only £66, and some of its land and that of the *caput manerii* had been taken into the Forest.[2] The whole system is obviously an artificial one, the £66 and £33 look like the division of £100 in the proportion of 2:1, and 3 × £52 6s. 1d. less 3 × £38 8s. 4d. is 9,999 pence.

In all, we have

	valued at	producing
	£ s. d.	£ s. d.
Royal manors	351 6 8	513 6 3
Bishop and cathedral monks of Winchester	183 0 0	243 2 6
Other tenants-in-chief	269 17 0	372 0 0
	804 3 8	1,128 8 9

[1] Could it be that, held by a certain Herbert of Walter fitzRoger, the pre-Conquest holder of the allodial manor, Wulfstan, or his heir, was having to pay this sum to continue to occupy the land?
[2] The 1086 value given for Neatham, £76 16s. 8d., must be an error. Basingstoke, Kingsclere, and Hurstbourne Tarrant (39a2) together rendered a night's farm, which Round showed was also £104 12s. 2d., though given as twopence less (*VCH*, i, pp. 401–2).

THE DETAILS OF DOMESDAY BOOK

The receipts, over 40 per cent above valuations, would go far towards making up the only small increase between 1066 and 1086, while the royal manors for which we have no values, and possibly farm-rents ignored by Domesday, might make the gap wider.

It might then be expected that there should be a deficiency of teams in Hampshire. In twelve entries a blank space was left where the number of ploughlands should have come, and they are not given in 21 others. Out of 306 entries, 78 give more teams than ploughlands, and 112 less. The potential deficiency is, however, only a small one, for where comparison is possible there are $1,992\frac{3}{8}$ teams for $2,075\frac{1}{2}$ ploughlands, which is only about 3 per cent.[1] It is interesting that if the apparent superfluities of teams are plotted, these are found on the alluvium and river gravels, as though here more oxen were needed than elsewhere. They come too, near Forest land, where the soil might also require more oxen to undertake the ploughing. There is a tendency also for excesses to appear on the larger and richer fiefs. At Abbots Worthy (42b) we do indeed find two villeins and nine bordars without a plough-team. But there are not a few instances of a superfluity. Nursling (41ai) had eleven teams for six ploughlands, and Hayling (43bi) 19 for 14. But in addition to the usual lack of information in many entries about the number of ploughlands, the suspicion that often their quantity has been arrived at by adding up the teams cannot be avoided. Neatham (38ai) had 52 of each, East Meon (38a2) 64, Whitchurch (41ai) 52, and Crondal (41a2) 29. In the last instance, as elsewhere, we probably are not given the ploughlands on the sub-tenancies at Itchell, Cove, and Clare Park, which had ten teams. But certainly there were apparently grave deficiencies. Bishops Sutton (44bi) had only 28 teams for its 50 ploughlands, but the latter might be an arbitrary round number. Micheldever (42b) had 72 ploughlands, but 34 teams on the demesne portion, and 26 in the scattered sub-tenancies.

Teamless villeins and bordars appear in numerous entries. In 37 others 244 villeins have $78\frac{7}{8}$ teams, averaging over $2\frac{1}{2}$ oxen per man. Only twice do we find a villein with an entire team (Odiham, 38ai; an anonymous manor, 47ai), while at Preston Candover (49b2) the three villeins had only three oxen between them.[2] In 13 entries 103 bordars had 13 teams, or an ox per man. Yet the twelve Basingstoke *coliberti* (39a2), though these are usually considered to be enfranchised slaves, had four teams. Here the villeins and bordars averaged $3\frac{1}{2}$ oxen apiece.

[1] I have assumed that where inhabitants were extremely few an absence of recorded oxen is correct. I have not included teams on sub-tenancies where the relevant ploughlands are obviously not mentioned: in a few fiefs it is clear that all the ploughlands are noted.

[2] The vill was one which, judging by the values, had suffered severely. Moreover, this holding had lost some of its land, which had been put in the royal manor of Odiham.

THE SOUTH-EAST: THE NEW FOREST

Villeins could afford to continue to rent the episcopal manors of Alverstoke (41bi) and Millbrook (41b2), worth £6 and £5 respectively. On the former 48 villeins had 15 teams, or nearly 2½ oxen each, at the latter 28 had only five teams. Since there were no demesne teams at the neighbouring manors of Hayling, Brockhampton, and Havant (43ai), it may be that the villeins (there were no bordars or slaves) were renting these. In all the three were worth £17 10s., and the 45 villeins had 13½ teams. At an anonymous holding in the manor of Micheldever (42b) four villeins were paying 7s., presumably as rent. Twice the rents of coliberts are mentioned; two at Kingsclere (39a2) paid 13s., while at Cosham (38a2) eight *buri* or *coliberti* had four teams and paid 49s. 4d. At Mottisfont a bordar paid 7d.

Pre-Conquest landholders or their heirs held nearly forty estates, several of them quite large ones. Some had purchased their land since the Conquest.[1] Cola redeemed his kinsmen's land from William fitzOsbern, but his son had mortgaged it. Ælfwine 'ret', whose three Tytherley manors (50ai) were in 1086 held by Ælfwige Thorbjornson, two of the previous tenants having been killed at Hastings, had managed to acquire them without the formality of livery or the royal writ. Some of the holders, and probably, from their names, several more than we are told of, were huntsmen, e.g. Ælfsige, Edwin, and Wulfric (50a2,bi,2). For a Cola was a huntsman (Ellingham, Langley; 50a2,b2), and several of the names occur as those of survivors in the New Forest section. It would be essential to maintain skilled men who had long known the ways of the hunting-grounds.

The New Forest

The six Hampshire Hundreds west of Southampton Water form a convenient unit, for the greater part of them was royal Forest and the entries have much to tell us about such land both before and after the Conquest. The principal complication is that some of the land attached to royal manors and one holding belonging to the Twynham canons were in the Isle of Wight, and no indication is given as to what proportion of the details was applicable to the island's statistics.[2]

The entries are conveniently classified in three groups; (a) no mention of Forest, (b) partly in the Forest, (c) wholly in the Forest. There are only four which are of no particular pattern.

[1] Oakhanger (49b2), Hartley Westpall (50ai)—a manor worth 15s. bought for two gold marks.
[2] Eling (38b2), Holdenhurst, Ringwood (39ai), Twynham (44a2), and parts of Breamore, Rockbourne, Broughton, and Burgate (39a2). Lyndhurst had contributed to the farm of the Wiltshire manor of Amesbury (39ai).

(a) In 36 out of the 135 entries the Forest is unmentioned.[1] Fifteen fell but little in value in the early years, by only just over 20 per cent; in all the total values in 1066 and 1086 were virtually the same. Thirteen, indeed, had increased in value; possibly these included men and equipment from land taken into the Forest.

(b) The vills where part of the land was in the Forest number 48. The non-royal ones had fallen in value by some 30 per cent by the time they had changed hands, and the unafforested portions were in 1086 worth less than half of their 1066 values. But in 17 entries we are told also what the land within the Forest is worth. Quite often the combined values of this and the unafforested land equal that of 1066. Ibsley (46ai), for example, had been worth £4 in 1066; in 1086 it was valued at £3, and 'what is in the Forest' at £1. Of 27 entries in which we are given values for both 1066 and 1086 and, by means of differing formulae, that of the land taken into the Forest, eleven together show no decline against 1066, and seven an apparent increase. But in some of these last it may be that the value of the land in the Forest is really included in the 1086 value. If not, manors such as Fordingbridge (46b2), though three virgates and all the woodland were in the Forest, had gone up in value from £3 to £4. Whether the value set on Forest land represents actual or only potential receipts is problematical, but the fact that the value of Forest land was supplied and recorded suggests that it was realistic. It suggests too that there inhabitants and teams had not been seriously reduced in number, and perhaps that there had been an influx from less fortunate holdings.

(c) Including Tatchbury (43a2), said to be waste, 47 holdings were in 1086 wholly in the Forest, except that for rather less than half of these a few acres of meadow were not included therein.[2] Many were quite small, and their total value in 1066 had been only £85 11s., less than one-third of the value of the whole area without the royal manors.

The effect of afforestation on the inhabitants cannot have been as devastating as it was once commonly supposed to be. Large sterile areas, the settlement map shows, had been unpopulated. When, in some entries, it is recorded that men and their dwellings had been 'taken into the Forest', this does not necessarily mean that they had been rendered homeless. The dispossessed may have been transferred to other manors; if so, this might account for appreciations in value. But many may not have been moved. So many holdings have a total value covering land both within

---

[1] It is probable that Burgate (50a2), where there was *silva sine pasnagio*, was to this extent in the Forest.
[2] At Canterton (50b2) the meadow was within the Forest, and at Burgate (39a2) and Bickton (44b2) the pasture.

THE SOUTH-EAST: THE NEW FOREST

and without the Forest that it is difficult to believe that their population had been substantially reduced. There may well have been less agricultural activity, for where land was wholly in the Forest, in 15 entries it is noted that there 'were' *n* ploughlands. But in 17 the formula is *terra est* n *carucis*, and it is questionable whether these ploughlands would have been recorded if they were not in use. To be 'taken into the Forest' did not imply total disappearance from the scene.

How far compensation was made for inclusion in the Forest is problematical. But its owner had received Milford (51b2) 'in exchange for land in the Forest'. The name of the owner, Ælfric, appears frequently; a man of this name held Efford in Milford, which had doubled in value. We cannot say, moreover, just how many holdings were affected by King William's extension of the Forest. Certainly he is said to have included *Achelie* (51ai) in it, but this was his own manor, and the frequent use of 'it is now in the Forest', and a reduction of assessment because so many hides or virgates were 'in the Forest', imply that inclusion was post-Conquest. But there was Forest in west Hampshire before King William came to England, and while the peasantry and small landholders may have suffered, it is doubtful if the baronage who had been granted manors in the district lost greatly by his appropriations. It is significant that even here several manors are said to be worth so much, but rendering a higher sum. These are not all royal ones; Stanpit (46a2), Sopley (48b2), and Dibden (51bi) were in all valued at £7, but were bringing £13 to their owners.

The whole or part of every royal manor was within the Forest, and the valuations set on them, even including that of the Forest land, was nearly one-fifth less than it had been in 1066. But they were having to produce more than their valuations. Eling, Twynham, Holdenhurst, and Ringwood (38b2, 39ai) were having to find £102 6s. 1d. against a valuation of £62 10s. Broughton (38bi,2) was outside the New Forest, but on fol. 39ai is linked with other royal manors, parts of which were within it, but we are not told the values of these.[1] If these could produce such sums, they cannot have lost many inhabitants and their equipment.

The royal property taken into the Forest is said to be outside the manors concerned, and with one exception (Hordle, 51a2), it is only in the entries for these that the past tense is used of villagers and their holdings, as it is of a mill at Ringwood (39ai). It is highly doubtful if closure or migration is implied; the fairly full details regarding land in the Forest were probably

---

[1] We are, however, told that one hide was in the Isle of Wight, and used to furnish £9 towards the royal *firma*. The holder, 'Gherui', is probably the 'Gerin' who had a hide at Ningwood (*Lenimcode*, 54ai), which had contributed £9 to King Edward's *firma*. Yet we are told it had been worth £6, perhaps after the Conquest; in 1086 it was worth £7.

recorded because royal Forest was most likely not the concern of the sheriff, Hugh de Port, or of farmers of royal manors.

In 15 entries the quantity of ploughlands is not given, and in 16 the teams outnumber the ploughlands. Instances of the latter occur almost invariably in the Avon valley and near Southampton Water, again suggesting the need for extra oxen where the soils demanded their use. Where comparison is possible, there were $197\frac{1}{2}$ teams for 203 ploughlands, a deficiency of only $2\frac{3}{4}$ per cent. But we ought to add 113 to the number of ploughlands where no teams are recorded and often the formula is *terra fuit n carucis*. In over half the instances of demesne teams no slaves are recorded.

We might suspect that sometimes, when the number of teams exceeds that of the ploughlands, some oxen had been transferred from land taken into the Forest. Seven of the eight virgates at Fawley were in the Forest, and on fol. 41b2 two teams appear for land for one team on the remaining virgate, but fol. 51ai says that earlier there had been land for twelve teams.

The occasions on which only villeins or bordars appear are few; eight for the former, six for the latter. The 26 villeins' teams work out at $3\frac{1}{3}$ oxen per head, the 65 bordars' at one ox for each two men, but without Chardford (44b2), where 20 bordars are said to possess a single team, the figure would become $1\frac{1}{4}$ oxen per man. Such quantities, even allowing for the unsatisfactory basis for deduction, do not suggest exceptionally low standards.

The Isle of Wight

The geographical situation of the Isle of Wight ensured that the life of its eleventh-century inhabitants should rarely be undisturbed. It was the natural base for an English fleet guarding the eastern Channel coast, and equally the natural target of pirates and raiders. Each would require to supplement provisions, and the island must have suffered in consequence of their needs. In 1048 it had been harried by vikings, and four years later by Earl Godwine during the campaign which ended his exile. It was raided in May, 1066, by Tostig Godwineson, and through the summer of that year it was the base of his brother Harold's fleet.

The strategic importance of the island may be indicated by its comparatively low assessment and the high proportion of demesne land. Though not much smaller than Middlesex, it was rated at less than one-quarter of the number of Middlesex hides, though it had half as many inhabitants. Of a little over 200 hides, only 54 per cent were not exempt, as fiscal demesne, from paying geld. That the common formula 'then it gelded for *a* hides, now for *b'* implies partial exemption, not a post-Conquest reduction in rating, seems to be indicated by the Calbourne entry (52bi): *Ibi sunt xxxii hidae. Sed tempore regis Edwardi et modo non geldat nisi pro xvii hidae.* Its strategic importance inspired the Conqueror immediately to place the island in William fitzOsbern's charge, and it must have been one of the first areas of England to receive a Norman garrison. Whether all his holdings passed to his son Roger we cannot tell, but we are told that Rainald fitzCroc claimed that Earl Roger had given his father part of Wilmingham (52a2). One manor (Sandford with Week, 39bi) refers to 'when the sheriff received them', and may indicate a date subsequent to Earl William's death in 1071 and his son's forfeiture after his rebellion in 1075.

Unfortunately we cannot determine how acutely the islanders may have suffered in the early days of the Conquest. Of 120 holdings 24 were in 1086 still in the possession of king's thegns, an unusually high proportion. Only two of these, however, had substantial valuations, but it is suggestive that only five had declined in value, and that on the whole they had slightly improved. We are given only 36 statements about values *post*.[1] The total fall is not very great, only 16 per cent, but it is noticeable that the royal manors in the eastern half of the island fell by 22 per cent. Strategically this side of the island must have been more important than the other, and may accordingly have suffered worst. The other holdings in the eastern half declined in value by 25 per cent.

Between 1066 and 1086 royal manors fell in value by $21\frac{1}{2}$ per cent, from £128 8s. to £100 18s. Of the twenty royal holdings for which we are given values both for *tunc* and *modo*, 13 declined in value, and seven showed no change. Again the principal decline was in the royal manors in the east, where it was over 25 per cent. The other 85 holdings appreciated from £240 12s. to £253 6s., or by under 9 per cent. Yet only 17 show an increase in value, and 25 no change.

But, as throughout the south-east, actual receipts were greatly in excess of values. In 22 entries, all but one of which was royal, the manors are said to be worth a certain sum, but paying more. What was valued at £164 13s. was in fact rendering £225 5s. Again there is the contrast between east and west. Payments in the west exceeded values by 61 per cent, but in the east by only 29 per cent. Twice we are told that the demand for additional profit was unreasonable. The demesne portion of the bishop of Winchester's manor of Calbourne (52bi) was valued at £30, but was being farmed for £40. It is added that it cannot bear or pay it. William

[1] Freshwater (52a2) has not been included, for though we are given a value for *post*, there is none for *modo*. The former should possibly have been *modo*.

fitzStur was paying £60 for four royal manors, 'but they are not worth so much' (52bi).[1]

There is here great variety of phraseology. Frequently we are told that the manor is *ad firmam*; a number of the sums payable by the eastern manors are to be in 'weighed money', or 'blanch', 'of 20d. to the ounce', of 'blanch farm'.[2]

The 36 royal manors represent half of the island's recorded wealth, population, and plough-teams. They include an unusually high proportion of slaves, 27 per cent of the total population mentioned, and these represent 59 per cent of all the slaves noted for the island. They alone, too, contain more villeins than bordars. The most striking figure is indeed the high proportion of slaves for the whole island, almost 23 per cent, a figure far higher than that for the Hampshire mainland (17 per cent), or for neighbouring counties. A high proportion of slaves argues a backward economy, but where the teams were numerous, slaves would be required in quantity for the ploughing of the demesnes. There was not far short of a slave per team or two slaves per demesne team, while on the royal manors there were 137 slaves for 43 demesne teams.

A short and uncomplicated text provides a convenient means of studying certain statistics in detail. Unfortunately those concerned with ploughlands, teams, and population confirm any latent suspicions that the statistical deficiencies of DB are considerable. The clerk at work here seems to have assumed that either there should be a team for each ploughland, or a lesser quantity of teams than ploughlands. Thus for Milford (53b2) he wrote: 'there is land for half a team; however, there is in demesne one team'. But thrice a space was left where the number of ploughlands should have come, and in twelve other entries we have no information about them. In how many entries teams or inhabitants should have been included but were not, we cannot tell, but it looks as if there were not a few omissions. A Nettleston manor (53b2) was worth £1, and there was a demesne team, but only the tenant is mentioned. In an entry such as that for Calbourne (52bi), probably we are given the ploughland figures for only the demesne portion, while those for the $9\frac{1}{2}$ teams on the sub-tenancies and churchland were at least in part omitted; possibly this occurred at Shalfleet (53bi) also.

In 28 holdings the teams exceed the ploughlands, though only twice is the surplus a really large one. Gatcombe (52b2) had eight teams for four

---

[1] These can hardly be the four preceding entries, as DB says, which were worth only £28. Possibly the reference should have been to Brook, Afton, Wellow, and Freshwater (52a2), worth £45 but paying £69.
[2] e.g. Knighton and the Down, Sandford with Week, Arreton, Nunwell, Haseley (39bi,2).

ploughlands, South Arreton (39bi) thirteen for five.[1] Demesne teams occur in 97 entries and sub-entries, if *et ibi est* implies a demesne team where distinction between demesne and villagers' teams is not made. Now the proportion of slaves in the island, we have seen, was a very high one, yet in 59 of these 97 instances of demesne teams no slaves are recorded.[2] At Milford (53b2) and at Atherfield (52b2), though there was a demesne team at each, there was a solitary bordar; at Binstead (53ai) two demesne teams but merely two villeins. At Shalcombe (52bi) there were a couple of demesne teams, but the sole person recorded is a bordar. Unless, in a good many instances, there were heads of families besides those reported in DB, the agricultural and animal husbandry simply could not be executed without help from outside, though the families of those set down in DB, and of the tenants of these holdings, no doubt helped with the work. The arrangements for cultivating the arable (and this applies to much of the country) must have been highly complex. Where there was a deficiency of teams, which occurs in 35 entries, the oxen may have been supplemented by loans from alternative holdings.[3] 299 teams for 314 ploughlands is a deficiency of under 5 per cent.

Exactly half the holdings, including sub-tenancies, were worth £1 or less. The statistics for these give us some idea of the inadequacies of these small farms. They averaged less than a team apiece, and though there was demesne land on the majority of them, the whole 59 could muster only 11 slaves, and only 25 included villeins. There was meadow in only 21, and wood in no more than five, yet seven had mills. Who operated the mill in places where there was a solitary bordar, as at Huffingford (54ai) or Milford or Sheat (53b2), is problematical. Perhaps it was the tenant, or help was obtained from elsewhere.

In 13 entries 61 villeins owned 27 teams, an average of 3½ oxen per head. In eleven others 61 bordars possessed 9½ teams, which represents 1¼ oxen a man. Only at Cheverton (52b2) and Bowcombe (52ai) do we hear of peasant rents. At the first a villein was paying 10s. for half a virgate; in the second eight 'men' produced 5s. The villeins of St Mary of Lire (52bi) held 1½ hides less a quarter-virgate 'in different manors'.

---

[1] It is of course possible that *viii* was miscopied as *iiii*, and that the *v* is an error.
[2] These 59 entries include six where no inhabitants whatever are recorded.
[3] The figure of 35 may be slightly too high, for it includes holdings where no teams are mentioned. But in these the number of inhabitants is very small; sometimes a solitary bordar appears (e.g. at Alverstone, 53ai). He may well have had no oxen.

Berkshire

The frequent references to the work of the Inquest and to alterations in the composition of manors are among the outstanding features of the county text. It is comparatively poor in its provision of triple valuations, which occur in only 42½ per cent of the 327 entries, and the majority of these occur for the royal estates and those of the ecclesiastical houses. But the general picture, with nearly 70 per cent of the holdings falling in value after the Conquest, and 45 per cent failing to reach their pre-Conquest values by 1086, is clear enough.

By the times described as *post* or *quando recepit* the relevant manors fell in value from £1,776 7s. 1d. to £1,485 8s. 9d., or by 17 per cent. Yet there were a few which apparently increased their worth. One royal manor at Sparsholt (57ai) went up from £9 to £15, the other (57ai) from £15 to £18. Cumnor (58bi), the wealthiest of the many manors of the abbey of Abingdon, is said to have appreciated in value from £30 to £50. But Cumnor was a complex manor; of its components Seacourt fell in value from 100s. to 70s., and two others lost by 1086 30s. of their 1066 valuation of 80s. A possible change in the composition of the manor must here be suspected.

The distribution of falls in value suggests that they were in the main the result of the Norman progress from Winchester to Wallingford. The tracks of three main columns seem to be apparent. That of the westward flank guard is not strongly marked; indeed, any decline south of Hungerford might be merely the natural ultimate effect of general disturbance on the high downland about Inkpen where the economic standard cannot have been a high one. If the former flank guard functioned independently, and had not merged with the main body moving northwards from Winchester, it seems to have moved to the Sheffords and then turned up the Lambourn valley. The main body crossed the Kennet in the Newbury neighbourhood and then in three parties restocked itself before, probably, coming to a temporary halt near the royal vill of Wantage. The flank guard proceeded close to the western boundary of the county, possibly as far as Highworth in Wiltshire, the only substantial vill in the neighbourhood, and then turned eastwards above the Thames valley to the Pusey district, where it would be in touch with the Wantage force. A detachment seems to have made a circuit above the line of the Thames, and a junction was effected about Sutton Courtenay, south of Abingdon, before moving on Wallingford.

The right wing had crossed the Loddon about Swallowfield, supported possibly by a small force which had moved through north Hampshire

THE SOUTH-EAST: BERKSHIRE

along the Portway. One section advanced on Reading and then joined the body of troops masking the western approaches to London; the other made for Pangbourne on the Thames and then concentrated in the Goring gap at Streatley (Fig. 7, p. 66).[1]

At Wallingford the submission of Archbishop Stigand was received. He would convey the temper of London to Duke William, and whatever was reported, any idea of a march on the capital was rejected, and the army proceeded north of the Chilterns on the final stages of the great encircling campaign. There can have been little of Berkshire which had not experienced Norman power, and small threat now of an assault from the rear.

By 1086 the county as a whole had recovered its total valuation of 1066, but only just. What had been worth £2,461 19s. 3d. was now valued at only £2,474 8s. 1d. A number of the royal manors, though now valued more highly than they had been, were worth considerably less than they were reckoned to be in 1066. Cookham (56b2), worth £50 then, was returned at £36 in 1086; Warfield (57a2) was only half as valuable as it had been. Some royal manors seem to have suffered from appropriations by Henry de Ferrières. Yet though he had acquired $2\frac{1}{2}$ hides at Shalbourne (57bi), the value of the manor had risen from £12 to £20, while at Sutton Courtenay (57b2), where he had 120 acres *de dominica terra regis*, a manor which had sunk from £30 to £20 was at the Inquest valued at £50. But where a priest had put a hide of the manor of Wargrave (57a2) 'in a manor of his lord's', the value had declined by more than £3. It rather looks as though, despite an overall decline in the value of the royal manors, some had had their commitments increased.[2] Though four of the ten hides of Winkfield (59a2) were 'in the king's Forest', the value of this Abingdon manor, £4, had not declined. Perhaps they had been Forest land in King Edward's day also.

Eleven royal manors, but only four others, were having to produce more than they were said to be worth, though it is never noted, as in other shires, that the demands were excessive ones.[3] Royal manors valued at

---

[1] Lemmon: *op. cit.*, p. 120, suggests that the Norman cavalry was at Wallingford and the infantry at Goring. Mixed forces may perhaps seem more likely.
[2] It is unfortunate that for Wantage (57ai), the most valuable royal manor, only values *olim* and *modo* were recorded. Here a £55 valuation had become one of £61.
[3] The non-royal manors are Woolstone (58a2), Moreton (61a2), an anonymous holding in Wantage Hundred (62a2), and Hanney (61b2). The first three were together worth £27, and only £33 was in fact being paid. Hanney paid an ounce of gold above its value of £6; this looks like a premium for a lease to the tenant. Appleford (59ai) at no time changed in value, but the 21s. said to be 'from gain of the demesne land' (*de lucro terrae dominicae*) must be additional to the £9.

£288 15s. were having to find £365 10s. In none is the difference exceptionally large. Of the farming of manors we hear practically nothing, except at Sutton Courtenay (57b2) and Winterbourne (58ai), but some

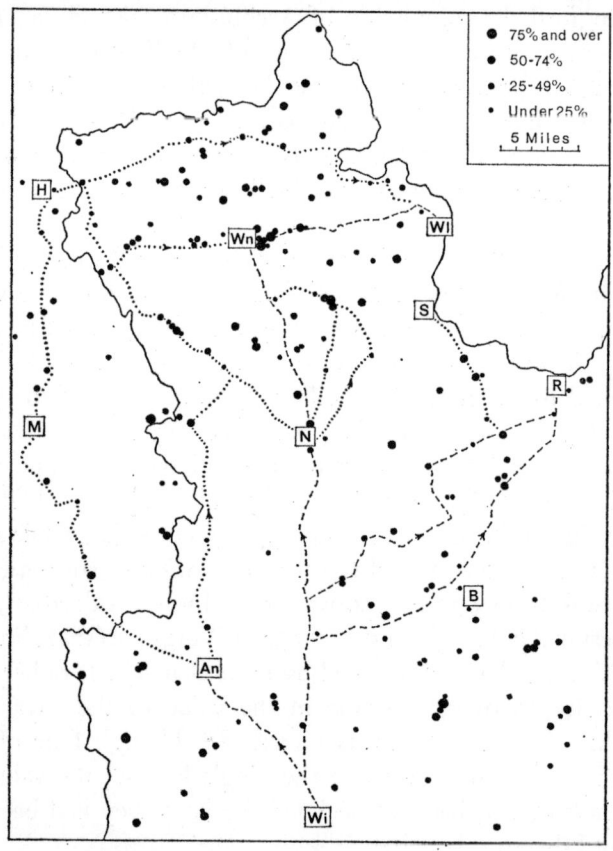

Fig. 9 The move from Winchester to Wallingford
Team deficiency, 1086
Suggested routes as in Fig. 7
An—Andover B—Basingstoke H—Highworth M—Marlborough
N—Newbury R—Reading S—Streatley Wi—Winchester
Wl—Wallingford Wn—Wantage

small properties are said to be 'in the farm of' Wantage or Sutton Courtenay (57ai). Pangbourne (58ai), too, was *in firma regis*, as had been the acquisitions of Henry de Ferrières, e.g. from Kintbury and Shalbourne and Sparsholt (57bi). Finchampstead (57a2) is said to 'render farm in Reading', and since it was valued at £8 it is suggestive that the value of the manor of Reading (58ai) had increased by the same sum.

THE SOUTH-EAST: BERKSHIRE

A map of falls in value *tunc–modo* repeats the picture, though with somewhat greater emphasis owing to the increased number of instances. As might be expected, the damage hardest to repair had occurred in the chalk downs between Newbury and Wantage. But it is also well marked in the extreme north of the county, and west of Reading. The need to reprovision before concentrating at Wallingford and Streatley may have been the cause (Fig. 8, p. 67).

We are here no better informed about a possible ploughland/team relationship than elsewhere, for a blank space was left for the quantity of the former in 19 entries, and they were not recorded in 36, but a dozen of these probably do not represent omissions. If the figures showing a deficiency of teams against ploughlands are mapped, it is apparent that this is greatest in the northern half of the shire, where the Norman ravaging seems to have been at its maximum because it was the best-equipped area in the county, and is also especially marked in the higher parts of the chalk downland south of Wantage.

The distribution of team-deficiencies (Fig. 9, p. 80) suggests that a detachment may have been sent through eastern Wiltshire by way of the Marlborough road to discourage local resistance, turning eastwards in the Highworth neighbourhood. Unfortunately information about possible falls in value in this area is scanty (p. 277).

On 135 holdings there was a deficiency of teams, and on 74 parity, out of 248 instances where comparison is possible. The proportion of holdings in which teams apparently exceeded ploughlands is therefore much less than in, e.g., Surrey. On the figures we have, there were $1,729\frac{7}{8}$ teams for $1,934\frac{5}{8}$ ploughlands, a deficiency of $10\frac{1}{2}$ per cent. But we cannot be certain that a disparity was always present. At Ashridge (60a2) there were ten ploughlands, but only four teams in demesne. Teams of the eight villeins and eight bordars could have been missed. But where there were no demesne teams and no slaves either, and a large difference between ploughlands and teams, the information may well be correct.[1] In a number of the holdings there may well have been no arable land, or else these were components of manors whose ploughlands were noted elsewhere. In several no inhabitants are recorded; some of these are manorial components.[2] Artificial quantities of ploughlands are not numerous. Decimal figures, from five to fifty, occur only 53 times, mostly for five or ten ploughlands, which might well be realistic numbers. Except for Reading (58ai), 56 teams for 40 ploughlands, the disparity is never excessive, for it is conceivable that

[1] e.g. at Whistley (59a2), Easthampstead (59b2), Midgham, and Maidenhead (61b2).
[2] e.g. Bucklebury (61bi, 63ai), Kintbury (61bi), *in eodem manerio* (63bi) which 'lies in Swallowfield' (58ai). If inhabitants are unrecorded, there are no teams either.

some of the excess teams were hired with profit to till underteamed holdings, or acquired with a view to breaking new ground.[1] Six teams is a high number for a recorded population of eight, if the latter was correctly transcribed (Frilford, 58b2); some of our figures could be deceptive. On those we have, excess teams did not necessarily improve the value of a manor. Shottesbrook (63bi) had twelve teams for eight ploughlands, but the manor fell in value from £7 to £6.

For the teams of the peasantry, we have only a score of entries for those of villeins which can be isolated, 14 for bordars, and eight for cottars. 164 villeins had $63\frac{3}{8}$ teams, or just over three oxen a man, with a maximum of half a team. 103 bordars had $14\frac{7}{8}$ teams, and 76 cottars ten. In this county the clerks seem to have seen no difference between bordars and cottars, and the above figures give either category only just over a single ox apiece.

The information about slaves furnished by the Berkshire text is puzzling. They represent about 13 per cent of the recorded population, but are unevenly distributed either geographically or feudally. Some were probably not recorded. In Shrivenham Hundred the servile population is only about 5 per cent, but in the neighbouring Hundreds of Wifol and Ganfield over 20 per cent. The figures are low in the eastern Hundreds (that of Riplesmere has a solitary slave recorded), yet just west of Reading Bucklebury Hundred had over 20 per cent. Similar variations are to be found for different landowners. On the royal estates only about 8 per cent of the inhabitants were slaves, and on the abbey of Abingdon's holdings some $9\frac{1}{2}$ per cent. But the other ecclesiastical foundations had slaves in number slightly above average, while on the lands of the five bishops it is above 20 per cent. The major lay landholders had on the whole an average number of slaves, but there are exceptions. On the estates of William fitzAnsculf one man in every four was a slave, on those of Miles Crispin one in twelve. There were none on Ghilo fitzAnsculf's $16\frac{1}{2}$ hides.

Such results encourage a further examination of the text. There is a total absence of slaves in 102 entries in which demesne teams are mentioned. In a high proportion of these there are no villeins either. None of these holdings had more than four demesne teams, and the average is just under $1\frac{1}{2}$. Apparently the lords could get much agricultural work done without the need to maintain slaves. It might be that in many manors they had found the retention of slaves to be uneconomic, and had emancipated a number of them. *Coliberti* and *buri* appear twice (Barton, 58ai; Letcombe

[1] It is possible, too, that fresh ground was being cultivated but that only the former ploughlands were recorded.

THE SOUTH-EAST: BERKSHIRE

Regis, 57bi), on royal and Abingdon land where there were but a couple of slaves on either manor.

Alternatively, the clerks failed to record all the slaves that they should have done. Manors with a recorded population approaching the century but with no slaves whatever seem anomalous.[1]

[1] Blewbury (56b2), Shrivenham (57bi), Reading (58ai); all royal manors. But elsewhere the inhabitants noted never exceed thirty, except at Buscot (60a2).

2
The South Midlands

From the formulae and from the type of information provided, there can be no doubt that the counties of Buckingham, Bedford, Cambridge, and Hertford, together with Middlesex, formed one of the Inquest's circuits, though Cambridgeshire and Bedfordshire are divorced from the others in DB, and Huntingdonshire appears between these last two. In each it is common for triple valuations to be furnished, and often we are told that there could be more plough-oxen employed than were available, while woodland is described largely by the number of swine pasturable therein and meadow by the number of plough-oxen it could support.

Much of the area included must have been traversed by the invading forces of 1066 during the great horseshoe march from Wallingford to London. The exact course these took is impossible to trace, but if falls in value both *tunc–post* and *tunc–modo* and deficiencies of plough-teams against ploughlands are mapped, the pictures presented are so similar that these must to some unknown degree represent Duke William's army's movements. There is virtually a gap west of Buckinghamshire, for the Oxfordshire text gives us but little relevant information. A detachment may well have moved from the Bedford neighbourhood to that of Cambridge by way of southern Huntingdonshire, but here we have no figures for any date between 1066 and 1086.

The percentage of falls in value over either period, and of plough-team deficiency, on the whole show remarkably small differences. In this circuit it is unlikely that many ploughland figures are artificial ones; certainly an excess of teams over ploughlands is a rarity. It is true that many of the Cambridgeshire figures are duodecimal, and Dr Hart is of the opinion that, though 'incomplete and inaccurate', they reproduce the assessments laid on Cambridgeshire vills about 877 and display a mathematical relationship with the hidage of 1066. But in that case we must suppose that the hard-pressed Inquest officials subtracted the existing teams from the ploughlands, not always correctly, and then were at pains to set down that there could be that quantity of teams more than there were.[1]

Percentage fall or deficiency	tunc–post	tunc–modo	Percentage deficiency: teams to ploughlands, 1086
Buckinghamshire	24	8	$10\frac{1}{2}$
Bedfordshire	$33\frac{1}{3}$	$23\frac{1}{2}$	14
West Cambridgeshire[2]	32	29	$14\frac{3}{4}$
Hertfordshire	$30\frac{1}{2}$	$20\frac{1}{2}$	20
Middlesex	40	18	27

The low figures for Buckinghamshire (where, incidentally, vills were divided among fewer holdings than in the more easterly counties) might be explained by (a) a march possibly more rapid than it was later in the year, (b) a higher power of recovery than that of districts which must have experienced the progress of troops during the rebellions after the Conquest. The above-average Middlesex figures might reflect the pressure in 1066 from every side except western Essex, and the needs of armed men and their companions based on London, while the last might encourage improvement in the value of a holding, even though the receipts might exceed true worth.

Buckinghamshire

The text for this county is among the simpler ones. There are only about a dozen entries which do not give us triple valuation figures, and of the total of 390 entries only 43 mention sums which are not integral numbers of pounds or include half-pounds. This may suggest the furnishing of only approximate values by those responsible, or a general absence of rented manors. Certainly over 60 per cent of the vills were undivided ones, and many had comparatively high values.

[1] Dr Hart's paper on the subject is not yet published. He considers that the assessment figures of 877 were preserved because they governed the extent of obligations other than fiscal ones.
[2] Much of Cambridgeshire does not seem to have been seriously affected by the events of 1066; these figures are for the six western Hundreds and four adjacent vills.

THE DETAILS OF DOMESDAY BOOK

In the early years of the Conquest 61½ per cent of the 379 holdings for which intermediate figures are given fell in value, and only thirteen, mostly small ones, show values higher than those of 1066. It is perhaps significant that six of these declined by 1086; the new owners may have demanded more than was equitable. The overall decline was 24 per cent,

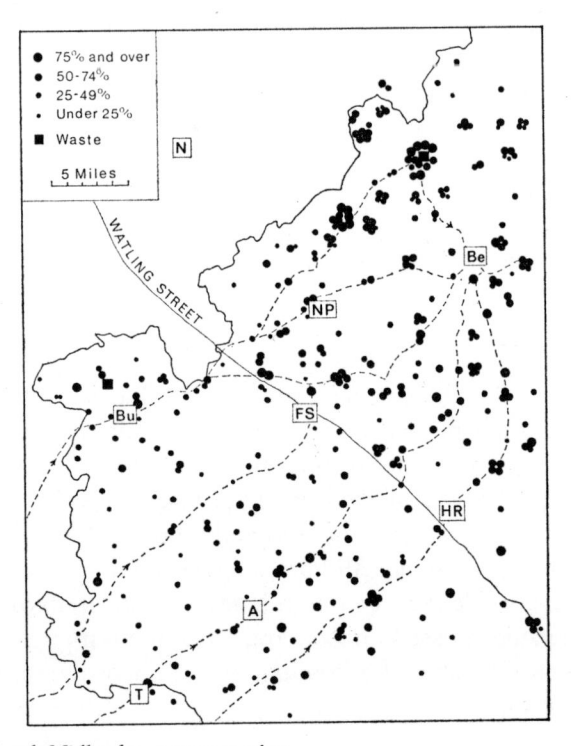

Fig. 10 The South Midlands: western section
Fall in value *tunc–post*
– – – Suggested routes of Norman forces
A—Aylesbury   Be—Bedford   Bu—Buckingham   FS—Fenny Stratford
HR—Houghton Regis   N—Northampton   NP—Newport Pagnell
T—Thame
Because of textual peculiarities, holdings recorded in the Northamptonshire and Oxfordshire Domesdays have not been shown

from £1,735 17s. 8d. to £1,318 18s. 4d. Where values show no change, the relevant holdings were mostly small, poorly equipped, and of slight value; because of this, many may have been left undisturbed as Duke William's troops marched through the shire.

His decision to embark on the encircling march through the counties to the north of London made the country beyond the Chilterns his first objective. He would naturally avoid the heavily wooded hills and the

THE SOUTH MIDLANDS: BUCKINGHAMSHIRE

defiles of the hill country. Here vills were few and potential supplies at a minimum, and the character of the terrain could conceal an enemy gathering. His immediate route from Wallingford cannot be traced, for the Oxfordshire text gives us few values for *post*. The only possible clue is the deficiency of Oxfordshire teams against ploughlands in 1086, which is an

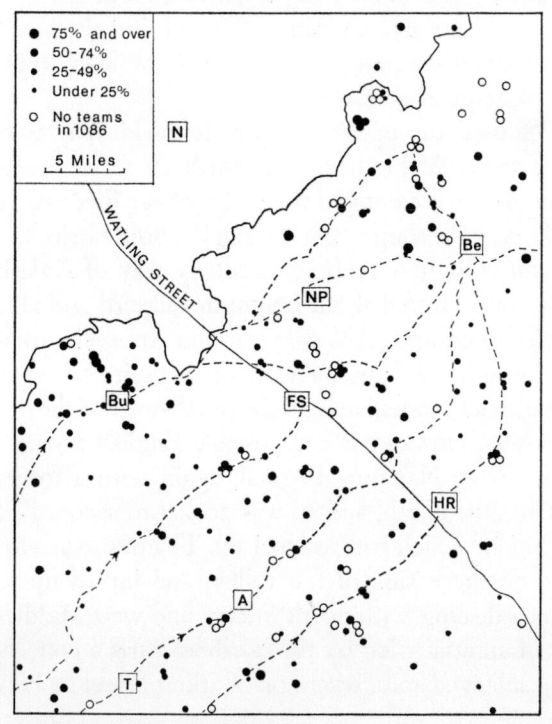

Fig. 11 The South Midlands: western section
Team deficiency, 1086
– – – Suggested routes and places as in Fig. 10
Holdings recorded in the Northamptonshire text not shown because its 'ploughlands' represent earlier assessments

unsatisfactory though somewhat suggestive guide. Along the general line of the Icknield Way from Wallingford there is a string of holdings with a team deficiency which may indicate the course of one column.[1] Another column may have moved first northwards and then on Thame, but here there are few deficiencies.[2] There is also the possibility that a body of

[1] e.g. Crowmarsh (157bi), Benson (154bi, 160bi,2), Ewelme (157bi, 159ai,b2, 160bi), Britwell Salome (159bi *bis*), Watlington (157ai), Ingham House (161a2), Kingston Blount (159a2), Henton (159bi).
[2] They do, however, occur at *Hunesworde* (157bi), probably near Stadhampton, Great Haseley (155b2), Rycote (157b2), Great Milton (155a2), and Chelworth Farm (159b, foot).

87

troops was despatched either to secure or to mask Oxford, and then to proceed to Buckingham, using the Roman road (**162**) through the Baldons to Bicester, and then the Towcester road (**160**) which passes close to Buckingham.[1] Deficiencies at Kiddington (158a2), Islip (160a2), Wendlebury (159b2), and Chesterton (159bi) might indicate the possible Oxford detachment joining the other body at Bicester. But the more easterly of these tracks would involve crossing Ot Moor and the wet Ray valley in late November, and may have seemed to Duke William to place his troops too far west to be profitable.

Certainly he used the upper or lower Icknield Way to reach Thame. It looks as if from Wallingford the northern force proceeded in four columns. One may have entered the county near Bledlow and moved by the Icknield Way through the country about Princes Risborough, Wendover, and Ivinghoe. Another went by way of Aylesbury, and the two probably concentrated about Leighton Buzzard and Houghton Regis in Bedfordshire to command Watling Street. Another turned northwards and passed through the extreme west of the shire to Buckingham, and occupied the district immediately to the north-west of the borough, where it could offer protection against a possible English assault from Mercia. Thence it moved to Newport Pagnell, again with a force masking the approaches from the north, and so was poised to secure Bedford.

The detachment which had reached the Thames seems to have crossed it, raided the northern side of the valley, and linked up with the force which had been dealing with north Surrey and west Middlesex (Fig. 14). In the event of an attack led by the northern earls a concentration could thus easily be achieved somewhere on Watling Street or between this and Ermine Street.

So maps of falls in value, whether by holdings or by vills, would suggest. Raiding, whether merely to acquire supplies or to demonstrate that English resistance to the Duke's coming had been and would be punished, seems to have been widespread. Its effects, it would seem, are still apparent in the figures of 1086.

By 1086 47 per cent of the holdings still showed values lower than those of 1066, and, including the royal manors, only $11\frac{1}{4}$ per cent had appreciated in worth. But even excluding the royal manors and those which had been Queen Matilda's, from which much more was now being gained than formerly, the holdings were within 8 per cent of their pre-Conquest value.

---

[1] Deficiencies are recorded at Marsh and Toot Baldon (155bi, 156ai *bis*, 160ai), Sandford on Thames (156b2 *bis*), Iffley (157bi), Walton Manor and Wolvercot (159ai), and, further north, Stanton St John (156ai *bis*), Woodperry (155b2), Merton (160a2), and in ten vills just north of Bicester.

THE SOUTH MIDLANDS: BUCKINGHAMSHIRE

Only twenty-two had fallen in value since King Edward's day or their transference, and nearly one-third of them had improved their worth. Perhaps Buckinghamshire had suffered less severely than neighbouring counties from the Norman advent. Behind the screen of the Chilterns it may have enjoyed comparative peace.

The lines of march are still clearly visible, though their effect had naturally lessened, on Fig. 10. They show the movement north of the Thames, north of the Chilterns, along the western border of the shire, and the concentrations beyond Buckingham and Newport Pagnell. Confirmation, to an inevitably limited extent, is obtained by the map of deficiencies of plough-teams in 1086 (Fig. 11), where the damage caused around the chief stronghold, Buckingham, is most marked. Everywhere they pass through the districts which in 1086 had the highest figures for population and plough-teams per square mile, which thus may have been higher still in 1066.

It is perhaps surprising that we hear so little of waste. Stowe near Buckingham (144b2) was received by Odo of Bayeux in a wasted condition, and in 1086 holdings at Biddlesden (146bi), Cheddington (150b2), and Chesham (151bi) were waste, though the last still had a potential value of 5s. Each, except Chesham, is in an area where Norman troops may be presumed to have passed. Values do not seem to have decreased because of inclusion in the Forest; this is mentioned only in the entries for Brill (143bi) and Oakley (149a2), and the value of the latter fell from £7 to £6.

The royal manors and the pair still credited in DB to the late Queen Matilda show enormously increased values. Those bestowed on the queen are given as increasing in value from £26 to £60 (151bi,2). They had their full complement of teams and were populous vills, but unless rents had been raised appreciably, or the extensive woodland and the fishery at Marlow had been newly and fully exploited, it is difficult to account for so large an appreciation. There is, however, always the possibility that the manors had been enlarged by consolidation of local holdings of Earl Ælfgar's adherents unmentioned in DB.

Certainly the royal manors (143a2,bi) had had their liabilities increased. Biddlesden had declined slightly after a former 100 per cent increase in value (or rent); Swanbourne now paid 30s. in blanched silver where formerly counted coin had been accepted. The other five, liable for £93 in 1066, now had to produce almost £200. Each had paid by tale in King Edward's day; now they must pay in weighed and assayed coin, and the differences are gigantic. Aylesbury's burden had been increased from £25 to £56, Brill's from £18 to £38, and Princes Risborough's from £10 to £46 18s. 8d. The £10 toll at Aylesbury and the £12 from the Forest at

Brill would seem to be additional impositions by the Conqueror. Buckingham with Bourton (143ai), too, a borough centred on a rural manor, had to find £16 where under King Edward it had paid £10 in counted coin. If some of these were farm-rents, the lessees were paying dearly for the privilege of exploiting the king's property. Had there earlier been overmuch leniency? But even if we include the royal manors, the value for the shire in 1086 is still only about £5 more than in 1066.

Manors said to be farmed are infrequent. Barton Hartshorne (145ai) had been worth £3, which fell to £2 after the Conquest. At the Inquest it is said to be worth the improbable figure of £14, while 30s. was obtained from the pasture, since it was deficient of 40 per cent of the plough-oxen it could have employed, and contained only three bordars and four slaves, unless the number of villeins was accidentally omitted. It may of course have been in a bad way before and after the Conquest, or the correct sum may have been £1 4s. or 14s.

The text suggests that the presence of woodland was often swelling manorial values. Eleven entries record money payments, five renders of iron for ploughshares.[1] These are probably far from comprehensive. The sale of surplus hay from the meadowland, or its provision towards the lord's *firma*, occurs five times.

The *ora*, as we might expect, is of infrequent occurrence. Its appearance is limited to a render from the woodland, occasional mill values, and, apparently, the profit from fisheries.[2]

If the quantities given for ploughlands indicate the approximate extent of arable available, there was a deficiency of teams of about $10\frac{1}{2}$ per cent. This is most marked in the districts where values fell after the Conquest and invading troops may be supposed to have passed. There are 130 instances in which the possibility of employing more teams than were at work in 1086 is mentioned; these include some where both demesne and villeins' land was understocked, but there are also entries where a total absence of oxen is noted, or fewer teams than ploughlands, but nothing is said about the possibility of employing additional teams.[3] But while there were some remarkable deficiencies, as at Wing (146a2), where there were only 25 teams for 40 ploughlands, and 15 more could have been used, though the value had fallen but little, some manors had an excess of teams, e.g. at Upton (143bi) and Wooburn (144ai), each of which shows a rise in value.

---

[1] See *Dom. Geog.*, iii, pp. 166–7.
[2] Missenden (147ai), Caldecote (146bi), Aston Clinton (150bi), Thornton, Chalfont (151b2); 26s. 8d., or 18 *orae*, from four fisheries at Wyrardisbury (149bi).
[3] e.g. Lavendon (152b2), Aston Abbots (145b2).

In 36 entries there are villeins and no bordars, and in these 199 villeins had 92½ teams, or 3¾ oxen per man. At Aston Ivinghoe (149b2), indeed, a villein is said to have 1½ teams, and in four holdings the number of villeins equals that of their teams.[1] The teams of bordars can be isolated in only four instances; in these 23 had eight teams, or 2¾ oxen a head. At Dunton (144b2) six had three teams. These figures are higher than those of some nearby counties. The reason might be that in a shire which had contained many minor thegns, but apparently few sokemen, the villein was often the equivalent of either in all but status. Sometimes he or his ancestor may have been of thegnly rank before the Conquest, but was insufficiently prosperous to maintain it, though still superior to the average villein.

The recorded surviving landholders and tenants are neither markedly more or less numerous and prosperous than elsewhere. In all they held in chief land worth under £50, and less than £50 as sub-tenants. The only really large manor in English hands in 1086 was Steeple Claydon (153ai), held by Ælfsige the cook, whose services were perhaps worth retaining. Leofwine of Nuneham and Svertingr each owned or leased property worth less than £10, and among the sub-tenants we find, besides those named, a dozen instances of Englishmen and sokemen. But some unnamed men may, like Ælfric at Marsh Gibbon (148b2), still have been struggling to retain their land, but under a new lord, and, like him, *graviter et miserabiliter*. The phrase may suggest that though valued at £3 10s. at all periods, it was really worth less, but the same rent was being demanded.

Bedfordshire

Bedfordshire was a county in which royal manors, none of them large, were few, and indeed it was one without any really extensive manors. Only a dozen were in 1066 worth more than £15, and the maximum value was £30. Though about half the vills were undivided in 1086, the number of individual holdings in a high proportion of them was large; there were eleven at Sutton and Sharnbrook, and ten at Biddenham and Little Stoughton. Some of these had been held by sokemen; a hide at Sutton (217bi) had been divided between six of them, while a Marston Moretaine estate (214a2) had been held by 21. Individual wealth must have been generally lacking, and any threat to the local economy extremely serious.

After the Conquest the inevitable decline may have been accelerated by

[1] Shenley Church End (147ai), Newport Pagnell (148b2), Tickford (149ai), and in Ixhill Hundred (152bi).

THE DETAILS OF DOMESDAY BOOK

one of the least scrupulous of the royal agents, Ralf Taillebois. He had included Biscot (209bi), which had been the property of an adherent of Ansgar the marshal, in the royal manor of Luton 'for the advantage this gave him'. He had disseised Nigel d'Aubigny of part of Clophill (214a2), and his injustices and those of John des Roches are frequently noted in

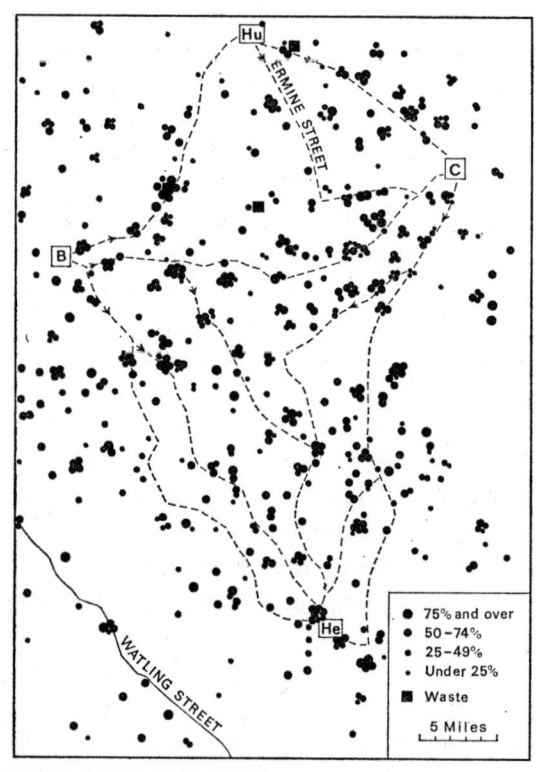

Fig. 12 The South Midlands: eastern section
  Fall in value *tunc–post*
  – – – Suggested routes of Norman forces
  B—Bedford C—Cambridge He—Hertford Hu—Huntingdon

DB. The sole occasion on which a farm-rent in excess of value is mentioned (Stotfold, 213ai) is said to have been in operation 'when he died'. The very large number of claims to land with which the Inquest was required to deal further testify to the untranquil history of the area.

The county seems to have suffered severely from the Conquest. Land worth £1,303 6s. 2d. in 1066 was later worth only £871 12s., a fall of one-third. This seems to have occurred principally on the medium-sized manors, those which in 1066 had a value of from £5 to £10. These, which

92

THE SOUTH MIDLANDS: BEDFORDSHIRE

amount to 60 per cent of the whole number, fell in all by 43 per cent, whereas the largest manors and the smallest holdings declined by just over and just under 30 per cent respectively. The very general impoverishment, with 72 per cent of the 331 out of 384 holdings for which we have triple figures having values less than those of 1066, must at least in part be attributed to the first descent of the invaders.

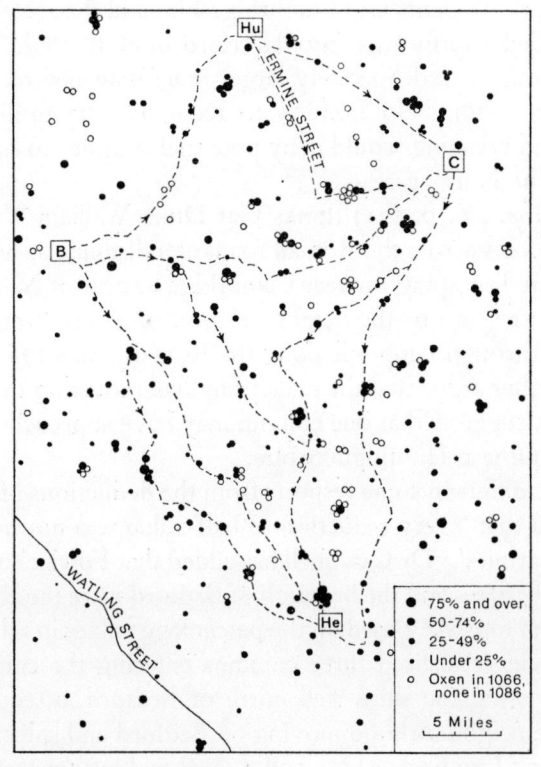

Fig. 13 The South Midlands—eastern section
    Team deficiency, 1086
    Suggested routes and places as in Fig. 12

It must have been late in November or early in December when Norman forces reached the county, and their situation was far from being a comfortable one. The weather was likely to grow worse, yet they could hardly as yet approach an unsubmissive London. There was the possibility that Northumbrian and Mercian forces, led by Earls Edwine and Morkere, might be on the way to attack an army which had enjoyed scant rest in the last six weeks. Supplies would be hard to get from neighbouring Northamptonshire, devastated by the Northumbrian rebels of 1065. We are given no idea by DB of the size of Bedford, but a borough assessed at 'half a Hundred' could hardly support or house Duke William's army.

To these conditions the general impoverishment of Bedfordshire may have been due. Fig. 12 shows few clear signs of the possible movements of a campaigning force; it suggests rather forcible requisitioning from as much of the countryside as possible, within fifteen miles of Bedford, especially to the east and south. Possibly, however, the first was intensified by troop movements into Cambridgeshire and the second as the army later proceeded southwards into Hertfordshire. It could be, too, that devastation was on a deliberately larger scale than before. The news of such conduct might help London to recognise the futility of further resistance, and ravaging would deny potential supplies to northern forces threatening the Norman rear.

Lemmon (*op. cit.*, p. 121) thinks that Duke William 'threw a line of observation posts across the Roman roads at a distance of fifty miles from London, from Trumpington near Cambridge to near St Neots and thence along the river Ouse to the neighbourhood of Stony Stratford', with a support line through Ampthill along the Roman roads **176** and **23a**. The last would rather argue that the main army had moved to the south of the shire. Fig. 12 suggests that one column may have approached Cambridge by way of southern Huntingdonshire.

The above differs in some respects from the deductions of Fowler, who rightly added that 'every reduction to half-value was not necessarily due to William's armies'.[1] Dr Campbell has added that Fowler's map 'suggests that the royal estates and the borough of Bedford were the chief objectives of the Norman forces'.[2] Based on the percentage values in relation to those of 1066, Fowler visualised three columns entering the county from the west, one crossing the shire well north of Bedford, a second from the Aspley Guise neighbourhood moving on Bedford and splitting into three before entering Cambridgeshire, and a third making for the royal manor of Luton in the south.

Whatever the actual course of Norman activities, the shire seems to have been so formidably stricken, then or later, that by 1086 values were in all only some 13 per cent better than after the Conquest, and still 23½ per cent lower than those of 1066. There is not much scope for doubt here, for we have 331 triple valuations, and a mere 24 entries give us only *tunc* and *modo*, and a further nine *modo* only. Of these 331, 53 had declined still further by 1086, and 144 show no recovery. In 1086, 72 per cent of the

---

[1] G. H. Fowler: *Bedfordshire in 1086* (Aspley Guise, 1922), and 'The devastation of Bedfordshire and the neighbouring counties in 1065 and 1066' (*Archaeologia*, lxxii, 1922, pp. 41–50).
[2] E. M. J. Campbell, in *Dom. Geog.*, iii, p. 26.

holdings were worth less than in 1066, and only 5 per cent had appreciated. Some of the appreciations, moreover, seem somewhat artificial. Clapham (212ai), worth £12 in 1066, was valued at £24 both *post* and *modo*, but in addition to its five hides there were two 'carucates of land' in demesne, which could be a post-Conquest extension of this manor appropriated by Miles Crispin from Ramsey Abbey, or geld-free land. Biggleswade (217ai) rose from £10 to £15 and then to £17, but this had been Stigand's manor. Stigand made the most of his property, and may have raised rents before his disgrace in 1070.[1] Unfortunately we are not given comparative values for the royal manors, three of which had to find half a day's provisions and numerous dues in addition to their renders, with additional payments which had been imposed by Ivo Taillebois. The sheriff had an ounce of gold from each, and the queen ten ounces in all. The dues included grain, honey, and 'other things', a packhorse and 'customary payments for the dogs'. The sums of money mentioned add as much as £36 15s. to the renders of £62.

Yet only twice is land said to be waste (Wyboston, 210b2; Beeston, 216b2), and Wyboston is none the less said to be worth sixteenpence, while we hear nothing of values lowered through inclusion in a Forest. The general impression gained is that few holdings had escaped depression, and that the smallness of their resources had made recovery no easy matter. The county, too, though apparently well supplied with teams for the arable land available, was not heavily populated, averaging about eight recorded persons to the square mile.

There may well be little or no artificiality about the Bedfordshire ploughlands. It is true that the royal manors have as many ploughlands as teams (Luton has 82 of each), as though the number of the former had been arrived at by summing the latter. Where, too, we are told that there could be more teams than there are, parity for totals exists in most cases. Only thrice, where the possibility of more teams is not indicated, do teams exceed ploughlands, and then only by a single team in each instance. There are indeed 86 per cent as many teams as there are ploughlands. Out of the one hundred instances of a deficiency, 18 are for minute holdings where there was land for less than an entire team. In 69 of these instances we are told in varying formulae that there could be more teams than there are, 151½ for 549 ploughlands, or a deficiency of 27½ per cent. The deficiency is rarely large, though at Stevington (211a2) there were only six teams for 24 ploughlands, and here the value had fallen from £30 to £14, while at Woburn on the same folio there were eight teams for 24

---

[1] Two of his other holdings, Dunton (216a2) and Stratton (217ai) show appreciations between *post* and *modo*.

ploughlands, and the value had declined from £15 to £5, as at Harrold (217a2) it had from £20 to £6 and there were but eight teams on the sixteen ploughlands, though there could be nine, not eight, more.

In 24 instances it seems as if we can isolate the teams of villeins, and if so, 195 had 78½ teams, or 3·2 oxen per head. For bordars we have only seven relevant entries, where the 37 recorded had eight teams, or 1¾ oxen each on an average. We can learn nothing about the teams of sokemen; usually no teams other than those of the demesne are mentioned where these survived. There were ten men's teams at Wilden (209b2), but in addition to the twenty sokemen there were a dozen bordars, so the sokemen may not have averaged half a team apiece.

Sections almost unique in DB record the rural properties of Bedford burgesses and of the royal reeves and almsmen. Many were very small; the maximum value even in 1066 was only 30s. Thirty sub-tenancies, also mostly small holdings, were in 1086 still in native hands, and several entries tell us that the sokemen of these were the men who were there in 1066 also.[1] But the thegns and sokemen of the county seem to have been drastically reduced in number as a result of the Conquest.

Sums which might be based on the *ora* are surprisingly few in a county which must have experienced considerable Scandinavian influence. Sixteen-pence appears among values only thrice.[2] Amounts of 4s., 8s., 12s., 16s., 24s., 28s., are, however, fairly common, and these might have an *ora* basis.

Cambridgeshire

For this county we possess the doubtful advantage of the existence of two documents which to some extent supplement DB, the *Inquisitio Eliensis* and the *Inquisitio Comitatus Cantabrigiensis*. Each supplies certain information omitted by the Domesday clerks, and each furnishes details of some holdings which in DB were combined into a single statement. But on a high number of occasions we find figures which differ from those of an alternative document, and it is only rarely that we can determine which of them is the more likely to be accurate. For example, DB (191ai) gives a Barham holding a value of 4s., but ICC (95a) and IE (40bi) one of 3s. 4d. DB is probably wrong, for 3s. 4d. is the amount recorded for Babraham (191ai, 199a2; 96a; 40bi).[3] But whether, for Horningsea, the £18 of DB (191ai) and IE (40a2) or the £16 of ICC (93b) was right, we cannot tell.

[1] e.g. at Bolnhurst (209b2) and Dene (211b2).
[2] *Newentone* (210ai), Wyboston (210b2), Rushden (212bi).
[3] Sums which derive from the third part of the £ are not infrequent, e.g. at Balsham (190b2; 92b; 41bi). In totalling the figures I have used those which seem to me to be the more probable ones.

THE SOUTH MIDLANDS: CAMBRIDGESHIRE

Nor can we say whether Shelford (198a2; 99b) fell from £8 to £6 or to £7. The ploughlands at Camps (199bi; 94) probably numbered 11, not the 12 of ICC, since the teams add up to 11. The £30 of DB for Bassingbourn (194a2) must be right, and not the 30s. of ICC (103b), for the manor had earlier been worth £26.

Some check on the adequacy of the statements may be obtained by comparing those of the manorial entries with the Summaries on IE fols. 48ai–9bi and the claims section in IE fols. 68b3–9a2. It must be remembered, however, that while IE is certainly based on the information provided for the Inquest, it was probably supplemented before the twelfth-century copies we possess were made. This would seem to apply particularly to the Summaries, and perhaps to the claims section also.[1] Differences in the three texts we do indeed find, and in addition the claims section does not cover all the relevant entries. But the differences are comparatively slight ones; e.g. the DB and IE figures are only just over 3 per cent in excess of the total value given to Picot's infringements of Ely Abbey's rights, which IE fols. 48b2 and 69ai both give as £29 6s. 8d. The clerks too had their difficulties. DB (191bi) and IE (43bi) give a Hardwick holding a value of 1s., ICC (111a) one of 7d., and IE (69a2) has 7d. corrected to 12d.

There are, it is true, three additional disturbing factors about these quantities. One is that where no change is indicated at any period, the holdings are on the whole very small ones, worth £1 or less. Another is that where we have information for *tunc* and *modo* only, the figures almost invariably show no change. The third is that frequently it is said that values changed at no period, and it is doubtful if *semper* should always be interpreted literally.[2]

The formula for the intermediate period is mostly given as *quando recepit*. Whether this invariably refers to the time of the Conqueror's land settlement must be doubtful. The Ely entries which in DB appear both in the Ely *breve* and that of the layman who had acquired them might refer to that date at which Symeon was appointed abbot, 1081. Westwick (202ai) may not have changed hands until after Earl Waltheof's death in 1076. Hardwin d'Escalers, Picot the sheriff, and others who appropriated Ely lands would hardly do so simultaneously. But, from IE fols. 210b–11a, Eudes fitzHubert seems to have done so after the death of Lisois de Moustières, whenever that occurred, and in many instances Ely lost estates before the time of the plea at Kentford in 1071/5.

[1] See Galbraith: *The Making of Domesday Book*, pp. 141–2.
[2] For a fuller discussion, see p. 242. Where DB has *semper* for a Trumpington holding (202a2), ICC and IE give no intermediate value.

But still we do not have all the information we desire. The difficulties *Terra Regis* presents are considered below, and here we are largely deprived of the assistance of ICC. Where Ely lands had been appropriated by a man who held all or much of a relevant vill in which these lay, we do not know whether the value IE gives to the former Ely land is included in the Domesday or ICC value of the manor or not. Rampton (201ai; 113a), a six-hide vill, was valued in 1086 at £5, £3 less than in 1066. Of these hides, 5⅝ had been held by Ely sokemen, to whose land IE (44a2) gives a value of £3, implying that the 1½ virgates which had been held by a sokeman of Edith the Fair were worth the somewhat surprising figure of £2. Had Picot or his tenant Roger demanded rents in excess of fair value?[1] Again, a virgate at Abington Pigotts held by Earl Roger belonged to his manor of Shingay (193a2). Was the value of the sokeman's virgate, 13s. 4d., included in the £7 value of Shingay, which had been held by the same sokeman, or not? There are uncertainties, too, of a different kind. Picot had two Croydon holdings (200bi), one of 1⅞ and one of 1¼ hides; each had been worth £2 in 1066 and when he received them. The larger, which was underteamed, fell to 30s.; the other, fully supplied with oxen but peopled only by five bordars and two cottars, rose to £4. Clerical error is here not impossible. It certainly seems likely that ICC's 2s. 8d. (two *orae*) is right for both Orwell and Kingston (108b, 110b), and not DB's 2s. (196a2, 194b2).[2]

What can be said with certainty is that Cambridgeshire values fell steeply after the Conquest, and in many manors had not recovered their 1066 value by 1086. There are enormous variations between the figures for different parts of the shire. They may be tabulated thus.

Values	tunc			post			Percentage fall
	£	s.	d.	£	s.	d.	
North	189	0	0	123	17	0	34½
East	645	3	8	604	4	4	6¼
West[3]	785	5	9	544	4	8	30¾
TOTAL	1,619	9	5	1,272	6	0	21½

[1] See also, e.g., Lolworth, Madingley, Oakington, Landbeach (191bi, 201a2,bi; IE 44bi, 45ai).
[2] For Duxford ICC (98a) has 6s. 8d., DB (196b2) 6s. The former seems the more probable figure.
[3] The six Hundreds of Armingford, Wetherley, Longstow, Northstow, Papworth, and Chesterton, excluding Waterbeach and Landbeach but including Foxton, Harston, Hauxton, and Trumpington from Thriplow.

THE SOUTH MIDLANDS: CAMBRIDGESHIRE

	tunc £ s. d.	modo £ s. d.	Percentage fall
North	189 0 0	167 4 0	11½
East	647 2 10	696 10 6	1¾
West	791 7 9	591 4 5	25¼
TOTAL	1,627 10 7	1,454 18 11	13¾

	ploughlands	teams	Percentage deficiency
North	131	126	3¾
East	728	668¾	8
West	749⅜	624¼	16¾
TOTAL	1,608⅜	1,419	11¾

The difference between east and west is demonstrated also by these figures.

Values

	instances	tunc–post + −	Percentage of falls
East	107	8 42	39½
West	216	3 156	72

tunc–modo

| East | 131 | 28 41 | 31½ |
| West | 224 | 9   154 | 69 |

Teams in relation to ploughlands: tunc–modo

| East | 134 | 3 43 | 32 |
| West | 229 | 3 106 | 46 |

Now these western Hundreds are just those that we should expect to have suffered most in 1066, assuming that Norman forces penetrated as far as Cambridge. If so, Figs. 12 and 13 suggest that columns which had been ravaging Bedfordshire entered the county near Tadlow and the main body followed the route Croydon—Wimpole—Wratworth—Whitwell—Barton to Cambridge. Possibly a detachment operating in north Bedfordshire had crossed the southernmost part of Huntingdonshire and linked up with the main force by way of Bourn, Kingston, and Eversden. Some of these vills fell by 40–60 per cent in value. The usual practice seems to have been followed; the vills to the north and north-west seem to have been occupied, blocking an assault from the north, and severely damaged. It is suggestive that a map of the deficiency of teams against ploughlands in 1086 (Fig. 13) seems to tell exactly the same tale. On the other hand, the picture presented could be attributed to some extent to the assault on the Isle of Ely during Hereward's revolt, and indeed this may well have been responsible for much of the decline north of Cambridge. But south-west of Cambridge it seems more probable that the damage was inflicted earlier. Whatever the cause—and the depredations of the sheriff and his associates stressed in the text may have been a contributory factor—the shire still shows a gravely disturbed economy in 1086. Eighty per cent of the falls in value *post–modo* are north-west and south-west of Cambridge, suggesting that they may be connected with the Isle of Ely campaign.

The decline in value on the manors and their berewicks in the Two Hundreds of Ely is more likely to have been caused by the campaign of 1071 in the Isle of Ely than by the immediate advent of the Normans. At Ely itself and south thereof the fall was over 40 per cent. Recovery by 1086, though substantial, was incomplete, and only three manors had increased since then in value.[1] But none shows a fall in value between *post* and *modo*, so *post* is probably subsequent to Hereward's revolt.

One further possibility presents itself, more apparent in Fig. 13 than in Fig. 12. In the rebellion of 1075 Earl Ralf of East Anglia advanced on Cambridge, but was outnumbered by the forces of the bishops of Bayeux and Coutances, defeated at *Fagaduna* (unidentified), according to William of Poitiers (ii. 263, p. 317), and retreated towards Norwich.[2] Such falls in values and deficiencies of plough-teams as there are in the east of the shire are largely on the line of these movements. The advance of the royal troops on Cambridge may have added to the lowering of values in the south, especially *post–modo*.

Six Hundreds, the texts show, had their assessments reduced. Four of these, to which Chesterton should perhaps be added, are among the ones where falls in value were at their maximum. It is tempting to suggest that they received this treatment during William's reign and because they had been so badly affected that the geld was for them too heavy a burden. But neither Staploe nor Cheveley Hundreds, which also enjoyed a reduction, seems to have been gravely affected by the Conquest. Nor, probably, did Earl Ralf's revolt greatly disturb them. Nor was it equitable that Wetherley, though less stricken than the other western Hundreds, for values declined by only about 15½ per cent, should receive no reduction. We do

---

[1] Doddington, Littleport, and Little Thetford (191b2), from £19 10s. to £28.
[2] Florence of Worcester, who says the rebels were defeated by William of Warenne and Richard fitzGilbert. Probably all four dignitaries contributed.

not know that the change in liability *was* post-Conquest; if it was, an alternative explanation could be that it was on account of good service during the Ely campaign.[1] This might seem the more likely because DB shows no trace of post-Conquest reductions in neighbouring counties, though, as Galbraith has pointed out, we hear in DB of reductions in Cambridgeshire only in undivided vills. For reductions elsewhere we are dependent on ICC.[2]

There is another line of substantial falls in values east of that described above, through Trumpington, Harston, Shepreth, Meldreth, and Melbourn which might mark the beginning of the march to Hertford, since it leads to Royston, where Ermine Street crosses the Icknield Way and is the most direct route to London. The plough-team deficiency is, however, here rather less marked, and at the outset of the journey it may have been less necessary to collect supplies.

It is not possible to determine how far the royal manors might have been affected. The seven which had been part of the ancient demesne had to find sums varying from £10 to £25 together with a payment each of £13 8s. 4d. of blanched coin, which was the equivalent of earlier food-renders in corn, honey, and malt, together with unspecified customary dues. In three instances we are told that the prime payment had not been increased since King Edward's day. It may have been impossible to extract more, if local trouble had affected them. Most of the other manors had fallen in value, and for Fulbourn (190ai) we have the strange statement that while in 1086 it rendered £8 of coin 'weighed and assayed', in 1066 the twenty-six sokemen rendered nothing to the sheriff. Exning (189b2) is given successive values of £56, £12, and £52, and Salzman has reminded us that it was here that the marriage which allied Earls Ralf, Roger, and Waltheof in rebellion was celebrated.[3] If the fall was due to the revolt or its punishment, *post* must here be 1075 or later.

Three royal manors at least were being farmed; Ditton (189b2), which Archbishop Stigand had acquired from Ely, Litlington (190ai), whose value had surprisingly remained constant, and Exning (189b2), in the hands of that supervisor of East Anglian manors, Godric. Outside the *Terra Regis*, the farming of Chippenham has been mentioned above,

---

[1] J. H. Round suggested that the reduction of Ditton (189bi) in Cheveley by 90 per cent instead of the 40 per cent applied elsewhere was because it had become a royal demesne vill; it fell in value from £15 to £12. Chippenham in Staploe (197a2) had its assessment halved by a pre-Conquest sheriff, because the farm was too high; its value had risen from £12 to £20. Not all the vills in this Hundred had their assessments reduced, so whatever the occasion and the basis were, the selection of Hundreds and vills seems to have been deliberate. See Round's *Feudal England*, p. 52.

[2] Galbraith: *op. cit.*, p. 127.

[3] *VCH*, i, p. 350. The figure of £56 is that often found in Yorkshire for 1066 (p. 196).

and the Ely manor at Fulbourn (191ai; 40ai) is said to be *ad firmam*.[1] Guy of Anjou held a Duxford estate (196ai) at farm from Earl Eustace, and 18s. 8d., or fourteen *orae*, sounds like his farm-rent for his hide.[2] Barton (201b2) had been part of Countess Judith's farm when William de Cahainges received it; the valuation given to Weston Colville (196a2), £16 and an ounce of gold, against a previous £10, sounds like a farm-rent. Many another manor, though DB does not say so, may have been farmed.

The *ora* appears in a number of entries. At Babraham (198ai, 199a2), Boxworth (195ai), and Orwell (197ai) we find the odd sum of 18s. 8d., which is 14 *orae*, and also sums of 6s. 8d., 5s. 4d., 2s. 8d., 1s. 4d., and 8d.[3] Values of £16, £8, 16s., etc., are common.[4]

There seems to have been an appreciable and intelligible deficiency of plough-teams in 1086, and numerous entries inform us that there could be more teams than were available, or that teams no longer operating could be restored. Teams exceed ploughlands in only six entries. The only considerable majorities are at Long Stanton (195a2), eight on land for five teams, though the value fell from £8 to £5 (perhaps one pair of figures became reversed), and Wilbraham (199bi), where the value rose.

In a great many entries there is no indication of the villeins, bordars, or cottars possessing plough-oxen. The quantity could be deceptive, for when the teams are not specifically described as being purely demesne ones, the general statement might really cover both demesne and other oxen. But the Cambridgeshire peasantry do not seem to have been well endowed. There are indeed only 22 entries where the oxen are definitely said to be those of the villeins only. In these 74 villeins had $23\frac{1}{2}$ teams, or about $2\frac{3}{4}$ oxen per man. Nine similar entries for bordars give 53 of these twelve teams, or $1\frac{3}{4}$ oxen each, much nearer the figure for villeins than in some counties.

Sometimes we are told how much land the peasantry held, and the entries show what vast disparity there was between men of the same broad category. At Ickleton (196ai) a villein had a whole hide, eleven half a hide each, and one a virgate, but seventeen had no land. We find villeins who possessed 5, 6, 7, $7\frac{1}{2}$, 8, 10, 12, and 15 acres. The holdings of bordars do not seem to exceed ten acres, and five is the more usual quantity, while at Cherry Hinton (193b2) 21 bordars had 21 acres, and at Horningsea (191ai) 'only their gardens'. Cottars, too, we find with no more than their gardens or closes; at Littleport (192b2) one had a solitary acre, and at Morden (198a2) another possessed three.

[1] Possibly an error for *in dominica firma*, a phrase applied to many Ely manors.
[2] So ICC, 97b. DB says half a hide.
[3] The 5s. 5d. at Pampisford (198ai) should surely have been 5s. 4d., which was the value of another Pampisford holding (202a2); ICC (96b) has *iiii orae*.
[4] e.g. at Steeple Morden (190a2, 193a2), Elsworth (192bi), Over (193ai).

The apparent contrast between the number of sokemen in Cambridgeshire in 1066 and 1086 has caused frequent comment. It has been reckoned that in King Edward's day there were between 800 and 900, whereas DB records less than 200. No doubt many had perished, or left the country, or through economic stress had become villeins. But we have no right to assume that their numbers had fallen quite so steeply as this. The Ely sokeman of 1066 was still on a Barham holding (191ai; 40bi). The same sokemen as those recorded for 1066 were on a Carlton estate of Countess Judith's (202a2). Ælfwine Hamelecoc the king's beadle still held at Abington Pigotts (190ai), and as he could not divorce his half-virgate from the manor of Litlington he was probably of sokeman status. There were probably many more sokemen in 1086 than are mentioned in DB.[1]

We can, as Maitland pointed out, see in many a vill the creation of demesne land where there had been none, but only the farms of free men and sokemen.[2] This would be easy to achieve where the sokemen owned individual shares in common fields. But were there in the east midlands no instances where some at least of the numerous sokemen in a vill possessed dispersed farms? Perhaps in Maitland's example of Meldreth (199b2, 191a2; 42bi; 104b) the five sokemen were all members of one family, and farmed a solid holding of a hide and a virgate. But were the other ten all farming their seventeen virgates in common? It would presumably be easy to reduce sokemen to villein status where land was held communally.

But the Cambridgeshire thegns were certainly far fewer than they had been; indeed, neither thegns nor free men are mentioned as such for 1086. But Colswegen still had his three virgates at Melbourn (194bi) and Sigar his land at Orwell and Shepreth (197a2), while Ælmaer of Bourn, perhaps the Ælmaer *cild* who was a Longstow juror (IE 38b2; ICC 110a2), had four hides at the vill from which he took his name, and land elsewhere also. These were probably above the sokemen class. So was Ordmær of Badlingham, a juror for Staploe Hundred and still the tenant of his holding of $3\frac{1}{2}$ hides (195bi; 38a2; 76ai). Few of the Hundred-jurors of 1086 are named in DB, but many must have been surviving tenants or officials. Sigar is styled *dapifer* (IE 38bi; ICC 98a2), Ælfric was Eudes fitzHubert's reeve (38b2; 110a2).

Hertfordshire

This again is a county where we have triple valuations for almost all the entries, and a majority of simple straightforward valuations. There are

---

[1] Bourn (200b2), Willingham (195ai), Elsworth (197a2), and Conington (197bi) furnish some of the entries mentioning sokemen.   [2] *DBB*, p. 63 (91).

what seem to be occasional errors; e.g. the 5s. Inquest value for a Shenley holding (136bi) should probably be £5, and the 1066 value for Rushden (142ai) £10 and not 10s. Nearly two-thirds of the vills were undivided ones, though there are some formidable exceptions, e.g. Bengeo (nine holdings) and Libury (*Stuterehale*, twelve). The chief difficulty is presented by the royal manors, especially as we have inadequate information about the enormous Hitchin complexity.

In the early years of the Conquest 77 per cent of the 311 relevant holdings fell in value, and only two had values higher than those of 1066. The overall decline was 30 per cent, from £1,810 8s. 2d. to £1,264 18s. 2d. As usual, it is on the whole the smaller holdings which display no changes in value. Some substantial manors were lessened in value by 50 per cent or more, e.g. Bayford (133ai), Westmill (138ai), Stanstead (138bi), Bennington (141ai), and Standon (142b2).

The Domesday county divides conveniently into two districts, the dividing line running rather to the north-east of Watling Street. West of this line vills were few, and while many manors fell in value, especially in the projection between Buckinghamshire and Bedfordshire, which was probably crossed by invading troops on their way to mid-Bedfordshire, the decline was here about 22 per cent, well below the county average. For the rest of the shire Fig. 12 suggests the movement of the Norman army in four or more columns from Bedfordshire and Cambridgeshire and concentrating near Hertford. The western column entered by Hexton and reached Hertford by way of Hitchin and the Welwyn neighbourhood. A second followed roughly a line through Baldock and Stevenage, whence it moved directly on Hertford. A third, coming in along Ashwell Street near the small borough of Ashwell, proceeded almost due south, following the valley of the Beane. A fourth, entering near Royston, appears to have split up. One portion may have linked up with the third column, another used Ermine Street, and another kept first east and then west of this, along the Quin valley.

Either there was deliberate ravaging to discourage resistance, or a halt around Hertford of some duration was anticipated, judging by the general devastation caused and the many falls in value south of Knebworth and at Watton at Stone and Bengeo. There is a suggestion, too, that raids were carried out from the base at Hertford. All four Brickendon manors (136bi, 139bi, 140bi, 142a2) fell in value, in all by nearly 45 per cent. So did those at Hoddesdon (137bi, 139a2,bi, 142a2), where the decline was 70 per cent. Probably it was known that supplies would not be easy to come by in the country between Hertford and London, in which vills were few and woodland extensive.

THE SOUTH MIDLANDS: HERTFORDSHIRE

In 1086 74 per cent of the holdings still showed values lower than those of 1066, and only thirteen had appreciated in worth. In all the county had a value almost 20 per cent less than it had in King Edward's day. It was only a little less than this west of Watling Street, but here the effects of the Norman take-over had probably been felt. Only just over one-third of the holdings had improved their worth since their transference, and 49 had fallen in value. Confirmation of the suggested effect of the Conquest on the county is supplied by Fig. 13, showing team-deficiencies. This is most marked along the lines by which the invaders may be supposed to have moved on Hertford, while beyond the borough there are some substantial deficiencies. There are frequent and heavy falls in the extreme east, and here declines may indicate the route of yet another Norman detachment. Only the abbeys of Ely and St Albans, with their vast resources, seem to have weathered the storm with fair success. Of the three Ely manors only Hatfield lost one-sixth of its value, and over one-quarter of its teams. The St Albans estates fell in value by almost one-quarter after the Conquest, but in 1086 were worth very slightly more than in 1066. They had, moreover, lost only about $13\frac{1}{2}$ per cent of their teams.

Even the royal manors (132a2–b2) seem mostly to have been worth less than they had been in 1066. They were indeed not of the order that we are accustomed to find in neighbouring shires, for they were for the most part small properties which had been held by minor thegns and sokemen, while Bayford, worth £20 T.R.E., had not been royal until King Edward acquired it, presumably after Earl Tostig's disgrace. A number of manors had been incorporated in Hitchin, some by Earl Harold, some by post-Conquest sheriffs and *ministri*. The value of some of these is given, and is presumably independent of that of Hitchin, but for six we have no information. Before the Conquest Hitchin produced £60 'for the soke' and £40 by tale; in 1086 £106 of burnt and weighed money and £10 of counted coin, but we cannot evaluate how much the services mentioned, probably of carriage on horseback of goods, which were owed by the components were really worth. We are not told that any royal manor was farmed, though the phrase 'when Peter the sheriff received it' suggests that Hitchin, Temple Dinsley, and Bayford were. The only other instance of a farm is that of Boorscroft (136b2), which Leofwine, the pre-Conquest holder, still held at farm, of Robert of Mortain. But Tring (137a2) paid in blanched silver, and Miswell (138ai) was worth £5 and an ounce of gold, which suggest manors at farm.

A number of the sums probably represent rents, e.g. the 84*s*. at Offley (133b2), the 52*s*. at Throcking (133bi), and the 34*s*. 8*d*. at Wallington (138ai). Boorscroft, mentioned above as being at farm, was worth 20*s*. 9*d*.

in both 1066 and 1086. Rents of one penny an acre are suggested by an elevenpenny value for the same number of acres at Libury (*Stuterehele*, 134bi) and one of threepence for three acres in the same vill (142a2).

If the quantities given for ploughlands indicate the approximate extent of arable available, there was a deficiency of teams of just under 20 per cent, which is a high figure. Where comparison is possible, there were 1,363¼ teams for 1,696½ ploughlands. There are no areas in which this is especially marked. Individual deficiencies are rarely large ones, but Great Berkhamsted (136bi) had only 15 teams for 26 ploughlands, while the value had fallen by one-third, a Therfield manor (136a2) had 32½ per cent less teams than ploughlands, though it was worth only £1 less than it had been in 1066, and Temple Dinsley (133b2), with unchanged liability to the king, had only 11 teams for 20 ploughlands.[1] There are in all 185 instances of the possibility of teams additional to those in existence being used.

In only a score of entries do we find only villeins besides slaves, and in these 131 held 52¼ teams, or 3·2 oxen a man. But there is no instance except that of Bengeo (141a2) where we can clearly see a villein with as much as half a team, though four at Alswick (138a2) had three teams. For bordars only four relevant entries, giving the 21 bordars 1·3 oxen per head, are insufficient data, and when two cottars are said to have 1½ teams at Hormead (137bi) it is probable that other categories of inhabitants were omitted.

In the IE (49bi,2) and in the entry for Sawbridgeworth (139b2) we are given information about the peasant holdings. The maximum villein holding is a virgate, which rather more than one-third of those enumerated held. The remainder have half-virgates. The Sawbridgeworth villeins, or some of them, had also 1½ virgates 9 acres in common, and rendered dues amounting to 17s. 4d. (13 *orae*: 14 of the villeins are said each to have a virgate). Assuming that a phrase such as 'nine bordars of one virgate' implies that they shared thirty acres, the average holding of a bordar works out at seven acres. But at Sawbridgeworth the 46 bordars had eight acres each, and six at Hatfield shared half a hide. Cottars are equated with bordars in the Ely Summary (48a2), but at Sawbridgeworth 20 had only 26 acres and 30 more paid one penny each. Seven at Hadham are said to have half a virgate between them, but DB mentions none here, merely fifteen bordars.[2] The occasional priests and a reeve have a whole or a half-hide.

[1] In each of these, teams which would make their number equal the number of ploughlands could have been used. Their absence at Berkhamsted might be connected with the development here of an urban element; it had 52 burgesses.
[2] Either IE missed eight bordars, or the *viii* of MS A refers to them. MSS B and C record no bordars, but list seven slaves, the number given in DB, but apparently omitted from MS A.

Of the use of the *ora* in reckoning amounts there seems to be very little trace. A Libury holding (141ai) was always worth sixteenpence, and the 17s. 4d. at Redbourn (136b2) might represent 13 *orae* and the 34s. 8d. of Wallington (138ai) double that number. Figures of 8, 12, 16, etc. appear but rarely; the tendency is rather for sums to be multiples of 20d., which could conceivably represent payments of twenty instead of sixteen pence to compensate for imperfect coins. Rents from woodland, pasture, and meadow appear intermittently.[1]

Middlesex

The Middlesex text includes three features which assist consideration of the position in 1066 and subsequent changes. In addition to frequent triple valuations of manors, there is regular record of the ploughlands and much information as to the potential employment of teams additional to those of 1086, and numerous statements as to the extent of the holdings of the various classes of the peasantry.

For only eight holdings, all small ones, are we not given the value at the time when its owner received it.[2] Between the Conquest and this nebulous date values declined considerably; from £905 3s. 8d. to £545 12s., or by 40 per cent. An appreciable decline is to be expected, for damage to the economy must have resulted from the Conqueror's advance through Hertfordshire on London and his occupation of the city. It is significant that the heaviest falls in values occur in the Hundreds—Edmonton, Gore, and the northern part of Elthorne—through which armed forces may be supposed to have passed. Enfield (129b2) fell in value from £50 to £20, and Tottenham (130b2) from £26 to £10; Harrow (127ai) from £60 to £20, and the two holdings at Stanmore (129bi, 130bi) from £20 to 30s.; Northolt (129b2) from £12 to £5, and Ruislip (129b2) from £30 to £12. These areas and the holdings in Ossulstone Hundred near the lines of approach indeed show a decline of almost 60 per cent.

To map the holdings, rather than the named vills, is not an easy matter. A settlement map shows many wide empty spaces, partly because some manors which must have been complexities, e.g. Harrow, were so immense, and partly because the components of other large manors, e.g. Stepney and Fulham, were some distance away from the *caput*. Fulham

---

The Summary has five more villeins than do DB or IE, and its 55 bordars seem to be made up of the 42 bordars and 19 cottars, giving six more than in the Summary. Otherwise the Summary agrees with DB and IE.
[1] Listed in *Dom. Geog.*, iii, pp. 77–81.
[2] All the other 87 entries read *quando recepit*; none, as elsewhere, *post*.

THE DETAILS OF DOMESDAY BOOK

probably included Acton, Brentford, Ealing, and Hammersmith; Stepney part of Hornsey and Hackney.[1] It must be remembered, too, that much of the north and north-west of the shire was then heavily wooded. Thus if all the holdings could be plotted, the decline in the area of the invaders' approach would possibly be even more marked.

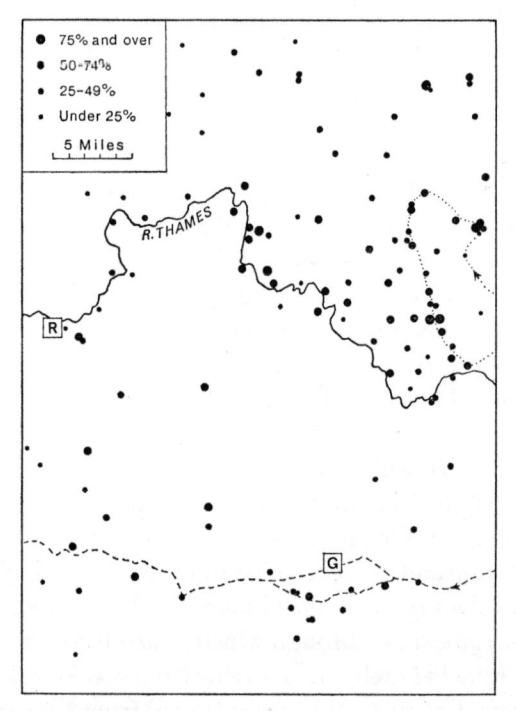

Fig. 14 The masking of London on the south and west: western section
   Fall in value *tunc–post*
   – – – Suggested route from Kent through Basingstoke to Winchester
   · · · Route of Southwark force to west Middlesex: its course in Berkshire is indeterminable
   G—Guildford R—Reading

  It is also noticeable that there are heavy falls in the south-west (Fig. 14); the Hundred of Spelthorne declined by 42½ per cent. It might be that troops left in mid-Wessex earlier in the advance, or reinforcements from Normandy, moved towards London to link with the main force.
  By 1086 a good many manors were again worth their pre-Conquest value, or at least the values had appreciated since the time described as

---

[1] See *Dom. Geog.*, iii, pp. 101–2. The information given there has been supplemented by notes of a discussion between Miss Jeffries Davis and Mr J. E. B. Gover.

THE SOUTH MIDLANDS: MIDDLESEX

quando recepit. What is startling is that apparently there was no recovery on any of the holdings of the bishop of London, St Paul's, or Westminster Abbey, except at a portion of the manor of Westminster itself, perhaps Paddington (128a2). Indeed, the only ecclesiastical lands which display an advance are the manors of the archbishop of Canterbury and

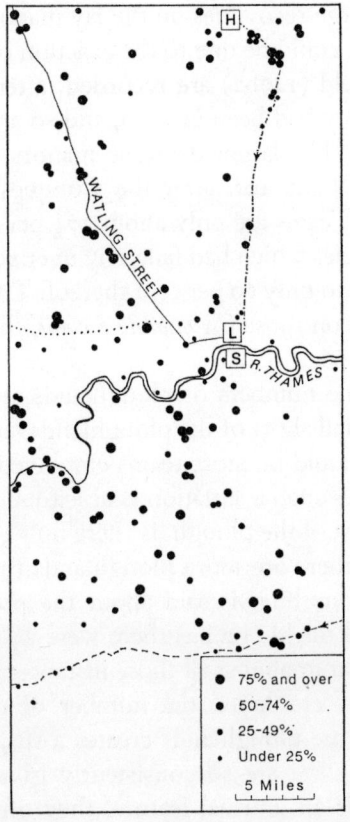

Fig. 15 The masking of London on the south and west: eastern section
Fall in value *tunc–post*
– – – Suggested route from Kent through Reigate to Guildford
· · · Route of Southwark force raiding in Surrey, then crossing the Thames and probably linking with a force from the Reading area
– · – · The final approach from Hertford to London
H—Hertford   L—London   S—Southwark

that of Holy Trinity, Rouen. It is of course possible that here fairly stable conditions persisted, and no general principle of raising rents obtained. Here, too, values had on the whole declined early in the Conquest less than the average of 40 per cent. The bishop's manors were down by only 15 per cent, St Paul's by 26½ per cent, Westminster's by 24½ per cent.

Plough-teams were apparently less than they had been by 35 per cent, and it may have been impossible to lease at higher rates, or to make the holdings more profitable. The archbishop's two enormous manors fell in value by 68 per cent after the Conquest, but though apparently well short of their proper complement of teams (110 ploughlands, 77 teams) they had recovered to 86 per cent of their pre-Conquest value.

If this is so, the large recoveries on the lay manors, which come chiefly on those in demesne, could be due to the exaction of increased rents. Both Edmonton and Enfield (129b2) are recorded, after a 55 per cent fall, as being worth what they had been in 1066, and so are Stanwell (130ai) and Kensington (130b2). The larger demesne manors had been worth £366 in 1066, but fell to £202 10s. after the Conquest. By 1086 they were valued at £321 15s. Teams are only about $17\frac{1}{2}$ per cent less than ploughlands. But sub-tenancies which had fallen by over 50 per cent of their 1066 values had recovered to only 60 per cent thereof. Though the figures show a rise of $35\frac{1}{2}$ per cent on those for *quando recepit*, they are still 18 per cent down on those of 1066.

On 40 holdings the numbers of ploughlands and teams are identical. But on 49 the teams fall short of the ploughlands, and in 38 entries we are informed that there could be more teams employed than are available. In three further instances such a situation is at least suggested; arable land is recorded, but no beast of the plough 'is there now', or a team is said to be 'wanting'.[1] In three there are more ploughlands than teams, and in two, less, but quite often nothing is said about the possibility of additional employment; e.g. at Enfield (129b2) there were 24 ploughlands, but only 20 teams. The fact that in almost all those instances in which it is said that more teams could be employed the number of existing and potential teams equals that of the ploughlands creates a suspicion. It may be that though for Middlesex we are so consistently given the number of the ploughlands, which is an unusual feature, they often were not, as such, supplied, and the clerk arrived at them by summing the existing and potential teams. It does seem strange that the figures should be the same for manors with as many as 70, 55, and 40 teams, as at Harrow (127ai), Isleworth (130ai), Hayes (127ai), and Fulham (127b2). Secondly, no explanation is given as to why, on five holdings, the teams exceed the ploughlands. However, 14 teams for 10 ploughlands at Tottenham (130b2) may well be because there was, besides the five hides of assessment and the ten ploughlands, land in demesne for two teams.[2] It makes us wonder whether

[1] Greenford (130b2), Ickenham (130ai), Stepney (127bi).
[2] The other instances are Hanworth, (129ai) Stanwell and Haggerston (130ai), and Tollington (130b2); a total of 37 teams for 27 ploughlands.

we can even here trust many of our ploughland quantities. The possibility of textual error where teams exceed ploughlands must exist.

At any rate, the formulae regarding potential teams argue a heavy decline in the number of teams at work after 1066. Over land for 476¼ teams these had fallen by 128¾. It might be that at one time, nearer the Conquest, they had fallen by a good deal more, but, like manorial values, had recovered substantially. At least a dozen instances come from the areas where falls in value were most marked, but some of the largest losses come from the manors of Isleworth and Hampton (130ai) in Hounslow Hundred and from Hayes (127ai) and Harmondsworth (128b2) in Elthorne. Further suspicion is inevitable: where the teams are said to equal the ploughlands, might there not also in fact have been a decline, and the clerk, as he seems to have done elsewhere (see p. 280), gave for the ploughlands the number of the existing teams? The total deficiency, on the figures, is 19½ per cent, 544½ teams for 676¼ ploughlands.

Some apparent absences of teams may be due to clerical error. Ruislip (129b2) is credited with 20 ploughlands but only three demesne and twelve villeins' teams; further teams owned by the four *francigenae* on their 3¼ hides may have been ignored. Similarly, the surplus of teams at Stanwell (130ai), 13 for 10 ploughlands, could be due to neglect of the ploughlands relevant to the 2½ hides of the *milites*. It is, however, only fair to say that a *miles* held two of the ten hides of East Bedfont (130ai), but here the teams equal the ploughlands.

Despite the dominance of heavy and cold London Clay in the north of the county, and the large amount of woodland, we should expect Middlesex to be a fairly prosperous area at the time. London must have furnished a constant demand for local agricultural produce. A two-shilling geld on the hide would make the assessment about 6s. per square mile, which argues a fairly high rating and thus ability to pay the tax. Only about 29 per cent of the hides were in manorial demesne, and if, as elsewhere, fiscal demesne did not differ greatly in quantity from this, exemption was thus comparatively small. A low proportion of demesne land implies, too, a high degree of peasant freedom from manorial demands.

It is arguable whether a high proportion of slaves makes for a backward economy or not. Since their number is highest in the least progressive districts, especially the south-west and the west midlands, it is probable that in a highly manorialised area a small servile element denotes a reasonably efficient economy. The Middlesex slaves represent only just over 5 per cent of the peasantry. It may seem an impossibly low figure, since for the counties other than Essex with a substantial common boundary with Middlesex it ranges from 12–16½ per cent. Only two slaves on the 100-hide manor of Harrow (127ai), with four demesne teams, may seem highly improbable. None is mentioned for the bishop of London's two large and dispersed manors, and only two on all St Paul's lands, but the Westminster Abbey estates had 8½ per cent. But many of the St Paul's estates were being rented by villeins, and on these we should not expect to find slaves. Possibly the individual fief failed to record them; of 25, eight report none, including that of Walter de St Valéry, of 105 hides and nine demesne teams. Still, small demesnes imply the maintenance of few slaves.

In the majority of the entries we are given the actual holdings of the peasantry. It does not seem as if the figures are those of geld liability, for if added to the demesne and sub-tenancy quantities they produce the quota of assessment in only about half a dozen instances. In the majority of the entries the details fail to reproduce the assessment by large amounts; e.g. Isleworth (130ai) was rated at 70 hides, but the itemisation falls short of this by 38⅝ hides. Sometimes, perhaps, a quantity not given for a category of inhabitant would supply the difference, but this could not be true for many holdings, e.g. for Isleworth only the holdings of six cottars are not described. It is true that no bordars are mentioned, against 93 villeins, but however many there were, they would hardly hold 38 hides. Both Maitland and Vinogradoff decided that these itemisations related to agrarian, not fiscal, hides.[1] Neither they nor Darby could find a relationship between these and ploughlands or teams.[2]

The holdings of villeins are given on 134 occasions; only four other entries give no quantity for these. The average holding is 28 acres, or little less than a virgate. But though 468 villeins are each said to hold 30 acres, and 432 half that quantity, variation is considerable. The villein at East Bedfont (129a2) held only eight acres. A Hanwell villein (128bi) had two whole hides, and one at Greenford (128bi) close by 150 acres. Eleven had a hide apiece, 19 half a hide. Thus the Middlesex villein of 1086 was far from being altogether impoverished. Two on the manor of Stepney (127ai) could pay 4s. for a house and 8s. for half a hide respectively.

Then we have ten entries telling us that villeins 'hold the land', or have it *ad firmam*, or 'from the Canons of St Paul's', which seems to imply the renting of manors.[3] The individual villein's land is here sometimes assessed at one or two hides, and the holdings average 2½ virgates. If the values given represent the rents, the hide is fetching 10s. 6d. in rent, and each

---

[1] *DBB*, p. 478 (549–50); *Eng. Soc.*, p. 168, with tables for this relationship on pp. 490–1.
[2] *Dom. Geog.*, iii, p. 107.
[3] Land in the manor of Harrow (127ai), Harmondsworth (129ai), Hatton (129ai), in Spelthorne Hundred (128b2), Willesden (127b2) and five instances on fol. 128ai.

villein is on the average paying 6s. 6d. Rents would of course vary with the character of the holding: at St Pancras (128ai) 24 'men' (*homines*) were paying 30s. for a hide.

But do all these represent our conception of the average villein? Maitland stressed that villeins must have been 'heterogeneous to a high degree'.[1] Those villeins who held or rented the land possessed on an average four oxen apiece, which is far more than many who are categorised elsewhere as villeins did. Few of those at, e.g., Feltham (129a2), can have owned two. May they not, often enough, here be the freemen and sokemen of 1066? Pre-Conquest sokemen are not often recorded. Two had held two of Harmondsworth's 30 hides (128b2), which 'they could not sell outside the manor'. In 1086 two of the villeins were also holding two hides. Again, two held a hide and a half at Hatton (129ai), and might well be the two villeins who in 1086 'held the land'.[2] Five sokemen had held six of Enfield's hides (129b2); they are unrecorded for 1086, but four villeins were holding 2½ hides. They may have been unable to keep all their land; at Greenford (129bi) one sokeman had held two hides and another a single hide, but at the Inquest we find two villeins with half a hide. Many a Middlesex sokeman (free men as such are never mentioned) may have died at Stamford Bridge or Hastings and left his family, if any, in no state to maintain his holding. Where in Ossulstone Hundred (129bi) there had been two of the king's sokemen, there were in 1086 only four bordars and a slave, and a sub-tenant of Geoffrey de Manneville's held it. There had been sokemen at East and West Bedfont and Hatton (130ai); the two at West Bedfont had held four hides, and in 1086 two villeins had the same amount, though at East Bedfont the three sokeman-holdings had averaged half a hide while in 1086 those of the four villeins averaged a virgate.

The holdings of bordars are noted in 51 entries, over one-third of which allot the bordar 5 acres of land, though the average is nearer 8 than 7 acres. The maximum holding for the individual bordar was at least 18 acres (seven held a hide at Greenford, fol. 128bi); at Stepney (130ai) eight held a hide.[3] Here, too, 15, though holding only 10 acres, could pay a rent of 9s.; and 46 at another Stepney holding (127a2) 30s. for the hide they shared. Sometimes, however, holdings were small. At another Stepney holding (127bi) six held only five acres, and seven at Ruislip (129b2) only

---

[1] *DBB*, p. 41 (67). He further pointed out that the *villanus* 'both is and is not a free man', p. 43 (70).
[2] The two sokemen who had held two hides at Harlington (129ai) might be represented by the sub-tenants in 1086, Alfred and Olaf.
[3] In Stepney, too, a bordar is said to hold as much as 75 acres, but probably this should be for a number of bordars, their quantity having been omitted.

four acres apiece. Obviously the prosperity of the men classed as 'bordars' varied greatly.

The holdings of cottars are specified in 22 entries. They average only two acres a man, though one at Westminster (128a2) and one at West Bedfont (130ai) each had five acres. But four at Edmonton (129b2) had only four acres between them, and three at Stanmore (130bi) a solitary acre. But in the same manor another three owned ten acres. Many an entry does not credit either cottars or bordars with any land. Eight cottars at Fulham (127bi) 'had only their gardens', but at Westminster (128a2) the 41 cottars were paying 40s. (? *recte* 41s.) for these.

The rents of bordars and cottars are not small ones, and we shall see that their wealth seems to be superior here to what it is in other areas. Probably, then, taking into account the decline in teams and values, they had been more prosperous still before the Conquest.

Sometimes we can isolate the teams they held. There were only villeins and slaves at Kensington (130b2), and the 18 villeins averaged over two oxen apiece. On a Stepney holding (127a2), the 14 bordars who are the only recorded inhabitants averaged nearly two oxen each. Lennard has calculated that over the whole of England the villein on an average possessed 2·9 beasts of the plough.[1] If we ascribe to a villein three times as many oxen as a bordar, as Lennard's figures suggest (though the average holding is rather in the proportion of 6:1), we can arrive at a very rough estimate for Middlesex. On this principle, 1,163 villeins and 364 bordars had 408½ teams, which would give only about two oxen per head, or three oxen between two villeins and one between two bordars, while the calculation ignores the possibility of cottars, here more numerous than bordars, having any oxen. It is highly possible that the text omits some peasants' teams, but it does not look as if Middlesex peasants possessed in 1086 an adequate quantity of oxen. We have seen above how the number of teams had fallen since the Conquest. We cannot, it is true, always be sure from the text whether teams are demesne or villagers'. What we can be sure of is that it tells us that almost half as many teams again as those actually at work in 1086 in the relevant instances could be employed. If this improvement were effected, it would have given the average villein at least a couple of oxen, and, so the frequent lack of information suggests, probably more.

Few Englishmen or Englishwomen above the status of villein held Middlesex land in 1086, so far as we are told. There is no list of king's or 'English' thegns, as there is for other counties. Two women hold estates *in elemosina* (130b2), a nun held Laleham of Robert Blond (130bi), and

[1] *Rural Eng.*, p. 352.

only nine other entries suggest English sub-tenants, one of whom was *miles probatus* (130ai). Four holders in 1066 had been housecarls; more than a score the thegns or men of the king or Earls Leofwine and Harold. Many of these must have perished before William was crowned; indeed no lay holder of a manor in 1066 is recorded for 1086.

NOTE: Some commentators see in the numerous falls in value between the Thames and the Reigate—Guildford road (Fig. 15) the movements of the raiding forces which attacked Southwark in November 1066 (p. 45). These may well be the reason for the obvious damage, but there is no indication of whether the invaders proceeded from Surrey to attack Southwark or moved from Kent and rejoined the main body near Reigate after the assault. Accordingly this potential movement has not been shown on Figs 3 and 4.

3
The West Midlands

There are obvious objections to including the counties of Oxford, Warwick, Worcester, and Gloucester within a single area, and to styling them all 'west midland'. They were parts of different Inquest circuits, and the Domesday records are consequently of varying character. The complexity and dispersed components of the larger manors in the last two shires is stressed in the text, and the country covered ranges from the Welsh March to the Cotswold Hills and from the Severn valley to Chiltern slopes.

But it would be difficult to include Herefordshire with Gloucestershire, though it was part of the same circuit, and exclude Shropshire, which was not, and the Domesday of which is of a largely different character, while Oxfordshire cannot be brigaded with wasted Staffordshire or a Northamptonshire using a Domesday valuation system almost unique. Three of the shires have at least one point in common, a large difference in the areas covered by the Domesday and by the modern county. Several vills were partly in one county, partly in another, the result of the wide dispersion of the property of the bishopric of Worcester and of transferences in liability, especially to the royal *firma*, and in ownership, many of which are ascribed to the influence over the district of William fitzOsbern in the early years of the Conquest.[1]

There is considerable difference in the character of the valuations at the time of the Inquest and in King Edward's day. The two easterly shires show substantial appreciation on the non-royal lands, the two westerly a slight fall. Even in Worcestershire life had probably been more insecure since the Conquest than in the central midlands, while much of Gloucestershire was uncomfortably near Welsh territory. The south-eastern

[1] See the maps in *Dom. Geog.*, ii, Figs. 2 and 72, pp. 2 and 217.

portion of the area had possibly been affected by the post-Conquest campaigns, and the more westerly and northern districts by the western rebels and their Welsh allies.

Oxfordshire

The Oxfordshire Domesday does not cover all the land then within the county. Thirteen entries which should have been included appear in error in the Northamptonshire text, and a few other holdings are to be found in the Staffordshire or Warwickshire Domesdays. These have here been considered as in Domesday Oxfordshire.

Although the Domesday text gives us a high proportion of possible values for both 1066 and 1086, and of the total quantities of ploughlands and teams, the results do not lend themselves to satisfactory deductions. There is little consistency in the distribution of changes in values, or of deficiencies of teams, and mapping the relationships yields few useful results. Since only eight entries give sums which are not simple multiples of 5s., and the majority are for whole numbers of pounds, the text, as regards valuations, is somewhat uninteresting.

Baring suggested that strikingly low valuations in 1066 might mark the advance from Northampton of the Northumbrian rebels on Oxford.[1] It is true that in the appropriate area the values in 1066 of some manors are small compared with those of 1086; e.g. Weston on the Green (158bi), worth £8 in 1066 but £12 in 1086, or Islip (160a2; £7–10) or Beckley (158bi; £5–8) or Shelswell (221ai; £5–10). But similar instances occur throughout the county. In the south, Crowmarsh (157bi) doubled its earlier value of £10, and the Dorchester holdings (155ai,2) rose from £44 to £77. In the west Taynton (157ai) went up from £10 to £15 and Brize Norton (158b2) from £9 to £13. In any case, the chroniclers do not suggest that the rebel forces approached Oxford, where negotiations seem to have taken place between Harold Godwineson and the Northumbrian leaders.

The statistics of DB lend only slight support to the theory. It is true that in the neighbourhood of the principal roads connecting Oxford with Northampton there was in 1086 a deficiency of teams well above the county average, over 18 per cent against under 10 per cent, and 24½ per cent north of Bicester. But, as will be demonstrated later, in this county interpretation of *terra est* n *carucis* is not necessarily straightforward, and it may be

[1] F. H. Baring: 'Oxfordshire traces of the northern insurgents of 1065' (*EHR*, xiii, 1898, pp. 295–7). See also G. H. Fowler: 'The devastation of Bedfordshire and the neighbouring counties in 1065 and 1066' (*Archaeologia*, lxxii, 1922, pp. 41–50).

THE DETAILS OF DOMESDAY BOOK

impossible to arrive at a true relationship between ploughlands and the teams of 1086. Moreover, the 1066 value of the ploughland is here only infinitesimally below the county average. On the other hand, appreciation in value between 1066 and 1086 is below average, as though some incident had affected the area.

After the Conquest, values seem in places to have risen. We are given post-Conquest values for 50 manors; eleven show appreciation and twelve a decline, while there is a very small total increase (less than ¾ per cent). By 1086 these same manors had increased their pre-Conquest value by 29 per cent, which is considerably above the average for the whole county. Some show spectacular appreciation between *tunc* and *post*: Lewknor (156b2) doubled its value of £10, while Pyrton (157a2) went up from £16 to £25. On the other hand Duns Tew (158ai) fell from £3 to 10s., and Hempton (159bi) from £8 to £2.

Generally speaking, Oxfordshire holdings were worth more in 1086 than they had been in 1066. Of the 354 entries which furnish comparable figures, 45 per cent display an increase in value, and 15 per cent a decline; no change in 1086 from the value of 1066 is recorded for the remaining 40 per cent. The total rise in value, excluding *Terra Regis*, is quite considerable, from £2,016 5s. to £2,460 13s. 6d., or 22 per cent. Frequently the value of King Edward's day had doubled by that of the Inquest; e.g. at Great Tew (155b2), from £20, or at Pyrton (157a2), where it rose from £16 to £30. But with these large manors one is always suspicious that the increase might be due to an enlargement of the manor.

Equally there are spectacular falls in value. Sandford on Thames (156b2) fell from £8 to £3, and had only about two-thirds of the teams it could have employed. Minster Lovell (157bi), though it had thirteen teams for ten ploughlands, went down from £10 to £7; Lashbrook (157bi), with only three teams for nine ploughlands, from £12 to 30s., after falling to £8 *post*. The 53 holdings which declined in value fall into five main geographical groups.[1] Their situation suggests that figures lower in 1086 than in 1066 might often be due to extension of the Forest. A number of the manors are in the neighbourhood of Shotover and Stowood Forests, and near Ot Moor, where wildfowl must have been hawked. Another group lies north-west of Woodstock, and yet another south and north of Wychwood. Added emphasis is given by the existence of waste land at Noke (161ai) by Ot Moor and at Chastleton (156bi, 157ai,b2) in the eastern Cotswolds. Again appreciation in value is below average around

[1] An apparent rise between 1066 and 1086 at Milton under Wychwood (161a2) from £1 to £7 should probably be a fall to 7s., for the manor declined to 15s. *post*, and had only a single team.

118

THE WEST MIDLANDS: OXFORDSHIRE

Wychwood and the eastern Cotswolds, in the Oxford area, and in the neighbourhood of the routes we might expect King William's troops to have used on leaving Wallingford in 1066.

It is unfortunate that we are given no indication of the extent to which the ten royal manors (155bi,2) might have appreciated in value. Somewhat unusually, only Benson and Headington have decimal values, £85 and £60. Bampton (£82) and either Wootton or Langford (£18) might have formed a £100-unit; four of the ten have nine as a factor in their amounts.[1] Five are said to pay *ad numerum*.

There is no indication that the royal manors were being farmed, except for Langford, which Ælfsige of Farringdon farmed at an unchanged sum of £18, though probably they were. Sydenham (16ai), a manor of Gilbert de Bretteville's which had been William fitzOsbern's, is the only other holding said to be *ad firmam*. Six properties are said to be waste; to these should probably be added the teamless Rycote (157b2), though there were three villeins there, for while it had been worth £4, *nil reddit*.

Ploughlands and teams (or an absence of teams) are fairly regularly recorded. A deficiency of teams for the ploughlands given occurs in rather under one-half of these, and a surplus in about one-fifth. On balance there is a deficiency of teams of about 9 per cent. But all such figures, 2,314½ teams for 2,553¼ ploughlands, are open to grave doubt as to their adequacy. In some entries the demesne teams or those of the villeins may have been omitted, e.g. at Cogges (156ai), consistently worth £10 but with only two demesne teams for its ten ploughlands and five hides. Again, we have no comparative figures for some of the largest manors. We are not, for example, told how many ploughlands there were at the *caput* of the manor of Banbury (155a2), where there were forty teams, or in several smaller manors. This is true also of seven of the royal manors, but for three of these we are told the number of teams in King Edward's day, which quite possibly implies the number of ploughlands, or nearly so, in 1086. It looks as if there was throughout a considerable deficiency of teams on royal manors, but the ploughlands may still have been worked to capacity by exacting heavy labour services from the peasantry.

Three entries in the fief of the bishop of Lincoln (155a2) deserve consideration. At Eynsham he had found, on becoming bishop of Dorchester in 1067/8, eighteen teams for the same number of ploughlands, and in 1086 there were still eighteen in all. But he had also in demesne 'inland for two teams', and in this phrase, which occurs in other counties, it is usual for the

---

[1] The two at £18 above and Shipton under Wychwood, £72 and £9. If *lxvii* was a mistake for *lxiii*, Bloxham with Adderbury could be added. The combined values of the remaining three, £197, is very near £200.

hides or ploughlands specified to be additional to those previously recorded. At Banbury, indeed, the bishop had 50 hides, and land in demesne for ten teams and three hides besides (? in addition to) the inland. He found on his succession to the bishopric as many teams, $33\frac{1}{2}$, as there had been in 1066, but he had 40 in 1086. Had he extended the demesne portion of his manor? And had he then land for $10 + 33\frac{1}{2}$ teams? He had at Cropredy land for 30 teams, though he found 35 there in 1067/8, and by 1086 he had 40. In addition to the 50 hides at which the manor was assessed he had demesne land for ten teams. Though he is said to have 30 ploughlands 'in all', one cannot help suspecting that he now had 40, and the same number of teams. At Waterstock (155bi) he had land for five teams, and there had been that quantity in 1066.[1]

The deduction of the authors of the Oxfordshire chapter in *Dom. Geog.* (iv, pp. 200–1) was that here 'the ploughland formula indicates the number of plough-teams in 1066, rather than the extent of arable land', and that 'to the scribe plough-lands and past plough-teams were one and the same'. Twice, where there was a surplus of oxen, he gave the amount of arable land and then stressed that there were, however, more oxen than might be expected.[2] But in the Cottisford entry (224b2), after noting three demesne teams, he added that there might be a fourth employed.

There does not seem to be any strong indication that there is an artificial basis for Oxfordshire ploughlands. If there was not, we are compelled to suppose that in about one-fifth of the manors more teams were at work than had been employed in 1066. Though Nuneham Courtenay (159ai) had consistently been worth £13, even after the Conquest, there were apparently seventeen teams operating where there was land for ten, and at Water Eaton (158a2) nine on five ploughlands, though there is said to be land for five only, and the value of £3 was half what it had been in 1066. If so, we do not know how many actual ploughlands there may have been at that date, though we may suspect that we should add to those where teams equal or are less than the ploughlands at least the number of apparently surplus teams, $143\frac{3}{4}$. If so, we have a deficiency of teams for the shire of about $15\frac{1}{4}$ per cent instead of under 10 per cent.

The distribution of these potential increases in the number of teams is curious. They occur only rarely in the Chiltern district or north thereof until the Icknield Way is reached; then, perhaps, the demand from Oxford for increased production begins to make itself felt. They are common on the gravels between Cotswold and Thames, and in the valleys which run eastwards to join that of the Cherwell. It may be that they are virtually

---

[1] At an anonymous half-hide (157ai) we are not given the quantity of ploughlands, but told that 'there was one team there'.   [2] Northbrook (159ai), Brize Norton (160b2).

absent from South Oxfordshire because this was the area traversed by invading forces in 1066, and the damage was such that here teams were fewer or no more numerous than before the Conquest.

We can look at the ploughland/team relationship in another way. The ploughland of 1066 was worth, on an average, about 16s.; that of 1086 a little over £1. But if the apparently surplus teams of 1086 represent teams operating in 1066 for which there was land available, the ploughland of 1066 was worth only about 15s. For each 1066 team the value of the land is just over 17s., for 1086 about 23s. 6d. Coupled with a balance of increase in value by 1086, the harmonies suggest that an apparent surplus of teams merely implies a number of teams at work higher than that of 1066. But, it should be added, the figures do not tell us the actual amount of arable land available, for there may have been more ploughlands than teams in a number of manors, and thus the figure for the apparent deficiency of teams in 1086 may be too low.

But it is not impossible that the ploughland figures may reflect, at least in part, an earlier assessment which had a duodecimal basis. Quantities of 24, 18, 16, 12, 9, 8, and 6 appear in almost one-quarter of the entries. The figures for a number of divided vills also give similar quantities, e.g. Fritwell (4 + 8), Marsh Baldon (7 + 5), Cassington (3 + 3 + 6), Ascot d'Oyly and Earl (5 + 7).[1] It is perhaps of significance that no figure is given for any of King Edward's former manors (154bi), which were presumably *mansiones de regno*, and had contributed a *firma* and so would not initially be assessed.[2] It is noticeable that as the limits of Mercian land are reached south of Oxford duodecimal quantities become far fewer than in the north of the shire.

In a very large number of entries, including the huge fief of the bishop of Bayeux, no information is given about the holders of manors in 1066. Thus, so far as we know, the surviving landholders were virtually limited to those recorded on fols. 160b2, 161ai, whose property was valued at no more than £53 10s. The occasional Englishman appears among the sub-tenancies; e.g. Godric at Showell (156bi) and Ælfric with six hides of the manor of Thame (155bi), but including the clerics of fol. 157ai they occupied only about a score of holdings.

Nor can we deduce much about the potential numbers of oxen owned by villeins and bordars. In fifteen holdings 81 villeins had 27 teams, or just

---

[1] Fols. 155b2, 161a2; 155bi, 159bi; 156ai,a2,bi; 158bi *bis*.
[2] Benson is an exception, but the ploughland figure is the arbitrary one of 50, if *T.R.E. erant ibi l carucae* represents this. It had 32 teams in 1086. In 1086 the manors were assessed, and it is suggestive that with the non-royal holdings Bloxham and Adderbury were rated at 50 hides.

THE DETAILS OF DOMESDAY BOOK

over 2½ oxen per man. Only thrice are the teams of bordars clearly given, and here the average number of oxen per head is less than two. Such figures are obviously unrealistic.

Warwickshire

The Warwickshire text is one which does not add greatly to our knowledge of conditions in the years following the Conquest. We are lacking a few manorial values for 1066, and have only 63 for what are probably varying times between 1066 and 1086, which is only about 17½ per cent of the 355 entries which give values at the time of the Inquest. Six places in Warwickshire wrongly became included in the Northamptonshire section of Domesday, and have here been treated as in Warwickshire, as has Cubbington (248ai), which was incorrectly inscribed in the Staffordshire text. The final four entries for Earl Roger's fief (239a2) are for places in Shropshire. It is possible that they should have been included in that county's text, but they have here been treated as part of Warwickshire in 1086. So have the county text's entries near the present boundary now in Staffordshire, Oxfordshire, or Worcestershire, but not Spelsbury (238bi), which was well inside Oxfordshire. A few entries possibly became duplicated, e.g. those for Flecknoe (238bi, 244bi), Barston (241ai, 242b2), and Middleton (242ai, 244bi), but have not been considered as such.

The fall *tunc–post* for these holdings was from £288 10s. to £258 10s., a decline of 10½ per cent. By 1086 the same holdings had recovered to a total of £403 10s., an appreciation of 53¾ per cent on 1066, well above the county average. But two at least of the entries may be deceptive. Coten End (238a2), a royal manor, went up from £17 10s. to £30 by the time 'Robert received it *ad firmam*'. When Earl Edwine had it the £17 10s. included 'the borough of Warwick and the pleas of the shire', and the revenue may have been increased when the manor became royal. Long Itchington (244a2) was worth £12 in 1066, but 'when the king gave the manor to Cristina' it was producing £36. Cristina, sister to Edgar Ætheling, and a nun at Romsey Abbey, may have received a manor enlarged in comparison with its former size. But though seven manors had improved their worth, 40 had fallen in value since 1066, Bishop's Itchington (238b2) by 70 per cent, and Bilton (239a2) by 87½ per cent. One would like to think that at Itchington land had passed from one manor to the other.

By the time of the Inquest values had improved by 25½ per cent from those of 1066, from £839 9s. 4d. to £1,130 17s. 8d. Some increases are so spectacular that we may doubt if we are reading of manors which had not been enlarged. Eatington (242a2) went up from £4 to £20, and Hampton

Lucy (228bi) increased in value from £4 to £20, Stratford on Avon (238bi) from £5 to £25 on valuations *post* which, except for Eatington's, £4, were then the same as in 1066. The last two were the bishop of Worcester's, and another of his manors, Alveston, improved from £8 to £15.

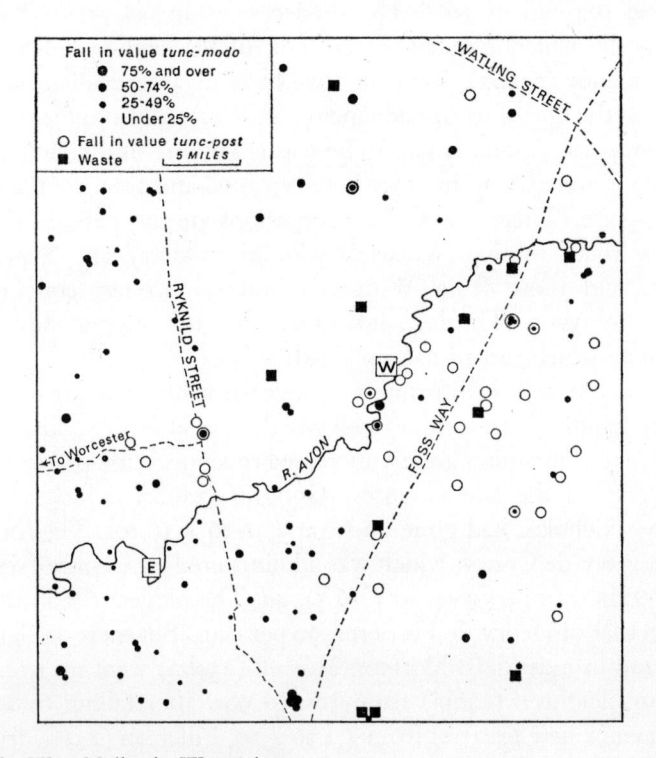

Fig. 16 The West Midlands: Warwick area
Fall in value *tunc–post* and *tunc–modo*
E—Evesham   W—Warwick

Falls in value between *tunc* and *post* are to be found mostly in the east and south of the shire. It might be thought that values *post* were altogether omitted for northern Hundreds, but this is not so. Their distribution rather suggests (a) a movement by royal troops from Oxford and Gloucester, perhaps connected with the foundation of the castle at Warwick in 1068, (b) another thence in the direction of Leicester, which could imply results from the march against the insurgents at York which saw the establishment of the castle at Nottingham, (c) a group in the west which might be the result of the West Mercian revolt of 1069 spreading through Worcestershire. It is possible that disaffection was active earlier, and that

123

the falls in value reflect a punitive campaign which virtually ended when Warwick was secured and a castle built there. Thorkill of Warwick, son of the former sheriff Ælfwine, may well have obtained his huge fief, which occupies almost two whole folios of DB, by virtue of the support he may have given the newcomers. He had made his peace with the king at Barking at the end of 1066. His predecessors in his 75 holdings were numerous; he had not obtained the bulk of his land by inheritance. A Harbury manor (238b2), for which we have no intermediate value, and which is on the line of troops advancing on Warwick from the south-east, fell from 10s. to 2s., and is said to be waste 'because of the king's army'.[1]

The manors declining in value between 1066 and 1086 are scattered all over the shire. There are slight suggestions of the passage of troops along the roads joining Warwick with Shrewsbury and Stafford and Leicester, and those from Worcester and Gloucester, converging at Stratford on Avon. The last, however, does not suggest any military operation of which record has survived.

We are given so little information about the values and attributes of the few royal manors that we cannot tell whether, as at Brailes, King William was apparently obtaining greatly increased revenue. Perhaps he was, since the property of the late Countess Godgifu (239bi), which was being farmed by Nicholas, had gone up from £36 to £45 10s. The former fief of Earl Aubrey de Coucy, which was administered by Geoffrey de Wirce, had appreciated from £9 5s. to £16 5s. 4d. The biggest rise in the larger fiefs is on that of Henry de Ferrières, 90 per cent. But there are large rises to be found in most fiefs. Moreton Morrell (239b2) went up from £6 to £11, Wormleighton (240bi) from 30s. to 90s. after falling to 20s., and another manor here (241b2) from £4 to £10, Pillerton (242ai) from £10 to £17, and Long Compton (243bi) from £15 to £30.

Warwickshire does not seem to have been particularly densely populated, though the fact that it had twice as many villeins as bordars may be of significance as an index of prosperity. It looks as though either by improved management or increased rents and services the newcomers were exploiting the county thoroughly. The chief area of appreciation is that of the open country of the Feldon and the Avon basin, roughly the part of the shire south of a line running across it south-westwards from Rugby, in which the recorded population average ten to the square mile.

Waste is mentioned in eight entries only, two of which show that only part of the holding was waste, and three of which still had some small

---

[1] Harbury occurs five times in DB (238b2, 239b2, 241bi, 242a2, 243bi). Between 1066 and 1086 the manors appreciated from £11 to only £12 7s., so more than one may have fallen in value.

THE WEST MIDLANDS: WARWICKSHIRE

value. These last and the remaining three were all small estates.[1] A few manors had suffered because their woodland was *in manu* or *in defensu regis*.[2] The importance of the woodland in the manorial economy is shown by the fact that though Kingston Grange was waste, it was yet worth 5s., and the woodland was worth 10s. a year; the value of woodland is recorded also for Wilnecote (5s.; 240ai), Arley (£3; 244a2), and Fillongley (10s.; 244bi). Few manors are said to have been farmed. In addition to Coten End only Radway (244bi) is given as in this category.

Since the county is unlikely to have received much influence from Danish settlers, it is not surprising that we find little apparently based on the *ora* in the values. The sums include 1s. 4d., 5s. 4d. (*bis*), and 10s. 8d.; at Myton (241b2) eight men were rendering 32d.[3] Very occasionally 4s., 8s., 16s., make an appearance. Most of the places concerned are in the east of the county, nearest the Danelagh.

The deficiency of plough-teams was not great, $1,916\frac{1}{4}$ teams for $2,174\frac{1}{2}$ ploughlands, about 12 per cent. It seems to have been at its highest in the southern portion of the shire, but it must be remembered that the appearance of Domesday maps is often deceptive. In the northern half of the county Domesday place-names and manors are far less frequent than in the south. But there is a strong similarity to the map of decline in values *tunc–post* as regards the approaches to Warwick from Oxford and Gloucester. There is, too, a marked broad belt of deficiencies of plough-teams running right across the shire from the Worcestershire border through Warwick to the neighbourhood of Rugby at its eastern boundary. Possibly, on the occasion of the frequent Danish and Northumbrian irruptions, troops had to be drawn from western shires and provisioned themselves on their way to the main roads leading to Yorkshire and Lincolnshire and the Isle of Ely. There is even a suggestion of damage along the road from Shrewsbury; if this seems an indirect approach to the seats of trouble, it must be remembered that the obvious routes would after 1070 have taken armed men in need of sustenance through the ravaged north midlands. Alternatively, though Earl Roger's revolt in 1075 is said to have been checked on the line of the Severn, some of his adherents, though we are not told so, may have been able to move in the direction of Cambridge and their East Anglian partners in rebellion.

But there is strong indication that the quantities given for the ploughlands have a duodecimal basis, and may represent an older assessment.

[1] Harbury (239ai), Kington Grange (240ai), Roundshill Farm (239b2), Weston under Wetherley (241bi), Bushbury (243ai), Eatington (244bi), Whitacre (224a, foot), Marston juxta Wolston (242bi).
[2] Southam (238b2), Erdington (243ai), Sowe (in part, 244bi).
[3] Marston (241bi), Bentley (243b2), Churchover (239bi), Long Lawford (241bi).

Over one-quarter of the figures are 32, 24, 18, 16, 12, 9, 8, or 6. Inclusion of those of 4 and 3 brings the proportion up to 45 per cent. Moreover, the total number of ploughlands attributed to a vill is often duodecimal; e.g. Austry (4 + 2 + 10 = 16), Napton on the Hill (8 + 5 + 3 = 16), Binton (2 + 10 = 12), and frequently we can see what may be combinations of neighbouring vills on a similar principle, e.g. Wootton Wawen and Offord (9 + 1 + 6 = 16).[1] This, perhaps, is why for the four manors anciently royal (238a2) no figures are given. Presumably they would then have been exempt from the geld and contributing a *firma*. For all we know some vills recorded in the Gloucestershire and Worcestershire texts, which omit ploughland figures, but are within the modern county, were once in Warwickshire. If so, more duodecimal figures and combinations might be discovered.

Ploughlands outnumber teams in 75 entries, and since the Warwickshire figures may not include a conventional element, it could be that teams had been transferred from one holding to another in the interests of manorial economy. The surplus is hardly ever a large one, usually of only a single team or pair of teams.[2] Deficiencies, too, are rarely great.[3] These might sometimes be due to a change from agriculture to stock-raising, or to mortality. At any rate, in almost one-third of the holdings there was a team for each ploughland, and this seems to have been expected, for where there was a surplus the clerks several times wrote 'there is land for n teams, however there are $n+$', e.g. at Elmdon and Wolfhamcote (241ai) and four times on fol. 241a2.

Too few entries give us the teams possessed by villeins or bordars alone, a dozen for the former and three for the latter. Fifty-nine villeins had $20\frac{3}{4}$ teams, an average of just over $2\frac{3}{4}$ oxen per man, and 13 bordars $2\frac{1}{2}$ teams, or $1\frac{1}{2}$ oxen each. In no instance is there clear indication of a villein owning more than half a team, but these entries can give no idea of the relative prosperity of the various classes of villager.

Only six properties, one of which was waste, were in 1086 credited to thegns. But the number of men with native names who held sub-tenancies is nearly seventy, and some of these, e.g. Ordric at Wishaw (243ai) and Hereward at Barnacle (240bi), had been the owners before the Conquest.

---

[1] Fols. 239ai, 242a2, 244a2; 240a2, 241a2 *bis*; 243a2,b2; 242bi *bis*, 242b2.

[2] Stretton on Dunsmore (239a2), Monks Kirby (243bi), and Nuneaton (241b2), where the value had doubled, are however said to have 17 teams for 7 ploughlands, 28 for 20, and 11 for 5 respectively.

[3] But we have Lighthorne (243a2), 8 teams for 18 ploughlands, where another holding was waste, Harbury (241bi), 4 for 9, Barford (243a2, 244ai), 4 for 14 in the two manors, Shrewley (242ai), $3\frac{1}{2}$ for 12, Ullenhall (242bi), 6 for 15.

Worcestershire

Domesday Worcestershire is in many ways an unsatisfactory unit, on account both of the numerous manors now well within the modern county boundary but included in the text for other shires and also of holdings recorded in the Worcestershire text but now in other counties. The extreme west would be best brigaded with Herefordshire, but to adopt such a system would make the treatment of certain other counties unnecessarily complex. Here the county Domesday forms the basis, with the addition of certain royal holdings geographically within the county but which had been in some respects attached to Hereford.

Various documents from the abbey of Evesham supplement the information derivable from DB. Of these the chief is that known as 'Evesham A', which has been described as 'a compilation of Domesday information ... arranged in Hundreds in preparation for the hundredal enquiry but before that enquiry took place'.[1] It contains 168 entries and covers a substantial portion of the DB text. While not infrequently it fails to record, in the relevant entries, a village mentioned in DB, it adds the names of a number of holdings anonymous in the Domesday text.[2] Sometimes it is more informative than is DB regarding sub-tenancies, gives the values of separate holdings where DB combines them, and occasionally has values different from those of DB.[3]

Omitting *Terra Regis* throughout, values for a date between 1066 and 1086 are given in only 28 entries, though if the phrase *wasta fuit* refers to the intermediate period, a further three should be added. These come from nine fiefs only, and sixteen of them are to be found in the *breves* for Evesham Abbey and Ralf de Tosny. Moreover, half occur near the northern portion of the boundary separating the county from Herefordshire. Thus little can be deduced from material so slender. They show a fall of from £131 to £98 5s., or 25 per cent, but by 1086 had recovered to £122 10s., though seven had declined still further. The western group east of Tenbury suggests a possible effect of the Mercian revolt of 1069 or Earl Roger's rebellion in 1075; those in the east of the shire point towards

---
[1] P. H. Sawyer, in *Worcester Miscellany I*, p. 8.
[2] *Halmelega* (Elmley Castle, no. 146), four components of the manor of Longden (Eldersfield, Chaceley, a further holding at Longden, Staunton; nos. 54–6, 63), an additional holding at North Piddle (no. 71), and Flyford Favell (no. 72), Bucknell Wood (no. 52), six components of the manor of Powick (a further holding at Powick, Bransford, Madresfield, Berrow, Pixham, and Clevelode; nos. 62, 64–7, 70), a Comberton holding (no. 154) and Ginstone (no. 165). If *in eadem terra habet Alaberge i hidam* should have been *in Alaberge* (no. 135), this would add another. It sounds more like a place- than a proper name.
[3] e.g. at Pendock (no. 106, DB fol. 173ai), where holdings were worth £1 and 6s. respectively, and Hambury (no. 8, DB fol. 174ai), where DB has £6 and Evesham A £5.

Evesham, and might be connected with the harrying of the north midlands which drove fugitives to the very gates of the abbey.

Only 200 entries enable us to compare values for 1066 and 1086. This is a small number compared with that of the individual holdings recorded, for many which were manors in 1066 had been combined with other manors by 1086, while berewicks and other components are exceptionally numerous. The great majority of the latter are indeed named, but we are given no values at all, or no 1066 value, for an unpleasantly large number of them. Thirty-nine show an increase and 99 a fall. There are some unfortunate omissions, notably on the lands of Westminster Abbey, from which sixteen values for 1066 were omitted. The figures show a slight fall in value, from £768 1s. 4d. to £707 17s. 4d., or 7¾ per cent. Few show a major decline, though Wolverley (174a2) went down from £4 to 30s., and Strensham (175ai) dropped by 50 per cent from £10.[1] The occasional entry may be deceptive. Kempsey (172b2), some of which manor was waste, is said to have fallen from £16 to £8. But to the £8 should perhaps be added the value of components of the manor for which we are not given a 1066 figure, which would bring the 1086 value up to £13. Of two of its other components, one fell and one rose, but their combined value remained unchanged. Appreciations in values are also rarely large ones. Elmley Lovett (176a2) went up from £10 to £16 and Worsley (176ai) doubled from £2 in value, but there are few suggestions of increases being due to enlargement of a manor.

Manors which declined in value are to be found all over the county except in the extreme south-west, where in any case settlements were infrequent and Malvern Forest limited cultivation. They are inclined to follow (a) the route from Herefordshire through Kidderminster into Staffordshire, a possible echo of the Mercian revolt or that of Earl Roger, (b) that from Worcester through Bromsgrove into Staffordshire, possibly reflecting the movement of a force drawn from the shire to challenge the rebels, (c) the Warwick—Worcester road, along which the newcomers must have moved in the early stages of taking over ungarrisoned country or reinforcements to check Earl Roger were sent. It is, however, noticeable that such manors do not for the most part actually lie on these roads, but slightly to the side of them.

The account of *Terra Regis* is lengthy and complex, but does not enable us to obtain much idea of possible changes in the royal revenue. It is necessary to include certain entries in the Herefordshire and Gloucestershire Domesdays (180bi,2; 163bi). Geographically in Worcestershire

[1] Other instances of large falls are Sheriff's Lench (176ai), £5 10s. to £2 2s., and Churchill (177a2), £3 to 8s.

THE WEST MIDLANDS: WORCESTERSHIRE

though the *caput* of each manor was, these had been obliged to render their farm to Hereford, probably at the instance of William fitzOsbern.[1] Three seem to be rendering less than they had done earlier. Martley had to pay £24 (and a *gersuma* of 12*s*.), Feckenham and Holloway £18, each *de xx denariis in ora*. Between them the values of Hanley Castle and Forthampton had sunk from £25 to £18. 'Six manors' are said to render £50, but it is not clear which six properties are meant. It would seem that they include these last two.

Fols. 172a2,bi contain the accounts of five manors and their berewicks, Bromsgrove, Kidderminster, Droitwich, Kinver, and Kingswinford, the last two of which are now in Staffordshire. Kinver is indeed said in the text to be in that county. They also include Suckley as paying £5 *in firma de Hereford*, repeated on 180b2, where a 25*s*. *gersuma* is added. Bromsgrove's contribution to the *firma* had been £18; in 1086 the sheriff paid £24 'so long as he had the woodland'. Kidderminster's had been £14; it had all been waste, but at the Inquest paid £10 4*s*. by weight. The Droitwich entry mentions as previous *firma* £52 to the king and £24 to Earl Edwine; in 1086 the sheriff paid £65 'while he had the woodland'. Kinver and Kingswinford paid £5 and £15 respectively *de xx denariis in ora*, and Tardebigg and Clent, which belonged to Kingswinford, contributed £11 and £4, the first sum also of 20*d*. to the *ora*. From such information it is impossible to determine the relative values for 1066 and 1086, though it looks as if the royal revenue may have been less than it had been formerly.

The values of holdings are for the most part too large for the existence of an *ora*-basis to be detected. However, Bucknell (174bi), though waste in 1086 and earlier, had at each time been worth 16*d*.[2] At Martley (176bi) a radman rendered 4*s*., and at Eastham with Bestwood (176a2) a man's render was 32*d*. A figure of 16*s*. occurs at White Ladies Aston (173bi) and at Lindon (176ai). Sums which are not proper fractions of the £ or whole pounds are comparatively rare. The sheriff's holding at Peopleton (175ai) was rendering 8*s*. 4*d*. (100*d*.), though there 'was nothing there'. Osmerley (177bi), valued at 13*s*., is one of the few divergencies from round sums.

Land is said to be waste, or to have been waste, in very few entries. The whole manor of Kidderminster (172b2) is said to have been waste, but the term may apply only to the *caput* and not to its sixteen widely dispersed berewicks. Since in 1066 the 20-hide manor produced a *firma* of

---

[1] Named components of some of the manors appear; the details for a holding are not identical in parallel passages, and Suckley at one point is said to have been taken by William fitzOsbern out of the distant manor of Bromsgrove.
[2] The holding is anonymous in DB, but Evesham A gives its name as *Bokindona*. The value of Edvin Loach (176b2) was 28*s*., or 21 *orae*, and of Cradley (177a2) 24*s*., or 18 *orae*.

only £14, the detached components would hardly be worth plundering. Five of Kempsey's 24 hides were waste, and earlier we saw that the manor may have declined in value; so was one of Tredington's 23 hides, though this manor with its member Tidmington had gone up in value from £10 to £12 10s.[1] Portions of Cropthorne with Netherton and Cleeve Prior with Lench (174ai) were waste, and the greater part of Cooksey (177b2) also. All had naturally declined in value. In 1086 Bucknell (174bi), Walter Ponther's virgate at Mathon (175bi), Hollin, Stildon, and Glashampton (177ai) in the north-west uplands, Bellington (177a2) and Hillhampton (178ai), were waste, while Himbleton (173b2) had been waste earlier (*fuit*), as had Bucknell, Hollin, and Bellington. Kidderminster had recovered, at least in part, for in 1086 it was paying £10 4s. and was a place of some importance, though it could have employed twenty more teams than the nineteen which were in use. Himbleton (with Spetchley) had recovered its 1066 value, Bucknell Wood was said to be worth 16d., the Mathon virgate 5s., and Glashampton 10s., so these could not have been entirely deserted, and the last certainly had a team and a half available. Bellington still had meadows, though they were worth no more than fourpence. The shire, if perhaps less prosperous than in 1066, does not seem to have suffered extensive or violent losses.

But an appreciable number of manors had suffered from their inclusion in a royal Forest. Many are near Worcester, some in the Forest of Malvern. At Ripple (173a2) the local bishop had 'the honey and the hunting and all profits, and 10s. over and above . . . its pannage and (wood for) firing and the repair of houses'. He had somewhat similar rights at Fladbury (172b2) and Bredon (173ai). At least a score of entries refer to woodland included in royal Forest; where it 'rendered nothing' (Astley, 176a2), or was 'put outside the manor' (several instances in the Herefordshire text concerned with Worcestershire; 180bi,2), it is to be presumed it had been similarly taken away from the manor's assets.[2] Evesham A tells us that Shell (no. 15, 176bi) was worth £2 with its woodland but only 15s. without it, and the woodland had been *missa in defenso*, in the king's Forest. The importance of woodland in the manorial economy is stressed in several entries. The sheriff pays given sums at Bromsgrove and Droitwich (172a2) 'so long as he has the wood'; if this were taken out of the manor he would no doubt make a loss unless the *firma* was appreciably reduced. Bromsgrove's woodland may not always have been among the manor's assets, for in

[1] Fols. 172b2, 173a2. Evesham A gives the value of Tredington as £15. But the £10 might represent the value of Tredington only.
[2] It is definitely stated to be 'in the king's wood' at Feckenham and Forthampton. Some of the manors concerned, such as these places and Kidderminster, were royal, or, as at Chadwick (172a2), a berewick of a royal manor.

King Edward's day the 'keepers of the wood' gave 300 cartloads of it for the 300 loads (*mittae*) of salt supplied from Droitwich.[1]

Ploughlands are recorded only twice, and in each case the holding was waste in 1086, so that the intention may have been to give some indication of potential prosperity.[2] But in 47 entries we are told how many more teams than were then in use could be employed.[3] Where 299 teams were at work in these, 158 more could have been used, a deficiency of $34\frac{1}{2}$ per cent. But if in the other entries there were as many ploughlands as there were teams, the deficiency for the county would be only about $7\frac{3}{4}$ per cent. At the end of the *breve* for the Church of Worcester (174a2) it is stated that 'in all these lands there can be no more teams than are recorded'. While this implies that the inquisitors expected the number of ploughlands in a manor to be furnished, it can be interpreted either as 'there is no deficiency (or surplus) of teams on our lands', or 'we could use more teams, but are unable to obtain them'.

The deficiencies are sometimes large ones. In the formerly wasted Kidderminster (172a2) there could have been 20 more teams in addition to the 19 employed, and at Pershore (174bi) 21 where there were in fact 12, while both Church Lench (175b2) and Sheriff's Lench (176ai) could have used three times the number of teams, four, which were at work. Elmbridge (176b2) and Hanley Child (177ai) could have found work for twice as many teams as they possessed. A surplus of teams is never recorded.

In three-quarters of the relevant manors for which comparable values are available, quantities of teams had fallen. Hollin and Glashampton (177ai) were both waste in 1086; the former had no team where one might have been used, the latter needed a further team to supplement the $1\frac{1}{2}$ at work. Willingwick (172a2) had half a team where there might have been two, and its value had fallen by 60 per cent.[4] Bockleton (174a2) had fallen in value by one-third, and was short of a quarter of its potential teams. Elmbridge, mentioned above as possessing only half the teams there might have been, was valued also at only half what it had been worth in 1066. A connection between a deficiency of teams and a fall in value seems

---

[1] See also Northwick (173bi), Fladbury (172b2), and Martin Hussingtree (174b2). Lennard has pointed out that no woodland is mentioned in the last manor, where there was also no demesne, but plenty at the demesne manor of Upton Snodsbury close by. The villeins from Hussingtree may therefore have had to cart wood from Snodsbury to Droitwich and bring back salt in lieu of labour on the demesne (*Rural England*, p. 247).

[2] Stildon (177ai), Bellington (177a2).

[3] The information is given for eleven out of the fourteen manors of Osbern fitzRichard, and out of all a score come from the north-west uplands, an area which may well have suffered some damage. It adjoins shires in which the same formula is used.

[4] This entry seems to be paralleled by that on fol. 177a2, though there the value has declined by 40 per cent.

strongly to be implied. If this is so, perhaps the overall decline in value for the county indicates that there were not necessarily as many teams as ploughlands where no figure for the latter is given.

Entries from which the plough-oxen owned by villeins or bordars can be deduced are infrequent. In twelve 80 villeins possessed 40 teams, averaging half a team a man. Most of the entries indeed give the villein half a team, and at Forthampton (180b2) seven villeins had five teams between them.[1] There are occasional suggestions of the holdings of villeins. In the portion of Martley (180bi) given by Earl William fitzOsbern to St Mary of Cormeilles two villeins seem to hold half a hide. But the phrasing may be deceptive, for in several parallel instances (e.g. Feckenham,180bi) he gave 'a virgate of land with one villein', and in these the villein may have held no land. But at Queenhill (180b2) the villein is said to 'hold' half a virgate.

In eighteen entries 155 bordars had $57\frac{1}{2}$ teams, averaging $2\frac{2}{3}$ oxen a head. This seems far too close to the figure for villeins, but in these arbitrary instances of holdings without villeins, the bordars may have been of wealth and status above the average. At Ham Castle (176b2) seven bordars had five teams, so one at least must have owned six oxen, while at Frankley (177a2) nine had five. Still, at *Halac* (176ai) five bordars could render 5s., while at Elmley Lovett (176a2) seven villeins were rendering only 3s. But we are told also of a bordar at *Hatete* (177b2) *qui nihil habet*, and three on the same folio 'had nothing'; so did three at an anonymous holding on the same folio. At Suckley (180b2) in addition to the 24 bordars, there were ten others of the same category described as *pauperes*.

In this county, where the Church lands were extensive, many a priest had a hide of land or half a hide, and often a full team.[2] They may have been monks rather than parish priests. While free men and radmen must have varied considerably in importance, we do not here find them on a par with the villeins. The free man at Wolverley (174a2) had a hide, four radmen at Blockley (173a2) six hides, two at Hallow and Broadwas (173b2) two, and two teams. Leofwine, 'serving as the bishop's radman', had held Bredons Norton (173a2), assessed at two hides and worth £1. In the royal manor of Martley (177ai) one radman rendered 6s., probably for his holding of a virgate, and another 4s. (176bi).

Exemption from geld, largely on the extensive Church lands, figures in the text quite frequently. It seems as if at least 186 out of an approximate 1,200 hides paid no geld. But in considering assessments, beneficial hida-

---

[1] A villein had half a team at Willingwick (172a2); see also, e.g., Phepson (174ai), Comberton (175a2). At Rock More (176a2) the villein had a whole team.
[2] e.g. Blockley and Ripple (173a2), Tenbury (174a2), Powick (174b2).

tion needs to be taken into account, and it may be assumed that some ecclesiastical properties had not been rated as highly as they might have been; e.g. Leigh (175bi), 3 hides worth £20 T.R.E.

Some immunities must have been of considerable advantage. Of Blockley's 38 hides, 25½ were exempt from geld (173a2); at Kempsey (172b2) five out of 24 were not liable, and at Acton Beauchamp (176ai) half of the six hides did not pay.

Where such a high proportion of land was the Church's, and many estates leased, it is difficult to estimate either the importance of pre-Conquest landholders or the extent to which these or their successors held land after the Conquest. It seems as if by 1086 very few persons with English names were holding lay land. Sæwold's son had succeeded his father on a small estate at Collingwick (176bi) as tenant of Ralf de Mortemer, and Hunulf held Rushock (177bi) of the sheriff. The only large manor is that of Eadgifu at Chaddesley Corbett (178ai) with its eight berewicks, still valued at £12.

Gloucestershire

The lack of coincidence between the Domesday and the modern county is considerable, and the number of entries for which we are given no comparative figures uncomfortably large. Both the ecclesiastical and the lay holdings furnish numerous examples of complex manors, for whose members we are only rarely given statistics. These include the bishop of Worcester's manors of Westbury on Trym, Withington, and Bishop's Cleeve (164b2), Westminster Abbey's Deerhurst and its berewicks (166a2), and the dozen properties of St Denis of Paris, for which a single value is given. When we find St Peter of Gloucester's manor of Abbots Barton (165bi) worth £8 in 1066 but three times that amount at the Inquest, and Kempsford (169ai) worth £30 before the Conquest, but bringing in £66 6s. 8d. in 1086, we cannot help wondering how far real comparison is possible. The virtual absence of anything but round figures in the valuations suggests frequent approximation. The impression is also gained that Gloucestershire valuations did not greatly trouble the Inquest officials. No one answered for certain lands in Langtree Hundred (166bi), but the shire-jury valued them at £8, nor for a manor in Swineshead Hundred (170a2), which some witnesses valued at 10s.

On fols. 162ai,2 appears a confused account of the country between the Wye and the Usk. Few places are given their names, and no pre-Conquest information is provided, for presumably little or none of it was then in English hands. A dozen Norman tenants are mentioned, and the names of the Welsh reeves of groups of vills, together with those of the holders of vills also unspecified. The properties mentioned early in the account are said to render in all £40 12s. 8d., but to have been given to William of Eu at a farm-rent of £55. The tenancies which follow are valued at £39 0s. 6d., and must be supplementary to the £55. The royal property was valued at £33 10s. 4d., or £12 less, but there is no clarity about the statements.

Of the 287 entries following *Terra Regis* 125 show a decline in value and 60 appreciation, while for 18 comparative figures are lacking. We might then expect to find a modest total fall in values, and so we do, from £1,832 2s. 8d. in 1066 to £1,742 5s. 2d. in 1086, a trifle under 5 per cent.

But some increases in value are large ones. Buckland had trebled its former value of £3, Abbots Barton went up from £8 to £24, Frocester from £3 to £8 (all fol. 165bi). It could be, of course, that the 1066 values of the three members of Abbots Barton mentioned in the text were not included in the £8; they may have been post-Conquest additions to the manor. Some enormous increases suggest heavy increases in the rents demanded. Northleach (164bi) had been worth £18, but Archbishop Thomas *misit ad firmam* for £27. Tetbury with Upton (168ai) was valued in 1066 at £33, but this manor of Roger d'Ivry was at farm for £50 twenty years later. No *firma* is mentioned for Kempsford (169ai), but since it had gone up in value from £30 to £66 6s. 8d. (note that this is two-thirds of £100), both the sum and the fact that it belonged to Arnulf de Hesdin, keenly interested in improving his estates, suggests that it was farmed.[1]

A decline in the value of a Gloucestershire manor is thus likely to be a comparatively small one. But Longborough (170ai) and Guiting Power (167a2) had fallen from £16 each to £5 and £6 respectively, and Lashborough (166b2) to a quarter of its previous value of £10. Twice a holding is said to be scarcely (*vix*) worth the value set on it (High Leadon and Down St Peter, 165bi). What is noticeable is that falls are heaviest, and most frequent, in certain areas. In the northern section of the Cotswolds, with much land above the 600-foot contour, the manors fell in value from £608 10s. to £513 6s., or by 16 per cent, more than three times the county average, and a small decline is also to be observed in the hilly district between the Windrush and the Evenlode valleys. It is, therefore, conceivable that manors on the less favourable parts of the Cotswold upland had found it impossible to maintain former standards, or that there had been some transference of men and equipment from the thin and light Oolitic soils. Unfortunately we are not told if there were large deficiencies

[1] See Lennard: *Rural England*, p. 69.

THE WEST MIDLANDS: GLOUCESTERSHIRE

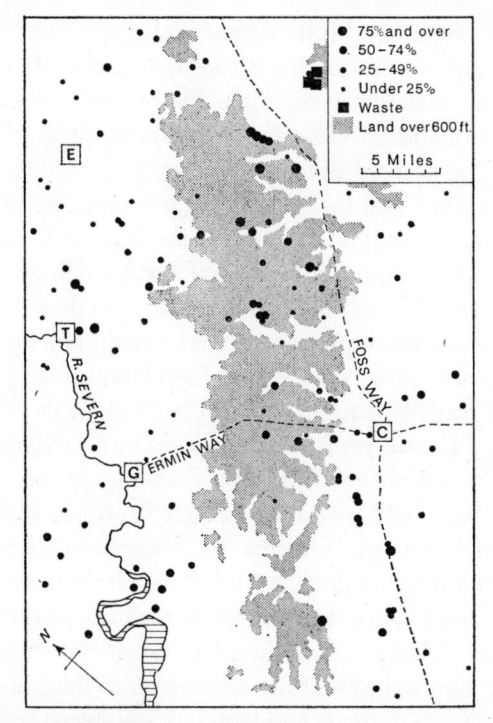

Fig. 17 The Northern Cotswolds
Fall in value 1066–86
C—Cirencester   E—Evesham   G—Gloucester   T—Tewkesbury

of plough-teams in this area. Certainly there were less teams to the square mile than there were to the north-west and north-east of the uplands. Another area where falls in value were frequent is around Cirencester, which stands at the junction of Foss Way and Ermin Way. Decline in the neighbourhood of Ermin Way betwen Cirencester and Gloucester and then along the Hereford road is fairly marked, as though the passage of troops might at some time have been responsible for this. Another line of lessened values runs across Cotswold close to the route between Oxford and Worcester. Only two other areas display marked falls in value, the area south of Cotswold between the roads from Gloucester to Bristol and Bath, the latter in the southern Cotswolds, and round the head of the Severn estuary. This last might be the result of a piratical raid, or even one from Wales directed against Gloucester. The decline in values on several of the estates of Winchcombe Abbey (165b2) might have been the result of the misfortunes of its Saxon abbot, who suffered imprisonment after the Conquest.

THE DETAILS OF DOMESDAY BOOK

Values which are not multiples of 5*s*., and really small properties, are so rare that the rents of minor tenants are not disclosed. Though the *ora* commonly appears as the basis for the value of a mill, there are few signs that it governed a manorial valuation. Occasional sums of 24*s*., 12*s*., 8*s*., 4*s*. might indeed be derived differently.[1]

Several times we are told that a manor was earlier not *ad firmam*, or no value for it is given, though at the time of the Inquest it was at farm for a large sum. Roger d'Ivry put a collection of royal holdings (162b2) at farm for £46 13*s*. 4*d*., and this possibly includes the £40 from Cheltenham and Kings Barton, for the small properties mentioned immediately before the note of this *firma* amount to only eight hides. Hempstead (164a2) had not been at farm, for Earl William fitzOsbern had held it in demesne, but the sheriff had set a £3 farm on it, nor had Beckford (164ai), which Roger d'Ivry had put to farm for £30, nor Tockington, nor Nass (164ai). Tockington had been held by a thegn called Wulfgar, who may have let it out at a farm rent, for it is said that 'he whose it was lived on the proceeds'. Down Ampney (164a2) had been worth £20, but in 1086 was rendering £26 *in firma regis*. Another farmer, who rented manors in other counties also, was Ælfsige of Farringdon (Great Barrington, 164a2). In some instances a standard rate of increase seems to have been adopted, or else Cheltenham, Kings Barton, and land in Cirencester Hundred (162b2) were treated as an unit; the render from each went up from £9 5*s*. to £20.[2] Cirencester (162b2) had been 'put outside the farm' by Earl William, but the next entry, Bitton, is for a manor which had to find a night's farm, and Westbury on Severn (163ai) still had to furnish this, though half a dozen of its components had been taken away from the manor. Sharpness (163a2) had been part of the manor of Berkeley, but Earl William had 'put it outside' in order to build a small castle there.

Certainly the king was getting all he could from his manors. Awre (163ai) had in 1066 rendered the farm of half a night; in 1086 the sheriff still had to find the whole (unspecified) sum, though half a hide was waste and three former components had been put outside the manor, so that it rendered only £12. The render from Marshfield (163a2) had risen from £35 to £47. It seems strange to read that the sheriff had in 1066 rendered 'what he would' from Lower Slaughter (162b2), but in 1086 he was paying £27, which included the profit from the Hundred in which it lay. He had

---

[1] Siddington (167ai), Windrush (168ai); Dumbleton (167a2); Shipton Solers (164bi), two anonymous manors in Langtree Hundred (166bi), Murcot (167bi); Duntesbourn Abbots (169b2), are the sole instances. Only once does 20*d*. occur (a virgate in Swineshead Hundred, 170a2).

[2] 5*s*. more (perhaps an error, echoing the 5*s*. of the 1066 value) for the last-named. Each of these had to furnish animal- or food-rents in addition.

enjoyed the same privilege at Dymock (164ai), but in 1086 paid £21; so had the reeves of Chedworth (164ai), but now they had to produce £40. Many of these payments, too, had to be made in blanched silver at 20*d*. to the ounce.

The lengthy account of royal property leaves us with no clarity as to how much it might have appreciated under the management of the king's *ministri* and reeves. Some royal manors certainly brought in less than they had done formerly. Godwine of Staunton paid only £3 *in firma regis* for Little Barrington (164a2), though it had been worth £5. We are given no indication of what the Berkeley complex (163ai), producing £170 of 'burnt and weighed money' in 1086, might have been worth earlier, nor most of the late queen's property (163b2). Hallasey (163a2) had fallen in value from £4 to £2 10*s*. But the greatest loss had occurred in the immense dispersed manor of Tewkesbury (163a2–b2). It had been diminished in size, possibly under the direction of William fitzOsbern. 'When it was all together in King Edward's day' it had been worth £100, but when Ralf received it, only £12. However, recovery of some of the abstracted components seems to have been achieved, for in 1086 it was valued at £40, though Ralf was in fact having to render £50. Here we are given the values of many of the components, some of which, on fol. 163bi, are said to have belonged, not to belong, to the manor. Two-thirds of these had fallen in value, and we are indeed told that the manor had been *destructum et confusum*.[1] We are not given comparative values for all the former components of the manor, but in seventeen a value of £103 5*s*. had become one of £68 5*s*.

Several other organisational changes are recorded. Earl William had made one manor at Lydney (164ai) out of four properties which had been the bishop of Hereford's, the Pershore monks', and two thegns'. Tidenham (164ai), which had furnished food for the monks of Bath, had been leased to Stigand, but Earl William acquired it and gave a virgate to his brother the future bishop Osbern; in 1086 it was producing £25 *de xx in ora et albas*. Edward the sheriff of Wiltshire had unjustly included Woodchester (164a2), which had belonged to no *firma*, in that of his county.[2]

It is obviously quite impossible to say what the royal revenue from the county might have been. On the figures we have, it looks as though it was not less than £750, or about the value of the whole county of Middlesex,

[1] Shenington in Oxfordshire, which belonged to Tewkesbury, showing a decline of 60 per cent, was *in manu regis*, but was held *ad firmam* by Robert d'Oyly.
[2] Of this manor no one gave an account to the *legati regis*, nor did anyone from it come to this *descriptio*. Edward may have been trying to conceal the illegality, or the inhabitants thought they should not attend the Gloucestershire proceedings.

together with the unspecified amount produced by manors rendering a night's farm. So much space has been given to it to demonstrate the complexity of many an account of *Terra Regis*, our inability always to interpret it, and the frequent post-Conquest changes in the extent of royal property.

We hear very little about Forest land, though the map shows much of the Forest of Dean as devoid of settlements. It is accordingly impossible to deduce whether some diminutions of values may have been due to inclusion in the Forest. St Briavels (167ai) had fallen in value from £4 to £2, and hard by is Wyegate (166b2), which, though worth £3 in 1066, was in 1086, by the king's order, 'in the Forest', as was Hewelsfield (167ai). There were several declines in value near Taynton, one virgate of which (167bi) lay in the Forest. There is but slight indication of the possible effect of the Forests of Kingswood and Horwood north of Bristol.

As only three times are we given indication of the number of ploughlands, we cannot try to connect a deficiency of teams with falls in values. At Hambrook (165ai) there was land for one team more than the four operating, and the value had fallen from £5 to £3. At Alderton (165b2) there could have been twice as many teams used as the three which were at work, and at Naunton on the same folio six teams in addition to the four recorded could have been employed. But the values of these two manors had not changed; possibly a higher rent than was fair was being asked for them.

So far as we know, there was here no major resistance to the Conquest, and in addition to seventeen properties held in 1086 by king's thegns with native names, about a score of sub-tenancies held by survivors are mentioned. In all they total almost 100 hides, and those for which we have values were worth over £70. In addition to farming Great Barrington (164a2), Ælfsige of Farringdon had 3½ hides of the Windrush estate of Winchcombe Abbey (165b2).[1] Edric Ketelson had 8¼ hides at Baunton and Alkerton (170bi), and if 'Chetel', who had held land in 1066, is his father, property at Windrush and Duntesbourn (170bi) was still in the family. 'Schelin', holding five hides of the church of Worcester at Notgrove (164b2), might be the man who appears in Somerset and Dorset. The holdings of free men and of radmen appear among the tenancies.[2] It is to be suspected that many other minor tenants were omitted from the record.

Taylor listed the smaller men who had teams of their own.[3] On his

[1] An 'Elsi', perhaps the same man, held five hides at Longney (170bi).
[2] Kings Barton, Cirencester (162b2). Westbury-on-Trym, Bibury, Withington (164b2), Duntesbourn (166b2), some Berkeley berewicks (163ai).
[3] C. S. Taylor: *An Analysis of the Domesday Survey of Gloucestershire* (Bristol & Gloucester Archaeological Society, Bristol, 1887–9).

figures the *milites* had about $2\frac{1}{4}$ teams apiece, suggesting that they were superior to those occurring further north, *francigenae* 7 oxen each, free men over $2\frac{1}{2}$ teams and radmen nearly $1\frac{3}{4}$; these, too, are figures higher than in the March counties. 197 villeins had 129 teams, averaging more than five oxen a head, and 67 bordars $13\frac{1}{2}$ teams, which would give each the unexpectedly low figure of 1·6 oxen each. The five villeins at Woolaston (166b2) had a team apiece.

4

The March Counties

Herefordshire, Shropshire, and Cheshire, all of which may have been in the same circuit, though there is doubt regarding the first, were three counties which both before the Conquest and in the years immediately following Duke William's expedition suffered continual disturbance. To them should probably be added western Gloucestershire, but there the results are far less clearly indicated. The border between them and land in Welsh hands was nebulous and continually fluctuating; it is not possible to determine where it should be drawn at any given moment.

In 1055 had occurred the irruption into England of the alliance between Gruffydd ap Llewelyn, king of Gwynedd and Powys, and the outlawed Ælfgar, then earl of East Anglia. Their forces burst into the county, defeated the local defenders, burnt Hereford, and fell back only when Harold Godwineson arrived with troops drawn from all over England. But within their own mountainous territory the Welsh could not be mastered, and Gruffydd probably retained the district known as Archenfield, between the Wye and the Monnow, which he is said to have laid waste in 1055 (181ai). The following year he defeated the local levies at Glasbury on Wye, and a second English force sent against him was unable to cope with the mountain warfare in which the Welsh excelled. In 1057 Ralf, King Edward's nephew, who had been earl of Herefordshire and had unsuccessfully tried to stem the Welsh threat by castle-building and employing mounted troops, died.[1] A year later Ælfgar and Gruffydd organised a further full-scale invasion about which we unfortunately know very little. Ælfgar lived another four years and was succeeded as earl of Mercia by his eldest

[1] For early Norman influence in the county, see Round: *Feudal England*, pp. 320–6.

son, Edwine, who was insufficiently mature to undertake the suppression of the Welsh power. But a campaign in 1063 generalled by Earls Harold and Tostig Godwineson, the former striking from Gloucester to Rhuddlan by sea and the latter through North Wales, ended with Gruffydd's death.

It is probable that the Welsh used the occasion of the invasions of Harald Hardraada and Duke William to make further raids, and thus further impressed on the new monarch the essentiality of strengthening the March defences. Before he left for Normandy in March 1067, he appointed William fitzOsbern earl of Hereford and Gloucester. The ruthless government of the king's lieutenants alienated the English, who in the west midlands had no previous experience of the effects of Norman arrival. Despite Norman settlement, especially in Herefordshire, though it cannot have been widespread, a high degree of independence was still maintained, and developed, in alliance with the Welsh, under a thegn known as Edric 'the Wild', whose lands had been ravaged by Normans.

Edric is often described as a Herefordshire or Worcestershire thegn, but his lands in these counties were scattered and of small value. He (or men of the same name, for in Herefordshire an Edric is styled 'salvage' at Burrington alone, fol. 183bi), appears in six entries for this county only, two of which are said to have been waste.[1] He seems rather to have been a Shropshire man; Florence of Worcester describes him as the nephew of Edric Streona, the traitor-magnate of the reign of Æthelræd II and later, so he must have enjoyed local eminence. In Shropshire an Edric appears in 40 entries as holding in 1066, but it is improbable that these all refer to the same person.[2]

In 1069 this movement for independence spread through Shropshire, Cheshire, and Herefordshire, and despite the presence of the fortifications established by the newcomers and those constructed before the Conquest, and the successful resistance of the Shrewsbury garrison, which was relieved by a force commanded by William fitzOsbern and Brian of Brittany, though we are told also that the town was burnt before they arrived, the local Normans were unable to suppress the revolt.[3] Florence of Worcester tells us that Richard fitzScrob lost many knights and squires, and that with the help of the Welsh princes Bleddyn and Rhiwallon Edric raided the country as far as 'the bridge over the Lugg', presumably where the Roman road from Kenchester (63) met the river. Obviously there had by then been further Norman settlement in the county of Hereford at least. King William was at the time occupied with the Danish invaders in

[1] *Hamenes* (180a2), Elton (183bi), Staunton on Arrow, *Elburgelega*, and Birley (183b2).
[2] See p. 165.　　　　　　　　　　[3] *VCH: Shropshire*, i. p. 288: Orderic, ii, 193.

the Humber, but led a force into Mercia which easily defeated the rebels in the neighbourhood of Stafford. The remaining dissidents were suppressed when his Northumbrian and Danish opponents had been dealt with. Cheshire too must have been affected by Welsh raids and by this rising, but the chroniclers do not give us much information about that county.[1] For some reason Edric seems to have escaped lightly, though his presence with the king in the Scottish campaign of 1072 suggests that it was thought politic to keep him under supervision and to prevent him stirring up further trouble.

We may expect DB, then, here to tell us of a good deal of waste, report low values and little improvement in these since the Conquest, depict the Marches as under the influence of major barons capable of protecting them and spreading Norman influence westwards, and show us few surviving native or Welsh tenants.

Unfortunately we do not possess information enabling a complete picture of conditions in 1066, some few years afterwards, and in 1086, to be constructed. It is impossible to say just when villages and their satellites became wasted, or to what extent, or with whom responsibility lay. It may even be that some of the waste was the enduring result of the devastation of Cheshire, Shropshire, and Staffordshire by Edmund in 1016 in order to deny Cnut and his invading forces the means of sustenance. Some is certainly the result of unsuitability for human settlement, and waste only in the sense that it was Forest-land.

Figures somewhat different from those which follow are obtained if the unhidated districts of Herefordshire, Archenfield, Ewias, and Clifford, are not included. Information about these is fragmentary and unsystematic, but no serious defects are induced by treating them as part of the Domesday shire.

Herefordshire

Herefordshire furnishes as good an example as any of the difficulties encountered in studying economic and political changes between the ends of the reigns of King Edward and King William. Here too the administrative county of 1066 or of 1086 is markedly different from that of today, and the land of some vills was in more than one shire. The farm of the shire had been considerably increased by William fitzOsbern by including within it the renders of manors now in other counties, and there had been frequent consolidation of holdings into single manors and

---

[1] Orderic was a Shropshire man.

THE MARCH COUNTIES: HEREFORDSHIRE

numerous alterations in the composition of royal manors.[1] Such changes make it difficult to determine which separated passages may refer to a single piece of property.

Moreover, we receive only slight information about certain areas intimately connected with attack upon and defence against the Welsh. We are told that certain vills or *terrae* are situated in the borders of Archenfield (181ai), a district in 1086 more or less Welsh but under English overlordship and not yet fully absorbed in the shire system. The area known as the castellary of Ewias (184ai, 185a2, 186ai) had only recently been reconquered from the Welsh. Both these and the castellary of Clifford (183a2, 184ai) were unhidated, the settlements within them are for the most part unnamed, and we hear little of money payments but more of renders in kind and practical obligations. Nor are we told much of the castellaries in the north of the shire, Wigmore (179b2, 180a2, 183bi) and Orleton near Richard's Castle (183b2, 185a2, 186b2). Monmouth (180b2) and Caerleon (162ai, 185bi) castellaries were recent acquisitions from Welsh territory, and we are not given the situation of any of their components or their quantity. Caerleon was valued at only £14 and Monmouth at £35.[2] Caerleon, 'in Earl Roger's time', i.e. *ante* 1075, rendered £16; in 1086 the king had £12 from it.

Monmouth and Caerleon, the entry for *in Hereford port* (181bi), and the royal manors on fols. 179bi–80ai, have been omitted from the initial discussion of valuation figures. The total number of entries and subentries in the remainder of the Herefordshire Domesday is about 450, but this figure can give no idea of the actual quantity of distinct settlements in 1066 or later. Many a large manor must have included several vills; even a modest manor was probably made up of dispersed hamlets and isolated small farms. When we are told that three of the seven hides of Little Hereford (182bi) were waste, we surely cannot think that all seven hides were contiguous. William fitzNorman had land which had been part of the royal manor of Marden (179bi); these were his holdings at Venne and Ferne (185b2), which had 'lain in the farm of the king's manor of Marden.' In 1066 four different men had held land all known in 1086 as Thornbury (186a2), but it is improbable that there was or had been a single settlement;

---

[1] Isolated examples include Earl William's donation of part of the king's manor of Kingsland (179b2) to Walter de Lacy, the diminution of the royal manor of Leominster (180a2), the wrongful inclusion in the farm of that manor by a sheriff, Ralf de Bernay, of two holdings at Woonton (181a2), the transference of *Niware* (181a2) to Gloucestershire, and the conversion of Gayton (181a2) from thegnland to reeveland.
[2] Much of the information about these is actually in the Gloucestershire and Worcestershire Domesdays. Caerleon is said to have been waste in 1066 and later, but this may imply 'of no profit to the English or Normans'.

some of the land had been waste. From the wording and arrangement of the text we may suspect that even allowing for potential parallel entries there were at least 550 distinct holdings, and probably a good many more than that. Balliol MS. 350 gives us a number of place-names unmentioned in DB.[1] Probably they represent settlements extant in 1086, but concealed by the form of the Domesday entry.

Waste in 1066 is mentioned for only thirteen holdings in ten places, some of which were only partially waste. By 1086 a few had made some recovery; Willersley with Winforton (182bi) was indeed worth £7 in 1086, with ten teams and 28 recorded inhabitants. It is, however, probable that holdings which had been waste at an unspecified date and which at the time of the Inquest were still waste had been waste in 1066 also. These number 32, and perhaps we should add 20 for which no information prior to 1086 is given. Certainly 62 places waste in 1066 seems a more reasonable quantity, especially as almost all are in the west of the shire. There were also 24 holdings said to have been waste about 1070/1 for which no pre-Conquest information is given.

Presumably some recovery from the Welsh raids took place over the three years which preceded the Norman Conquest, though the map shows that little of the shire west of the river Lugg had been unaffected. The holdings which were waste in 1066 are naturally found mostly to lie along the border near the source of Welsh raids, and clearly mark the irruptions down the valleys of the Wye and the Dore to the neighbourhood of Hereford. There is a good deal of waste land in the north of the county, but it looks as though the existence of Richard's Castle had proved a deterrent. What is puzzling is that towards Wales some manors were not waste. Monnington on Wye (183a2) and Lyonshall (184bi) is each said to have been worth £3 in 1066, and the valuations of several others are given.

William fitzOsbern was killed early in 1071, and was succeeded by his son Roger. Roger forfeited his lands for his share in the baronial revolt of 1075, but DB, though it records some of William's administrative changes, gives no clue as to when most of the landholders of 1086 may have acquired their estates.

Waste at a time between 1066 and 1086 is only twice recorded (Pembridge, 186ai; Thornbury, 186a2). But it is to be presumed that when the past tense is used (*fuit*), the holdings were then waste. In addition to Pembridge and Thornbury, 57 places are so described, to which we should presumably add 24 which are said to be waste, or partially so, in 1086,

---

[1] V. H. Galbraith and J. Tait: *Herefordshire Domesday*, circa *1160–1170* (Pipe Roll Soc., London, 1950).

THE MARCH COUNTIES: HEREFORDSHIRE

and perhaps the eight waste in 1066 for which no intermediate information is given, a total of 91.[1]

The 60 holdings for which we are given information for all three dates display only slight changes in total value; £271 7s. 4d. in 1066, £242 10s. later, £274 14s. in 1086. But the figures may be highly deceptive. Twenty-five instances come from the fief of the local bishop and his canons, and all but nine of these show no change in value at any date. It may be, then, that those responsible for the return made no attempt to estimate what had been the earlier value of the holdings; certainly their *breve* includes the statement that they had made no return for 33 of the 300 hides of the bishopric, but then these may still have been waste. Moreover, the manor of Bromyard (182bi) alone accounts for £45 10s. of the above sums at every date, though three hides were waste, and thus makes comparison of the figures useless. It is further stated that 40 hides were waste 'when Robert came to the bishopric' in 1079 (181bi). DB reports only 26½, but probably failed to specify all.

There is, however, a slight suggestion of damage caused by a westward movement of troops, either those of the rebels of 1069 or of Earl Roger in 1075. But since Roger seems to have been checked before he could pass the Severn, his rebellion may not have greatly affected his own earldom. The disposition of the places with lowered values rather suggests the passage of rebels into west Worcestershire and south Staffordshire, with a hint of junction with the men of Shropshire (Fig. 18).

At the Inquest waste is mentioned in 72 entries. In eleven of these the waste is only partial, and in nine, though the land is said to be waste, it is none the less producing a small rent.[2] Partial waste probably indicates detached manorial components.

Values for both 1066 and 1086 are given in 266 entries. Some show a fall in value, and for 86, a score of which were the bishopric's, no change is reported. It looks as if about one-third had increased their worth and one-quarter were less profitable. In 25 entries it is said that *wasta fuit et est*. What had been valued at £654 6s. 2d. was in 1086 reckoned at £699 14s. 8d., an increase of only 6¾ per cent. If we omit the lands of the bishopric, the figure becomes 3¼ per cent.

---

[1] Willersley with Winforton (183a2) is said to have been worth 10s. earlier (*valebant*).
[2] Didley with Stone, Preston on Wye, Burton (181bi), Preston Wynne, Ullingswick (181b2), Cradley, Coddington (182ai), Huntington (182a2), Bromyard, Little Hereford (182bi), Clehonger (186bi). Kinnersley (187bi) was waste 'except for three acres lately ploughed'. At Walford (182ai) six villeins were paying 10s. 'for the waste land', and at Fownhope (187a2) 12s. 4d. was received 'from the waste lands'. Land is said to be waste, but to produce small rents, at Leadon (184bi), Yarsop (185a2), Brampton, Whitney (182b2), Chanstone (187a2), Rowden (187bi).

But we are going to see that such figures may not give the true picture. Four out of Huntington's ten hides were waste (182a2), yet its value *post* and in 1086 was £4 as it had been in 1066. Either the four hides were waste also in 1066 and later, or rents had been increased, or the economy of the manor had been improved, or the 1066 figure is probably fictitious, and this is by no means an isolated instance. It is difficult to believe that Yarsop (185ai) improved in value from 15s. to 60s. if the extent of the manor remained constant; an even more striking disparity is the difference at Letton (184b2), 2s. in 1066, 30s. in 1086. True, there were here *hospites*, settlers, but they and the priest rendered only 5s.

Land said earlier to have been waste had a value at the Inquest of £77, just over £12 of which is for land waste in 1066, while it is doubtful if a further £27 should be reckoned in the £77. It is suggestive that fifteen places classed as 'waste' no longer appear on the map.[1] Though some of the properties must have been very small, e.g. Yarpole (180bi) and Webton (184a2) were valued at only 3s. each, a number of values are at first sight surprisingly large. Even near the March Staunton on Wye (180b2) and Monnington Stradel (186ai) were worth £3 and 30s. respectively, though earlier they had been waste. As will be discussed later, there had obviously been some re-colonisation and settlement since the Conquest, but we doubt if Staunton on Wye had really been exploited to the extent of stocking an empty vill with six plough-teams and by the importation of 14 recorded persons. Probably such vills had never been entirely waste, though where we find a deficiency of plough-teams we may suspect that they were and had been partially waste. At Wolferlow (183b2, 185ai) there could have been six teams more than the 6½ which were operating, and there are a dozen instances where waste is not mentioned but ploughlands are recorded and there is an absence or deficiency of teams. In the castellary of Ewias (184ai) Roger de Lacy received fifteen sesters of honey and the same number of pigs *quando homines sunt ibi*; the degree of habitation obviously fluctuated.

Falls in value between Conquest and Inquest could in part have been due to the forces of Edric's allies or of Earl Roger, but it must not be forgotten that both the advent of Norman lords and their movements towards acquiring Welsh land could damage manorial economy. But much waste may have been due simply to the extension of Forest land, or to the abandonment of small March holdings where the profit from woodland and wild animals was more rewarding than rents and services.

Several times the wood of a manor, or a portion of it, is said to be in the king's Forest, e.g. the two Bullingham manors (184a2, 186a2), or 'in the

---

[1] Wigmore castle (183bi) had been built 'on the waste land called *Merestone*'.

royal demesne' (Burton, 181bi; Dinedor, 183a2), or *in defensu regis* (Madley, 181bi; Ross, 182ai).[1] The numerous occasions on which we are told that 'the wood renders nothing' (e.g. Clehonger, 186bi; Eastnor, 182ai) may also reflect its inclusion in the royal or a baronial Forest.

Much of the shire, especially in the west, was probably more profitable as a hunting-ground than if cultivated. William fitzNorman was paying the king £15 for his position as forester (181a2), and in the north-west Osbern fitzRichard had eleven waste manors which furnished no geld, on which had 'grown up woods in which he hunts, and thence he has whatever he can take' (186bi). Ailey (187ai) had 'a large wood for hunting', Harewood (and perhaps Middlewood also; 187ai) had all been converted into woodland and rendered nothing; at Cascob (186b2) there was 'nothing but woods'. These are all on or outside the present Welsh border. It may have been the woodland which was valuable where a holding is described as waste but rents were none the less derived from it, e.g. Whitney (182b2), where no inhabitants are mentioned, or Brampton (182b2).

Woodland, and the hays for taking the deer, indeed, figure so prominently in the areas where waste and fallen values are most common that *vasta* must often imply a well-wooded area. At Rushock (185bi) there was 'one hay in a large wood'; *Mateurdin* (187bi) was waste, but there was a hay there. Where there was partial waste, it was the woodland which was frequently singled out for mention. The woodland in the manor of Bromyard (182bi) and at Clehonger (186bi) 'rendered nothing', and this may well imply that it was in the same case as that of Burton (181bi), where 'the king has it in his demesne'.

But some of the woodland had been reclaimed; 58 acres at Marcle (179b2), and enough to produce 17s. 4d. at Leominster (180ai). At both Weobley and Fernhill (184b2) land for a single team had been cleared, one intake rendering 11s. 9d., the other 4s. 6d. There had obviously been some re-settlement of wasted manors; Woonton (181a2) had been waste in 1066, but in 1086 contributed 5s. 2d. to the *firma* of Leominster. On a few occasions we are told of *hospites*, settlers who had been invited to take up vacant land, who paid rent, e.g. at Hope (184bi), 10s. 8d., or eight *orae*. The instances of Kinnersley, Walford, and Fownhope have been mentioned earlier.

Pannage is mentioned twice only; in the manor of Leominster (180ai) each villein with ten pigs gave one to discharge this due. Wood was

---

[1] Twice (Eardisley, 184b2; Ailey, 187ai), we are told of a *domus defensabilis*. Each place is in the March, where a fortified dwelling would be appropriate. But they are also in the heavily-wooded district, and might be hunting-lodges, *defensabilis* being akin to *in defensu*.

required for inland salt-making, and its possession was therefore of value, as may be seen from the relevant entries relating to Droitwich, which was not far distant from the county.[1]

On 32 manors which had been waste, six of which were royal, plough-teams were operating in 1086, which argues re-settlement, though for 52 holdings we are told that there could be more teams employed than there were actually available. In the 28 entries in which we are told that there is 'land for *n* teams', 170 in all, teams are recorded only rarely. Nine of these entries refer to waste land. In places where there were $344\frac{7}{8}$ teams, we are told that there could be $88\frac{1}{2}$ more, a deficiency of 20 per cent. If this is combined with the ploughland statements, the deficiency becomes 38 per cent. An assumption that where no deficiency is reported there were as many teams as ploughlands would obviously have its dangers, and would give us a deficiency figure of about 10 per cent, which seems too low to be probable.[2] For some entries induce doubts as to the adequacy of these figures. There was a demesne team at Hampton Court (180ai), but the only occupant mentioned is a bordar, who could not have managed it single-handed. There are a number of entries where teams are recorded but no inhabitants, e.g. Woonton (181a2) and Pipe (182bi). On occasion, no doubt, oxen operated on more than one holding, where men and oxen were few, but there are entries in which inhabitants surely were omitted, e.g. Credenhill (187a2), where there were two teams. It is accordingly impossible to deduce the extent to which such a county was underteamed.

Yet there were three manors with a surplus of teams, in contrast to the three where it is definitely stated that in 1086 there were less teams than there had been.[3]

Valuations in terms of the *ora* of sixteenpence, or of a Welsh unit, inevitably suggest actual rents received. The men who had settled at Hope and at Lyonshall (184bi) were rendering 10s. 8d. and 8s. 4d. respectively. Bullingham (181ai) made a customary payment of 1s. 4d. Hamnish (180a2) was valued at 3s. 4d., which might represent the payment of two *orae* at 20d. to the ounce of silver. Evesbatch (184bi) was and had been worth 28s., or 21 *orae*. A Thornbury holding (186a2) had been worth 13s. 4d., or the value of one silver mark. Odd sums such as 5s. 2d. (Woonton, 184b2) or 5s. 5d. (Hatfield, 180a2), may be clerical errors for 5s. 4d. or four

---

[1] See *Dom. Geog.*, ii, p. 94, and *VCH*, i, p. 196.
[2] For ploughlands and teams, see *Dom. Geog.*, ii, pp. 97 (Fig. 34) and 69–72.
[3] Preston on Wye (181bi: 'the villeins have more teams than arable land'), Mansell (182bi: a team was idle or superfluous (*ociosa*), Bartestree (183ai: four teams on three ploughlands); Leominster (180ai: 260 teams had become 230), Rotherwas (186b2: there had been ten villeins with thirteen teams where the villagers now had only two), Wellington (187a2; 'there were more teams than there are now').

THE MARCH COUNTIES: HEREFORDSHIRE

orae. Sums of 4s. and 8s. (and of 2s., 3s., 6s.) are quite numerous, and may have been based on the *ora*. In values under £1 they occur 29 times.

As everywhere in DB, the royal manors (179bi,2) present their own special problems. We are not told what Cleeve (179b2), rendering £9 10s. blanch in 1086, had paid in 1066. Linton (179bi) had before the Conquest rendered a quarter of a night's farm, but while we are told that the manor 'is now greatly decreased', and in 1086 rendered £10 blanch, we can have no idea if it was partly waste, or whether the implication is that in this county a night's farm had been worth far more than £40.[1] Marden (179bi) had gone up in value from a render of £9 to £10, though it too had lost some of its land (184ai). A higher farm-rent may have been set on it, or a premium for the lease demanded. Lugwardine (179bi) had not been farmed in 1066, and 'therefore it is not known what it was worth'; presumably less than the £10 blanch plus an ounce of gold received in 1086. Leominster (180ai) was being farmed for £60, but had the obligation of maintaining the nuns of its dissolved abbey, and it was added that if it could be freed from this and other claims £120 might be asked for the property. How its numerous components may have fluctuated in value we do not know, but its composition had certainly changed.[2] The 10s. paid *de firma* for Rowden (181a2) may also have been part of Leominster's revenue. This was 2s. less than the 1066 value, and the other holding here (187bi), worth 3s. in 1066, rendered 2s. although it is said to be waste.[3] Indeed, DB tells us that the pre-Conquest hidage of Leominster was less by one-quarter (Stanford Regis and Marcle had previously been components), and of 28 holdings which had formerly been part of the manor, with the dues paid by fourteen of the 1086 tenants. It is interesting that all are multiples of 20d., suggesting, as so often with royal manors, that this sum had been demanded for every 16d. due to compensate for imperfect coins.

Some entries for the royal manors in this county give an idea of the many sources of manorial revenue. Kingsland (179b2) was farmed for £13 3s. Wood and pasture brought in 8s, 'the customs', mills, villeins, and socage £4 15s., wood 3s. 4d., and the coliberts of the manor rendered 3 sesters of wheat and 2½ of barley. Kingstone (179bi) furnished a hawk,

---

[1] A virgate of Linton was in the possession of William fitzBaderon (185bi); the 'decrease' might be the loss of land, though no other instance is specifically mentioned. £40 would seem about right for the *firma unius noctis* of a March manor.
[2] Woonton (181a2) had been put in Leominster 'unjustly'. It contributed 62d. to its *firma*.
[3] It is possible that whenever a sum is given as *de firma* the holding, though not specified as such, was really a component of a royal manor, let to farm; e.g. Westwood (181ai), Sugwas (182a2), Pixley (187ai), Gayton (181a2), Ash Ingen (181ai). A sum paid blanch, e.g. Stanford Regis (180ai), may also really indicate a farm-rent.

Bach (187ai) a hawk and two hounds, Cleeve (179b2) six sesters of honey and six sheep with their lambs, *Turlestane* (179b2) 50 masses of iron and six salmon.[1] It is interesting that while we should expect hawks and hounds, and perhaps honey as well, to come from the heavily-wooded districts, almost all the instances derive from the March or from land which had a Forest connection. Commutation of rents had obviously not yet been organised in these outlands.

Despite the century's vicissitudes, the Herefordshire peasantry do not seem to have been altogether impoverished. In the upper strata, free men, *franci*, reeves, radmen, and priests seem to have averaged a whole plough-team apiece. The Welshmen, who from the fact of their being recorded as such were probably of at least moderate equipment, several times had a whole team per man, and on average five oxen. Thirty-seven times we are given the quantity of teams which belonged to villeins alone, and twenty-nine times those of bordars on a similar basis. In six manors villeins had an entire team, presumably of eight oxen, or more, and the 161 concerned averaged just over $4\frac{3}{4}$ oxen apiece. In eleven manors bordars possessed half a team; at Hampton (180a2) one had a whole team. On average the 142 for whom isolated figures are given owned $2\frac{1}{2}$ oxen apiece. *Homines* are frequently to be equated with villeins, but may here sometimes include lesser men, for 91 had 33 teams, averaging just under three oxen apiece. But one at Ash Ingen (181ai) had $1\frac{1}{2}$ teams, while at Baysham (181ai), Eaton in Foy (187a2), and Ledicot (184bi) the 'men' had each a whole team. If these figures seem to be high, it must be remembered that Herefordshire soils probably demanded much labour and so many oxen. We may well think, too, that each category of inhabitant is here a highly nebulous term, and that the villein of one place might have been styled a bordar in another.

Immunity, total or partial, from liability to geld, would help to make a manor profitable. Some exemptions probably date to the Confessor's reign or earlier. Six of Cowarne's fifteen hides (186a2) were quit by King William's grant, and he had remitted the geld of Ley (187bi) to Meredydd and his son. A large disparity between hidage and value or ploughlands may sometimes indicate earlier unrecorded exemptions; e.g. *Elburgelega* (183b2) had six teams at work but was rated at a single hide; Shobdon (183bi) was worth £7 and had 12 teams, yet was assessed at four hides only. The castellary of Orleton (185a2) did not geld, no doubt because of its defensive responsibility; the hides of Bromyard (182bi) were only two-thirds of its value in pounds. Of the amount of fiscal baronial demesne,

[1] See also Ewias (184ai, 186ai) for a honey-render, and *Dom. Geog.*, ii, pp. 104-5, for renders in kind generally.

THE MARCH COUNTIES: HEREFORDSHIRE

exempt at the levy of the six shilling geld, we are told little, but of Monkland's five hides (183a2) one was in demesne, and 'therefore it does not geld', and of Kingstone's four hides (179bi) 1¾ were in demesne.[1] In eighteen other entries some of the land does not geld. Waste land could not pay geld, for there were none to find it (see Bromyard, Little Hereford; 182bi). Some holdings are said to be quit of geld and 'the king's service' and 'customary duties'.[2] Clifford (183a2) and Eardisley (184b2) were 'in no Hundred' and paid no geld; Archenfield (181ai) neither gelded nor gave customary dues. The Kilpeck men (181ai) rendered 10s. but 'do not give any other geld'. Some of these holdings, especially those now in Wales or in the March, and especially those within a castellary, never had been hidated.

The majority of landowners in the county in 1066 seem to have been mostly men of little importance. On the Marches, perhaps, it was not easy to grow rich. Most of them possessed from one to four properties only; less than a dozen had substantial estates.[3] But three are styled *cilt* or 'noble', and of these Edwi, father of an Ælfwine who may have been the sheriff mentioned in a Wolferlow entry (185ai), had a score of holdings. If Thorkill King Harold's thegn and Thorkill the White were the same man, he had fourteen properties.[4] We hear too of thegns of Earl Ælfgar, of Earl Odda, and of Odda's sister Edith, all of whom had been dead some time when the Conquest began.[5] The Pencombe entry (186ai) suggests that Alfred of Marlborough, William fitzOsbern's adherent, was a landowner before the Conquest, which is not improbable, and Robert fitzWymarc, the half-Breton pre-Conquest sheriff of Essex, had a couple of manors. He had been given the profits of a canonry in Shropshire also. Were these given to him so that local property was available to him if he accompanied King Edward when he hunted? The pre-Conquest Norman influence, at its height in a county of which the half-Norman Ralf, King Edward's nephew, had been earl, is represented only by the manors of Richard fitzScrob and his son Osbern, and by those held by Osbern the kinsman of Alfred of Marlborough, whose son-in-law also held local property.

In 1086 the named survivors are few. Only fifteen bear English names, and of these all but three were sub-tenants. None, unusually, is said to be connected with the Forest in an official capacity, but one was a priest, and

[1] At Street (184bi) half a hide was royal demesne and did not geld; the other half-hide did.
[2] Bowley (183ai), Brampton Abbots (182b2).
[3] If the various instances of an Ælmar, an Arnwine, an Edwine, and the Leoflæd who occurs fourteen times represent individuals.
[4] A Thorkill is also said to have been the man of Wulfmær.
[5] Yazor (185ai), Mathon (184bi), Leadon (186ai).

one an interpreter.[1] In a few holdings seven of the 68 radmen were designated sub-tenants, and Grifin son of Meredydd still held eight properties in chief and one as a tenant. The only other Welshman named is Madoc (Ashperton, 187bi). If the major figures of Edwardian Herefordshire still lived, they were nowhere recorded as still holding land, except as tenants of Norman lords. Still, some surely aided the newcomers when Edric or Roger rebelled, and profited thereby, though they are unlikely to have retained all their former land.

Shropshire

Shropshire would seem to have suffered from the Conquest almost as much as those counties which are specified by the chroniclers as having been ravaged by King William's forces. The deficiency of plough-teams in 1086 was large, at least 50 per cent, and the manors had failed to recover the value of King Edward's day by some $8\frac{1}{2}$ per cent. At the time of the Inquest there were indeed far fewer properties waste than in 1071, but there was still a good deal of waste land, and many manors with grievously depreciated values.

Certain difficulties in dealing with the text are quickly apparent. A number of manors had appreciable quantities of berewicks. Morville had 18, and Condover 10 (253a2). The situation of a berewick is very rarely named, and when we find that Wrockwardine had $7\frac{1}{2}$ berewicks and Whittington $8\frac{1}{2}$ (253a2,bi), suggesting, since here alone fractions occur, that these two previously royal manors, a score of miles apart, shared an interest in a single place, the difficulties of satisfactory cartography become even more obvious. Nor can we say just how manors such as Cause (253bi), with five sub-tenancies, and 38 out of 40 hides waste, or Stanton Lacy (260bi), which included three sub-tenancies, the land of four *servientes*, and a member of the manor, were composed. While the great majority of the entries give us information about plough-teams, the quantity of ploughlands can often only be deduced by assuming that there was a team for each ploughland where the text does not record that there could be more teams than there are.

Then there are several instances in which 'the Hundred', implying the profits of justice in the Hundred-court, is mentioned (253a2,bi). Wrockwardine yielded £6 13s. 8d. in 1066, and the king, whose manor it was, had two-thirds of 'the Hundred' and the earl one-third. In 1086 the manor was at farm for £12 10s.; 13s. 8d. should probably have been 13s. 4d., thus making £10 for Wrockwardine and Hodnet together. Was the large

[1] Ashperton (183bi), Yarpole (180bi).

increase caused by the imposition by Earl Roger of an over-large farm rent, or because he was now getting all the profits of jurisdiction? Condover benefited the king similarly in 1066, and used to yield £10. But even with 'the Hundred' it produced only £10 in 1086 for the earl. Hodnet brought the king £3 6s. 8d. in 1066; in 1086, with 'the Hundred', it produced £8 for Earl Roger. Morville, with two-thirds of the profits of the Hundred of *Alnodestreu*, had yielded £10. In 1086 'what the earl has' was worth only £3. Corfham produced in 1066 a *firma* of £10 with 'two-thirds of the Hundreds of Culvestan and Patton': in 1086, with 'the Hundreds', it brought the earl only £6. Morville had a deficiency of teams of 61 per cent, Corfham of 50 per cent, Hodnet of $47\frac{1}{2}$ per cent, Condover of $42\frac{1}{2}$ per cent, so any apparent decline in receipts might be due to vicissitudes the manors had suffered since the Conquest. Maesbury had been waste in 1066, but with 'the Hundred' of *Mersete* it was worth 40s. at the Inquest, while Alberbury, to which manor was attached 'the Hundred' of *Ruesset*, had gone up in value from 5s. to 20s. Hence the complex previously royal manors will here be dealt with separately.

I reckon the number of holdings in 1086 as at least 505, plus 138 unnamed berewicks and three 'members' of manors, and 90 properties which were classed as having been manors in 1066, but which by the time of the Inquest had been combined to form fewer manors.[1] Seventeen manorial components might well be added also. The total of holdings is not likely to have been less than 800, for probably DB often fails to tell us that a manor did not consist of a single settlement.[2]

Berewicks are very rarely named where a manor possessed many such detached holdings, though Hopton (256bi) is said to be one of the $7\frac{1}{2}$ berewicks of Wrockwardine, and *Wlferesforde* in *Mersete* Hundred (259b2), since it had been King Edward's and no value is given for it, was possibly one of the $13\frac{1}{2}$ unnamed berewicks of Maesbury or Whittington. Minton and Wittingslow (259b2) formed part of the *firma* of Church Stretton (254ai), and may have been two of its four berewicks. Broom (259a2) is said to belong to Welshampton. Thus when the number of 'entries' is mentioned it must be remembered that the actual holdings represented must be many more.

---

[1] The wording of DB suggests that this figure of 90 should probably be 97.
[2] Tait (*VCH*, i, p. 282) for some indeterminable reason gives 480 manors and three berewicks. I have not included the 57 berewicks mentioned in the entry for the city of Shrewsbury (254ai). The text speaks of King Edward's 'twelve manors with 57 berewicks thereto pertaining'; he is said to have held thirteen manors, and these possessed 53 berewicks, which are not, I think, supplementary to the 57. The small discrepancy is characteristic of Domesday arithmetic, akin to that regarding Montgomery which was noted by Tait (*op. cit.* p. 318; n. 33).

THE DETAILS OF DOMESDAY BOOK

Thus it is hard to say how many holdings may have been waste or partially waste in 1066. It might have been as low as a dozen, which however incorporated 21½ berewicks, but it seems more probable that we ought to

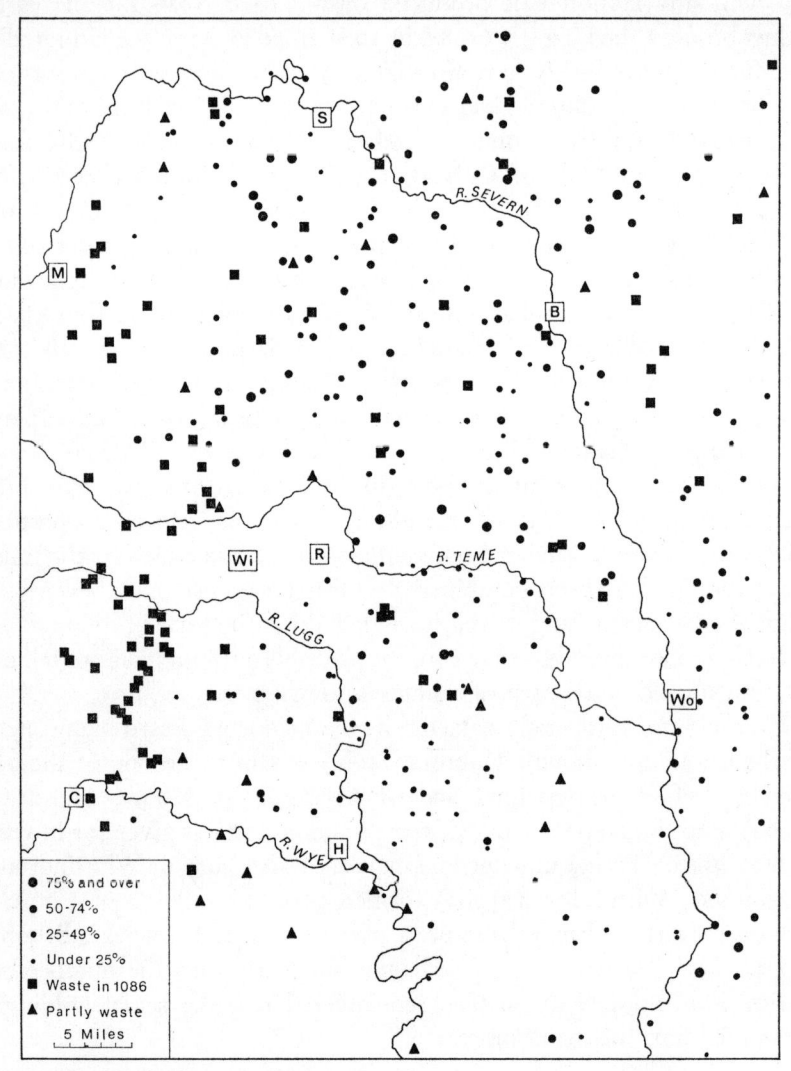

Fig. 18 The March Shires: southern section
    Fall in value *tunc–post*
    B—Bridgnorth   C—Clifford   H—Hereford   M—Montgomery
    R—Richard's Castle   S—Shrewsbury   Wi—Wigmore   Wo—Worcester

add 72 entries for places which are said to have been waste at an unspecified time and for which we have no 1066 value, and perhaps a few which were partly waste at the time of the Inquest. Most of them are in the west

154

THE MARCH COUNTIES: SHROPSHIRE

and south of the shire, where pre-Conquest waste might be expected to be found. The neighbourhood of Montgomery contributes 22 of them.

It need hardly be said that we are not regularly furnished with informa-

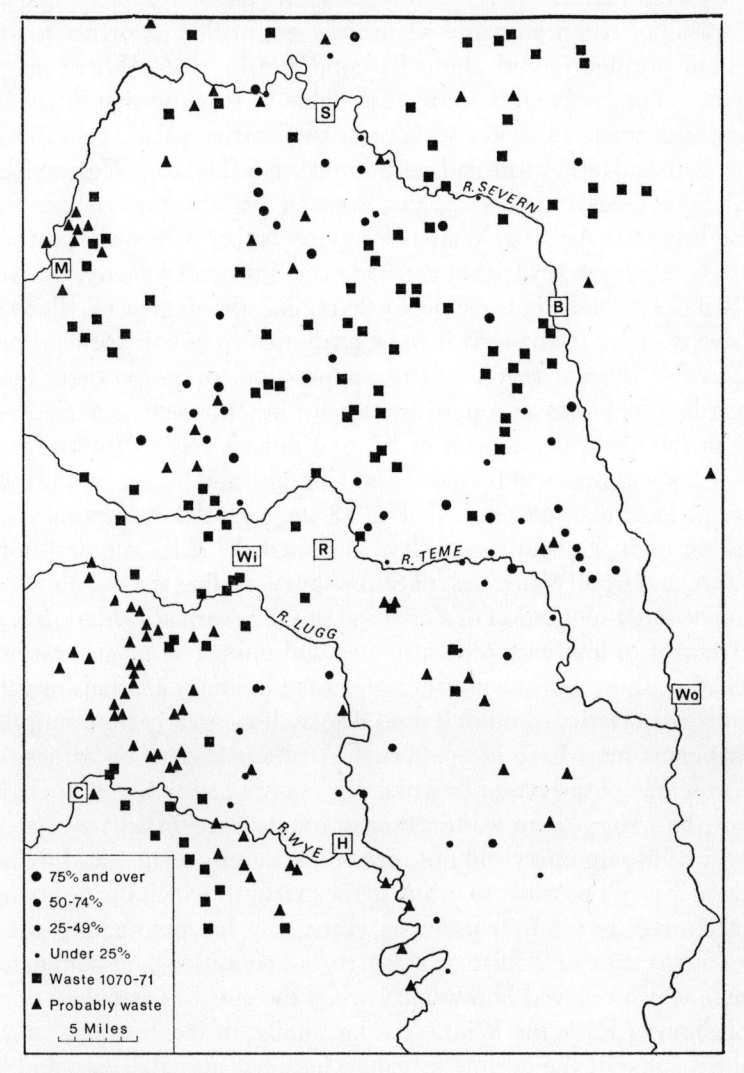

Fig. 19 The March Shires: southern section
Fall in value 1066–86
Places as in Fig. 18

tion, even for manorial valuations, for all three dates. Fortunately we are given most of the necessary figures for 1066 and 1086. But Baschurch (253a2) 'used to yield' £7, but when, we are not told. For 1086 we are

155

given only the value of the earl's demesne, £6. Netley (259b2), waste in 1086, 'used to be worth' 12s. Eyton on Severn (252bi) had been worth £14 'when it was given to the church' of St Peter's, Shrewsbury.

As in Herefordshire, we are all too frequently told that a manor had been (*fuit*) waste, or had been waste when received, or that its owner found it waste, but nothing is said about its condition in 1066. Where no pre-Conquest value is given, it seems reasonable to suppose that many such manors were waste in 1066 also. For in two entries we are told that the manors both had been waste and were found waste (Halston, Weston Rhyn; 254b2). Sometimes, too, it is specifically stated that a manor had been waste in King Edward's day, e.g. Wattlesborough (255b2), Chirbury (253bi). It is unlikely that by 1071 such manors had made substantial, if any, recovery.

It is unfortunately impossible to determine the degree to which the extensive waste of about 1071 is to be attributed to initial Norman settlement, to the Mercian revolt and its suppression, or to the desertion of unrewarding holdings as opportunities for resettlement occurred elsewhere in the final fifteen years of King William's reign. We know that Shrewsbury was besieged by men from Cheshire and burnt, and presumably some local damage resulted. Fig. 18 suggests that raiders may have moved through the southern valleys and then the dales running north-eastwards, and from Wales west of Shrewsbury, raiding around the county town. There is a suggestion of a crossing of the Severn at Bridgnorth, and of movement to link with Cheshire men and ultimately concentration in west Staffordshire. But the plotting of wasted holdings and falls in values offers no great clarity, though it does display how greatly the county and its inhabitants must have been affected. An Inquest clerk or witness was fully conscious of the extent to which the county had suffered: 'these two manors', he wrote, 'were waste as many others were' (254b2).

Roger of Montgomery did not receive the county as his earldom until 1071, and it is not possible to estimate the extent to which the newcomers had taken over in the four previous years. Tait has pointed out the influence on the shire of William fitzOsbern, who is said to have commanded the force which relieved Shrewsbury when the city was assaulted during the rebellion of Edric the Wild.[1] To the coming of the Normans may be attributed some of the decline in values between *tunc* and *post*, and it is possible that some defensive works were then constructed or improved in the Marches. A castle was at some time built at Oswestry (253bi), and another at what is now Castle Holdgate (*Stantun*, 258bi). The prosperity induced by the security this gave is perhaps indicated by the fact that there were here 5½ teams for 6 ploughlands and that the value had risen

[1] *VCH*, i, p. 288; Orderic, ii, 193.

from 18s. to 25s. Some of the immense rises in values by 1086 may perhaps be explained by the need for immediate concentration at danger-points. Ellesmere (253b2) doubled its value between 1066 and 1086, while that of Ford (253b2) rose from £9 to £34 and of Great Ness (253b2) from £3 to £13 10s. Whittington and its berewicks (253bi), said to have been waste in 1066, were valued at £15 15s. at the Inquest.

163 entries mention waste at times variously described as *post* or *quando recepit*, or land which was (*fuit*) or found (*invenit*) waste, representing well over 200 holdings. In 1066 these had been worth £123 17s. 8d., and it must be remembered that in 72 entries we have no figure for that year, so that the decline might have been even greater. In 1086 what had previously been waste was valued at £103 14s. 4¼d., a fall against the pre-Conquest figure of 16 per cent, assuming that the 72 mentioned above were waste also in 1066. If they were not, the fall was about 30 per cent.[1] Nearly sixty entries recording waste in 1070/1 were still waste in 1086, or partially so.

Only about 30 per cent of the entries which mention a time between Conquest and Inquest give us clear information about values. They show a total fall since the Conquest from £378 16s. 8d. to £102 10s. 4d., a decline of 73 per cent. In 1086 the same holdings show a decline on the 1066 figures to £291 9s. 10¼d., or 23 per cent. Some of the falls in value in the early years of the Conquest are enormous: Lydbury North (252a2) fell from £35 to £10, Clun (258a2) from £25 to £3. A very few show, rather surprisingly, appreciation, and not only those like Ruyton (257b2) which were waste in 1066. Pitchford (258ai) doubled its value of 8s., Meadowley (268bi) rose from 30s. to £2 'when received'.

Between the time or times described as *post*, etc., and the Inquest, these waste holdings recovered in value by just over £100. More than sixty had remained waste, or partially so. Few were worth more than £2, and some, e.g. Wollaston (255bi) and Lack (259bi), are accorded a small value though said to be waste.

Some of the manors for which we have triple values had declined still further by 1086. Myddle (255ai) had fallen in value from £4 to £3 10s., and Caynham (256b2) from £3 to £2. But in some manors the rise is staggering. Worthen (255b2) had increased from 10s. to £9 10s., Clun (258a2) from £3 to £10, Idshall (256b2) from 6s. to £15, Stoke upon Tern (256bi) to £7 from a wasted condition.

But the county as a whole had not recovered the standards of 1066.

---

[1] From the above Cause (253bi), Womerton (256ai), and Bratton (257bi) have been omitted because of the difficulties these entries present. It looks as if what in 1066 was worth £5 was largely waste later and worth £4 10s. in 1086.

The little which then is clearly said to have been waste was indeed in 1086 worth £25 5s., indicating some post-Conquest development. But holdings which had been worth £842 2s. 6d. were at the Inquest valued at only £766 13s. 4¼d., a decline of 9 per cent. On the whole the manors of Earls Edwine, Morkere, and Harold show slight improvement.

These figures do not include the manors which had been King Edward's, the difficulties regarding which have already been stressed. Most were in Earl Roger's hands, and an apparent appreciation of from about £50 to £82, which includes three manors waste in 1066 but later bringing in £19 15s., may be deceptively large.

Now while there had obviously been a large amount of restocking of damaged manors, as indicated by a map showing plough-teams on former waste, and encouragement to settle on wasted land had been given, some of these figures seem to be quite incomprehensible.[1] *Hospites* appear only thrice in the Shropshire text (259ai,2; 259b2), and are but seven in number, but possibly many men not so described might have been given this classification. The statement that Meole (252a2) was *nunquam hospitatus* may imply that many other manors were furnished with newcomers. No inhabitants here are mentioned, but it looks as if the 17s. 4d. it paid must have been contributed by unmentioned survivors, diminished perhaps in number, for in 1066 it had paid 20s. Possibly, where a holding is described as having been waste, the potentiality was still there, but until it had been restocked, land temporarily uncared for recultivated, and buildings repaired, none would be prepared to rent it, especially if the peasantry were in no position to pay rent or dues. We can hardly imagine that all these manors, which in 1086 possessed over 350 teams and nearly 900 inhabitants (excluding priests), had previously been completely empty. Stoke upon Tern (256bi), though a complex manor, cannot have acquired in about fifteen years over a hundred oxen and perhaps a population of 120 from elsewhere. Nor can we reasonably account for the only small total increase here in values between 1066 and 1086 by visualising wholesale transfers of men and oxen to wasted land from less affected manors.

On only one occasion is value said to be in excess of worth, but probably, as elsewhere, rents in excess of what was reasonable were being demanded. Bausley (255bi) was worth only 2s., but was *ad firmam* for 6s. 8d.; a heavy rent for the two Welshmen with their solitary team. Whether this was because their hide was exempt from geld, or whether they were unable to pay it in consequence of the excessive rent, we cannot say. The text merely says that it did not geld.

[1] See the map in *Dom. Geog.*, ii, p. 146 (Fig. 51).

THE MARCH COUNTIES: SHROPSHIRE

Sometimes, however, it looks as if potentiality could not be achieved. Marton (253ai) was worth 10s. in 1066 and 8s. later, but paid only 6s. 8d.; there was a 36½ per cent deficiency of teams. Mytton (252b2) had been worth 12s., but was *ad firmam* for only 11s.; presumably it was being rented by the four villeins there.

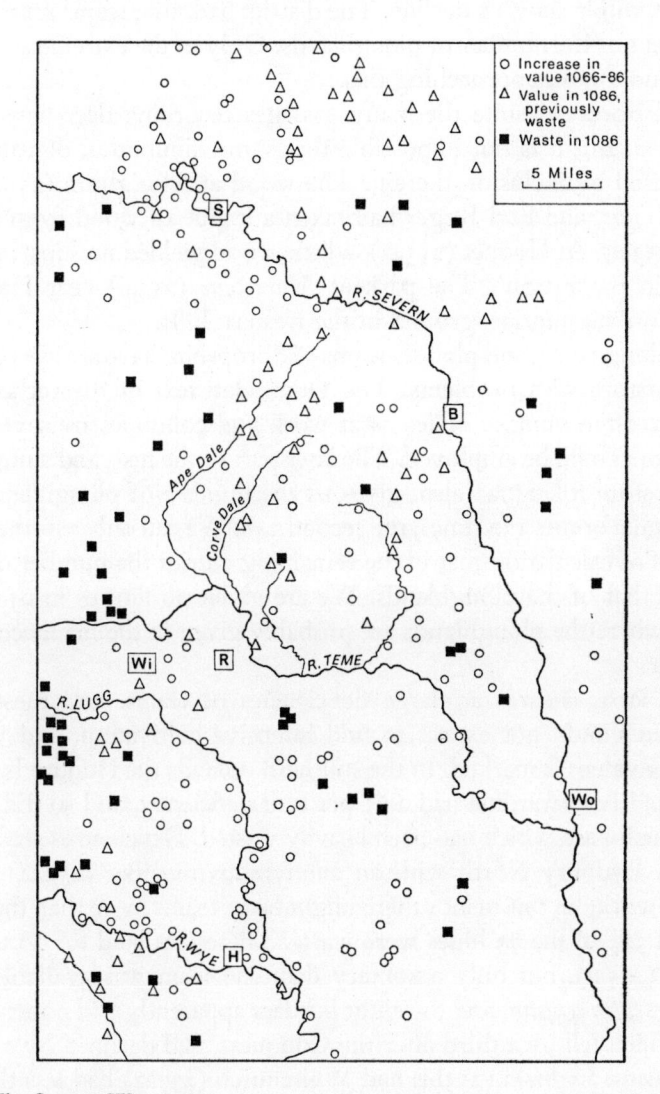

Fig. 20 The Severn–Wye area
    Increase in value *post–modo* and waste in 1086
    B—Bridgnorth   H—Hereford   R—Richard's Castle   S—Shrewsbury
    Wi—Wigmore Wo—Worcester

The district where recovery is most apparent, other than those settlements guarding against Welsh raids, is in the neighbourhood of Shrewsbury. The influence of the city on local economy seems to have been such as we might expect. Even if we omit the manor of Ford, referred to above, the value of the settlements within a radius of six miles from Shrewsbury rose in the score of years following 1066 by over 25 per cent, whereas the shire as a whole shows a decline. The district had, too, teams representing 86 per cent of the number of ploughlands. Only in the extreme south-east do we find a ratio approaching this.

Royal Forest, despite the many passages recording deer-hays, is unmentioned. But it is not impossible that some diminution of values had been caused by inclusion therein. The wood at Albrighton (259a2) was *in manu regis*, and Earl Roger had taken a league of wood from St Alkmund (253ai). At Hodnet (253a2) 'a little wood yielded nothing'; perhaps it was 'in the Forest'. The park at *Marsetelie* (252ai) near Habberley implies a royal hunting-ground in the western hills.

The ploughlands and plough-teams of Shropshire have always provided commentators with problems. The Domesday text of the earlier folios often gives the number of teams at work and continues by saying how many more could be employed. The later part of the text, and a number of entries before fol. 257a2 also, gives us the number of ploughlands. The first formula occurs 132 times, the second 248. We can only assume for the purposes of calculation that in the remaining entries the number of teams equalled that of the ploughlands. We are given no figures in 95 entries, plus 31 where the ploughlands are probably given in the main account of a manor.

Some areas show very large deficiencies of teams, and these occur where we should not expect to find intensive cultivation, and where a decline in values is marked. In the southern uplands the Hundreds of both *Rinlau* and Leintwardine had a 65 per cent deficiency, and so did the extreme north-east, which had been heavily wasted. Deficiencies are at times gigantic. Lydbury North with an anonymous member (252a2) had 28 teams at work; 'in this manor there might be 92 teams more than there are', but then $32\frac{1}{2}$ of the 53 hides were waste. There was land for 20 teams at Myddle (255ai), but only a solitary demesne team was available there. The priest, *francigena*, and the eight bordars apparently had none, and the value, which fell by a third after the Conquest, had declined by a further $12\frac{1}{2}$ per cent. Lydham (253bi) and Whitchurch (257a2) had less than half the number of teams which could have been employed, while at Onibury (252a2) there had been nine teams in King Edward's day, but four less in 1086. There were six teams at Clunbury (258ai) in 1066, but in 1086 this manor and Kempton had between them but nine on land which could occupy 14. Their joint value fell from £8 to £3, and recovered to only £6. It is then not surprising to find that for about 80 holdings, most of which had been or were waste, teams are unmentioned. Nor is it surprising that some of these cannot now be identified; the settlements appear to have decayed completely. In only 38 holdings were there as many teams as there were ploughlands, unless an absence of information implies parity.

Some entries, however, indicate revival. Great Sutton (258b2) had been waste, but in 1086 the five ploughlands were being worked by the same number of teams, and the manor was valued at 5s. more than the £1 it had been worth in 1066.

Only twice are holdings overteamed. Pulley (260bi) had seven teams for its five ploughlands; its 1066 value had been maintained, and increased by 1086. On the holding of the *servientes* at Stanton Lacy (260bi) there was land for three teams, but four were there. However, immediately after the ploughland figure is added 'and one ferling and ten acres', which might represent further arable land and not assessment.

Some statements are difficult to disentangle. Cause (*Alretune*, 253a2) is said to have land for 40 teams, while land for 31 teams is waste. We might then expect to find nine teams at work, but there were four for the demesne land and $9\frac{1}{2}$ on that of the *milites*. It looks as if the waste land was not in the demesne portion of the manor, but in detached components. Worthen (255b2) had 41 ploughlands, and in all 21 teams. We are told that there could be four more teams on the demesne, so Roger presumably had $16\frac{1}{2}$ ploughlands and $12\frac{1}{2}$ teams, and his four tenants $24\frac{1}{2}$, of which 16 could not be tilled. Again the demesne, as we should expect, is the least affected portion of a presumably complex manor.

Sometimes, when land was waste, no ploughlands were recorded (e.g. on fol. 258a2), which may make the deficiency figure for the shire too low. Also, a grave shortage of teams in a manor may well often imply unrecorded waste.

While a number of the peasantry were apparently without oxen, those who possessed them do not seem on the whole to have been poorly equipped. There are 58 entries in which we can be reasonably sure that the oxen were owned solely by villeins. In these 286 villeins had $108\frac{1}{2}$ teams, an average of just over three oxen a man. The villeins at *Udeford* and Ruyton of the XI Towns (257b2) were in a position to rent five fisheries. Bordars in 22 holdings where they alone, save for slaves or *bovarii*, are represented, had $21\frac{3}{4}$ teams among 88 of them, giving a fraction under a couple of oxen each. The figure for 19 radmen is almost $4\frac{1}{2}$ oxen per head, for five *hospites* over three, and for forty Welshmen $2\frac{1}{2}$. A free man at

Sleap (257bi) had a whole team, another at The Lowe (256a2) had half a team, but he had land for another. A priest possessed half a team (Broughton, 252b2). In two holdings (Clee Stanton, 252b2; Morton and *Aitune*, 254b2) six *homines* averaged half a team apiece.

Some of the villeins who had appreciable numbers of oxen may have been former free men or radmen who had sunk in the social scale. A villein on fol. 252b2 had an entire team, and so did radmen at Norton in Hales (258bi), Moston (259a2), and Rhiston (259bi). Seven villeins at Wistanstow (260b2) owned an equal number of teams, and five at Peplow (257ai) had 24 oxen between them. A Long Stanton bordar (256bi) had half a team, and six at Harcourt (259b2) 32 oxen in all. Many of the Welshmen with oxen had a whole or a half-team, and no radmen with oxen had less than four.[1] There were, however, 125 holdings in all where the peasantry had no oxen. Their inclusion would reduce the figure for bordars to an ox apiece.

Over half the instances of such figures for teams come from the manors or holdings in which there was no demesne land. In these, as we might expect, the average number of oxen per head is in excess of those associated with *terra villanorum*.

More than one hundred holdings seem to have included no demesne land. A precise figure cannot be given, for while in a number of entries demesne is unmentioned, the presence of slaves suggests that it must have existed in these. About one-third had been waste, or partially so, at some period. The deficiency of teams, $57\frac{1}{2}$ per cent, is well above the county average. Values are naturally small, usually under £1, and many had earlier been much smaller still. The frequent use of *reddit* harmonises with the fact that many of these holdings were peopled only by free men, *francigenae*, radmen, Welshmen, *servientes*, *homines*, or a *miles*; such categories occur comparatively rarely elsewhere.[2] It is on such holdings, too, that we encounter bordars, or a villein and two slaves, 'who own nothing' (*Corselle*, 257a2; Bratton, 257bi), or no inhabitants are recorded (e.g. Soulton, 253ai; Lack, 259bi; The Eye Farm, 256b2), though there may have been resident an unrecorded survivor and his family.[3]

It is suggestive, too, that eight of these small properties were *ad firmam*.[4] Moreover, a number of values are sums which surely represent rents cal-

---

[1] See, e.g., Weston Rhyn, Maesbrook (254b2), Melverley (255ai), Church Stoke (259bi), Meadowley (258bi), Stanton Lacy (260bi).
[2] e.g. Sutton (252b2), Halston (254b2), Harcourt (257a2), Charlton (255b2), Beckbury (259a2).
[3] On a half-hide, probably at Shelton near Shrewsbury (253ai), two burgesses were 'working on the land' and paid 3*s*. rent for it.
[4] e.g. Mytton (252b2), Haughton (259a2), Bausley (255bi).

THE MARCH COUNTIES: SHROPSHIRE

culated in terms of the *ora* of sixteenpence; e.g. Merrington and Soulton (256ai, 253ai—64d. each), Melverley (255ai—32d.) Brockton and Lack (257a2, 259bi—16d.). Seventeen are of either 4s. or 8s., three or six *orae*.

As in many other counties, the values of mills are often given in terms of the *ora* (e.g. Ford, 253b2; Leintwardine, 260a2; Eardington, 254ai); the High Ercall entry (253b2) records 'ounces of pence'.

Sometimes we are told of the money contributions of the peasantry of varying categories. The Edgbold free man (260bi) was paying 8s. *de firma*, though he had no oxen and none but his own family to help him; three at Grinshill (257bi) rendered 7s. for two hides and two ploughlands which had been held by four men as three manors and which had been worth 32s. A *miles*, who may not have been a foreigner, rendered 4s. for his hide at Morville (253a2), and one at Beckbury (259a2) 20d. Seven radmen at Priestweston (256ai), where there had been six minor thegns with a virgate apiece who might be represented among the radmen of 1086, paid 20s. The land of four of these thegns had been waste, and they may in consequence have declined in status. The two *hospites* at Leaton (259b2) were paying 4s. 8d., four at Colemere (259a2) 3s. 4d., and one at *Etone* (259ai) 2s. Unspecified occupants were making varied contributions. One man at Houghton (259a2) paid 6s. *de firma*, another at Longslow (259ai) 3s. 4d., and three at Prees (252a2) 10s. Of Welshmen, 25 paid £1 at Whittington (253bi), four at Wootton (255ai) 4s., four at Clun (258a2) 2s. 4d., and two at Kempton (258ai) 1s. 2d. Two villeins at Great Ness (253b2) were paying 5s.; here, too, six Welshmen paid £1. Most of these suggest small farms outside the relevant villages.

As we might expect, if land is said to be waste, no teams or inhabitants are mentioned. But waste land, or land for which no occupants other than the owner are mentioned, might still have a value. Hawksley (259a2) was apparently unpopulated, but was at farm for 6d., perhaps because it had woodland for fattening 60 swine, and the free man who owned it may have continued as a swine-farmer.[1] There were no men at Strefford (255ai), but Rainald's tenant none the less had 20s. from it. There must have been some asset here which DB does not mention.[2] So far as we are told there was one ploughland and one villein, and nothing else at Stapleton (255bi), but it was worth 12s. Again DB may be defective. A radman at Charlton (253ai) had no team, and neither ploughland nor woodland is mentioned, but the holding yielded 5s. It may have been part of another manor, as may

---

[1] At Haughton on the same folio a man was paying a *firma* of 6s., but for what there is no suggestion. The geld-liability and its two ploughlands alone are mentioned. At Edgbold (260bi) a free man paid a *firma* of 8s., and here there was wood for fattening 20 swine.
[2] See also *Estone* (259a2), Little Eaton (253ai), Brockton (257ai, 259b2).

the holding in Beckbury (259a2) for which a *miles* paid 20*d*. Two holdings, the first of which was worth one shilling, but had been worth £2, while the second was almost waste, were peopled only by bordars who 'owned nothing' (*Corselle* and Bratton, 257bi). Buttery on the same folio was worth 2*s*., though 'only three oxen are there'; no peasantry are recorded.

Rents in kind are occasionally mentioned. Two Clun radmen rendered two *animalia de censu*; the Welshmen of the commote of Edeyrnion eight cows (258a2, 255ai). A falcon supplemented the 20*s*.-value of Calverhall (259ai), and a falcon was the *firma* of a Welshman at Kinnersley (259a2).

Of the advance of Norman power into Wales we hear less than we should like to do. The lands forming the castellary of Montgomery had apparently been English in 1066, for three thegns held them of King Edward 'for the chase'. They had been waste, and in 1086 still mostly were waste, but Earl Roger received six pounds of pence from a portion of his castellary. Other districts and their profits have been discussed by Tait.[1]

One of the characteristics of the larger Shropshire manors is the fluctuation in values between 1066 and 1086. These are often so curious that we can only suspect that many had changed in composition during the period. We find, for example,

			1066 £ s. d.	1086 £ s. d.	
253a2	Wrockwardine	King Edward	6 13 8[2]	12 10 0[3]	Earl Roger
	Hodnet	,, ,,	3 6 8	8 0 0[2]	,, ,,
260bi	Meole Brace	Queen Edith	7 0 0	13 5 6	Ralf de Mortemer
252bi	Emstrey	Earl Edwine	5 0 0	11 0 0	St Remy of Rheims
253b2	Ellesmere	,, ,,	10 0 0[2]	20 0 0	Earl Roger
254bi	Cound	Earl Morkere	4 7 0	10 0 0	Rainald *vicecomes*

Of the thirteen manors which had been King Edward's, three had been waste in 1066; the remainder brought in £52 13*s*. 4*d*. In 1086 they were valued at £86 5*s*. 2*d*. Morville (253a2) had certainly altered in composition. Of its twelve hides, four were in Earl Roger's demesne; St Gregory's eight hides had become St Peter's five, of which a *miles* held one and the earl's chaplains three, while Richard the butler held two. Unless these were demesne hides, the manor had been enlarged, and no hides of *terra villanorum* are recorded for the 47 recorded inhabitants with their thirteen teams.

[1] *VCH*, i, pp. 287–8.
[2] With 'the two pennies of the Hundred'; i.e. two-thirds of the profits of justice.   [3] *de firma*.

THE MARCH COUNTIES: SHROPSHIRE

Earls Edwine and Morkere had between them possessed 20 manors valued at almost £200. In 1086 they were worth very little more. Edwine's properties had frequently been worth £20, as though this was the farm-rent set upon them.[1] Their grandmother Godgifu had had four smaller manors; their grandfather Leofric only Eyton on Severn (252bi) besides those which had presumably passed to his son Ælfgar and so to his grandsons, and this had been given to St Peter's, Shrewsbury. Earl Harold had held only Whitchurch (257a2), and Queen Edith half a dozen manors which had appreciated slightly in value. The fall in values had obviously been chiefly on the lands of lesser men.

The pre-Conquest landholders have been discussed by Tait.[2] Thoret of Wroxeter probably acted as sheriff of Shropshire or Cheshire before the Conquest. His Shropshire lands had not been extensive: 14¾ hides valued at £7 17s. In 1086 he held three of his former estates as tenant of the then sheriff, Rainald of Bailleul, and had acquired Langley also.

No section of the text is headed 'land of the king's thegns', presumably because the county was now palatinate. The Englishmen surviving are mostly said to hold of the earl, not in chief; all may have been his tenants. Only some sixteen are recorded, holding a little over 37 hides valued at £12 10s. 4d. A few, possibly only a dozen, survived as tenants of other newcomers, holding rather more than 40 further hides.[3] Each (if the individual is represented) seems also to have lost estates he had formerly held.

Interest naturally centres on Edric the Wild. An Edric appears in 40 entries as holding in 1066, but it is improbable that all refer to the same person.[4] Edric *salvage* is five times named, holding 26¾ hides worth in 1066 £17 9s.[5] Six times an Edric is styled 'free man', and the instances include Hopesay and Clun (258ai,2), rated at 22 hides and worth in 1066 £35; Siefton, Culmington, and Halston (254ai,2), of 17 hides worth £10, were also an Edric's. At any rate, as befitted a descendant of Edric Streona, he can have been no small man.

But many of the free men of King Edward's day had held only one or two manors. A few, such as Hunni and Earnwine, were well-endowed, but when Ælfric appears eighteen times and Wulfric twenty, we suspect that we are not reading of individuals. A rich man called Siward is mentioned as having been concerned with the dispute between the bishop of Worcester and the abbot of Evesham. In 1086 a man or men of this name held six

[1] High Ercall, Wellington, Donington, Stottesdon (253b2, 254ai).
[2] *VCH*, i, pp. 299–300.
[3] Precise figures cannot be given, as assessment or value are not disclosed in some entries.
[4] Twice 'Edric' held jointly with Leofwine (257bi), and thrice jointly with others.
[5] Lydham, Loppington (253bi), Middleton (256ai), Weston under Redcastle (256b2), Hope Bowdler (256b2).

THE DETAILS OF DOMESDAY BOOK

manors valued at £6 14s. 4d., and for 1066 the name (also as Saward, Seward) occurs frequently, sometimes as holding quite large manors, e.g. Upton Magna (254b2) and Myddle (255ai), but also occasionally in conjunction with others.

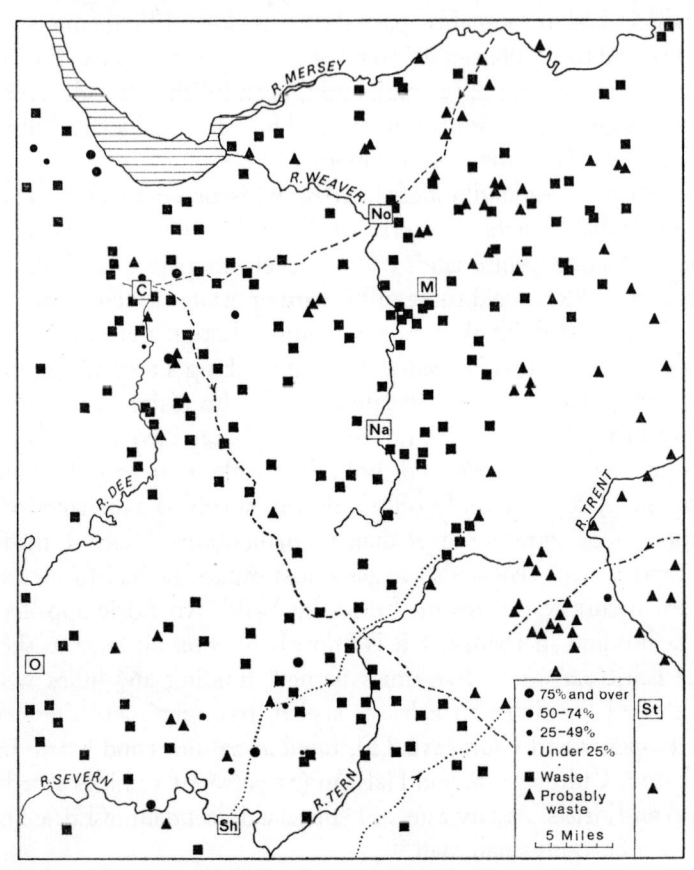

Fig. 21 Cheshire with north Shropshire and Staffordshire
  Fall in value *tunc–post*
  Suggested routes of – – – royal troops in 1070
  – · – · royal troops in 1069   · · · West Mercian rebels in 1069
  C—Chester   M—Middlewich   Na—Nantwich   No—Northwich
  O—Oswestry   Sh—Shrewsbury   St—Stafford

Only in about a score of entries do we receive any suggestion of immunity from geld, and these include four where it is to be assumed that the existence of demesne implies partial exemption.[1] A few very small holdings are said not to pay geld, two (Clunbury and Neen Sollars, 258ai, 260ai)

[1] Condover, Baschurch, Morville (253a2), Caynham (256b2).

THE MARCH COUNTIES: SHROPSHIRE

had never been hidated, and seven, five of which belonged to St Milburga, paid geld only for about four-fifths of their assessment. But then the total assessment of the county in 1086 was less than two-thirds of the 2,400 hides with which the County Hidage credits it. Tait thought that a reduction

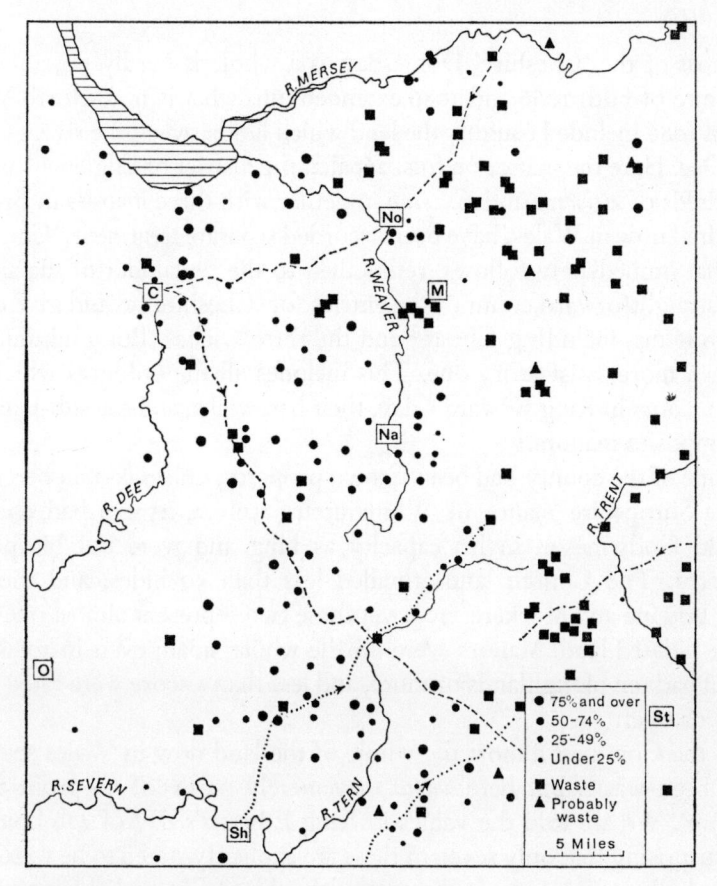

Fig. 22 Cheshire with north Shropshire and Staffordshire
Fall in value *tunc–modo*
Suggested routes and places as in Fig. 21

may have taken place in or before the reign of Cnut: it is certainly suggestive that Much Wenlock (252bi) is said to have enjoyed partial exemption in that reign.[1] The 52½ hides around Montgomery (254ai) had been 'quit of all geld', for they seem to have been regarded as royal Forest. No doubt Shropshire had always been a poor county, and some reduction of liability had been necessary. A quantity of teamlands in number more than twice

[1] For a discussion, see *VCH*, i, pp. 281–2.

that of the hides suggests that assessment had been made to relate more closely to capacity to pay. But we do not hear of post-Conquest reduction, and the geld must have borne heavily on so wasted a shire.

Cheshire

To treat of the 'Cheshire' Domesday as a whole is hardly possible. The Cheshire of both 1066 and 1086 extended into what is now North Wales, and in 1086 included roughly the land which lies between the rivers Clwyd and Dee. Here the matter on fols. 269ai,2, the district of Englefield and the Hundreds of *Atiscros* and *Exestan*, together with three manors in Broxton Hundred now in Wales, have been accorded separate treatment. 'Cheshire', in what immediately follows, refers then to the remainder of the area.

A straightforward count of the entries for 'Cheshire' would give a total of 316 items, including Chester and the three wiches. But a minimum of 400 is a more satisfactory one. This includes all the holdings which had been manors in King Edward's day, their berewicks, and the sub-tenancies in composite manors.

None of the county had been Crown property, unless certain berewicks of the Shropshire manor of Whitchurch (256bi,2, 257a2) had come to Harold Godwineson in his capacity as king and were not his private property. The Church lands totalled less than 50 hides, and those of Earls Edwine and Morkere 110½, yet these two represent almost one-third of the hidated land. Manors were on the whole small; even in 1086 only fifteen had ten ploughlands or more, and less than a score were rated at ten hides or over.

At the Conquest almost the whole of the land now in Wales seems to have been waste, but here *wasta* may merely mean 'of no profit to the English'. We are told the values in King Edward's day of 229 holdings. It is surprising that only seven of these are explicitly stated to be waste, and that only three should be in the west of the shire.[1] But probably we should include nine of which it is said *wasta fuit et sic invenit*, or some similar phrase.[2] Possibly, too, we should add 44 which were waste or found waste at some date between 1066 and 1086.

The rising of Edric and his associates, we are told, spread northwards from Herefordshire and Shropshire into Cheshire, but ultimately concen-

[1] Huntington (263a2), Mollington Banastre in Wirral (264b2), Caldecote (266bi), but this last was none the less rendering 2s.; Wheelock, Tetton (267a2), Lach Dennis, Ollerton (267b2).
[2] Edge (264a2), Crewe by Farndon (264bi), Great Mollington in Wirral (264b2), Carden (265ai), Bowden (266bi), Congleton, Wimboldsley (266b2), Wincham, Kinderton (267ai). Goostrey and Marton (266bi) are said 'always' to have been waste.

THE MARCH COUNTIES: CHESHIRE

trated in Staffordshire. Accordingly some of the damage in the manors said to be waste or 'found waste' after the Conquest might have been caused by English rebels or their Welsh allies. Certainly there had been much destruction in the neighbourhood of the roads joining Chester with Malpas and Whitchurch (**6a**), and near the road leading from North Watling Street (**70a**) through the salt-towns to Staffordshire. Equally, however, this could be attributable to royal forces moving south-east after the march from York to Chester in the winter of 1069–70. Along the line of North Watling Street (**7a**), the probable route of this march, no holding about which we have information escaped damage.[1]

To punish the rebels, and to ensure that Mercia should not again revolt, the shire was harried unmercifully. For only 175 holdings are we given information for the intermediate period, 153 of which are said to have been waste or were found waste. Here again we should perhaps add four which had been waste in 1066, and 21 which were waste in 1086 for which we have no earlier information. Where we have comparable figures, what in 1066 had been valued at £179 12s. 10d. was later worth only £24 8s., a fall of 86 per cent.

The holdings for which values are given are all in the extreme west of the shire, and largely in the Wirral peninsula. Rather surprisingly, five manors had appreciated in value by 1071, and three had the same value as in 1066.[2]

Much of the eastern half of the shire was so thoroughly devastated that it had made no recovery when the Domesday Inquest was held sixteen years later. More than thirty manors here were still waste then. But this must have been at least partially because the Pennines and their westward slope formed a thoroughly unrewarding countryside. The inhabitants may never have seen really formidable bodies of Norman armed troops, but economic decline to the westward might have encouraged them to leave their infertile plots and, perhaps on their lords' instructions, take the places of those who had perished or fled since King William's coming.

For the moment of the Inquest we have values for 239 holdings, while 65 are recorded as waste, and three are 'in the Forest'. For five holdings said to be waste, small values, of one or two shillings, are given also.[3]

---

[1] A map of post-Conquest 'waste' suggests that King William moved south-west from York by way of Huddersfield and Manchester (**712**), not by the more southerly route passing near Sheffield and Buxton (**710**).
[2] Mollington Banastre (264b2) had been waste T.R.E.; the others are Heswall (264b2), Ledsham (265a2), Raby (266ai), and Saughall (265a2). No change is recorded for Great Neston or Capenhurst (266ai) and for Poulton by Pulford (265ai).
[3] Little Edge (264bi), Butley (264b2), Nether Peover (266ai), Butley (267b2), Odd Rode (268ai). It is possible that the Butley entries refer to the same holding.

Of those waste earlier, 109 had now some value. What, about 1070/1, had been worth £24 8s. was now valued at £125 12s. 10d., of which holdings for which an earlier value is given contributed £41 14s. 4d. But for 1086 against 1066 there was a fall in value of 34½ per cent, from £264 8s. 9d. to £173 2s. If the ploughland figures represent capacity, there were teams for less than half of them (451⅞ teams for 930½ ploughlands). At least 122 ploughlands were waste in 1086.

Some areas, e.g. the Pennines, the Knutsford, Northwich and Nantwich districts, show a decline far more than the average fall in value. The renders from the wiches (268ai,2) show how grievously these had been affected, and devastation of the industrial areas may have been deliberate policy. Nantwich had rendered £21 *de firma*, which included the pleas of the Hundred, but when Earl Hugh received it only one salt-house survived; the rest was waste, and in 1086 was farmed for only £10. Middlewich had been farmed for £8 and the Hundred (? pleas) worth 40s. The latter value was still extant in 1086, but the farm was only 25s. and two cartloads of salt. Northwich had been farmed for the same sum, but at the Inquest was worth only 35s. Waste in the northern wiches is also mentioned in the entries for Weaverham (263bi), Hartford and Wincham (267ai), and Tatton (267a2) entries—all near Northwich and the road from Manchester to Chester, and for five holdings just south of Middlewich (264ai). Without salt for preserving the winter meat, the life of the peasantry became increasingly insecure.

The waste holdings were mostly in the eastern half of the county, where the soil is least fertile and there was an absence of towns to stimulate commerce. Over a large area here more than half the manors were waste. It may well be that from some of these the inhabitants had been transferred to manors in the plain. Only three *hospites* are recorded for Cheshire (Hampton, 264a2), and they 'had nothing'. But there may well have been more colonists and settlers than these. Some 'waste' manors had woodland, one meadow, and one pasture producing 3s. Equally, though Macclesfield Forest is not mentioned, some of the more easterly holdings in the neighbourhood may have been 'put in the Forest', as were some in Delamere.[1] Some few, though said to be waste, are none the less given values. No waste holding is said to contain inhabitants or teams.

But there had been appreciable recovery since King William's devastation, notably around Chester and in the Wirral, and, it seems, where the the castle at Halton offered protection. Here Halton, Weston-on-Mersey, and Aston by Sutton (266a2) had more than doubled their 1066 value.

[1] Part of Weaverham and Conewardsley (263bi), *Aldredelie* and *Done* (263b2), and the Kingsley woodland (267b2).

There is no obvious indication that increases might have been due to enlargement of a manor, and the only really spectacular rise in value is at Eccleston (267ai), from ten to fifty shillings.

Many of the valuations obviously represent the rents actually paid. Carden (265ai), which had been waste both in 1066 and after the Conquest, was *ad firmam* for £3, and of several manors it is said, *reddit de firma*.[1] A few entries have *reddit* and not *valet*.

What is marked is the frequency with which the *ora* enters into the sums. A number of the instances come from the entries in which a *firma* is mentioned; they recur both T.R.E. and T.R.W. We find what seem to be instances of a single *ora* (Cuddington, 264bi), and of 3, $5\frac{1}{2}$, 7, 8, 9, 13, and 14 *orae*.[2] The very large number of examples of multiples of the *ora* which result in whole shillings is extremely marked; over 30 at both 4s. and 8s., 14 at 12s., and 16 at 16s. The *ora* is of Scandinavian origin, and the Scandinavian influence is markedly apparent in the shire.[3]

Ploughlands are recorded in 307 entries. Duodecimal figures are not particularly frequent, occurring in only about 28 per cent of the instances for three and over, and in about 8 per cent for six and more. Many of the quantities are very small indeed. An excess of teams over ploughlands occurs only at Ness (265a2; 3 teams for 2 ploughlands) and at Fulk Stapleford (267a2; 4 for 3).

About much of the land now part of Wales we are told very little, except where this formed parts of the Domesday Hundreds of *Atiscros*, *Dudestan*, and *Exestan*, east of Offa's and Wat's Dykes, where we have details similar to those given for the rest of the shire. There the manors in Broxton Hundred now in Wales were all waste after the Conquest, and in 1086 worth very much less than they had been in 1066.[4] The deficiency in teams was over 40 per cent, but from the fact that a 'new mill' is mentioned at Worthenbury and a saltpan of 24s. at *Burwardestone*, there must have been appreciable recovery.

For *Exestan* and the hidated portion of *Atiscros* there are 29 entries, and

---

[1] Manley (263bi), Neston and Raby (263a2), Guilden Sutton (264b2), Oulton Lowe (267b2). It has been pointed out (*Dom. Geog.*, iv, p. 351) that no resources other than ploughlands are recorded for places said to be 'at farm' except Guilden Sutton. Were these really components of manors described in full elsewhere?

[2] e.g. Wybunbury (263ai), Worleston (265b2), Hatton in Waverton (267bi), Broxton 264bi), Norton (266ai), Neston (263a2), Bartington (267b2). Eight *orae* made the 'mark' of 10s. 8d.

[3] The 1066 value of Malpas (264a2), £11 4s., represents 168 *orae*, but this may be mere coincidence. The *ora* is mentioned by name only at Chester (262bi) and Worthenbury (264a2).

[4] Bettisfield (86 per cent down), *Burwardestone* (? Iscoyd, 57 per cent down), Worthenbury (264a2). A straight comparison of values is here not possible.

probably the total number of holdings was not under 40. For 1066 waste is mentioned in only three entries, and a value in only two; in 1086 only two are said to be waste. In the intermediate period waste is recorded nine times, but since values are only twice given, there was probably a good deal more in a wasted condition both then and before the Conquest. The total value in 1086 was only £17 2s., which would make the local ploughland worth as little as 8s. But the deficiency of teams is only about one-third, and it may be that exploitation of the land immediately west of the Dee had been general.

The unhidated portion of *Atiscros* (269a2) included at least thirteen vills. The whole had been waste in 1066 and when Earl Hugh received it. In 1086 there were only 6¾ teams on 7 ploughlands, and the total value is given as no more than 66s.[1]

The number of places, including the borough of Rhuddlan, mentioned for the district of Englefield (269ai,2) is 62, six of which are twice named. All had been waste in Earl Edwine's time and when Earl Hugh received this area. We are not given individual values for many of the berewicks attached to the manors of Bryn and Rhuddlan. The values of Earl Hugh's share add up to £8 10s., but are also given in the text as £2 less. Robert of Rhuddlan's portion was worth £17 3s., which would make the average ploughland worth about 18s. Moreover, there is a team deficiency of only ¾ team on 29 recorded ploughlands. Teams on Earl Hugh's land are largely credited to his villeins, who seem to have possessed about 2¼ oxen apiece.

The only slight deficiency of teams west of the Dee is surprising. It is well below the average in east Denbighshire and south Flintshire, and only about 7½ per cent in north-east Flintshire. Thus it would appear, if the vills had really been completely deserted, that over 500 plough-oxen had somehow been acquired in fifteen years for the district. Had some of them been transferred from other manors, especially those manors which had been allowed to become waste or to remain so? It argues a formidable movement towards colonisation, and while many of the teams are said to be demesne ones, here and there villeins possessed two or three oxen apiece.[2] But 'waste' may here again not imply 'deserted', but rather that early in the Conqueror's reign the land was not in English or Norman hands. Perhaps the wasted condition of east and mid-Cheshire had made it essential to exploit to the full the territory newly in Norman occupation

---

[1] The seven teams which King Gruffydd had had at Bistre may no longer have been there. In the manor, together with four other holdings, there were in 1086 only two teams. Gruffydd had forfeited *Atiscros* by his rebellion of 1063, and land now in Wales had been returned to the bishop of Chester and his men.

[2] Formulae such as '... land enough for one team. It is there with 4 villeins and 8 bordars' (Mostyn, 269a2) probably imply a demesne team.

in compensation for unprofitable holdings in the ravaged districts. Alternatively, the 'ploughlands' may represent a basis for potential assessment, which would make comparison with the teams valueless.

The woodland of the manor of Bistre had been included in the earl's Forest; the districts known as Rhos and Rhufoniog, in north Denbighshire, consisted, save for 20 ploughlands, of woodland and moorland, and could not be ploughed. Much former Welsh land can have been of small profit, save for the products of the woodland and the chase. But Robert of Rhuddlan was paying the king a *firma* of £40 for 'the land called North Wales', and presumably hoped to make a profit from it, and a borough had been newly established at Rhuddlan.

From the comparatively few appropriate entries, the minor tenants and the peasantry do not in 1086 seem to have been less well-endowed than these were elsewhere. A *miles* had a whole team (Hartford, 267ai), eight *francigenae* six teams between them, seven priests $4\frac{1}{2}$, and a thegn half a team (Mobberley, 266b2). In 23 instances of villeins' teams 75 had $27\frac{1}{4}$, which would give them almost three oxen apiece. In several entries villeins are recorded as possessing an entire team.[1] There are few occasions in which the teams of bordars can be determined, but in the twenty where they can the bordars had almost two oxen each. At Larkton (264bi) one was able to pay a rent of 2s. The radmen, as we might expect, had rather more oxen than the villeins: they average five apiece. But their pre-Conquest lords seem mostly to have disappeared.

Earls Edwine and Morkere seem to have been allowed to retain their estates after the Conquest. Gherbod, a Fleming, must have been appointed earl of the county before their revolt in 1071, for he was at the battle of Cassel in February of that year, and did not return to England. The king then gave Hugh of Avranches the earldom. Possibly Gherbod's appointment, perhaps after the harrying of the shire in 1070, had been a factor in inspiring Edwine and Morkere to defect. The bestowal of the earldom on Hugh of Avranches, and his apportionment of it between his men, must have been accepted by these on the score of future potential exploitation rather than contemporary worth. The four manors allotted to Hugh fitz-Norman (266bi) were all waste in 1071 (and were still waste in 1086, though Butley was producing 5s.), so were the eight holdings of Hamo de Maci (266bi). Of Bigot de Loges's fourteen properties (266b2), only two are not said to have been waste. Gilbert de Venables received only six manors out of twenty which had not been waste, though as a forester he

[1] e.g. Peckforton (264b2), Shipbrook (265ai), Hatton (267bi). If holdings where villeins seem to have had no oxen are included, the figure falls to $1\frac{3}{4}$. The same principle would reduce bordars to an average of half an ox each.

would acquire also other sources of revenue. Robert of Rhuddlan, Earl Hugh's cousin, who had been attached to the Confessor's court, probably vividly appreciated the potentialities, including those of conquest and exploitation of lands beyond the Dee.

In the hidated part of the shire there were just over 400 properties to dispose of, a few of which were berewicks which should go with the manors of which they were part. Over fifty ceased to remain independent manors, holdings in 45 vills being combined and in each case being given to a single owner. All but about thirty properties had been in lay hands in 1066. Earl Hugh did not, for the most part, distribute the remainder to his barons on a basis of previous ownership. This would in any case have been difficult to organise, for nearly 70 per cent of the holders had possessed a single manor or only a couple of manors.

There had been, in 1066, a minimum of 108 named landholders and 21 more who are anonymous and might include some of the 108. Earls Edwine and Morkere excepted, none compares in status or wealth with the great men to be found in the south and the midlands. A common name may not represent the individual, and thus some of those who would seem to have possessed a dozen or more may really have been less influential than they might appear to have been. For example, a Wulfric retained Butley and Ollerton (267b2). But probably two Wulfrics are represented, for the holdings are both in Macclesfield (*Hamestan*) Hundred, but are not consecutively entered in DB, as those of Gamel are. Equally two holdings in the south of the shire and one in the Wirral may not have belonged to a single Edric, though it does seem possible that some men, though owning property in the east of the county, had acquired holdings in what is now Wales. A Wulfheah had four properties, three of which were in the Delamere Forest area, and a further holding at Broughton near Hawarden (263bi, 265a2, 265b2, 266b2, 268b2). No pre-Conquest figure is styled 'forester', nor is land said to have been 'in the Forest'. But it is noticeable that the *venatores* of 1086 naturally obtained property in the neighbourhood of the post-Conquest Forests, and thus the 1066 owners, e.g. Dodo (267ai), may have been concerned with the Forest land.

Even if we assume that individuals are concerned, the scattered estates of no native were large. Only about 16 or 17 hides appear against the names Dot and Godwine and Leofnoth, less than 7 for Godric; the largest agglomeration was Thoret's, $27\frac{1}{2}$ hides. He may have been sheriff of the county. A few men had single highly-rated manors; Orme at Halton (266a2) had ten hides, and Lyfing at Saughall (265a2) six. But these had been worth only £2 and £1 respectively. Since so many entries give no figure for 1066, we cannot estimate relative wealth. Possibly it is significant that in the text so few men are styled 'thegns' in 1066. The only occurrence of the term is at Caldecote (266bi), where Wulfgar the priest had held 'with three other thegns who were free', and at Bickerton (264bi), where there were 'three thegns who were free men'. The others are all said to be *liberi homines* or to have held freely. While thegn and free man could be equatable, so that the predominance of the latter in Cheshire might be an accidental of the clerks, the size of the individual holding suggests that here few men can have had much local influence. Thegnland makes a solitary appearance under Chester (266b2).

Only seven men with English or Danish names held manors in 1086, assessed at just over eight hides. Fifteen further properties of about 18 hides were held as tenants of the earl's barons by the men who had held them in 1066, though the occasional absence of information about sub-tenancies might, if supplied, have added a few more. Only two persons, Edward and Edwine, occur more than once. Four more were in the hands of men who had not held them in King Edward's day, though they may have succeeded relatives. Thus the bulk of the pre-Conquest landholders seem to have disappeared by 1086. Some, no doubt, died or were dispossessed after the Mercian revolt; others may have gone overseas or joined the Conqueror's forces.

5
The North Midlands

One of the leading characteristics of this section of England, though by no means confined to it, is mention, usually by name, of numerous berewicks and extensive sokelands forming portions of manors often dispersed over a wide area. Unfortunately we are rarely given information, or clear information, about their contents. Thus we can often have no idea of how plough-teams and inhabitants should be allotted to the different components. Some may have been devoid of either. In some the value may have fallen steeply, and indeed some may well have been waste, or almost so. But we must not blame the witnesses and clerks for the unsatisfactory text overmuch. In an area much of which had been deliberately ravaged, and in which some settlements had probably ceased to exist, it may have been hard to obtain any but the most generalised statements.

Again the relationship between plough-teams and the amount of land for which teams existed is frequently so eccentric that we can only assume that some artificial conception, connected perhaps with earlier assessments, lies behind the often mysterious figures. The social or economic categories of the inhabitants are equally puzzling. The Derbyshire text mentions few sokemen, that for Nottinghamshire very many, and neither records many free men. Yet in Lincolnshire, which is adjacent, while free men are unrecorded, sokemen form half of the population. Here, too, no slaves are mentioned, and they are so few in Derbyshire and Nottinghamshire that we can feel sure that they were often omitted. It is hard to imagine how the demesnes, or the extractive industries, could have been worked without some slave element.

Staffordshire

The Staffordshire text fills the Domesday student with a sense of frustration. About 30 entries describe manors 'with their appendages', and in comparatively few instances are we told where these components lay. This makes mapping unsatisfactory, and prevents determination of how many settlements there may have been in 1066 or 1086. It is not easy, too, to determine how to treat the county. Three entries in the Northamptonshire Domesday and three in that for Warwickshire were certainly part of the Staffordshire of 1086.[1] A few places mentioned in the Staffordshire text are now in Shropshire or Worcestershire. Cubbington (248ai) must have been in Domesday Warwickshire, and Sibford Gower and Drayton (250a2) in Oxfordshire; these have been omitted from the figures which follow. Dudley (177a2), a detached portion of Worcestershire, was included in that county's statistics.

Secondly, for a large number of manors we have the values for 1086 only. For less than a hundred are we given the value in 1066, and for only three a value for a date between 1066 and 1086. Over 90 per cent of the values in 1066, moreover, come from six fiefs only. The ploughland and plough-team figures, too, present difficulties.

This would give us a total of 377 holdings, some covering more than one place, to which should be added the numerous unnamed members of manors and those properties distinct in 1066 but amalgamated to form a manor of 1086.[2] We are here told little of vills held for two or more manors, but frequently of manors held by two or more persons, e.g. Wulfgeat and six thegns (Ellestone, 249a2) or five Englishmen (Maresyn Ridware, 248a2). We can, then, make no estimate of the number of holdings in 1066, and reckon how many were affected subsequently.

We are not, as a rule, given the values of the individual components of manors. The result is that even for 1086 we have values in only 302 entries, including those partly waste, and 66 wholly waste. Only three figures for *post* gives no scope for comparison with 1066 or 1086; the manors concerned declined from £8 10s. to £2 10s. and recovered by 1086 to £5 17s. 2d.[3]

But only 89 entries enable us to compare the valuations of 1066 and of 1086, and we can hardly use even all of these. The 24 manors of William fitzAnsculf have all the same value ascribed to them for both 1066 and

---

[1] Lapley, Marston (222b2), West Bromwich (226a2); Essington and Bushbury (243ai—an entry repeated in the Staffordshire text on fol. 250ai), Chillington (243a2).

[2] In this total have been included entries titled 'in the city (borough, vill) of Stafford' (247bi,2; 248b2) and the castle of Tutbury (248ai).

[3] Wetmoor, Stretton, and Darlaston (247bi). Such as they are, they confirm those of other wasted counties.

1086, which, in view of the deficiency of plough-teams upon them, seems unlikely to be accurate. *Terra Regis* accounts for 27, which had improved in value from £111 19s. to £151 19s., but includes Cannock (246bi) with its appendages, said to have rendered nothing in King Edward's day, but £20 in 1086. This rather suggests that it might have been Forest land in 1066; it had in 1086 only three teams for fifteen ploughlands. This leaves us only 38 holdings, which together had fallen in value by about 5 per cent. We can conceive of a handsome rise in the receipts from royal manors, though none shows a really large increase, for some may have been let to farm at inflated prices and increased rents demanded.[1] Even so, out of 73 entries and sub-entries 32 royal holdings are said to be waste, and four more partly waste. This ravaged county must have been worth much less in 1086 than in 1066, but how much less it is impossible to determine.

Some of the increases in manorial values may reflect the deliberate abandonment of unprofitable settlements and the transference of their equipment to manors more favourably situated. This might account for the value of Rocester (246bi) becoming doubled, or the increase at manors on the fringe of a wasted district, e.g. Leek (246bi) or Ellastone (247ai). Claverley (248ai), which appreciated from £7 10s. to £10, might have profited from movement of people and stock caused by extension of the Forest land about Wombourne and Kinver.[2] Probably something besides possible increased rents caused the value of five small holdings of the Wolverhampton clergy to rise from 9s. to £2 15s.[3] The value of Wigginton (246a2) might have gone up from 30s. to 80s. because of the proximity of the borough of Tamworth and its requirements.

At least 70 holdings were waste or partly waste in 1086. Eleven components of the bishop of Chester's manor of Eccleshall (247ai) and six of his manor of Lichfield (247a2) are said to be waste. Loxley (248a2) alone is said to have been waste before 1086 (*fuit et est*), but probably many others were also. Some of these properties were 'waste' because of inclusion in the Forest, e.g. Ashwood near Kinver (247b2) and Chaspel or Chasepool (249b2). From their situation, certain other manors might also have been 'waste' because they were in the Forest, though DB does not say so. Twice it tells us that the woodland of a manor was in the king's

---

[1] If, where there were appendages, we are given the 1066 value for the *caput*, but that for 1086 for a manor to which properties had lately been added, the rise, if any, is incalculable. It has been pointed out (*VCH*, v, p. 16) that 'the values for King Edward's time must obviously not be taken literally. The jurors' memories cannot have been clear concerning the exact situation twenty years before.'
[2] On the other hand, Claverley had only 28 teams for 32 ploughlands.
[3] Hatherton, Kinvaston, Hilton, Penkridge, and Gnosall (247b2).

Forest (Enville and *Cippemore*, 249b2), but no diminution of value on these holdings of William fitzAnsculf is noted. Possibly fourteen holdings for which we are given ploughlands but no teams or inhabitants were also waste.

Thus the degree to which Staffordshire had suffered since the Conquest is indeterminable. The map suggests that the recorded waste was due to three causes: (i) the movement of royal troops to Stafford from Cheshire, and perhaps the later stages of the Mercian revolt, (ii) the desertion of the hills and mosses in the north-west of the county in favour of less marginal land, and (iii) inclusion in the Forest (Figs. 21–3).

The ploughlands in this shire may well bear little or no relation to arable capacity, and may represent an earlier basis of assessment than that of the hides. If so, it would seem that something over 1,300 'ploughlands' had been converted to about 500 hides. For the majority of entries the quantity of ploughlands is from one to six, and a duodecimal basis would seem to have been employed, for there are a number of instances of 8, 12, 16, or 32.[1] Moreover, teams in excess of 'ploughlands' appear in 42 entries, and the disparity is often so great that it hardly seems probable that the cause had invariably been the transference of men and oxen from deserted holdings, though this may have occurred in some instances. Clifton Campville (246b2) had only four 'ploughlands', but thirteen teams are recorded, while Rolleston (248bi) had eighteen teams for eight 'ploughlands', and here it was reported that the arable was two leagues long by one broad.

But occasionally we do get statements about agricultural potentiality. Burton (248bi) is said to possess four teams, all its lord's, though in King Edward's day there had been twelve. The entry for Weston under Lizard and three other places (250bi) says that there had been land for six teams; in 1086 five more were at work, but there had been eleven when King Edward was alive.[2] Of Wolverhampton (247b2) it is said that while there is land for three teams only, there were eight working in 1066, and nineteen at the time of the Inquest. The figures suggest a low assessment in favour of the Church. Land is occasionally described in terms of the 'carucate of land'.[3] There was 'land for three teams' in demesne at Bishop's Offley (247ai), and it is noted of Syerscote (249a2), where there were $2\frac{1}{2}$ teams, that 'there could be a team'. The 'ploughlands' are not given; perhaps there were 3 or $3\frac{1}{2}$. Six times an alternative quantity for the 'ploughlands' is interlined, always for land which was waste (246b2). Had

[1] e.g. Norbury (248ai), Shenstone (248bi), Kinver (246bi), Claverley (248ai). They form nearly 20 per cent of the total, and those of 3 or 4 bring the figure up to nearly 50 per cent.
[2] The 'land for six teams' might really represent an older assessment. There had here been nine manors, held by nine thegns.
[3] e.g. at Bescot (246a2), Cheadle and the next two entries (246b2), Maresyn Ridware (248a2).

an older assessment been forgotten, or did it seem that the arable could be increased if the vills were re-populated?

We should, even with the small amount of information available, expect Staffordshire to furnish some information about actual rents and the *firma* of manors, but this last we do not find. The only values of interest are those which seem to be based on the *ora*: four at 16s., one at 12s., four at 8s., one each at 6s., 5s. 4d., and 3s., and a brace at 2s.[1] We are told that a certain Eddulf was holding Okeover with its appendages from Burton Abbey *ad censum* (247bi), but of the abbey's *censarii* of a later date we hear nothing.

Between thirty and forty Englishmen or Anglo-Danes were still holding land, though as tenants, in 1086. None appears frequently, but some of their estates were quite substantial ones. Five were in 1086 worth more than £1, and three holdings at Madeley Holme (249a2) were together valued at £4. At Maresyn Ridware (248a2) five *Angli* held 2½ 'carucates of land', twice the holding of a well-to-do villein. Only two men, Wulfgeat and Godric, appear more than once, or seem to have been holding in 1066 also, but some of the holdings are credited merely to *Angli* or to a *liber homo* (248a2,bi; 249a2,bi). Much of the land is ascribed for 1066 to Earl Ælfgar or to his mother, and so the extent of either of Ælfgar's sons' holdings cannot be determined. Many of Ælfgar's manors became part of *Terra Regis*. Earl Harold had a solitary manor (King's Bromley, 246a2).

Few entries, except where villeins are concerned, yield suggestions as to individual ownership of oxen. Six free men possessed 4½ teams on four holdings, one priest had a whole team and another a pair of oxen, a *miles* at Stretton had a full team, and three *Angli* five teams. Only five entries give us the teams of bordars; sixteen had six teams, or an average of three oxen apiece. At Fauld (248bi) two are said to have held a hide, but this does not seem very probable. In 26 entries 124 villeins had 38½ teams. This would give an average of about 2½ oxen apiece, but this, as we might expect in a still impoverished county, is less than we find further west and north. The apparent superiority of the average for bordars is probably the result of insufficient figures. In Staffordshire plenty of bordars, and villeins also, are not recorded as possessing any oxen.[2] There were manors with teams but apparently without a peasantry (e.g. Kingsley, 250bi).

[1] 10s. 9d. (Hixon) might be a mistake for 10s. 8d. There is one sum of 13s. 4d. (Fradwell), and one of 3s. 4d. (Wolseley). These occur together on fol. 247ai, and the holdings all belonged to Great Haywood.
[2] e.g. eight bordars at *Monetville* (249bi) or six at Fauld (248bi). At Talke (250b2) four villeins had none, while at Great Barr (250ai), which was teamless, there was 'nothing in demesne, but only one villein with one bordar'. Here the three hides were worth only 5s.

The inevitable impression is that we have nothing like the full story of post-Conquest Staffordshire. It seems always to have been one of the less prosperous shires, and probably suffered more during and after the Mercian revolt than is disclosed by the Domesday text.[1] It was to a limited extent recovering by 1086, and it still contained a fairly strong native element above the peasant level, but it was none the less a poor county.

Derbyshire

All the counties of the North Midlands furnish a problem encountered elsewhere also, that presented by large complex manors about the components of which we are given singularly little information. The Derbyshire text deals with a little over 500 holdings, including 78 properties which had been manors in 1066, but by the time of the Inquest had been absorbed into other manors. Probably this figure should be higher, for, among several similar instances, Risley (278a2) is not said to have counted as two manors, though Wulfsige and Godric had each possessed half. It is impossible to give an exact number of holdings, for there are a number of apparently parallel entries, e.g. for part of Breaston (276b2, 277b2). Moreover, a number of entries cover two or more places, e.g. Shottle and Wallstone (274ai), while though in 1066 there had been seven landholders in Shirley (274b2), it had apparently counted for only five manors.

It is the royal manors which yield least information. For six of these no components are mentioned, but the other seventeen had over one hundred berewicks and parcels of sokeland attached to them. Very rarely are we told anything about the value or teams of the constituents, and for eight manors we are not even given information for the values of the *caput* of each, but only totals for one group of five and another of three.

It was not only the royal manors which were complex ones. Bupton (273a2) had *appenditii*, but they are not named, nor is it stated how many they were. Scropton (274bi) had three berewicks, but these too remained anonymous.[2] For over fifty non-royal holdings we have virtually no information except the name of the place concerned. It is accordingly impossible adequately to present the information in the form of maps, since so often we do not know which holdings had fallen in value, or how much, or which were teamless. Fortunately many royal manors were situated in the districts which include the Pennines, the Peak area, and the moorlands. Here a general decline in values, or the abandonment of unrewarding settlements, is to be expected.

[1] Some statistics regarding the values of vills in 1086 are given in *VCH*, v, p. 12.
[2] Two of these might have been Sudbury (274bi) and Hatton (274b2), where sokeland and thegnland 'belonged to Scropton'.

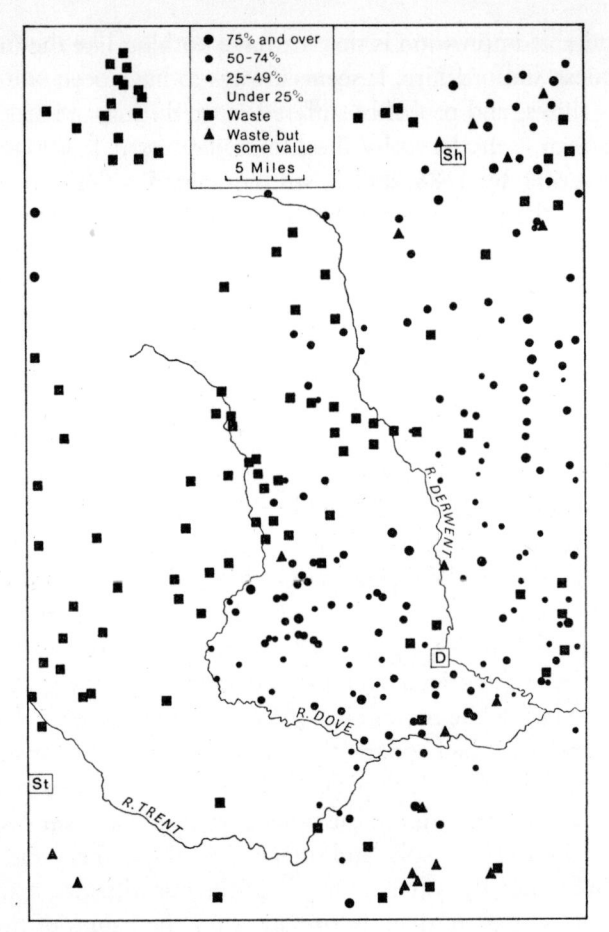

Fig. 23 The North Midlands: western section
Fall in value 1066-86
D—Derby Sh—Sheffield St—Stafford

Derbyshire, devastated on the king's order for its share in the northern risings, was far poorer in 1086 than in 1066. Where values can be compared, omitting the royal estates, land worth £474 1s. in King Edward's day was valued at only £307 4s. at the time of the Inquest, a fall of 35½ per cent. Ballidon (277a2) declined to 12s. 6d. from £3, and several manors in the highlands were in 1086 worth only half what they had been in 1086.[1] But the decline over the whole area is very little above the county average.

Some falls in the north-east are equally outstanding. Dore and Norton (278a2), each valued at £1 in 1066, were worth only 5s. 4d. and 1s. 6d. respectively in 1086. Duckmanton (277ai) declined from £4 to 19s., and

[1] e.g. Hathersage (277a2), Brassington, Tissington (274ai), Edensor (276ai), Youlgreave (275bi).

both Ashover and Newton (277ai) from £4 to 30s. The southern half of the county can show similar figures. Denby (277bi) fell from £5 to £1, Egginton (276b2) from £8 to £3, Snelston (275ai) from £8 to £2, Repton (272b2) from £15 to £8, and Mickleover (273a2) from £25 to £10. Repton was, and Mickleover had been, royal.

Terra Regis, despite the royal manors which appreciated in value, shows a small decline against the 1066 figures, but one of only about $5\frac{1}{2}$ per cent. The combined manors of Bakewell, Ashford, and Hope (272b2) dropped in worth from £30 to £10 6s., and there was much waste land among royal property.

The only fief which shows appreciation is that of Walter d'Aincourt (276bi), and its rise from £12 15s. 4d. to £19 5s. 4d. is due to that in the two manors of Elmton and Stoney Houghton, which together increased in value by 300 per cent. These are close to the Nottinghamshire border and may have escaped the worst of the shire's troubles.[1]

The decline in value can hardly be altogether attributed to the harrying of the north. It is highly improbable that a punitive force visited the thirteen properties in Longdendale (273ai) and so utterly destroyed the district that what had been worth £2 became utterly valueless, save for the woodland which was of service only for the chase. It is far more likely that the inhabitants migrated, voluntarily or under compulsion by a royal reeve, to land less bleak than the moorland. This, too, probably happened in many a manor in or near Peak Forest. The five royal manors with their berewicks, Darley, Matlock, Wirksworth, Ashbourne, and Parwich, paid £40 of pure silver in 1086 against £32 earlier. The value of Darley rose from £2 to £4; that of Wirksworth is not given. The other three are said to be waste or partially so, and Ashbourne was liable for a payment of £1 only.

If there was migration of peasants and peasant-farmers with their teams, we might expect a number of the lowland manors to display increases in value caused in part by transference to them of peasants and oxen from less rewarding settlements. But less than a score do so. Again the general decline need not be attributed to the ravaging of 1069/70. When the Conqueror's march from Warwick to Nottingham was accompanied by the foundation of castles at both, it is unlikely that he altogether neglected the Derbyshire lands which lie each side of the Trent and close to Nottingham. The district may, in addition, have suffered severely as north Leicestershire seems to have suffered as a result of the revolt of the northern earls. There was in 1086 a good deal of waste in Domesday Derbyshire south of

---

[1] In contrast, Geoffrey de Alselin's fief, the manors in which lay no great distance from Derby, fell in value by over 40 per cent. Perhaps his principal *antecessor*, 'Tochi', had in the king's eyes merited punishment.

Trent, especially in those manors now in Leicestershire. There were also heavy falls in value here. Melbourne (272bi) was worth only £6 in 1086, but had to find £10, its value in 1066. The Hartshorn manors (274a2) fell in value from £6 to £1, and both were partly waste. Derby (280a2), too, with fewer mills than previously, rendered £30 with the vill of Litchurch against £24 in King Edward's day, though 103 *mansiones* which then paid rent were waste in 1086.

In 1086 at least 51 holdings were waste and 15 perhaps partially waste, since these latter are said to have some value, though usually only a small one. The highest figure is that for Willesley (274a2; now in Leicestershire), 16s., where there were three villeins with five oxen, but most are valued at from two to thirty-six pence only. But these quantities cannot represent the complete tale of waste. The royal manor of Matlock Bridge (272a2) is said to be waste. Six berewicks belonged to it, and since the whole manor had only six teams and a recorded population of 23, more than one settlement was surely waste. The same applies to complex royal manors such as Ashbourne and Parwich (272bi). Ashbourne, with six berewicks, could render £1 though said to be waste, and 28 villeins and bordars had 1½ teams. A holding at Barrow upon Trent (275bi) is said to be waste, but none the less was worth 2s., and the villein there had half a team. 'Waste', it seems, is a relative term.

In addition to the entries in which waste is mentioned, there are some holdings which were apparently without inhabitants or beasts of the plough. How many these might have been, or whether they too were waste or partly waste, cannot be determined. Where they are components of a manor, it is probable that any inhabitants or oxen would be included in the figures for the *caput manerii*. In some instances, statistics were probably inadvertently omitted. Hathersage (277a2) was still worth as much as 30s., half its former value; Aston on Trent (275b2) had risen in value from 6s. to 8s. But manors such as Atlow (274a2), which had declined from 20s. to 2s., or Norton (278a2), worth only eighteenpence, 7½ per cent of its former value, may well have been at least partly waste.

Values in terms of the *ora* are less frequent than might be expected. There are only ten for 1066, though in many manors units of 16d. may have entered into sums given in round figures. There are only seventeen instances in all in 1086 of 16s., 12s., 10s. 8d., 8s., 6s. 8d., 5s. 4d., 4s., 2s. 8d. But Beighton (278a2) was valued at 32s., Codnor, etc. (276a2) at 41s. 4d., and Risley (278a2) at 22s. 8d., which sums probably had an *ora*-basis. So may the frequent instances of £1, £2, £4, £8, £16; they number 68, and there are no fewer than 35 instances of £1 or 15 *orae*. At Weston upon Trent (273ai) four *censarii* or rent-payers were contributing 16s. At Trusley (274b2) five paid 5s., as did two sokemen; at Egginton (276b2) six rendered 14s. 4d., and at Ockbrook (276b2) four rendered 14s.[1] Unfortunately we are not told of the rent paid by *censarii* on the three other occasions in which they occur. On the two occasions on which we are told of a villein's rent, it is two *orae* at Osmaston by Derby (275b2), 1s. at Normanton by Derby (275b2), while an Ashbourne man (*homo*; 272bi) rendered 1s. 4d. It is significant that at Risley (278a2,b2) the value of one of two holdings rose from sixteen to seventeen *orae*, while that of another was half the eight *orae* it had been in 1066. The *ora* must have formed the basis of many Derbyshire valuations and rents.

Villeins form so high a proportion of the peasantry (over 60 per cent), and sokemen are relatively so few (about $4\frac{1}{4}$ per cent), that many a Domesday villein may be a former sokeman or even a thegn.[2] The devastation of the land may have sent many a man lower down the social scale. It is perhaps partly on account of local devastation that Derbyshire villeins do not seem to have possessed a substantial number of oxen. In 41 entries 211 villeins had $61\frac{1}{8}$ teams, or only 2·3 oxen per head. The only two relevant entries give nine bordars twenty oxen, which gives a figure probably purely accidental. Thirty-nine sokemen in four manors had $19\frac{1}{2}$ teams, or half a team a head. The solitary *censarius* at Palterton or one of its berewicks (277ai) and at Swadlincote (278ai) each had a team, and eighteen at Duckmanton (277ai) possessed five teams, so that some of these had no more oxen than a villein, and some may have owned none.

The great majority of the entries include the statement that 'there is land for n teams'. But it is most improbable that all such entries are giving us the arable land available. Possibly none does so. We should expect this county, with its heavy decline in value, to possess in 1086 far fewer teams than ploughlands. But where entries give figures for both, we have almost 900 teams for just over 700 ploughlands.

Deficiencies of teams we do indeed find. Ashbourne (272b2) and its berewicks had only nine teams where there was land for 22, and Sutton Scarsdale (273bi) two teams for five ploughlands. A fair number of manors had as many teams as reported ploughlands. But what are we to make of instances such as Fenton with Sturston (275ai), where there is said to be land for six oxen but six villagers' teams in the manor, while its value fell by 50 per cent, or Barton Blount (274bi), where there was land for four teams but ten available?

[1] Eleven *orae* would be 14s. 8d.
[2] The proportions are probably too high, since only 20 slaves are recorded for the whole county. There must have been many more, especially where demesne teams were numerous or lead was mined.

Probably the ploughland is here an artificial conception. In over 50 per cent of the relevant entries the quantity of ploughlands is the same as that of the carucates for geld. It might, indeed, where there is no parity, point to a revision of assessment. It is highly unlikely that an excess of teams over ploughlands implies that the amount of arable had been increased. Nothing in the history of Derbyshire, pre- or post-Conquest, suggests that there would be men and capital to enlarge the arable. Moreover, if an extension of the arable was due to the arrival of the Normans and their anxiety fully to exploit the land, values should surely have risen on the relevant manors, which they have not. Nor can it be said that a large free element in the population, dispersed over small farms worked uneconomically, had resulted in teams unnecessarily numerous. There were manors where teams exceeded 'ploughlands', but no sokemen are recorded.[1]

Some slight suggestion of a possible explanation is furnished by plotting the figures given in DB on a map. The deficiency of teams against 'ploughlands', though general, is particularly marked in the north-west, where we should expect an abandonment of unprofitable settlements. An excess of teams over 'ploughlands' occurs chiefly in the river-valleys, in the north-eastern lowland, and especially where the foothills meet the plain west of Derby. It is not marked in the areas in which we should expect the earlier troubles of the county to have occurred, or around Derby itself.

Nottinghamshire

Complex manors, with little or no information about the resources of their components, are even more frequent in this county than in Derbyshire. Out of 648 entries and sub-entries, to which should be added at least 108 holdings, manors in 1066, but which by 1086 had been amalgamated with other manors, we have comparable values for only 56 per cent of the holdings of the time of the Inquest.[2] Though this point is of minor importance, it is often by no means clear whether a property was a berewick or sokeland of a manor. The twelve berewicks of Southwell (283ai) are not even named. There are, too, obvious omissions from the text. Holdings are said to be sokeland of named manors which are nowhere described, e.g. of Bathley (291b2) or of Colston Bassett (292ai). A Thrumpton estate (291bi) is said to 'lie in Sandiacre', but Sandiacre is a Derbyshire manor.

The royal manors naturally furnish many of the difficulties. A combined

---

[1] For a full discussion of the problem, see *Dom. Geog.*, iv, pp. 291–5.
[2] This includes waste or partially waste land. A few entries record only mills, 'gardens' (*orti*), or meadow.

THE NORTH MIDLANDS: NOTTINGHAMSHIRE

statement covers Dunham (281ai) and its four berewicks, after which come separate statements for seven sokelands. Mansfield (281a2) had thirty-one berewicks and sokelands or other holdings associated with the manor, and in addition, fifteen sokelands in Oswaldbeck Wapentake in the north-east of the shire, roughly twenty miles from the *caput*. Often we know nothing of these components beyond the assessment of the holding.

So far as can be determined from an incomplete text, royal property (281ai–b2) had declined in value. But we are not given values for the enormous manor of Mansfield (281a2), except for portions of its distant sokeland in Oswaldbeck Wapentake, and then only for 1086, or for some of the final entries. Of the nine holdings which permit comparison, only four had appreciated in value, while Thorpe in the Glebe (281bi), though said to be worth 2s., was waste. On balance, almost one-quarter of the 1066 value had been lost.

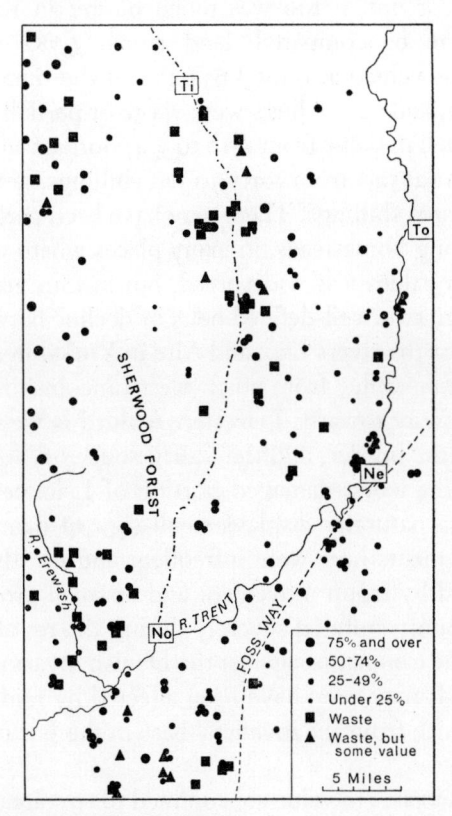

Fig. 24 The North Midlands: eastern section
Fall in value 1066–86
–·–· Possible route of royal force between Nottingham and York
Ne—Newark   No—Nottingham   Ti—Tickhill   To—Torksey

But not all the difficulties arise from the royal manors. Newark (283bi), for example, is described together with two berewicks in a single statement, while its sixteen sokelands are covered in three statements, for a single holding, for eight holdings, and for the remaining seven. Very frequently land in two villages is described in a single entry, e.g. Epperstone and Woodborough (285b2, 289b2). All this makes cartographic representation of the information highly unsatisfactory. The manor of Sutton (283a2) did not change in value between 1066 and 1086. But we cannot be sure that the *caput* or some or all of its berewicks and nine sokelands did not. Fortunately the components of a manor are only infrequently far distant from each other.

Nottinghamshire is in the Evesham Chronicle mentioned as having been one of the counties which did not altogether escape the devastation of 1070. Whether it was ravaged as thoroughly as the shires more prominently mentioned or not, it too was much poorer in 1086 than in 1066. Where values can be compared, land worth £782 15*s.* 8*d.* in King Edward's day was valued at only £634 18*s.* at the time of the Inquest, a fall of 19 per cent, and 72 holdings were waste or partially so. Gringley on the Hill (286b2) fell in value from £10 to £4, Bothamsall (281ai) from £8 to £3, Babworth (285ai) from forty to ten shillings, and Kelham (291ai) from sixteen to three shillings. There may have been partial waste, though perhaps on outlying homesteads, in many places where values fell steeply.

The decline in values was widespread, but in four areas is particularly marked. There are two well-defined belts of decline between Newark and the passages across the rivers Don and Aire in Yorkshire. Another follows the line of the Trent valley from north-west Lincolnshire to Newark, and then along Foss Way towards Leicester. A third is west of Nottingham, near the Derbyshire border, and the fourth south of Nottingham and the Trent, north of the worst-damaged portion of Leicestershire. The Sherwood Forest area naturally displays small sign of damage, except at its fringes, for settlements here were infrequent and mostly poor, so that it would be avoided by troop movement and of small profit to ravagers. It looks as if the county suffered severely during the revolt of the northern earls, and from the campaigns against the Danish invasions and Northumbrian irruptions. It may even have been affected by raids from the king's enemies: an advance from the invaders' base in the Isle of Axholme is not impossible.

By contrast, increases in value are confined to two areas. A few are to be found in the north-east of the county, and the remainder on each side of the Trent between Newark and Nottingham, and to the south-east thereof. In neither area is waste frequent. The picture rather suggests a northern

THE NORTH MIDLANDS: NOTTINGHAMSHIRE

district which largely escaped the consequences of the revolts and invasions, and the influence on local prosperity of the two principal towns in the shire. A Clarborough manor (286b2) appreciated from six to twenty shillings, and the two Granby manors (289ai, 292ai) from £20 to £35. But only about fifty holdings had in 1086 a value higher than in 1066. On a solitary occasion (Gunthorpe, 285b2) the *tailla*, additional to the value, so prominent in Lincolnshire, is mentioned.

In 1086 49 holdings were said to be waste and 23 partially waste; these 72 instances occur in 61 entries, for several times the relevant passages refer to more than one place. Teams are recorded in only three entries where the extent of waste is specified or a few inhabitants noted.[1] Fenton (286bi) was waste 'except for one bordar'; at Willoughby on the Wolds (293ai), partially waste, there were five bordars, but no teams. A Carlton on Trent holding (289a2) was inhabited by two sokemen 'having nothing'; of Owthorpe (289bi) it is said, *nil ibi habetur*; and of Leake (282b2), *nil est ibi*. Normally no inhabitants are recorded on waste or partially waste holdings. An East Bridgford estate (286a2) was uncultivated (*terra non colitur*), but though Broadholme (291bi) is classed as waste, it seems that there may have been villeins there, for their service belonged to Saxilby in Lincolnshire. But they may have lived at Saxilby and paid some due to Broadholme. Only once is a holding said to have been waste earlier, but at what date is not indicated (Ranskill, 283a2).

We are given pre-Inquest values in only a score of the relevant entries for waste, and are not always given their assessments, so that the potential extent of the waste cannot be gauged. Manors which had in 1066 been worth as much as 40s. (Normanton on Soar, 282bi) or 30s. (Oldcotes, 285ai) were waste in 1086; on the partially waste holdings what had been worth £14 6s. was later valued at only £3 14s. 4d. Some figures may represent not actual but potential values; Haughton (290a2), with no inhabitants or teams, had a value of £1 set on it, and the value of Normanton on Soar (286ai) was given as 4s., as in 1066.

Waste holdings resemble in their distribution decline in value. They occur for the most part in the neighbourhood of the roads joining Newark and south Yorkshire, west of Nottingham, and south of Nottingham near the Leicestershire border. This suggests that their origin was for the most part the disturbances of 1067–71, though some on the north and east of Sherwood might be due to inclusion in the Forest or to abandonment of unprofitable hamlets and farms.[2]

[1] Babworth, *Odestorp*, and Ordsall (281ai), Clumber (285a2); Costock and Rempstone (286a2).
[2] See *Dom. Geog.*, iv, Figs. 68–70, pp. 265–7, and for the relation to population, Fig. 64, p. 252.

In view of the appreciation of the Derbyshire fief of Walter d'Aincourt it is suggestive that here his lands had increased in value also, from £49 1s. to £60 13s. 4d. Only four of his seventeen manors had fallen in value. He was the owner of Granby (289ai), which shows a rise of two-thirds of its former value; it is interesting that the other Granby manor (Osbern fitzRichard's, 292ai) had appreciated by well over 80 per cent. It is also interesting that in Walter's fief there were but $83\frac{3}{8}$ teams for $72\frac{1}{4}$ 'ploughlands', 1·15 teams per 'ploughland' against a county average of 1·6. It suggests that Walter had an efficient steward who made the most of the land, though perhaps to the distress of his peasantry.

In contrast, the fief of Roger of Poitou had declined in value by over 40 per cent. Since it was scattered over the county, it was not inevitably poor in quality. We do not know what Roger's relations with the king were at the time of the Inquest, but it might be that there was a connection between the decline and possible royal disfavour. No other local fief of moderate size shows a comparable figure.

It has been suggested that some of the inhabitants in Roger de Bully's south Yorkshire fief had been transferred from his lands in north Nottinghamshire to make good the losses suffered in the harrying of Yorkshire.[1] But his lands now in North Clay Wapentake had depreciated in value by only 15 per cent, and those in Hatfield by 30 per cent. Any transference can at most have been only slight in its effects.

Values in terms of the *ora*, as might be expected, are extremely common. Including values both for 1066 and 1086, we find:

16s.	19 instances	4s.	13 instances
10s. 8d.	5 ,,	2s. 8d.	1 instance
8s.	12 ,,	1s. 4d.	1 ,,
5s. 4d.	16 ,,		

Decimal values of £1 or over are comparatively rare; there were only 34 holdings valued at £1 in 1086, and £1 is 15 *orae*. Thus occurrences of £16 (2 entries), £8 (10), and £4 (29) may suggest an *ora*-basis. So may such quantities as 64s., 48s., 32s., 24s. There are, too, copious instances of sums which happen to be multiples of sixteenpence, e.g. 25s. 4d. (Colwick, 292bi), 28s. (Kelham, 285bi), and 17s. 4d. (West Drayton, 285ai). The mark of silver is three times mentioned, but whether this represents the *ora*-mark of 10s. 8d., or that worth 13s. 4d., is not stated.[2] On the sole occasion on which the customary rent paid by sokemen is mentioned (Leverton, 281bi), twenty-two were paying 20s.

[1] T. A. M. Bishop, in *Essays in Economic History*, 2, p. 9 (1962).
[2] Epperstone and Woodborough (285b2), Sturton le Steeple (286bi), Burton Joyce (289a2).

THE NORTH MIDLANDS: NOTTINGHAMSHIRE

The Nottinghamshire text has more than the normal quota of difficulties. The county was apparently grossly underrated, as Maitland noticed.[1] Even when allowance is made for the general fall in values, inequalities are striking. East Stoke (288bi) and Fiskerton (288b2) had each been worth £3 in 1066, but the first was assessed at six bovates, with two 'ploughlands', and the second at twenty-four bovates, with five 'ploughlands'. Yet despite heavy gelds East Stoke fell in value to £2, while Fiskerton rose to £4. A Kelham manor (290ai), worth £2 in 1066, was rated at only $2\frac{1}{3}$ bovates, while on the same folio Costock and Cosgrave, of equal value, had assessments of 14 and 16 bovates respectively. We must often suspect beneficial assessment; e.g. at the bishop of Lincoln's manor of Coddington (283b2), worth £2 in 1066 but rated at a single bovate, or Bole (286b2), with the same value, yet assessed at only $1\frac{1}{2}$ bovates.

To relate the teams to the 'ploughlands' is impossible. In nearly three-quarters of the entries the number of teams for which there is said to be land exceeds the teams recorded, sometimes ridiculously so. Littleborough (281bi) had five teams where there was land for only one, Serlby (285a2) four teams for half a ploughland, and Kirkby in Ashfield (289bi) fifteen for two. It has rightly been argued that such figures cannot be explained by a possible increase in arable land since 1066, or be due to over-stocking because of a large free element in the population and a multitude of small uneconomic farms.[2] Both Maitland and Stenton came to the conclusion that here also the 'ploughland' is an artificial conception 'remote from real agrarian life', and represents fragments of 'an obsolete system of assessment' as conventional as that of the carucates for geld.[3] There is, however, no logical relationship between 'ploughlands' and carucates for geld. If the 'ploughlands' have to do with an earlier assessment, this had been drastically diminished. Possibly a re-assessment took into account contemporary standards. But to map the carucate/'ploughland' relationship would be a laborious business, and seems unlikely even then to yield indication of areas needing especially generous treatment.

The proportion of sokemen to the total recorded population, 30·6 per cent, is here far higher than in the shires to the north and east. In consequence the villein element is, though numerous (46·9 per cent), less strong than in Derbyshire or Yorkshire. But the figures may be entirely erroneous because only 24 male slaves are recorded, and these occur in three fiefs only. It seems highly improbable that these were all the slaves in the county in 1086.

---

[1] *DBB*, p. 462 (532).
[2] *Dom. Geog.*, iv, pp. 245–8.   [3] *DBB*, p. 471 (542); *VCH*, i, p. 213.

THE DETAILS OF DOMESDAY BOOK

An unusually high proportion of entries tell us of oxen owned by sokemen or by villeins only. There are, it is true, also many where neither appears to possess any beasts of the plough. Sokemen's teams can be isolated in 42 entries; 223 have $82\frac{1}{4}$ teams, or an average of 2·95 oxen per man. At Manton (288a2) three possessed an equal number of teams; one at Sutton on Trent (285b2) had a whole team. Possession of a half-team is not rare, but the sokeman at Headon (284bi) had only two oxen. In 48 relevant entries 247 villeins had $81\frac{5}{8}$ teams, or 2·65 oxen per head. Between the impoverished sokeman and the well-to-do villein there can have been at most only a difference in status. A Thrumpton villein (287a2) had a whole team, but two at Clifton (284ai) no more than an ox apiece, and three at Kelham (290ai) had but a pair of oxen between them. Only eight times can bordars' teams be isolated; sixteen had merely 27 oxen, or 1·7 oxen per head. But a Perlethorpe bordar (281a2) had six and one at Babworth (285ai) four; though a single ox was all the four bordars at Knapthorpe (292bi) could contribute.

6
The Northern Counties

Yorkshire and Lincolnshire contain even more instances of dispersed manors with numerous berewicks and sokelands than do the shires already examined. In the Domesday Yorkshire text 40 per cent of the entries and sub-entries are concerned with the berewicks and sokelands of manors. Composite or 'linked' entries affect some 64 per cent of the Yorkshire places mentioned.[1] The form of these varies; sometimes we have a statement covering the manor as a whole, sometimes information is given separately for the *caput*, the berewicks, and the sokelands, while the last may not be dealt with in a single passage. Several other variations occur, while it is not uncommon for sokeland and inland to be described in an entry well separated from that of the manor.[2] Hence we can often have no idea how statistics should be allotted. While sometimes we are given details for an individual berewick or a piece of sokeland, it is more common to find combined figures. Sometimes we are told that all the components are waste, except that one or two have a small number of inhabitants. Several entries give us no information beyond an assessment and perhaps that the holding is sokeland of an unnamed manor. Many of these might be presumed to be waste. A few give a value for 1086 only.

For Yorkshire we have two documents additional to the *breves*. The section entitled *clamores* (373ai–4a2) adds but little, save as regards the actual claims and facts concerning them, though it does record a few places unmentioned elsewhere. The Summary (379ai–82a2), which tells us only the names of landholders and the assessments of the places listed,

[1] Figures from *Dom. Geog.*, iv, pp. 473, 502.
[2] e.g. Earl Alan's holding at Dinsdale (309a2) was sokeland of the royal manor of Northallerton (299ai), where it is included without mention of Earl Alan. Part of Thornton Steward was in the soke of East Witton; the first entry is on fol. 311b2, the second on 311a2.

supplements the *breves* considerably, though differences regarding the information in either are frequent and often large ones. Entries in the *breves* sometimes have no parallel in the Summary. The latter includes over 120 holdings which do not appear in the Domesday text, but it is probable that some of these are covered by Domesday entries which mention a manor but not the fact that it had components. Certainly the Summary lists the berewicks of Wath upon Dearne (330bi) and some other manors where DB does not.

Assessments, though often more detailed in the Summary, are not always the same as in the *breves*. Nor is the ascription of ownership always identical. Many holdings credited in the Summary to the king appear in DB in the *breve* for the king's thegns. A few further outstanding instances include

Hemingbrough	299a2	the king	381a2	bishop of Durham
Persene	304bi	bishop of Durham 6 bovates	381b2	William de Perci 4 bovates, the bishop 2 bovates
Penistone, Darton	301a2	the king, but on 316b2 Ilbert de Lassi	379bi	Ilbert de Lassi
Cherry Burton	307ai	Robert of Mortain; Nigel held it, but yields it up	381b2	the king
Barnby & Silkstone	316bi	the king	379bi	Ilbert de Lassi

Some of the discrepancies would be readily explicable if, as seems to me to be highly probable, the basis for what became in DB *Terra Regis* was compiled earlier than that for at least many of the fiefs.

It is not even possible to separate the Ridings. Hallikeld Wapentake is now in the North Riding, but at the Inquest it belonged to the West Riding. Here the holdings in Hallikeld now in the North Riding have been treated as part of that Riding. The *caput* of a manor might be in one Riding, its sokeland in another. Nor did a manor with its berewicks and sokelands always lie within a single Wapentake. The *caput* of the manor of Buckton Holms (314bi) was in *Scard*, but of its four sokelands one was in Acklam and three in *Toreshou*. Scrayingham (327b2) was in Acklam Wapentake in the East Riding; its three berewicks in Bulmer Wapentake in the North Riding.

It is thus impossible to say how many holdings there may have been in Yorkshire in either 1066 or 1086. Collation of the text with the *clamores* suggests that there must in 1066 have been more holdings in a vill than are indicated by the feudal *breves* of DB. What in 1086 was a single manor often counted in 1066 as from two to eight manors, and many of these must have been isolated hamlets or farms. Such an assumption seems to acquire support from the fact that in many vills some holdings retained a constant value or declined in worth, while others were waste. At Guisborough (300ai, 305ai,bi, 320bi) one holding was always worth 64*d*., one fell from £2 to 16*s*., one was waste, and the last probably waste. The larger holding at Hackforth (310b2) increased in value from 14*s*. to 16*s*.; the smaller, earlier worth 8*s*., was waste. It may have been a farm slightly distant from the vill and abandoned, any men and oxen being absorbed by the larger holding and helping to increase its value. That the sum mentioned is often the rent being paid is shown by the occasional use of *reddit* and figures which can only represent a rentable value, received or demanded; sometimes the amount is said to be paid by *censarii*.[1] Occasionally it is noted that 'now it is cultivated', as though it had been waste earlier (e.g. Radfarlington, 327ai, worth 5*s*.). We find holdings which are given a value but seem to be uninhabited (this might imply the rent to be asked of anyone who will engage to bring it back into cultivation), inhabited holdings to which no value is given, and holdings said to be waste but to which a value is attached, which sometimes also might be the rent to be asked of anyone who will re-settle them.

The figures given here for any category of information must then be regarded as approximations. It is necessary to guess, where combined figures are given, how many of the sokelands of a manor might have been inhabited. Five holdings which were in the soke of Wheatley (308a2) were inhabited by a sokeman, seven villeins, and eight bordars. One or more may well have been waste. Sokeland of Laughton en le Morthen (319ai), in eight places, could muster ninety inhabitants; possibly none of these was waste.

Increase in value	78
No change in value	73
Fall in value	434
Inhabited: 1086 value given	43
Inhabited: no value given	166
Waste	440
1066 value given, waste in 1086	256
1066 value given only, presumably waste in 1086	137
No value given (a high proportion must have been waste or had fallen in value)	667
	2,294
In the Summary only	121
In the *clamores* only	3
Holdings in 1066 absorbed in other manors by 1086	417
	2,835

[1] e.g. at Helperby (303a2), Warthill (306a2), Pickhill (313ai); Burton Agnes (299b2), Bugthorpe (303a2).

The uncertainties as regards valuations are formidable ones. Hovingham (327b2) had fifteen berewicks, in which there were two of Hugh fitzBaldric's men and 43 villeins. It is improbable that all these berewicks were inhabited, but we can have no idea as to which were and which were not. Moreover, we are given values for the manor as a whole. Pickering (299a2) had sokeland in eighteen places. In these there were only ten villeins; 'the rest is waste'. There is no clue to the holdings which had villeins. Where a manor fell heavily in value, we must suppose that most if not all of its berewicks and sokelands became worth less, but for all we know the *caput* may have increased its worth. There had been three holdings at Patrick Brompton (312bi), made into a single manor after the Conquest. This had improved in value, but there is no guarantee that every holding in it had done so.

A feature of the Yorkshire values is the number of manors which in 1066 were valued at £8 or multiples thereof. The highest value is £112, and eight were of half this value; forty in all were worth £12 or more, assuming that amounts such as £60 and £28 represent 7½ and 3½ £8 units.[1] They are most numerous in the East Riding, while the West Riding has six and the North Riding a dozen. Now obviously the higher values at least evolve from an artificial system. Most of the manors concerned had been in the hands of the greatest national or local figures; the king, the archbishop, Earls Harold, Siward, Tostig, Edwine, and Morkere; Gospatric, Orm, Ulf, Haward. It looks as if the manors had once all been royal or the property of an earl, and that some had been bestowed upon local magnates. Where in 1066 we find such a manor shared by seven men for seven manors (Brandesburton, £40, 324bi) it may originally have been a single property and had descended to a man's heirs or been broken up.

Secondly, the number of carucates in the manors with a value of £56 has a wide range, and bears no obvious relationship to the values, but carucates and teamlands are sometimes identical in quantity or almost so. The valuations, which must represent the sums the manors had to find, may have been equitable; they may still have been fairly valid in 1066. But in 1086, though each had been valued at £56, and at the Inquest at £12 or £6, Mappleton had 15 teams and 57 recorded inhabitants other than a priest, Hornsea 5½ and 17 respectively. Howden, worth earlier £40, had 21 teams and 98 recorded inhabitants, while Great Driffield, of similar

---

[1] There is some doubt whether the value of Whitby (305ai) was £112 or £88. The text reads 'T.R.E. it was worth £100 and £12', which is twice the common value of £56, but if 'and' should have been 'less', it would have a value equal to that of Pickering (299a2), £88. But 112 + 88 = 200, so the two manors may have been associated.

value, was entirely waste.[1] A connection with another artificiality, the figure of 504 which seems to have governed the apportionment of assessments, is not obvious, but $9 \times 56 = 504$.[2] This again suggests artificiality. So do the frequently enormous falls in value. Northallerton (299ai) was completely waste, though returning £80 in 1066, Flamborough (305ai) and Burton Agnes (299b2) each fell from £24 to 10s., and this last was merely a rent-payer's contribution, Pickering (299a2) from £88 to 20s. 4d.

A number of entries duplicate information given elsewhere, and some furnish conflicting information. Normanton is on fol. 299b2 said to have fallen in value from 12s. to 10s., on fol. 301a2 from 12s. 8d. to 10s. 8d. The latter seems the more probable figure, and may make us wonder if in other instances pence suggesting an *ora*-basis were omitted. On fol. 300b2 Brafferton is given as assessed at one carucate, with land for half a team and a villein with a team rendering 2s. On fol. 330a2 the villein is said to have half a team and the land to be worth 2s. 6d.

'Waste' presents further problems. It seems fairly safe to assume that where we have a value for King Edward's day, but none for 1086, the land was waste. For all we know it may have been waste where we are given no value for either date, and no inhabitants are recorded. At Manfield (309ai) three sokemen had 1¾ carucates of the sixteen at which this sokeland was rated, 'the rest is waste'. Can we be sure, then, that there was no land waste in places for which a value is given? No value is given to Manfield, which was part of the huge manor of Gilling, worth T.R.E. the conventional figure of £56, in 1086 only £4, so Manfield probably paid merely a small rent. The next entry, for Hutton Magna, also Gilling sokeland, says that its six carucates are 'for the most part waste'. It had meadow and underwood 'in some places', which may make us think that holdings similarly equipped, but to which no value is given and for which no inhabitants are recorded, were not necessarily altogether waste. 'Pasturable woodland' (e.g. Wortley, 331bi) implies that the king's thegn who held the manor had a use for it, and someone must have tended and guarded the beasts who used it. But 'useless woodland' in some of the sokelands of Hexthorpe (307bi) suggests that it was serviceable for hunting only. Some holdings for which no value is mentioned had a few inhabitants, e.g. Upsall (306a2); these obviously cannot be classed as waste. Sometimes we are told that a group of named holdings are in part waste, but not which of these were deserted. Since the seven sokelands of Clifton (313a2) contained only four sokemen and nine villeins with five teams, some of these may have been waste; indeed Clifton itself is said to have been waste, but

---

[1] Maitland: *DBB*, p. 473 (544), spoke of the value of such manors as 'a legal fiction, though a fiction which is founded on fact'.   [2] See *VCH*, ii, p. 141.

the entry probably contains errors.[1] Sometimes a holding is given a value for 1086, but is also said to be waste, e.g. Dalton (310a2). If analysis of such entries is difficult, synthesis must obviously be highly unsatisfactory. Still, there is something to be learned even from such complex and opaque statements.

For the whole county (excluding Craven), where comparative figures are given or implied, the information furnished by DB gives

	1066 £ s. d.	1086 £ s. d.
Increase in value	129 9 4	210 13 4
No change in value	170 13 6	170 13 6
Fall in value	2,554 3 0	677 6 9
Value 1066, waste 1086	351 14 4	– – –
Value 1066 only	125 17 8	– – –
	3,331 17 10	1,058 13 7

The total fall is 68 per cent of the 1066 value.

We can never be sure as to just how many holdings were in native hands in 1086. A newcomer who was a sub-tenant may often have had under him an English tenant unrecorded in DB; Farrer quoted the instance of Ryther.[2] In the *clamores* (373bi) the wording suggests that Ketel and his brothers had land here in 1086; on fol. 315bi Hugh holds it of Ilbert de Lassi. Nor can we be sure that where a small manor appears to be in demesne it was not really leased by a native.

At least 121 properties in the West Riding were still in English hands in 1086 in some form or other, and these had earlier been valued at well over £100. Almost one-third of these were waste, but a few had retained their former value, e.g. Birkin, Fairburn (315bi) and Plumpton (322ai). The greater part of the sub-tenancies were in the fief of Ilbert de Lassi; a list of these is given in *VCH*, ii, p. 163. But the impossibility of determining whether a name is that of the individual or not prevents any estimate of the number of surviving landholders or tenants. Here there seem to have been at least twenty-four. Gospatric had 24 holdings in chief, and in the whole county four more, while the name occurs also in sixteen sub-tenancies on Earl Alan's land in the North Riding. In Craven fourteen properties were held by king's thegns.

In the East Riding sub-tenancies in native hands were very few, though king's thegns had over thirty properties. The surprising factor in the

---

[1] It begins by saying that its 18 carucates were waste, but T.R.E. were worth 20s. Later it shows Earl Alan's land to be inhabited, but states that the land of the canons of St Peter's, York, is waste. Yet it also says that the land is still worth 20s.   [2] *VCH*, ii, p. 164.

THE NORTHERN COUNTIES: YORKSHIRE: THE WEST RIDING

North Riding is that out of 46 relevant entries seven show an increase in value and another eight parity or only a small decline, though 17 were indeed waste. Over two-thirds of the holdings were tenancies on Earl Alan's lands. He had an English steward, Godric (Cowton, 309ai), and it may have been that he had chosen natives to be his tenants in those manors in which an increase in value may suggest a transference of men and oxen from elsewhere, or to use their local knowledge and leadership in the event of Scots raids.[1]

The number of holdings said to be waste and in the hands of natives suggests that the barons were ready to rent these to any men not obviously disloyal who were in a position to redevelop them. Equally the quantity of waste holdings where no tenant is mentioned is a mute reminder of the enormous number of Englishmen and Anglo-Danes who must since 1066 have disappeared from the scene, and perhaps of the death-roll during the events which culminated at Stamford Bridge.

Yorkshire: The West Riding

If for the moment the district of Craven is excluded, it is probably fair to say that this Riding saw more of King William's armies than did any other part of the county except the lands near York. The ways to York from the south lie within it, and so does the path of the king's march across the Pennines into Cheshire. In addition to the frequent desertion of the bleak Pennine moorlands in which subsistence, after the Conquest and reprisals for rebellion, would be difficult or impossible, we should expect to find a general lowering of standards west of the Humberland Levels.

Allowing for the discernible parallel entries, the information about valuations may be itemised as shown on the next page. Probably there were in addition a number of settlements unnamed in DB.[2]

It may seem strange that any manor should have improved in value. But three of those which did so were places of strategic importance, and half the remainder were no great distance from York, whose proximity

---

[1] As early as 1907 it was suggested that Hugh fitzBaldric, in his capacity as sheriff, may have transferred surplus population from one manor to another (J. Beddoe and J. H. Rowe: 'The ethnology of West Yorkshire' (*Yorks. Arch. Journal*, xix, p. 59, Leeds, 1907).

[2] e.g. Kippax (315ai) probably included Roche Grange, and Saxton (315ai), Woodhouse: *VCH*, ii, pp. 230, 231. A number of places not mentioned in DB appear in earlier surveys: see W. H. Stevenson: 'Yorkshire Surveys and other eleventh-century documents in the York Gospels' (*EHR*, xxvii, 1912, pp. 1–25).

may have made them more valuable than before.[1] If Conisbrough is omitted, the increase is only from £48 1s. to £57 12s. 8d. Of the 36 entries for which no change in value is reported, 30 were worth thirty shillings or less. But we may well feel some doubt that there had really been no alteration at Sherburn with its sixteen berewicks (£34 16s.; 302bi), or at Kippax with Ledston (£16; 315ai).

Increase in value	18
No change in value	33
Fall in value	213
Inhabited, or 1086 value given	104
Waste	111
1066 value given, waste in 1086	96
1066 value given only, presumably waste in 1086	37
No value given, but indeterminable quantity waste	154
	766
In the Summary only	40
In the *clamores* only	2
Holdings in 1066 absorbed in other manors by 1086	178
	986

Where a value is given for 1066, but none for 1086, we are probably entitled to presume that it was waste in the latter year. We may think so the more when we consider parallel entries such as those for Penistone and Darton (301a2, 316b2). The first pair merely gives values, but the second says that the sums reported are the values T.R.E. and that the manors are waste.[2] Against this it may be said that on fol. 298bi Skelton is said to have been worth 6s. in 1066 and 8s. in 1086, while on fol. 301a2 a single value of 8s. is given. Unless a mistake was made, here is an instance in which a single value does not imply waste in 1086. Some of the holdings, though said to be waste, are also given small values. Halton (315a2) is said to render 2s., Seacroft (315a2) to be worth 20d., Middlethorpe (321ai, 327ai) to be waste, but the first holding was worth 3s., while of the second it is said 'but nevertheless it renders 8s.'. Great Braham (328b2), though waste, rendered 16d. None has any population mentioned, but they have not been treated as waste in the figures given here. The rents were probably those of settlers prepared to try to exploit deserted farms. Some waste holdings

[1] The three were Dadsley with Stainton and Hellaby (319ai), a nascent borough (though the 'burgesses' were perhaps rather rent-paying settlers), Conisbrough (321a2), and Tadcaster (321bi). Conisbrough went up from £18 to £30 plus £10 of *tailla*; it may be that not all its 28 sokelands of 1086 were included in the 1066 value. One holding, said to be 'near the city' of York (302bi), includes the value of 'what the archbishop had in the city'.
[2] See also Studley and Cluden (322ai); former values are given, but at the end of the account of a group of holdings we are told that 'they are waste', except for Askwith.

THE NORTHERN COUNTIES: YORKSHIRE: THE WEST RIDING

had wood for pannage (e.g. Elland, 318a2; Gipton with Colton, 315a2, where there was a church—waste, but worth 2s.). Ilkley (321bi) is said to be waste, but a church and a priest are mentioned; this does not suggest

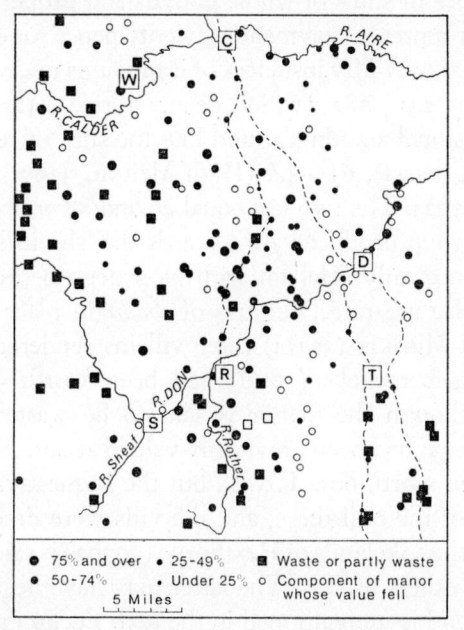

Fig. 25 South Yorkshire
Fall in value 1066–86
– – – Suggested routes of royal troops
C—Castleford D—Doncaster R—Rotherham S—Sheffield
T—Tickhill W—Wakefield

that the church was in ruins. Whixley (329bi), though waste, is credited with two churches. At none of the holdings in these vills are inhabitants recorded. There are parallels elsewhere.

The entries in which comparable values are given may be itemised thus:

	1066 £ s. d.	1086 £ s. d.
Increase in value	58 1 0	87 12 8
No change in value	95 9 2	95 9 2
Fall in value	702 5 0	306 17 7
Value 1066, waste 1086	115 13 4	— — —
Value 1066 only	32 10 4	— — —
	1,003 18 10	489 19 5

The total fall is 51 per cent of the 1066 value. The great majority of the waste holdings had only small values; 83 per cent were in 1066 worth less than £2. These are just the less profitable manors which one would expect to become deserted.

The *ora* is of less frequent occurrence than might be expected. Unless the preponderance of sums of whole pounds and proper fractions thereof had this basis, or represent payment of twenty pence for every sixteen due, there are only just over fifty instances of it for sums under £1. A few other amounts such as 24*s*., 28*s*. (which occurs thrice), 32*s*., 36*s*., may also reflect it.[1] Occasional amounts sound like the sum of rents, e.g. 42*s*. 4*d*. (Long Marston, 329a2), 61*s*. 4*d*. (High Melton, 319bi), 90*s*. 8*d*. (South Elmsall, etc., 315b2). The two last equal 46 and 88 *orae* respectively. The South Elmsall group produced £6 towards the 'sheriff's due'. The silver mark appears once only (Hallam with its sixteen berewicks, 320ai).

Exotic formulae are rare. The use of *reddit* in place of *valet* appears occasionally. At Minskip (301bi) three villeins rendered 5*s*. 4*d*. Knaresborough and its berewicks (300ai) had been worth £6, but in 1086 rendered 20*s*., though the manor is said to be waste; Halton (315a2) rendered 2*s*. when it had been previously valued at 20*s*. *Newose* and Sutton (315b2) had been worth 60*s*. T.R.E., but the Inquest value of 6*s*. represented the rent of the mill there, and the vills were described as 'waste'.

The wood in the sokelands of Hexthorpe (307b2) is said to be pasturable in places and in others useless. The latter may have been 'in the Forest', though Forest land is unmentioned in the text. Eccup (307bi) had woodland 'not pasturable'.

We cannot be certain that when villeins are said to possess teams they actually did so When demesne is not mentioned, a phrase such as 'one villein is there with two teams' (Keresforth and Barnsley, 317ai) might well mean that some if not all of the oxen were the lord's. The 58 entries in which villeins' teams seem to be mentioned give $133\frac{1}{4}$ teams for 325 villeins, but $3\frac{1}{4}$ oxen per head seems high for stricken Yorkshire, though the character of the soils may have necessitated the employment of a large number of oxen. The 19 entries in which demesne teams are also mentioned give 115 villeins as possessing 39 teams, which averages $2\frac{1}{4}$ oxen a man. There is no instance, where there were demesne oxen also, of villeins on a holding averaging more than a half-team except at Clifford (307bi), where three villeins had two teams. Thus that six villeins should have five teams (Aldborough, etc., 229bi) seems too high a figure. The villeins and bordars of North Milford (315b2) 'do not plough', and Winksley (330ai) was not cultivated. The two sokemen, the six villeins, and the bordar at Hambleton (315bi) are said to have no teams.

Eight entries where the teams of bordars only are mentioned are too few

[1] e.g. Barrowby, etc. (328b2); Upper Poppleton (329a2); High Melton (319bi).

to produce reasonable figures. In these 33 had 9 teams, or just under $2\frac{1}{4}$ oxen per head. The instances vary from two bordars with a team at Hessay (329a2) to twelve with one at Hensall (299bi). In five entries a sokeman has an entire team, but the average for 35 of this class is only about $4\frac{1}{4}$ oxen, and at North Anston (321a2) four shared a team. We find a priest with a team (Barton Hall, etc., 315bi) and fourteen *censores* with seven teams (Acomb, 303bi).

Six entries relating to holdings in a comparatively small area say that the land is cultivated, though in none are teams mentioned.[1] Though they are not all in the same Wapentake, the phrase probably owes its inclusion to clerical idiosyncracy. They may be holdings on which teams from other estates were employed.

Yorkshire: The East Riding

In some respects the smallest of the Ridings yields the most information. Also, very few holdings are anonymous. The information about valuations may be classified thus:

Rise in value	20
No change in value	18
Fall in value	115
Inhabited: 1086 value given	25
Inhabited: no value given	35
Waste	117
1066 value given, waste in 1086	47
1066 value given only, presumably waste in 1086	48
No value given (probably about 50 were inhabited and the rest waste or fallen in value)	261
	686
In the Summary only	61
In the *clamores* only	1
Holdings in 1066 absorbed in other manors by 1086	147
	895

Possible reasons for increases in value here are not easy to suggest. They occur in only seven fiefs, while in Gilbert Tison's *breve* four out of nine entries giving comparable values show appreciation, and five out of eleven in that of Hugh fitzBaldric. Buckton Holms (314bi) had doubled its pre-Conquest value of £4, yet its four sokelands are all noted as being waste. It is true that there were thirteen teams where there was land for ten,

[1] See *Dom. Geog.*, iv, p. 34.

and two mills, but these will hardly altogether account for the rise. Perhaps the seven sokemen 'who are there now' had been outside the manor earlier, they had nine teams and twelve villeins and six bordars. For in addition to the four named sokelands the manor seems also to have had sokeland in four other places.[1] Extension of a manor may account for some of these appreciations, but hardly for that at Bugthorpe (303ai). Though a substantial manor of $4\frac{1}{2}$ carucates, it had been worth only 5s. in 1066, yet in 1086 two *censarii* were rendering 20s. 4d. But it could have been in a bad way in King Edward's day, and the possibility of clerical error must never be discounted. Sutton upon Derwent (322bi), worth 20s., is said to have been worth both 36s. and 20s. T.R.E. The latter is obviously an error. The majority of the improvements in value are to be found north-east of York, between the river Derwent and the Yorkshire Wolds, the district in which we should expect recovery to be most rapid, though it would seem to have been less densely populated than mid-Holderness or the area immediately north of the Humber.[2]

Where a manor had fallen in value, we are not infrequently told that part of it is waste or partly waste, e.g. Great Kelk (304ai) with its two berewicks. In 1086 it was worth only one shilling where it had been valued at forty, and it was all waste except for three villeins with a single team. The berewicks and sokelands of many a large complex manor are said to be waste.[3]

Thus many more holdings than are said in DB to be waste probably were so. But we may perhaps doubt if the whole of such manors as Great Driffield (299bi), with its four berewicks and eleven sokelands, was, as the text would suggest, totally waste. There had been two churches and eight mills upon it, and though no inhabitants or teams are mentioned, it seems unlikely that it was altogether uninhabited. Quite often a holding is said to be waste except for a few men. At North Cave (302bi) a *censarius* was paying 10s. 8d.; at Weaverthorpe (303ai), which had three berewicks and seven sokelands, two sokemen with a team and three bordars produced a rent of 10s.[4] But where we are given a value for 1066 but none for 1086 it is to be presumed that in the latter year the holding was waste.

[1] *VCH*, ii, p. 324, n. 108. Hugh fitzBaldric's Buckton Holms manor (328a2) was waste.
[2] See *Dom. Geog.*, iv, Fig. 49, p. 196.
[3] e.g. Welton, Howden (304bi). North Cave (320bi), where no berewicks or sokelands are recorded, is said to be waste 'for the greater part'. It was composed of six former manors, some of which were presumably deserted.
[4] See also Middleton on the Wolds (306bi), Nunkeeling (324bi), North Ferriby (325a2—the Hessle sub-entry). Thoralby Hall (331ai) is definitely stated to be 'let', but to whom is not said.

The entries in which comparable values are given may be itemised thus:

	1066 £ s. d.	1086 £ s. d.
Increase in value	32 11 0	53 12 4
No change in value	48 0 0	48 0 0
Fall in value	1,158 8 0	270 1 0
Value 1066, waste 1086	141 8 0	– – –
Value 1066 only	53 0 0	– – –
	1,433 7 0	371 13 4

The decline of 74 per cent is largely due to the enormous falls in value of the complex manors with values in 1066 of £24 or more. These show a fall of 84 per cent, the remainder one of $38\frac{1}{2}$ per cent.

The Riding is one which we should expect to have suffered severely during the campaigns inspired by Northumbrian revolts and Scandinavian invaders, and perhaps from Scots raiders also. Though there seems, according to the information of DB, to have been comparatively little waste near the lower Humber or in Holderness, the impression given might be deceptive. Falls in value in Holderness are so frequent and extensive, totalling over 80 per cent of the 1066 figure, that there must have been much waste here. The fourteen holdings which were sokeland of Bridlington (299bi), rated at $58\frac{1}{2}$ carucates, were apparently inhabited by a single sokeman and three villeins; 'the rest is waste'. Thus, though the text does not say so, many of the berewicks and sokelands of the many complex manors must have been waste, for the population figures given do not allow all to have been inhabited in 1086, and those which were had probably been waste earlier. Withernsea (323bi) had eleven sokelands, peopled by only 22 recorded inhabitants with seven teams between them; Pocklington (299bi) also had eleven sokelands, and 15 burgesses are the sole persons recorded.[1] To what extent Holderness had been ravaged on the king's orders we cannot know, but probably it had suffered also from the raids of foreigners. Harald Hardraada had burnt Scarborough and fought a minor battle further south on his way to his defeat and death at Stamford Bridge.[2] In the south-west of the Riding there was comparatively little waste, except around the lower reaches of the rivers Ouse and Derwent, some of which may have been caused by failure to recover from the Danish assaults on York. Waste is at its most extensive along the York—Bridlington roads

---

[1] Brooks (*Domesday Book and the East Riding*, pp. 25, 45; York, 1966) very reasonably suggests that the 'burgesses' at Pocklington and Bridlington were free men renting land and bringing the waste back into cultivation.
[2] 'King Harald's Saga', cap. 83, in *Heimskringla*.

and north thereof, especially on and about the Wolds. Some of the holdings may have been deserted in favour of more attractive settlements. Vills in the condition of Kilham (299bi, 301ai, 329b2, 331ai) are not uncommon; here three of the four holdings were waste and the fourth probably so. Recorded population and plough-teams were at their lowest in the north of the Riding.[1]

This invites consideration of one of Domesday's mysteries. We are told practically nothing about the value of St John of Beverley's lands here, but Drogo's principal manors (323bi–5ai) were in 1066 valued at multiples of £8. Five had been worth £56, two £40, two £32, one £20, one £12, and two £8. The first nine were in 1086 worth £6, £8, or £10. Seven of these had been in the hands of Earls Morkere, Tostig, or Harold. That this is the result of an artificial system is obvious. The number of carucates in the manors with their berewicks and sokelands ranges from 28 to $54\frac{3}{4}$, and bears no obvious relationship to the values, but carucates and teamlands are always identical in quantity or almost so. There are ten other manors which had been worth £56, £40, £32, £30 (? an error for £32), or £24. One had been royal, two the archbishop's, six Earl Morkere's, and one Earl Harold's. As was said earlier, it looks as if the arrangements date from a time when all were royal or attributes of the earldom.

If, elsewhere, an *ora*-basis is not markedly apparent, this is because the size and character of the holdings make for values of £1 and over. Sums of 16s., 12s., 10s. 8d., 8s., 6s., 4s., 2s. 8d., 2s. occur only 26 times. Many of these are said to be rents.[2] One hundred pence appears at Marton (303a2), and 6s. 8d. at Newsholme (325a2).

The proportion of bordars is small ($18\frac{3}{4}$ per cent), and consequently we have many apparently isolatable examples of the oxen owned by villeins. In 48 where there are demesne teams also 431 have 122 teams, averaging $2\frac{1}{4}$ oxen per man. If we include the 24 instances where no demesne teams are recorded, the average would rise very slightly. But a phrase such as 'Drogo's man has one villein there with one team' (Marton, 325ai) does not necessarily mean that the villein owned the oxen. A villein at Newsholme (325a2) had two oxen, and we find villeins averaging only a single ox apiece (Leconfield, 306b2; Dunnington, 322bi). But at Molescroft (304ai) two villeins had a whole team, and at North Frodingham (324a2) five had four teams. Six villeins could render 10s. for their land at Monkwick (304a2), and five the same sum at Kirk Ella (306b2). But on the Burstwick sokelands (323bi) the six sokemen and sixteen villeins 'did not

---

[1] See *Dom. Geog.*, iv, Figs. 53–5, pp. 214–15, 219.
[2] e.g. at North Cave (302bi), Lowthorpe (304a2), Goodmanham (306bi), North Dalton (307ai).

plough'. Does this mean that they possessed no oxen, but hired the lord's five teams?

A few instances of the teams of *milites* often credit them with a team apiece.[1] Entries giving the teams of sokemen or priests only are rare. The priest at Beeford (324a2) had a team, and the one at Swine (302a2) half a team, the 'clerk' at Leven (304a2) a whole one. Three sokemen had two teams at Howden (304bi), but two at Brantingham (306bi) only a half-team.

Yorkshire: The North Riding

There were very few settlements above the 800-ft. contour in either the Pennines or the North Yorkshire moors, but the situation of many holdings argues the existence of much marginal land. Scots raids and Norman reprisals added to the number of marginal holdings which became waste between 1066 and 1086. It looks as if something like 70 per cent of the properties may have been waste in the latter year. The information about valuations may be classified thus:

Increase in value	40
No change in value	22
Fall in value	106
Inhabited: no value given	70
Waste	212
1066 value given, waste in 1086	113
1066 value given only, presumably waste in 1086	52
No value given	131
No value given, but indeterminable quantity waste	96
	842
In the Summary only	20
Holdings in 1066 absorbed in other manors by 1086	92
	954

Increases in value, over half of which occur on Earl Alan's estates, are rarely large ones. Twenty-two out of forty are in the neighbourhood of the main Roman road, Leeming Lane, running from the Tees to York. Another nine lie on a curiously straight line almost due west of Filey; five are close to York. Stanwick (309a2) went up from 3s. to 12s., but with so low a pre-Conquest value this 3-carucate manor must have been in a poor state earlier. Aldbrough (309bi) doubled in value from £2. Scorton (310a2) increased its worth from 5s. to 50s.; nothing in the text suggests a reason, though it is close to the junction of Leeming Lane and Swaledale,

[1] e.g. at Burton Constable, Great Cowden, Catwick (304a2), and Brandesburton (324bi).

and not far off is Ainderby Myers (310bi), which went up from 5s. to 40s. These were all Earl Alan's. Kirby Misperton (314ai) increased from 3s. to 20s., and Coxwold (327a2) from £6 to £12. Some of the six components of this manor may not have been reckoned in the earlier value. Equally, these increases might have been caused by the transference of men and oxen from less rewarding settlements.

Where a manor had fallen in value, it is sometimes said also to be 'waste', which presumably implies that some of its constituents were deserted, as at Dalton (310a2), which fell from 20s. to 3s., Thorpfield and Irton (323ai) or Inglethwaite (323ai). Sometimes, too, we are told that the berewicks and sokelands of manors are waste; e.g. at Helperby (303a2). Here Helperby itself is said to be waste, but since it was in the hands of a tenant who was rendering 6s., only the four sokelands, of which it is noted 'the rest are waste', are probably implied. Lofthouse (305ai) and its twelve sokelands were waste, save for Easington. The manor is said to be 'worth nothing'; the woodland was 'useless', but no value is given for Easington's church with a priest and villein with a team. Hutton Rudby (305b2) fell in value from £24 to 26s. 8d., and all but one of its sokelands was waste.

Thus many more holdings than are said in DB to be waste probably were so. The king's principal manors had declined from £256 to £3 10s. 4d., and here it is stated that the components were mostly waste.[1] Northallerton with its eleven berewicks and 24 sokelands are all classed as waste. Whitby (305ai) fell in value from £112 (or £88) to £3.[2] Nearly all the sokeland and berewicks are classed as waste. Thus some of the holdings at Manby (309a2) and similar manors may well have been waste even though DB does not say so.

Quite often a collection of properties is said to be waste except for a few inhabitants. At the end of a list of four estates of St Peter's, York (303ai), assessed at 14 carucates, we are told that they were waste except for eight villeins with five teams. Cold Ingleby (305ai) was the only one of eight sokelands of Acklam not waste; here there were three sokemen with the same number of teams.

The entries in which comparable values are given may be itemised as shown on the next page. The total fall is 78 per cent of the 1066 value.

Waste was at its most considerable in the Pennine valleys, between these and the eastern moors, the natural route to and from the extreme north of England and Scotland, and along the north-eastern coast.[3] Here recorded population per square mile was at its lowest.

[1] Easingwold, Falsgrave, Pickering (299ai,2).
[2] See p. 196.   [3] See *Dom. Geog.*, iv, Figs. 33--5, pp. 140, 143, 146.

In this Riding we again find manors with earlier arbitrary valuations which are multiples of £8; £88, £80, £56, £48, £32, £24, £12, £8. They had been the properties of the leading men of Northumbria, Earl Siward, Earls Edwine and Morkere, Earl Tostig, Gospatric, Orm son of Gamel, and Hawart.[1]

	1066			1086		
	£	s.	d.	£	s.	d.
Increase in value	38	17	4	69	8	4
No change in value	27	4	4	27	4	4
Fall in value	693	10	0	100	8	2
Value 1066, waste 1086	94	13	0	–	–	–
Value 1066 only	40	7	4	–	–	–
	894	12	0	197	0	10

The *ora* is more prominent in amounts under £1 than in the East Riding. Sums of 16s., 12s., 10s. 8d., 6s., 5s. 4d., 4s., and 1s. 4d. occur on 73 occasions. There are a dozen instances of 24s., 28s., 32s., 36s. One-third or two-thirds of a pound occur only thrice. It looks as if 26s. (14½ *orae*) might have some significance; it appears four times for 1066, thrice consecutively.[2]

It has been suggested that valuations may have been arrived at on the following basis: a sokeman's land 6d. an acre, that of a villein 4d., and of a bordar 2d., other elements being calculated in terms of the *ora*, e.g. 40d. for a demesne team and 16d. or 32d. for a team of the peasantry, with meadow valued at 2d. an acre.[3] Some manors do have values which correspond with such principles, but it is extremely doubtful if it was a method in general use.

The entries in which villeins' teams are isolated yield no appreciable difference between those where there were also demesne teams and those in which they are unmentioned. In 96 entries 773 villeins had 310½ teams, just under 3¼ oxen per head. So high a figure might result from the transference of teams from abandoned holdings, or from the need to employ relatively more oxen to till somewhat unrewarding soils. We do not find a villein with an entire team except where demesne oxen are

---

[1] Easingwold, Northallerton, Falsgrave, Pickering (299ai), Whitby, Lofthouse, Acklam (305ai), Hutton Rudby (305b2), Gilling (309ai), Bagby, Kirby Moorside (327a2), Stokesley (331a2). It has been pointed out that the values of Northallerton and Falsgrave work out at almost exactly £1 per team (*VCH*, ii, pp. 146–7).
[2] Hunton (312bi), Sutton under Whitestone, Marderby, *Fridebi* (327a2,bi). Possibly it should have been £1 6s. 8d., giving £4, a common quantity, for these three last manors.
[3] W. Hornsby: 'The Domesday Valets of the Langbargh Wapentake' (*Yorks. Arch. Journal*, xxv), pp. 334–40. Leeds, 1920.

unmentioned, though where they are, four villeins with three teams between them occur.[1] But we find also eight villeins with a single team between them, and a villein with only a pair of oxen.[2]

At Kildale (331a2) eight bordars are said to have two teams, but this is an isolated instance of their oxen. Some sokemen seem to have averaged a team apiece (Cold Ingleby, 305ai; Manfield, 309ai), but equally we find eight sharing a team (*Prestebi* and *Sourebi*, 305ai). Three *censarii* had a couple of teams at Henderskelfe (314a2), but for all categories other than villeins we have insufficient data.

Craven

The Summary (380a2) mentions only Bolton and the nineteen places which belonged to this manor. But lands within *Cravescire* appear in six *breves* besides those for *Terra Regis* and the land of the king's thegns.[3] In four of the seven the land is said to be waste, and since neither inhabitants nor oxen is ever mentioned, but merely the quantity of carucates, the probability is that the whole district was classed as 'waste'. In over 120 vills there were 164 distinct holdings, plus 22 former properties absorbed since the Conquest in other manors.

Possibly some vills in Craven were in fact inhabited in 1086, but it may be that no Inquest for the district was held, nor returns demanded from the landholders. Assessments could surely be obtained from documents connected with a geld-levy.

North Lancashire, Westmorland, and Cumberland

Entries for these districts are found only under *Terra Regis* (301b2, 302ai) and in the *breves* of Hugh fitzBaldric (327bi) and Roger of Poitou (332a2). 140 holdings are named in north Lancashire, in the districts of Amounderness, Lonsdale, and Furness with Cartmel, 27 in Westmorland, and five in Cumberland. Again we know nothing of them besides their names and assessments, except that we are told that of 62 vills connected with Preston (301b2) sixteen were inhabited by a few people, whose number was unknown, but that the rest were waste. In the Preston complex there were three churches, and a church at each of four other places, so that it is possible that here too there was also a small population. But it has been

[1] Knayton (304b2), Nunnington (305b2).
[2] Huntington (306a2), Marske sokeland (305bi).
[3] Fols. 301bi,2 (intermingled with places outside the modern Yorkshire), 322a2, 327ai,bi, 328b2, 329bi, 332ai. But the two places on fol. 327bi were probably not in Craven but in Cartmel in Lancashire.

suggested that the wasted condition of Amounderness could have been due to reprisals against Earl Tostig's adherents by his enemies after his exile in 1065.

South Lancashire

The district described in DB as 'between the Ribble and the Mersey' (269bi–70a2) consisted of six Hundreds which were said also to be manors. Only for that of West Derby (the coastal Hundred) are we given the names of the component vills, though place-names occur also in Blackburn and Salford Hundreds. What information was provided is slight and largely uninformative. The number of settlements seems to have been not less than 175 and only doubtfully exceeded 200.

Comparison of valuations in 1066 and 1086 is impossible. We have a 1086 value for only four Hundreds, and then merely for the demesnes of Roger of Poitou and his barons. For 1066 we have a value for each Hundred. The total for the district, for which we are given slightly varying figures, was about £145, which by the time Roger received it had fallen to £120. This suggests that the area had not suffered materially from the Conquest, and indeed it lay outside the parts of England principally affected. Only three places are said to be or to have been waste.[1]

With a solitary exception (though 30*d.* is probably a mistake for 32*d.*) the values of all the pre-Conquest holdings in West Derby Hundred are multiples of sixteenpence. It is noticeable also that the sums certain Hundreds used to render are also multiples of sixteenpence or eightpence, e.g. Salford's £37 4*s.* Obviously the *ora* had been the basis of rents and the royal *firma* in this district.

Ploughlands are only twice mentioned, and teams are given only for the demesnes of Roger and his barons. The entire recorded population number only 266, of whom villeins contribute 44 per cent, bordars 30½ per cent, and slaves 7½ per cent. We are told something of the obligations of the former thegns, which were not uniform over the whole area, but the record is one which otherwise furnishes us with singularly little information.

Lincolnshire

The numerous berewicks and extensive sokelands of Lincolnshire make this county as difficult to deal with as those of the north midlands. The

---

[1] Altcar in West Derby (269bi), three hides or twelve carucates in Salford (270ai), and some of Leyland (270ai).

sokeland of Folkingham (355b2, 356ai) lay in twenty-five villages and hamlets, of Greetham (349ai) in thirty-two, and of Kirton in Lindsey (338a2,bi) in twenty-seven. The totals for figures in individual entries do not always agree with the summarised totals given, and there seem to be many textual omissions.[1] A considerable number of estates describe by means of combined figures estates in more than one village. Some such villages seem to have been dealt with simultaneously on each occasion of their appearance, e.g. Appleby, Risby, and Sawcliff (346ai, 353b2, 354bi), or Scawby and Sturton (354bi, 359ai, 363ai, 364a2, 365ai), though Scawby once appears by itself (365b2).

Figures which enable the manorial valuations of 1066 and 1086 to be compared appear in 824 out of 1,635 entries.[2] The quantities of instances in which values had risen, remained constant, or had fallen, shows no preponderance of any; 287 show an increase, 270 a decrease, while 267 show no change. Over the whole county there seems to have been only a slight increase in values, of about $8\frac{1}{2}$ per cent. But if the holdings are classified, we get this picture:

	1066 £ s. d.	1086 £ s. d.	%
Royal holdings	292 0 0	452 10 0	+ 57
Other holdings, £20 and over	582 18 8	619 0 0	+ $6\frac{1}{2}$
£5–20 holdings	1,045 8 0	1,040 8 0	− $\frac{1}{2}$
Under £5	1,125 6 8	1,189 7 8	+ $5\frac{3}{4}$

Territorially, we have:

	1066	1086	%
Holland	146 10 8	198 17 0	+ $26\frac{1}{4}$
Kesteven	1,210 19 8	1,236 18 0	+ 2
Lindsey: North Riding	580 19 0	609 17 4	+ 5
Lindsey: West Riding	529 9 8	523 6 4	− 1
Lindsey: South Riding	577 11 4	732 12 0	+ 27
	3,045 10 4	3,301 10 8	

Thus the apparent gain in wealth is almost entirely due to that on the royal manors. The other fiefs in which values increased considerably are those of Odo of Bayeux, Earl Alan, Ivo Taillebois, and Robert de Veci. The last looks rather as if here sokemen had been added to manors to which they were not attached in 1066.

[1] A royal manor of Washingborough is mentioned (337bi), but there is no descriptive entry for this place, nor for Crowland, though the properties of Crowland Abbey and of a berewick of Crowland are recorded (346b2). Winghale (376ai) and Long Sutton (377b2) appear only among the *clamores*; they are omitted from the main text.
[2] The eight which appear also on fols. 293bi,2 under *Roteland* are considered in the section dealing with Rutland (p. 240).

THE NORTHERN COUNTIES: LINCOLNSHIRE

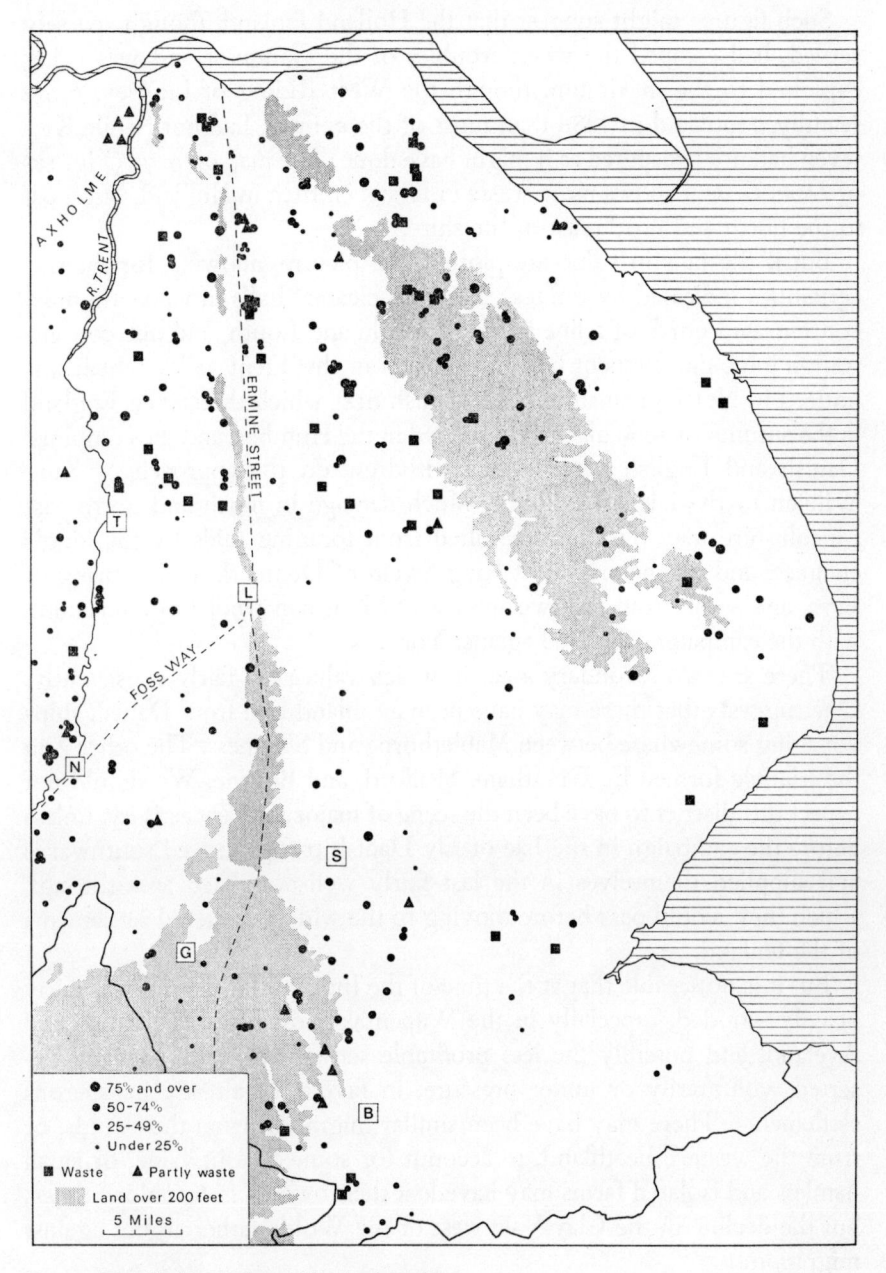

Fig. 26 Lincolnshire and east Nottinghamshire
Fall in value 1066–86
– – – Suggested routes of royal/opposing forces
B—Bourne G—Grantham L—Lincoln N—Newark
S—Sleaford T—Torksey

Such figures might suggest that the Holland fenland, though sparsely settled, had escaped the worst troubles of the Conquest and was being exploited to the maximum, though the West Riding of Lindsey, more scantily populated in 1086 than most of the county, had not, while Kesteven had not prospered as it might have done. The map on p. 73 (Fig. 17) of *Dom. Geog.* i shows more waste in Kesteven than in Holland, but most in the north and north-east of the shire.

But if the falls in value are plotted, the picture, allowing for the uncertainties indicated by the text, becomes clearer. Falls in value are most concentrated north of a line joining Lincoln and Louth, and one concentration joins the frequent falls in value about the Trent valley which was noticed in Nottinghamshire. The Danish fleet which threatened England in the autumn of 1069 ultimately arrived in the Humber, and the combined Danish and English rebel armies withdrew on the approach of King William to the Isle of Axholme. Much damage in north and north-east Lincolnshire may then have resulted from foraging raids by the king's enemies, and on the arrival of King Swein of Denmark in the spring of 1070, and some from the two marches of Norman troops in connection with the campaigns directed against York.

There are two secondary areas in which values fell fairly consistently. One suggests that there may have been an inland raid from Danish ships voyaging somewhere between Mablethorpe and Skegness. The other is in the triangle formed by Grantham, Sleaford, and Bourne. We should not expect this district to have been the scene of major military activity, unless before the campaign in the Isle of Ely Danish troops moved southwards and supplied themselves in the last fairly well-populated area through which they would pass before moving to the widely scattered settlements of the fenland.

But it is noticeable that at the time of the Inquest this district was fairly heavily wooded, especially in the Wapentakes of Threo, Beltisloe, and Aveland, and possibly the less profitable settlements were partially deserted, voluntarily or under pressure, in favour of already prosperous settlements. There may have been similar migration from the Wolds, or from the western heathland, to account for some falls in value, or small hamlets and isolated farms may have lost their owners in troublous times, but the decline in the Clay Vale west of the Wolds rather argues against migration.

But in the north midlands it is difficult to arrive at satisfactory deductions. In the rectangle whose limiting points are SK 80 60 TF 16 15, which includes the Grantham—Sleaford—Bourne triangle, values over all rose by $12\frac{1}{2}$ per cent, partly because of the increase in the Grantham figure

(337b2) from £52 to £100. If appreciations, declines, and constant values are plotted, a rather different picture appears.[1] The main appreciations lie north of a line running east and west from Grantham, north of Bourne, and in the extreme south-west of the area. The falls in value are found between the main roads running southwards from Grantham and Sleaford, in the well-wooded region of Kesteven Clays; yet the northern half of the district had 18 recorded persons to the square mile in 1086, which is a much higher figure than appears over most of the county. It almost looks as if the three principal settlements had improved the prosperity of the neighbouring countrysides, and that local trade had caused villages near the roads connecting them to prosper. Lincolnshire was apparently not well endowed with lines of communication in 1086. It is suggestive of the decay of Ermine Street (2c) and of other Roman roads (26, 26o, and 58a) that they have comparatively few villages, and very few prosperous ones, on or near them.

The variations in value in the individual vill are considerable. Though there was no change in any of the four Skillington manors (340a2 *bis*, 368a2, 371ai), or at Hacconby with Stenwith (364bi, 368b2, 369ai); at Silk Willoughby (345ai, 365a2, 368b2) one holding showed no alteration in value, one fell by 50 per cent, and a third rose from 30s. to 50s. At Creeton (358a2, 366a2, 368bi, 371ai) two holdings had the same values in 1086 as in 1066, the other two fell from 60s. to 20s. and from 40s. to 20s.[2]

In any case, we can never hope to know the full causes of changes in value. That of the manor of Drayton in Swineshead (348a2) rose from £30, 'with all things belonging', to £70. Of three other holdings in this vill, one remained constant at 16s. and the other two fell from 8s. to 5s. Had the manor been greatly enlarged since 1066, had rents and services been formidably increased, or had a multitude of small holdings been amalgamated and a common policy instituted with a notable improvement in agricultural efficiency?

Some of the changes in the values of royal manors are extraordinary. Kirton in Lindsey (338a2), worth £24 in 1066, was valued at £80 at the Inquest; Gayton le Wold (338b2) trebled its pre-Conquest value of £15; Horncastle (339ai) appreciated from £20 to £44. If these figures are due to the prices charged for leases or for custody as demanded by royal officials, the newcomers must have deemed such manors capable of enormous exploitation in comparison with the returns in earlier days. On the other hand, Bassingham (338ai) fell from £25 to £16, and Wellingore

[1] The area contains thirty villages for which the information does not enable values to be plotted.
[2] The entry on fol. 371ai records no inhabitants, so 20s. may be a potential, not actual, value.

215

(337bi) from £30 to £15. Both are on the road from Lincoln to Grantham, hard by Ermine Street, and may have suffered from military action.

There are gigantic appreciations, too, on non-royal manors. Ruskington (369b2) was worth twice its 1066 value, £25; Caythorpe (363a2) went up from £30 to £50, Market Overton with Stretton (366b2) from £12 to £40, Belchford (350b2) from £15 to £33, and Caistor with Hundon (338bi) from £30 to £50. Equally there were immense declines. Castle or West Bytham (360b2) fell from £19 10s. to £10, Waddington (349b2) from £96 to £20, and Doddington Pigot (346a2) from £20 to £4. We might expect manors with fairly low values in 1066 to furnish a high proportion of falls, but this is not so. Many manors of from £4 to £8 in value had declined. It is interesting that again Walter d'Aincourt's manors (361ai,2) show overall appreciation. Though Ingoldsby was partly waste, his thirteen properties rose in value from £54 to £64 18s.

In addition to the stated value, a *tailla* is mentioned in 268 entries, 32 per cent of those where comparative values are given. This is 'a sum of money paid directly to the lord by both free and unfree, standing outside the lessees' rent'.[1] Large sums are so mentioned; Spalding (351b2) was worth £30 in 1086, and the *tailla* was also £30. At Folkingham (355b2) it was £50, £10 more than the stated value of this large manor, while Bolingbroke (351a2) was valued at £40 but had a *tailla* of £80. There are several similar proportions, but the majority of the instances are of a few shillings to £3, with great variation in the values of the manors.

The total recorded value for *tailla* is £718 8s. 4d. It is unlikely that it bore any relation to manorial value, and certainly the proportion varies tremendously with the area. In the South Riding of Lindsey it is as much as 36 per cent of manorial values, but this is much higher than in any other administrative area. The figure is indeed only about 15½ per cent in the West Riding and 13½ per cent in Kesteven. It is, however, slightly suggestive that it is highest where falls in value are most numerous. If the figures are added to those of manorial values, they would give an appreciation over the county of 32 per cent in all.

It is never recorded for royal manors, but the huge appreciations on these suggests that its equivalent was being obtained. We hear little of it on the lands of the bishops of Lincoln or Durham, or in connection with those of the archbishop of York or on those of Roger of Poitou which pose so many problems. But it is very large in the fiefs of Ivo Taillebois (£179), Gilbert of Ghent (£118), and of Earls Hugh and Alan. In the

---

[1] Stenton, in C. W. Foster and T. Longley: *The Lincolnshire Domesday* (Horncastle, 1924), p. xxiii. It might be a parallel to the *gersuma* charged to exact the full value from socage land where land values were increasing while socage dues remained fixed.

lesser lay fiefs it is of infrequent occurrence, and it looks as if the more important a local landlord, the more extensively it had been imposed.

We do not find it mentioned in many large manors where we might reasonably expect it, but often it occurs on all or almost all the holdings in a vill. It appears five times at Scawby with Sturton and once at Scawby, in all three estates at Messingham and Ingleby, and in both at Covenham and Healing.

Some of the figures might suggest that the intention was to bring the 1086 value up to that of 1066. West Rasen's (362b2) declined from £16 to £10, and the *tailla* was £6; Thornton's (363bi), where the *tailla* was £1, from £5 to £4. But on too many occasions we find the *tailla* where the value had risen substantially. Indeed, where the increase is equal to the *tailla* we might wonder if here it represents this increase, e.g. at Melton Ross (363a2), where the value went up from £6 to £8, with £2 *tailla*. But this could apply in only a limited number of instances. Again, something like one-third of the relevant passages might suggest that the basis had been one shilling for each recorded member of the population, and others are very close to this relationship. Including the priest, there were 40 persons mentioned at Nocton (362ai), and the *tailla* was 40s. At Hibaldstow (350bi) the *tailla* was 20s. and there were 18 villeins and two bordars; while at Flixborough and its Thealby berewick (361b2) there were 41 recorded inhabitants for a 40s.-*tailla*. But equally there are many entries which in no way suggest this equation, and it is hardly likely that all sokemen and villeins could contribute identical amounts. A solitary villein appears at Messingham (344a2), but the *tailla* was 5s.

The *ora* is perhaps less prominent than might be expected, though it may well have formed the basis of sums which do not obviously reflect it. The sums most frequently occurring are 16s. and 8s.; 10s. 8d., 5s. 4d., and 2s. 8d. occur only ten times in the fifty-six instances of an *ora*-basis in values under £1. A high proportion of the instances occur for 1066 only. Values of £4 and £8, however, are extremely common. It is curious that there should be a number of high values which are integral multiples of the *ora*, e.g.

81	*orae*	£5 8s.	[1]Candlesby (360ai)
64	„	£4 5s. 4d.	Wyville/Denton (353a2), Belton (369a2)
25	„	£1 13s. 4d.	Tattersall Thorpe (341a2)
24	„	£1 12s.	[1]Navenby (365a2), [1] Goxhill (344a2)
20	„	£1 6s. 8d.	[1]Blyborough (350a2)
18	„	£1 4s.	Great Coates (357b2)

[1] 1066 value.

347 *orae* seems an unlikely quantity, yet this is what Spalding's £23 2s. 8d. represents. The *ora* not infrequently occurs in the renders of mills, fisheries, and salt-pans, e.g. at Evedon (337bi), Heckington (355ai), Bicker (368ai). The turbary at Grainsby (347a2) rendered 5s. 4d.

The mark of silver appears only rarely. Half a mark was the constant value of Riseholme (354b2), Boultham (368bi) had been worth 13s. 4d., and we have noticed above Blyborough (350a2) as having been worth £1 6s. 8d.

It is to be suspected that rents demanded and obtained were often in excess of true value. Such a situation is, however, only once mentioned; the Grantham church-land (337b2) was farmed for £10, £2 more than its value in 1066, but it was in fact worth only £5. Mention of leases and manors at farm are also rare. A holding at Gunby St Nicholas (369ai) was being leased for 6s., and the *censores* ploughing at North Stoke (360bi) rendered 7s. A decline in the value of Broughton (363b2) was a recent one. In 1066 it had been worth £10, but in 1086 it was valued at only £7, though 'in the past year it had been worth £10'. Half an estate at Little Lavington (371ai), the whole apparently worth £1 in 1066, was worth only 5s. at the Inquest, but for nine years had been mortgaged for £1. In four entries, peculiar to the Wapentake of Loveden (347b2, 348ai), the amount paid for horse-provender additional to the values of the manors is given.

Waste or partial waste occurs in 56 entries. For the most part they occur in the areas where concentrations of falls in value are apparent. It has been pointed out that most 'reflect the hazards of farming or were due to some special local cause ... the distribution bears no relation to the natural waste of heath and fen'.[1] Wrangle (367b2), it is true, is said to be waste 'on account of the action of the sea', and other coastal villages where waste is recorded may have suffered loss from a similar cause. A number of the holdings said to be waste possessed meadow and/or underwood, and several are definitely stated to be only partially waste. Garthorpe with Luddington (369bi) was rendering 3s., 7s. less than the 1066 value. Four only of the nine bovates at Addlethorpe (360ai) were waste; land for four oxen at Keisby (371ai) was waste except for three villeins who actually possessed four oxen. Here there were also four acres of meadow and two of underwood, and the value of 10s. had not lessened. Helpringham (357ai) was 'almost waste'; there were a villein and two acres of meadow there. Of two holdings at Bicker (367ai, 340ai), one was waste 'except for one salt-pan', the other was both waste and had a wasted salt-pan. Scottlethorpe (353ai), worth 100s. in 1066, was in 1086 worth 10s. 'at most'; the

[1] *Dom. Geog.*, i, 72.

two bovates at Elsthorpe with Balby (368a2) were *vacuae*, but none the less were being tilled.[1]

To relate teams to ploughlands is here again impossible. In a number of villages 'ploughlands' outnumber teams; in a number of entries the quantity of 'ploughlands' equals or is double that of the carucates for geld. There seems to be an artificial element about so many of the statements that, while the 'ploughlands' might be used to give some idea of agricultural reality, detailed exploration of their relationship with teams or geld-carucates is unlikely to prove profitable.

Nor can we learn much from the figures for recorded population, since sokemen outnumber villeins and bordars combined, while slaves are altogether omitted, except to presume that in 1086 there were still a large number of individual farms and small communities.

Entries in which the plough-teams of sokemen or of villeins only are recorded are here extremely frequent. In 217 there were 2,303½ sokemen with 521⅞ teams, averaging 1·81 oxen per man. Some sokemen, of course, had more; one at Thorpe on the Hill (338ai) had half a team, and one at Fulsby (339ai) a whole one, but such quantities are rare ones. At the other end of the scale a Rothwell sokeman (342a2) had a single ox, nor is this an isolated instance.[2] The sokeman at Beesby (347bi) had no beast of the plough; nor had three at Rippingale (364bi). Twelve at Torrington (362bi) are said to 'have nothing'.

In 192 entries 920 villeins possessed 169¼ teams, which produces an average of 1·79 oxen per head, akin to that for sokemen, so that the majority of sokemen and villeins cannot have been notably unequal in wealth. But the occasions on which villeins are not said to possess any oxen are numerous (e.g. Creeton, 358a2), though this may sometimes have been because they had occupations unconnected with the plough. Five at Drayton (346bi) 'do not plough'; perhaps, since there were four salt-pans here, they were concerned with these. Nor did ten at West Wykeham (364ai), but there is no indication of how these might have been employed. Often a villein had but a single ox (e.g. at Grasby, 338b2), while at Thrunsco (350ai) five had but one ox between them. But at North Kelsey (347ai) one had six oxen.[3]

[1] Presumably by men from a neighbouring holding. Seven other Lincolnshire entries refer to ploughing apparently being done in a similar manner; Uffington (366b2), Houghton (370bi), Brattleby (340bi), Fotherby (354a2)—though this last is a doubtful instance—, North Stoke (360bi), Claxby by Normanby (350ai). At the last there were two villeins 'who do not plough'. Little Grimsby (340b2) had been waste, but was being cultivated at the time of the Inquest.

[2] Sometimes the oxen of *homines* are recorded; in each instance except that of Carlton (370b2) such sokemen or villeins had a single ox.

[3] Stenton claimed that 'the ordinary Lincolnshire sokeman and villein . . . was a man of two

Bordars without oxen are common; only in half a dozen entries are these ascribed to them. Two at Burton by Lincoln (353b2) are said to have a team, but in all eleven had only 18 oxen, though this gives an average little less than that for villeins. But all these figures are somewhat arbitrary, for the number of entries in which no inhabitants are mentioned is large, as is that where men of more than one classification appear. If their equipment seems small, we must remember that the soils may have required fewer oxen than elsewhere, and that many teams must have been made up on a co-operative principle. A teamless Uffington holding (366b2) was tilled by the oxen of Belmesthorpe (376b2). No oxen are recorded for a Houghton manor (370bi), but Abbot Thorald of Peterborough held it of Colegrim and ploughed it with his own demesne (see also fol. 345b2). Land for half a team at Ravendale (341a2) is said to have been ploughed by Walbert, the Bishop's man, with three oxen. In this vill two villeins had two oxen (365bi), and there were other teams.

A feature of the text is the insistence on the presence of meadow and its importance, though the infrequency of mention of pasture may imply that much styled *pratum* was really of the nature of *pastura*. Its dimensions are sometimes given, or its extent in terms of the carucate or virgate; occasionally an entry is solely concerned with it. Peterborough had 48 acres of meadow exempt from geld at Uffington (346a2), and this was worth 90s. Several times we are told that a holding contains nothing but some acres of meadow, e.g. Yaddlethorpe (338bi) and Owmby (338b2), or is waste except for a little meadow, e.g. Barkwith (329bi), Snelland (339b2), Clee (342bi). At Sutton in the Marsh (348b2) two villeins had 20 acres of meadow.

Native survivors are only rarely mentioned as sub-tenants, and the number of those who are given on fols. 370a2–71bi is not large. Nor did they hold much land; no manor is said to be worth more than 50s., while over thirty were valued at less than £1 or were waste. On the fifty manors the *tailla* appears once only. The native element in the county above the sokeman level must in 1086 have been quite unimportant.

---

or three oxen' (*op. cit.*, p. xx). The above suggests that the possession of three oxen was not common.

7
The East Midlands

It is impossible to use what one normally thinks of as 'the East Midlands' as a Domesday unit. Its counties were in four different Inquest circuits, and the texts of two of the former treat valuations in an unique manner. Accordingly, the area now to be considered has been limited to two shires from circuit VI and two from circuit VIII, even though the Rutland text has specialised anomalies and Huntingdonshire was brigaded with the north of England.

Two counties, Leicestershire and Northamptonshire, furnish valuations in which, in the majority of instances, the *valuit* is frequently extremely small and less than the *valet*, and often very greatly less. The explanation seems to be that for the former county *valuit* refers to a time fairly soon after the Conquest, for the latter just before it, displaying the results of the Northumbrian revolt of 1065. Since comparatively little waste is recorded for 1086, general recovery seems to be implied. But whether it was full recovery or not is uncertain.

The differences between *valuit* and *valet* display so wide a range that it is difficult to determine whether a large disparity indicates that holdings with this feature had been greatly impoverished but had made a good recovery or not. It could be argued that a small difference implies post-Conquest troubles, but equally that it suggests inability to recover substantially from former disaster. A choice between such opposite points of view depends largely on the geographical distribution of large or small differences and on their proportions in relation to the values of 1065 or 1068. It is convenient to consider separately, where comparable figures occur, *valuits* of £1 and over and of smaller sums.

Valuit less than £1

	instances	
Leicestershire	203	75% have *valuit* 50% of *valet* or less, 64% 40% or less, 49½% 30% or less
Northamptonshire	236	68% have *valuit* 50% of *valet* or less, 48½% 40% or less, 36½% 30% or less

Valuit £1 or more

Leicestershire	142	34½% have *valuit* 50% of *valet* or less, 22½% 40% or less, 6¼% 30% or less
Northamptonshire	211	32½% have *valuit* 50% of *valet* or less, 17½% 40% or less, 7¼% 30% or less

There is here such similarity of figures for the two counties, and such large difference between the small holdings and the larger ones, that it looks as if the lower the proportion of *valuit* to *valet* on a small holding, the more probable it is that damage had been considerable, while the higher it was on a substantial holding, the less this had suffered. This seems logical, for a small and poorly equipped holding would find recovery difficult, though the addition of only a few men and oxen might make considerable difference, and troops in need of supplies would expend least time and energy by raiding intensively the larger manors. Hence the maps for this section (Figs. 27–8) show separately holdings with a *valuit* of less than £1 and those with one of £1 or over. The royal manors in Northamptonshire have however been omitted from these, for the figures given for them could be altogether misleading. The manors might have changed in structure, or in liabilities.

Huntingdonshire

The structure of the Huntingdonshire Domesday is a fairly simple one. Comparatively few manors in this hidated shire are said to be complex ones, with berewicks and sokelands, for which we are indeed frequently given statistics, though more manors were complex ones than the text would disclose, and a great many villages were in the hand of a single lord. The worst complication is that the land of a dozen villages lay in more than one county. It is convenient, therefore, to use the Domesday county as the basis.

Comparative values are given in 122 entries, 80 per cent of the total. In just under half the instances, there seems to have been no change in the valuation between 1066 and 1086, and only about 15½ per cent show appreciation. An apparent fall in overall value, omitting *Terra Regis*, is only a slight one, from £677 5s. 4d. to £652 0s. 4d., or 3¾ per cent. Stenton pointed out that 'though a prosperous county, it was bearing a

THE EAST MIDLANDS: HUNTINGDONSHIRE

burden of taxation out of due proportion to its wealth'.[1] This may have militated against full exploitation.

Even a small county like Huntingdonshire, the text of which includes few obscurities, can provide problems in the interpretation of values. For example, was the 1086 value of Eynesbury (207a2) £21 or, including that of the sub-entries, £26 10s? If the former, the manor fell in value by 12½ per cent; if the latter, it increased by 10¼ per cent.

The entries and sub-entries may be classified thus:

	all relevant entries	sub-tenancies omitted
valet in excess of *valuit*	19	15
valet and *valuit* identical	59	58
valet less than *valuit*	44	39
waste	3	3
no information	3	3
manorial components	24	24
	152	142
Fall in value 1066–86	3%	5%
ditto, omitting *Terra Regis*	1¼%	3¾%

The quantities are small, but produce quite large differences in percentage falls in value.

Of the eight royal manors (203bi), only one improved its worth. Bottlebridge went up from £5 to £8, possibly because the king had sokeright in 3½ hides of Orton Waterville which, though said to have been Godwine's land, was really the abbot of Peterborough's. Yet on fol. 205a2 it is stated that the soke over 2¼ hides which Godwine had held at this place had formerly been the king's, but had been given to St Peter.[2] Though the values of four manors remained constant, Hartford with King's Ripton fell from £24 to £15, and Gransden from £40 to £30. We have the unusual situation in this county of royal estates declining in value from £156 to £139 10s.

The appendix to the Huntingdonshire Domesday (208ai–bi) which deals with claims and disputes makes it clear that the king may often have been deprived of rights and revenue, largely at the instance of Eustace, his sheriff, who had been far from scrupulous in the conduct of his office. In a number of entries we are told that land which he seems to have acquired had been part of the royal *firma*, e.g. Keyworth, until Eustace

[1] *VCH*, i, pt. 8, p. 321.
[2] Possibly the accounts of *Terra Regis* and of the Peterborough lands were constructed at different dates.

became sheriff, or a berewick in a royal manor (Gidding), or in the king's soke (Graffham). Eustace did not, however, supervise the royal manors. With the exception of Godmanchester, they were in the custody of Ralf the brother of Ilger. Appropriations by Eustace, together with some of King Edward's gifts, probably reduced the royal revenue.[1]

It is rarely easy to deduce a reason for marked appreciation in value. Gidding (207a2) may have doubled its 1066 value because this may at that date have been abnormally low; £2 is a small value for a 4½ hide manor. William of Warenne seems everywhere to have made the most of his property, and Kimbolton (205bi), which had been Earl Harold's, rose in value from £7 to £16 4s., with a sub-tenancy worth £1. There was sokeland attached to the manor, the value of which in 1066 is not given. In 1086 this was worth £4 10s., and its value may not have been included in the £7. An appreciation of nearly 55 per cent is not a rarity; moreover, a complex manor may have been enlarged. A Hundred of Kimbolton is mentioned (206ai,2), and William might have had the profits of sokeright in it.

Possible reasons for falls in value in 44 holdings are not altogether obvious ones. Waste is only twice mentioned for an entire holding, but Waresley (206bi) was partly waste, and one of the ten hides of Ellington (204b2) was waste 'because of the king's wood'. Certainly there was royal Forest in the neighbourhood, for the jurors agreed that 36 hides in Brampton were royal demesne, and did not, as was claimed, belong to the Forest (208a2). The royal manor of Brampton (203bi) is credited with only 15 hides, but the paucity of named settlements in what was later Weybridge and Harthay Forests may imply that other assessments, and perhaps vills, did not find their way into DB, especially if the construction of the record for *Terra Regis* preceded that for non-royal land. To the south-west a number of manors declined in value, and may have been affected by extension of the Forest. Buckden (203b2) fell from £20 to £16 10s., one Offord manor (206bi) from £2 to 12s., and another (206b2) from £6 to £5. Near Alconbury, later if not in 1086 connected with the Forest, a holding in Stukeley (206ai) and one in Hemingford (207a2) were waste, perhaps because they may have been placed in the Forest, though DB does not say so.

Several instances of decline are confined to the individual vill. The three Hail Weston manors (206bi *bis*, 207a2) fell in all from £8 10s. to £5 5s. Nearby, Southoe (206bi, 207a2), worth £7 in 1066, was valued at only £4 10s. at the Inquest. But, despite apparent loss at Eynesbury (206b2, 207a2) and at Waresley (206bi, 207ai), where a half-hide was partly waste,

[1] King Edward had given the land of Leofric to the bishopric of Lincoln (Orton, 203bi).

there is really nothing in the figures to suggest violent disturbances in the south of the county (Figs. 12 and 13).

But falls in value in the neighbourhood of Peterborough might reflect movement of troops to or from the Northumbrian campaigns, or even earlier troubles. It is unlikely that the activities of Hereward and his associates had no effect on the district. One of the Chesterton manors (205a2) was worth only half what it had been in 1066, £4. The Orton Waterville and Longueville properties (203b2, 205a2, 206ai *ter*) declined from £10 to £4 15*s*. A few manors near Ermine Street—Denton (203b2), Yaxley (205ai), Woodston (205ai), Folksworth (205bi), Sawtry (206ai), and Caldecote (206ai)—show falls in value. Perhaps they suffered from the march from York through the shire which culminated in the raising of a castle at Huntingdon. In view of Eustace's unscrupulous tendencies, it is surprising that he should not have improved the receipts from his manors. But at the Inquest they were worth only about three-quarters of their pre-Conquest value. However, they were not large ones, and mostly in tenants' hands.

There is a distinct possibility that here the ploughlands do not indicate the actual arable, but 'preserve a record of the taxation imposed by Danish earls soon after the settlement of 877' on a duodecimal pattern.[1] Over 50 per cent of the figures are 2, 3, 4, 6, 8, 9, 12, 16, 18, 24, and others may have combined to produce similar quantities. At Stilton they were $2 + 2\frac{7}{8} + 3\frac{1}{8} = 8$ (203bi,2, 206ai); at Broughton (204a2) there were $7\frac{1}{4}$ on the demesne and $8\frac{3}{4}$ on the sokemen's land, 16 in all. Thus the 23 instances of an apparent excess of teams over ploughlands may not indicate a surplus at all. On the other hand, the hidage, ploughland, and plough-team quantities rather suggest that the ploughland figures are not too far from actuality. If so, there were, where comparison is possible, $999\frac{1}{8}$ teams for $1,130\frac{7}{8}$ ploughlands, a deficiency of only about $11\frac{1}{2}$ per cent.

The text includes a feature which is inclined to remind us of the 'carucates of land which never gelded' of the south-western shires. With varying formulae, we are told of 'land for *n* teams' apart, not from the ploughlands recorded, but from the hides of assessment. All but three of the sixteen instances come from the Hundred of Hurstingstone, in which, we are told (203ai), 'demesne ploughlands are exempt from the king's geld'. Such information is limited to four fiefs, three of which are ecclesiastical ones. It suggests the existence of arable land made available since the last assessment to the geld, though it was not necessarily all arable or indeed being cultivated at all. But a more probable explanation would be that the demesne ploughlands represent land which had been freed from the

[1] C. Hart: 'The Hidation of Huntingdonshire', pp. 55–6 (*Proc. Camb. Ant. Soc.*, lxi, 1968).

obligation of gelding; which, indeed, had been accorded beneficial hidation. To add this land to the given ploughlands would turn an $11\frac{1}{2}$ per cent team-deficiency into one of about 15 per cent. The number of demesne teams is almost always that of these additional ploughlands. In 29 entries, also, we are given the hidage of the demesne; these occur in 13 of the 29 fiefs.

Occasionally what seems to be a surplus of teams is encountered, e.g. at Denton (203b2), where there were six teams on land for two teams. But two ploughlands for five hides which had been worth £5 seems an over-small quantity, and may be a scribal error. Surpluses where the value had fallen, e.g. at Yaxley (205ai) or Folksworth (205bi), seem somewhat improbable, unless we are being given potential values or the manor had ceased to be largely arable. An excess of teams can hardly have been due to a quantity of uneconomic small farms owned by sokemen, for by 1086 sokemen, unless omitted from many entries, were few in the county.

The number of entries in which bordars are unmentioned is very high; in nearly fifty where villeins are noted none is recorded. Villeins accounted for nearly 80 per cent of the persons specified. Some may well have earlier been free men or sokemen, reduced in the social scale.[1] The teams of sokemen cannot be isolated, but when the numbers are compared with the total of villeins and sokemen in a holding, it does not look as if they can here have owned many oxen. 513 villeins from 40 entries had $195\frac{1}{2}$ teams, which averages just over three oxen per man. The statistics suggest that at Elton (204bi) some must have had six or more, and at Dillington (204b2) and Conington (206b2) five.[2] Stenton considered that 'the higher grades of peasantry had suffered material depression in the years preceding the Domesday enquiry ... men whose immediate predecessors had been free from strict seignorial control ... appear ... under the indefinite definition of *villani* ... their condition tended to become assimilated to that of the lower peasant ranks'.[3]

In some entries the bordars have no oxen; in the three available instances eight had only eleven oxen. But at Keysoe (207bi) the solitary villein had only two oxen, and at Boughton (206bi) five villeins had only four.

Slaves do not appear, but though omitted from DB they figure in the *Inquisitio Eliensis* for all four Ely manors in the county. Thus Huntingdon-

---

[1] It is said that at Orton Longueville (206ai) 'seven sokemen were there': no villeins or bordars are noted. There had been eight thegns at Catworth (206bi), and in 1086 there were ten *homines* with seven bordars under them.

[2] At a Northamptonshire holding in Elton (221a2), a village some of whose land was in Huntingdonshire, six sokemen had three teams, which suggests that some sokemen were less well-to-do than villeins, or that sokeman and villein were sometimes practically interchangeable terms. [3] *VCH*, i, p. 324.

shire as a whole may well have had a servile element of some 10 per cent of its population. It certainly seems unlikely that manors such as Gransden (203bi) or Eynesbury (207a2), where in each case there were seven demesne teams, should have had no unfree labourers. Ely had ten demesne teams on her Huntingdonshire lands, and demesne land available for additional teams. It is interesting that the IE figures show that on two of the Ely manors, Colne and Bluntisham, the number of villeins had declined by one-third, though it had increased slightly at Somersham and Spaldwick. Had we statistics for the whole county, we might well find the number of villeins less than they had been at the Conquest.

The list of king's thegns occupies only seven entries, and the total value of their holdings was a mere £6 11s. 4d. A very few survivors are noted as sub-tenants. Sæmær was still holding his quarter-hide at Hargrave (204ai), Ælfwold a hide at Holywell (204a2), Edric 2½ hides at Lutton, and Swegen five at Yelling (204bi). So far as we can see, the thegns of Huntingdonshire had largely disappeared from the scene. Ælfric, the tenant of St Benedict of Ramsey, was killed at Hastings (208ai), and doubtless other local thegns fell with him. But some may still have had tenancies, though unrecorded in DB.

Leicestershire

The Leicestershire text would present no special difficulties if it were not for the uncertainty of the implications of the varying formulae indicating the number of ploughlands, and the existence of certain large manors with dispersed berewicks and sokelands for which we are rarely given individual information. Rothley (230a2) was not in itself a particularly large royal vill, but it possessed twenty-two dependencies some of which were not within fifteen miles of the *caput*. Five other manors were also highly complex ones.[1] On the other hand, holdings in two or more vills are less frequently treated as units than they are in shires further north. Translation of the statistics on a cartographic basis is, none the less, more satisfactory than for some neighbouring shires.

The Leicestershire text, in recording two or more values for holdings, never states that one is that of 1066. Occasionally we are told that a value is that current when the holder received the manor, but in some instances, e.g. Burbage (231ai), this may not be *circa* 1067–70, but the date at which it later changed hands. In two entries we are told about values at three dates, and the earliest of these may well be 1066. Donington le Heath

[1] Great Bowden (230bi), Retby (232ai), Melton Mowbray (235bi), Barrow on Soar (237ai), Loughborough (237ai).

(236ai) had been worth 20s., but was waste 'when received', and by 1086 was valued at only 2s. Earl Hugh's fief (237ai) as a whole had been worth £40 earlier as it was at the time of the Inquest, but when he received it only £10. Such entries point to damage within the county caused possibly by the Northumbrian revolt of 1065, but probably to a greater extent by the movement of royal troops during one or both of the campaigns of 1068–70 when Danes and Northumbrians challenged King William.

The *valuit* of the text is frequently a very small sum. In over one-third of the holdings it is 5s. or less, and just one or two shillings commonly appear; sometimes it is as little as fourpence or sixpence.[1] For the whole shire the total is under £400, which would give the carucate an average value of only about 3s. 6d. By 1086 the figure was almost twice as much as this, and the difference between *valuit* and *valet* is often very large. At a Shenton holding (234ai) the value in 1086 was thirty shillings, but earlier it had been only a shilling; Worthington (233a2) had also been worth only one shilling, but in 1086 was valued at twenty. The entries may be analysed as follows:

valuit less than *valet*	258	holdings
valuit and *valet* identical	74	,,
valuit greater than *valet*	14	,,
single value, waste, or no information	54	,,
components of manors	68	,,
	468	

Where comparative figures are available, a total *valuit* of £386 4s. 2d. had become a *valet* of £761 15s. If *Terra Regis* is omitted, the figures become £364 3s. 2d. and £707 15s. The largest differences are on the great local fiefs; that of the lands of Henry de Ferrières is 70 per cent of the 1086 value, and on those of Robert de Buci 68 per cent. On the ecclesiastical lands it is rather lower, 42 per cent, but on the king's estates nearly 60 per cent.

Maitland styled Leicestershire a 'miserably poor' county, and was of the opinion that 'the *valuit* speaks not of the Confessor's day but of some time of disorder that followed the conquest, for in truth it seems to give us but "prairie values" '.[2] Stenton suggested that this time might well be that of the Conqueror's march from Warwick to Nottingham in 1068.[3]

No army of the period could campaign without drawing on the countryside through which it passed for much of its sustenance. But depletion of the resources of many a holding may often have exceeded the limits of

---
[1] Slawston (234a2); Coleorton (233bi), Husbands Bosworth (236ai), Seagrave (233a2).
[2] *DBB*, p. 468 (540).   [3] *VCH*, i, p. 282. It is a view not universally approved.

THE EAST MIDLANDS: LEICESTERSHIRE

essential requisitioning. The operations of 1068 had been necessitated by growing disaffection north of the Trent, enhanced by the support given to the movement by Earls Edwine and Morkere. It would be altogether in keeping with King William's common military policy to ravage parts of Edwine's earldom and thus discourage his subjects from supporting their lord's defiance.

The variations in the changes of value in the holdings known by the single place-name are often considerable. Swinford appears nine times:

fol.	valuit	valet	fol.	valuit	valet
231ai	not given	1s.	234a2	21s.	20s.
231a2	,, ,,	5s.	,,	10s.	20s.
232a2	2s.	5s.	,,	2s.	20s.
232a2	5s.	10s.	235b2	not given	waste, but worth 2s.
,,	6s.	10s.			

Here the *valet* is usually higher than the *valuit*. But at both Sutton Cheney (231a2, 232bi) and Market Bosworth (231bi, 233ai) one holding displays this relationship also, and the other the reverse.

It seems that, as we might expect, holdings with a low *valuit* increased their values most. For with a low value a few more men and oxen and slight exploitation would vastly improve almost derelict property. On the whole values had always been higher east of Foss Way than west thereof, and it is also probable that the east of the county had been least affected by post-Conquest troubles. Most of the differences between *valuit* and *valet* of 40 per cent or more are west of Foss Way, and while it must be remembered that a 50 per cent difference in a holding previously worth £1 or less has an implication different from that of a similar increase in a holding valued more highly, the distribution of either category does not disturb the picture presented. Holdings in which no change in value is reported are also far more numerous in the east than in the west. Many values in the western half, which included Charnwood Forest, were always low, and in the northern half thereof were the majority of the holdings which were or had been waste. The map suggests that the main Norman force had proceeded from Warwick to Tamworth to gain a major road leading to Nottingham and skirting Charnwood Forest. The varying soils are here mostly of low fertility, and consequently recovery would be all the more difficult or uneconomic to organise.

But while it was important that William should approach York as rapidly as possible, he could not well afford to ignore the danger presented by two large towns on his flanks, Derby and Leicester, for they

THE DETAILS OF DOMESDAY BOOK

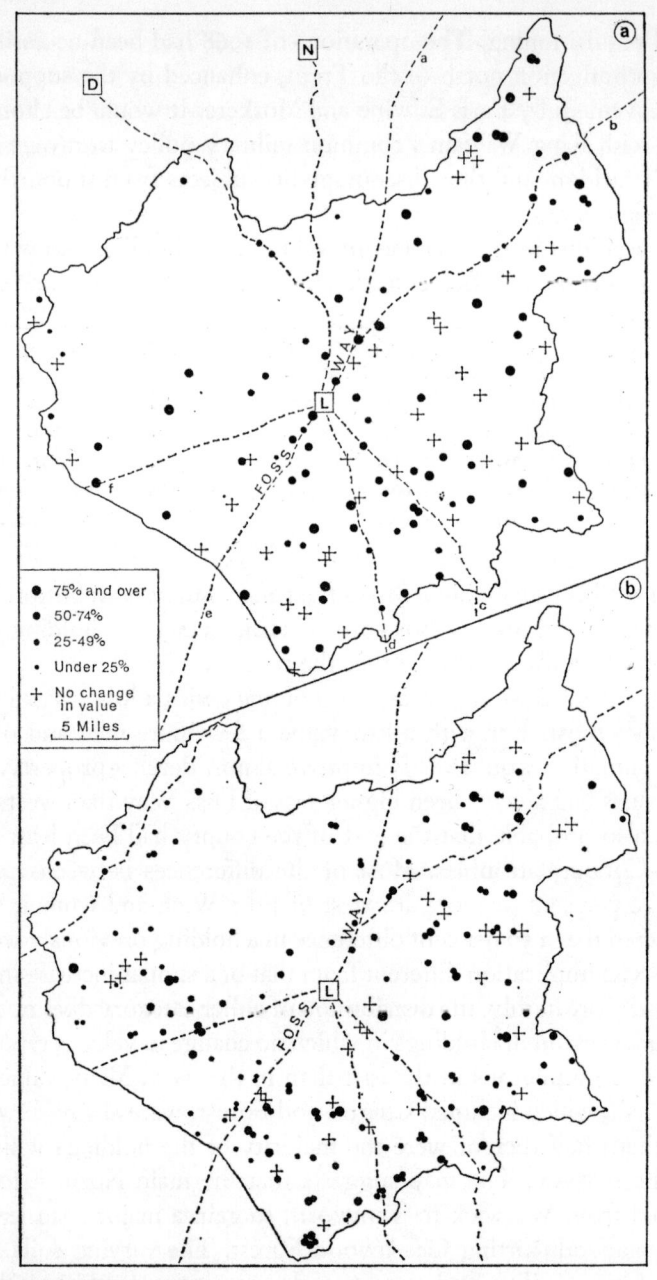

Fig. 27 Domesday Leicestershire
valuit as percentage of *valet*
(a) *valuit* £1 and over (b) *valuit* less than £1
– – – Main strategic roads from (a) Lincoln, (b) Grantham,
(c, d) Northampton, (e) Warwick, (f) north Warwickshire
D—Derby L—Leicester N—Nottingham

THE EAST MIDLANDS: LEICESTERSHIRE

might serve as rallying-points for opposition. The waste and lessened values south of the former (Fig. 23) may reflect a subsidiary campaign of the period.[1] The map further suggests that a portion of the royal force may have been detached to threaten Leicester, and rejoined the main body by moving along Foss Way, accumulating supplies on its way.

Such an hypothesis receives partial confirmation from the fact that little else suggesting large-scale ravaging can be seen in east Leicestershire save near Foss Way. There is, however, a suggestion of fairly concentrated damage parallel and close to the southern limits of the shire. This is possibly attributable to the advance in 1065 on Northampton of the men of south Lincolnshire, moving first on Stamford and then linking in the Market Harborough neighbourhood with other men of the north who had come down Foss Way or from Northumbria by way of the crossing of the Aire at Pontefract.

If the above is the correct explanation of Leicestershire values, recovery had been considerable, but only partial. There was still an appreciable amount of waste in 1086, while the facts that just over 15 per cent of the holdings had the same *valet* as *valuit*, that some values had fallen by 1086, and that the extent of recovery is frequently small, further suggest that Leicestershire had suffered severely from King William's advent. Norton juxta Twycross (231b2), though there were six hides, seven 'ploughlands', and four plough-teams, had a *valuit* of five shillings but a *valet* of only six. Stockerston (232ai), with three teams in excess of its 22 'ploughlands', and 61 recorded inhabitants, of whom 33 were sokemen, improved only from £8 to £9. Unfortunately we do not know to what extent most of the complex manors such as Rothley or Great Bowden or Barrow on Soar may have improved in value. But Melton Mowbray went up from £5 to £8, and its eight members from £4 10s. to £15 10s.

Some of the appreciations may indeed be the result of the imposition of increased rents and liabilities on the peasantry. Five royal manors (230a2,bi) were in 1086 *ad firmam*, and had appreciated from £20 10s. to £43, an increase of 110 per cent against the shire's average of just under 97 per cent. On the whole of *Terra Regis* the increase was nearly 150 per cent. Shepshed (230b2) was 'found waste', but by 1086 had to find a *firma* of £6 'for the service of the Isle of Wight', a due imposed by the Conqueror's half-brother Bishop Odo. Birstall (232a2,b2), where the two holdings had together been worth £2 10s., had to find eight ounces of gold, worth presumably £6. Weston (235ai) had been waste, but in 1086

---

[1] Derby lies less than ten miles from the direct line between Tamworth and Nottingham. Many holdings now in Leicestershire but recorded in the Derbyshire Domeday were waste in 1086.

is said to be worth £3 10s., Husbands Bosworth (236ai) had a *valuit* of sixpence but a *valet* of £1. But the 2s. said to be the value of Burbage (231a2) 'when the abbot received it' could be a mistake for 20s. or £2, since in 1086 it was worth £4.

In view of the fact that sokemen were still numerous in the county in 1086, representing almost one-third of the total recorded population, we might expect to find numerous expressions of value in terms of the *ora*. There are, however, comparatively few. Small sums which suggest reckoning by the *ora*, 5s. 4d., 2s. 8d., or 1s. 4d., occur less than a dozen times.[1] £16, £12, £8, occur only rarely, and so do 24s., 16s., 8s. There are two instances of 1s. 8d. and one of 10d. which might derive from the silver mark of 160d. or twenty pence paid for sixteen.[2]

The twenty-two entries which give us the teams of sokemen only, and the eighteen which supply those of villeins, yield unsatisfactory results. No doubt some villeins were here as well-equipped as were the lesser sokemen, but on average these villeins have $2\frac{1}{2}$ oxen apiece, the sokemen $2\frac{1}{4}$. Yet in no entry, unless there were major differences in the number of oxen owned by the sokemen of a manor, do these seem to possess more than half a team. Two sokemen at Walcote (231ai) and two at Harby (234bi) had each a team between them, while ten at Walton (231b2) had only a couple of teams. But villeins at Desford (232ai) and at Boythorpe (233bi) each had a whole team, though there were only three oxen between the same number of villeins at Sharnford (236b2). The solitary occasion on which the oxen of bordars can be isolated allots a team to five at Wigston Parva (231bi). There are plenty of instances of apparently teamless villeins and bordars, e.g. at Shenton (231b2, 233a2). Leicestershire, in Maitland's opinion, was an over-rated county, and a heavy geld would not make for appreciable capital equipment for most of the peasantry.[3]

In this county also it is not possible to relate teams to 'ploughlands'. The Leicestershire folios employ four different formulae for the latter:

(a) there can be *n* teams
(b) there is land for *n* teams
(c) in King Edward's time there were *n* teams
(d) *n* teams were there.

Possibly there is no real difference between (a) and (b) or between (c) and

---

[1] 'Part of Leicester outside the walls' (230b2), Twyford, Willoughby Waterless (232bi), Walton on the Wolds (231b2), Sharnford (236a2), Ragdale (234bi), Sysonby (236a2), Bogthorpe (233bi); Heather (236a2). Wyfordby (233a2) was valued at 8d., and Slawston (234a2) at 4d.
[2] Cotes de Val (231ai), Walcote (234a2); Cotesbach (232b2).   [3] *DBB*, p. 462 (532).

(d), and it may be that all are intended to tell us, though sometimes perhaps approximately, how many teams had been operating in 1066. Even if this is so, we cannot arrive at a full idea of the proportion of teams at work in 1086 to those of 1066, for the number of entries in which the ploughlands is not given is high. Where figures for both 'ploughlands' and teams are given, the deficiency of teams is about $12\frac{1}{2}$ per cent. This does seem a highly possible proportion, in view of post-Conquest troubles, but it may well possess no reality. An excess of teams over 'ploughlands' occurs in 68 entries. The instances are not confined to any one area, though the southern half of the county includes about two-thirds of them.

Maitland confessed to 'the horrible suspicion' that the teamland here might be 'as artificial and as remote from real agrarian life as is the hide or the gelding carucate'.[1] Moreover, 'in entry after entry the number of ploughlands bears a simple ratio to that of carucates in a suspiciously convenient manner'.[2] Probably there is an artificial basis to many of the Leicestershire ploughlands, though in the present state of our knowledge it is impossible to say if it might reflect an earlier geld-assessment.

What does seem plain about the information is that the formula employed seems very often to depend on the fief in which it appears. In only the last entry under *Terra Regis*, probably a postscriptal one, is a figure given. For the entire fief of Hugh de Grentmaisnil, which occupies four columns of the text, formula (b) is employed; so it is for the lands of Guy de Raimbeaucourt and of William Peverel. Formula (d) persists throughout the record of the estates of the Countess Judith and of the men of the Count of Mellent, while for the members of the manor of Barrow on Soar, for which we alone have figures for Earl Hugh's land, (c) is used. In some small fiefs more than one formula appears. The suspicion is aroused that there was no general return made by the holder of a small local fief, or that different reeves or juries in these gave varying information. But what here was in someone's mind when he stated that 'there is land for one team; however there is one in demesne and another of the villeins', etc. (there were also a priest and three bordars; Cadeby, 232bi) is problematical.

Northamptonshire

The text of the Northamptonshire Domesday was badly produced. Either through carelessness, or because the provincial draft did not clearly indicate the county in which a holding lay, a number of entries describe estates which were neither geographically nor administratively within the

[1] *DBB*, pp. 427, 471 (493, 542).   [2] *Dom. Geog.*, ii, p. 326.

THE DETAILS OF DOMESDAY BOOK

shire. Some villages included holdings which did not all belong to a single county, but here the basis has been only fols. 219a2–29a2, except that the manors now in Oxfordshire, Staffordshire, or Warwickshire have been

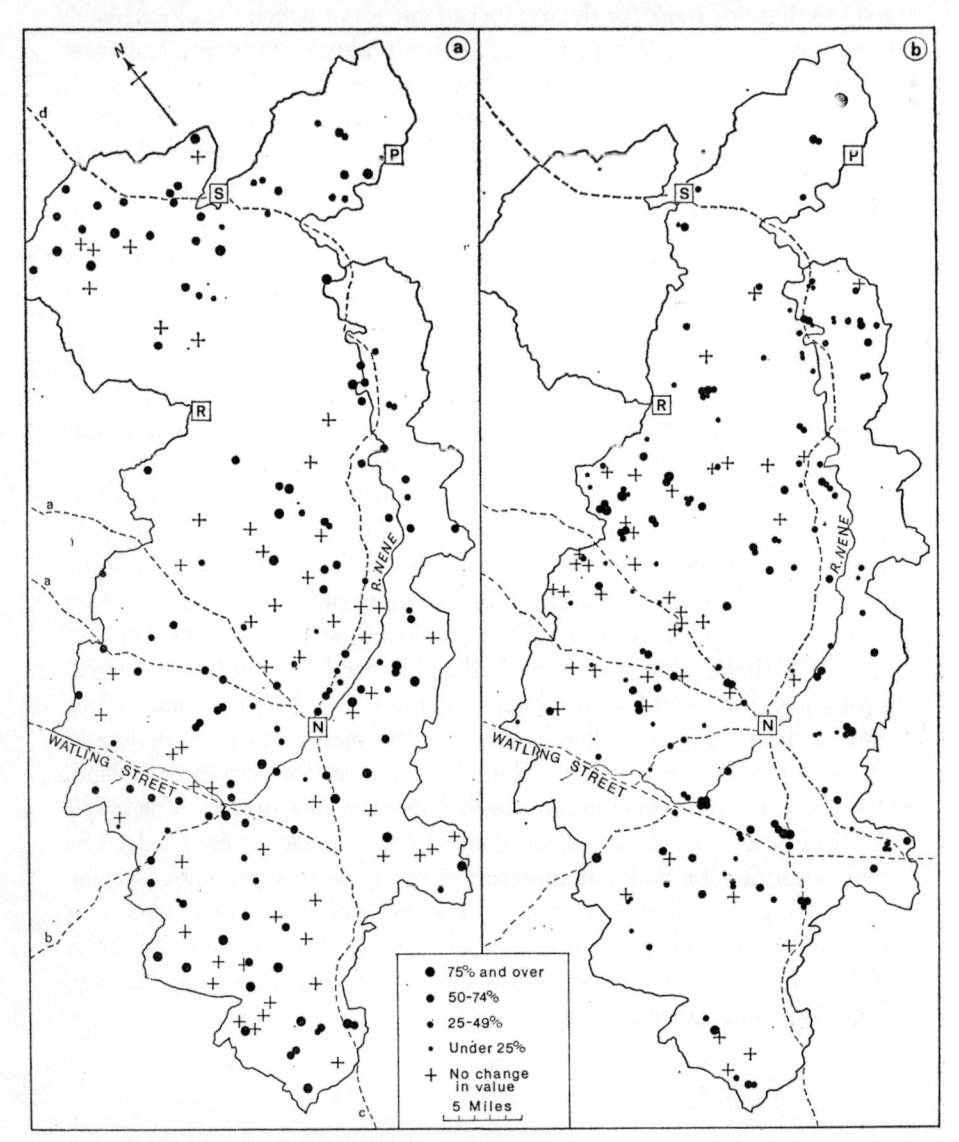

Fig. 28 Domesday Northamptonshire and Rutland
valuit as percentage of *valet*
(a) *valuit* £1 and over (b) *valuit* less than £1
– – – Main strategic roads from (a) Leicester, (b) Warwick, (c) to Oxford,
N—Northampton P—Peterborough R—Rockingham S—Stamford
(d) from Lincolnshire

THE EAST MIDLANDS: NORTHAMPTONSHIRE

omitted. The Domesday county includes the two Hundreds of Witchley now in Rutland.

This is another of the counties for which, in the majority of the entries, the *valuit* is less than the *valet*. The former value is, indeed, very frequently less than 10s., but not, as a rule, because the relevant holding was small. In twenty-four holdings the *valuit* was greater than the *valet*, and since most were south of Northampton, these will need special consideration.

The entries, including those vills now in the modern Rutland, may be analysed as follows:

valuit less than *valet*	313	holdings
valuit and *valet* identical	113	,,
valuit greater than *valet*	24	,,
single value, waste, or no information	66	,,
components of manors	57	,,
	573	

In 1065 the county had suffered appallingly from the ravages of Earl Morkere's forces from Northumbria and northern Mercia during their revolt against the government of Tostig Godwineson. The effects were still apparent ten years later, for the Northamptonshire Geld Roll, which cannot refer to a date later than 1075, shows almost one-third of the shire as 'waste'. By 1086, as the manors were re-stocked, recovery seems to have been fairly general; the *valet* shows an appreciation of 58 per cent if *Terra Regis* is excluded, and of just under 50 per cent for the whole shire.

The figures of the Geld Roll would suggest that the worst of the ravaging was in the Nene valley, where in the three modern Hundreds of Polebrook, Willybrook, and Nassaborough with Uptongreen over 50 per cent of the land was returned as 'waste', and was also severe where bands of rebels coming from the neighbourhood of Leicester and Derby entered the county. Maps of the differences between *valuit* and *valet* (Fig. 28) show the effect more clearly. In the Nene valley, in the country near Oundle, many values were very low at the time of the Conquest. The lines of approach from Leicester and Derby on Northampton are also plainly apparent. It looks as if the main body of the insurgents did not proceed to Oxford as their leaders did, but remained in the south-west of the shire during the negotiations with King Edward and his ministers and that its need for supplies seriously damaged the local economy, though the Geld Roll shows only about one-quarter of the land here as 'waste'. A string of low values about Watling Street possibly reflects Earl Edwine's Mercian and Welsh troops joining those of his brother at Towcester.[1]

[1] J. H. Round commented on the probable routes in *VCH*, i, p. 262.

THE DETAILS OF DOMESDAY BOOK

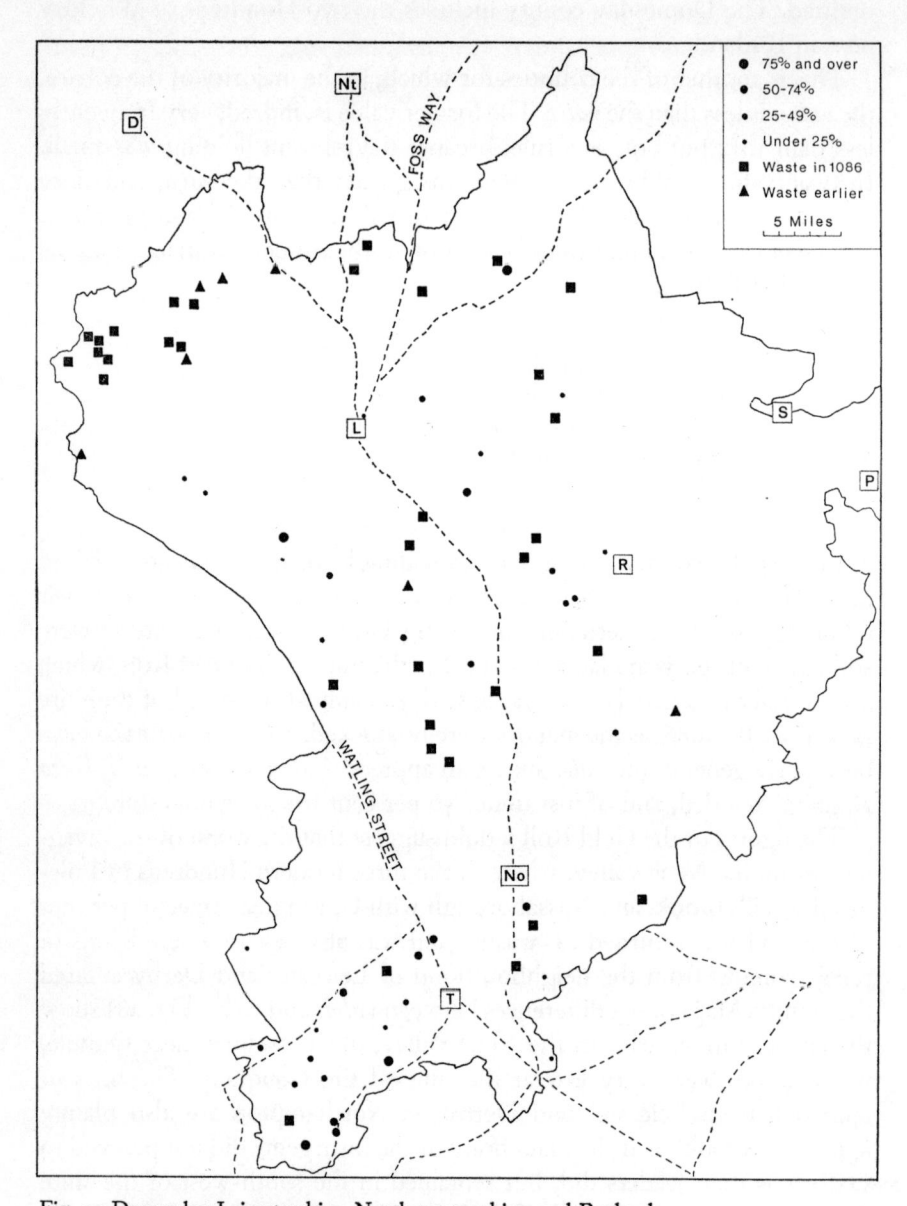

Fig. 29 Domesday Leicestershire, Northamptonshire, and Rutland
Fall in value 1066–86, and waste
––– Main strategic roads (north) from beyond Trent and south Lincolnshire, (south) to Oxford and Warwick
D—Derby   L—Leicester
No—Northampton   Nt—Nottingham   P—Peterborough
R—Rockingham   S—Stamford   T—Towcester

THE EAST MIDLANDS: NORTHAMPTONSHIRE

By 1086, recovery, if substantial, can only have been partial. The concentration of falls in value and of *valet* less than *valuit* on the larger holdings, mostly south of Watling Street, suggest that these may have been caused by the passage of royal troops into Warwickshire on the occasion of the revolts of 1069. An alternative or supplementary explanation would be that a detachment of the invading army passed through the district in the winter of 1066 during the stage which saw its passage from Buckingham to Bedford. The situation and distribution of the holdings for which *valuit* and *valet* are identical, suggesting only limited or no recovery, probably further indicate the movements of royal troops northwards to combat the Northumbrian revolt. They lie with some frequency along the two main roads from Northampton to Leicester, and in lesser degree in the neighbourhood of the Northampton—Stamford road. There is some suggestion that one detachment left the line of Watling Street where it enters the county and moved northwards to Northampton and so to Leicester. Static values are infrequent in and above the Nene valley, for Peterborough lies well to the east of the approaches to York. They are virtually absent from the neighbourhood of Rockingham Forest, where supplies would be hard to obtain.

The distribution of proportion of *valuit* to *valet* is inclined to vary with the size and wealth of the holding. In considering the maps, it must be remembered that the larger the symbol, the less the difference between the two values. This is especially marked south of Watling Street and in the neighbourhood of the common boundary with Leicestershire, where there are signs of post-Conquest decay in some large manors. It happens that neither the modern Rutland nor the Soke of Peterborough furnishes many examples of a low *valuit*, while there were naturally few settlements in the Rockingham Forest area.

It is somewhat surprising that so little waste is recorded for the county in 1086, but this is true also of neighbouring shires which saw the passage of Norman forces, while there had been ample time between 1069 and 1086 for recovery. Wellingborough (222bi) had been worth £2 10s., presumably in 1066, for we are given the value *post*, £2, whereas in 1086 it was valued at £6. Only three holdings are mentioned as having been waste prior to the Inquest; Rockingham, where a castle had later been built (220ai), connected with Forest land, Cranford (220b2), and Woodford (222a2). In 1086 only nine were totally waste.

The entries which in one way or another mention waste in 1086 are illuminating. In addition to the holdings which indicate only partial waste, we are told that a church in Guilsborough and a mill-site at Hollowell, with the land associated with each, were waste (224ai), though the wording of the text suggests that the church itself was unusable. Of two royal manors, Corby and Gretton (219bi), it is said that 'many things are wanting which in King Edward's time belonged to them in wood and ironworks and other proceeds', though no change in their values is indicated. This might be the result of illegal appropriation, not of wasting. Though not said to be even partly waste, the manors forfeited by Aubrey de Coucy on resigning the Northumbrian earldom mostly show a fall in value; however, a holding of Odo of Baycux (Roade, 220a2), in 1086 his half-brother's prisoner, was 'in the king's hand', and waste. A most significant entry is that for Aldwinckle St Peter (222ai); it had been worth £1 and in 1086 was valued at thirty shillings, 'but if it were worked well' (*bene exerceret*) it would be worth as much as £5. It is to be presumed that the opinion was that of the Hundred-jury, not of Peterborough Abbey who owned it. Forest is only once mentioned (Brixworth, 219b2), but some low values may have been caused by the presence of Rockingham Forest.

The royal land had not improved in value to the extent that it did elsewhere, or to that displayed by the shire as a whole; in all it had increased only by about 33 per cent. Hardingstone (219bi) had indeed fallen from £30 to £12. But some royal manors were much more profitable than they had been. Towcester (219bi) went up in value from £12 to £25, Finedon (220ai) from £20 to £40. The increase at Rothwell (219b2), from £30 to £50, might be connected with its extensive dependencies, as might that at Barnwell (220ai) from £13 6s. 6d. to £30, which included Tansor. It may even be that these manors had been enlarged in composition since 1065/6.

The most spectacular increase in value is that of the Church fiefs. The estates of Peterborough Abbey, worth only £63 9s. earlier, were in 1086 valued at £193 3s. 4d.[1] The holdings of Ramsey Abbey had more than doubled their previous value. The Peterborough manor of Warmington (221bi), worth only 5s. earlier, was valued at £11 at the Inquest, and that of Ashton on the same folio had gone up from 8s. to £7. But the bishop of Lincoln's few manors show an overall decline, and the appreciation on the Bury St Edmunds estates is a modest 19 per cent. The ecclesiastical authorities may have had more capital than some to restock their estates; they may have been in a position to extract larger rents and increased services from their tenants and peasantry.

Some lay fiefs certainly show large increases. That of Eudes fitzHubert (227ai) appreciated from £2 2s. to £12 10s., that of Geoffrey de Wirce (227bi) threefold from £2 10s. Robert of Mortain's immense local fief

---

[1] As Round said (*VCH*, i, p. 261), it is 'not so much a rise as a sharp recovery in value'.

went up in value by just over 80 per cent. A large increase for a modern Hundred demonstrates how much it must have suffered in 1065. The values in Polebrook, Willybrook, and Nassaborough with Uptongreen had risen by 66 per cent, in Corby and Huxloe by 70 per cent, and in Navisford by 150 per cent. Five southern Hundreds, however, appreciated by only 7½ per cent.

Sokemen, though less numerous than in Leicestershire, accounted for about one-eighth of the total recorded population of the county. We are only infrequently told of the rents paid, but where we are, the *ora* is often the unit employed, and the rents are usually those of sokemen. The northern Hundred of Corby provides many of the instances. There are four of varying numbers of sokemen or unspecified persons paying 5*s.* 4*d.* One group of four, one of five, one of six, and one of eight sokemen each produced 10*s.* 8*d.*[1] A single *ora* or a brace of *orae* appear on three occasions, and it might be that the 21*s.* 4*d.* of Scaldwell (228b2) and Sutton Basset (225a2) and the 41*s.* 4*d.* of Broughton with Cranley and Hennington (228a2) were based on the *ora*. Sums of £4, £8, £16, or 4*s.*, 8*s.*, 16*s.*, often occur. Mill-renders which are multiples of 16*d.* are frequent. The two mills at Denford and that at Raunds (220bi), with their eel-renders, were worth 50*s.* 8*d.* and 34*s.* 8*d.* respectively. Each is a multiple of sixteenpence.

The silver mark is unmentioned, but might lie behind two values at Dingley (225a2, 228a2) of 13*s.* 4*d.* and 6*s.* 8*d.*, one at Hanging Houghton (228b2) of the former sum, and one at Weedon Beck (223a2) of 6*s.* 8*d.* 3*s.* 4*d.* occurs at Thurning (221a2) and Lamport (222a2). Small clerical errors might account for 2*s.* 9*d.* at Moulton Park (228b2) and 5*s.* 8*d.* at Hargrave (226ai); perhaps 2*s.* 8*d.* and 5*s.* 4*d.* were the actual sums. We can hardly doubt that the £26 13*s.* of Nassington (219b2) and the £13 7*s.* of Barford (220ai) were connected and together made a pre-Conquest rent of £40.

The 'ploughlands' recorded are not ploughlands at all, but represent earlier assessments. It is accordingly useless to consider the relationship between ploughlands and plough-teams. For there are in this county varying ratios between ploughlands and hides, the ratio depending, for the most part, on the district. In the south-west it is 5:2, in the central area 2:1, and in the north not of constant character.

Northamptonshire hides and 'ploughlands' are the subject of a recent detailed study of their relationship.[2] This develops the earlier work of

---

[1] Stoke Albany (220ai), Boughton (222a2), Brampton Ash (225a2), Ashley (228a2); Brampton Ash, Ashley (225a2), Weldon Parva, Sutton Bassett (228a2).
[2] C. Hart: *The Hidation of Northamptonshire* (Leicester, 1970).

Maitland, Round, and Baring, traces successive reductions in the county's assessments from 3,200 to 2,663½ and then to 1,242 hides, and displays how the Domesday figures for 'ploughlands' indicate the reduction of assessment in the individual Hundred and holding. The Northamptonshire Geld Roll, it is convincingly argued, represents a sheriff's explanation of why the receipts were so poor from a shire which had clearly proved incapable of recovery in the decade following its devastation by the Northumbrians and North Mercians in 1065, and from possible damage during and after the Conquest.

Rutland

The modern county covers an area unlike that of Domesday *Roteland* (293bi–4ai). The Hundred of Witchley was included in the Northamptonshire Domesday, and eight of the twelve manors in Alstoe Wapentake appear also in the Lincolnshire text, with slight variations in the details. In 1086 *Roteland* 'belonged to the sheriffdom of Nottinghamshire for the requirements of the king's geld', while Alstoe Wapentake was half in Thurgarton and half in Broxtow, both Nottinghamshire Wapentakes.

Composite entries are here not so troublesome as in other midland counties, though we are not given the names of the nineteen berewicks forming part of the three royal manors which made up Martinsley Wapentake, and no indication is given as to the situation of Albert's land. There is the added handicap of the absence of values at the time of the Inquest for the greater part of Martinsley. Hence comparison is limited to thirteen entries and one sub-entry. Moreover, the sums may represent, not manorial values, but contributions to the royal *firma*.

Roteland appears to have been a fairly prosperous area. Population figures and those for teams are high; in 1066 it was valued at just over £200. We are told that in 1086 it paid the king £150 of blanched coin, yet most of its manors are accorded values higher than those of 1066. What is said to have been worth £69 earlier was at the Inquest valued at £97. We cannot, moreover, be sure of these figures, for in the Lincolnshire text (366b2) Market Overton with Stretton is said to be worth £40, but on fol. 293bi £20. On the same folio a Thistleton manor is valued at £3, but on fol. 358bi it is said that the value was included with that for South Witham, which is given as only £2 10*s*. It looks as if the district was in fact more profitable to the king than it had been to members of the Godwine family and others in 1066; on the other hand, if the royal manors of 1086 had to find only £150, this sum is not far from their pre-Conquest values.

Teams are so grossly in excess of 'ploughlands' that artificiality in the latter would be suspected even if the text did not happen to stress the fact. Alstoe is said to contain 24 carucates and 'land for 48 teams'. But the text lists 'land for 84 teams', 42 for each of the anonymous 'Hundreds' of the Wapentake. Perhaps the clerk should have said that there was land for 48 teams in each Hundred. Yet 102½ teams for the 84 'ploughlands' are said to be available. In Martinsley each of the three royal manors is said to have 'land for 16 teams', and each was rated at four carucates for geld, but 120 teams are recorded to serve 48 'ploughlands', and the possibility of employing more teams is mentioned. There could be four more at Oakham where there were already 39 for the 16 'ploughlands', and 16 teams are said to plough the land Albert had, where 'land for eight teams' existed and nine are recorded, while despite the 'land for 16 teams' in each of the Martinsley royal manors and the statement that there could be 48 teams on it, it is added that there was land—further land?—for 14 teams. The artificiality of many of these quantities, probably connected with a former arbitrary system of assessment, is obvious.

Villeins greatly outnumber any other element in the population; 86½ per cent of the recorded inhabitants are of this category. No slaves are mentioned, but the existence of over forty demesne teams makes their total absence improbable. Yet the peasantry do not seem to have been well equipped with oxen. In three entries 58 villeins have only 104 oxen between them.[1] Perhaps in this area they did a considerable amount of labour on the demesnes and thus made many slaves unnecessary. In all 844 recorded persons had 187½ teams, which averages less than a pair of oxen per man. At Ridlington (293b2) two sokemen had an equal number of teams.

If by misadventure only the *Roteland* section of DB had survived, we should have strange ideas about eleventh-century England. As it is, its contribution is somewhat negative.

[1] Thistleton, Teigh, Exton (293bi).

8
The Eastern Counties

As we turn the folios of the second volume of Domesday Book, and see so much information for not only 1066 and 1086 but for an intermediate period also, we may feel that we are here being presented with better opportunities of studying post-Conquest changes than are afforded by the Exchequer text. But before long difficulties and doubts manifest themselves. Information about any one aspect of the economy does not appear with anything like regularity, while all too frequently no basis for comparison of the statistics is available. Occasionally we are given a figure for *post*, but none for *tunc*. Frequently we have information for *modo*, but no earlier statistics. We can never be sure whether these were omitted, or whether the clerk could have said that previously there had been no teams, or none of a particular category of inhabitant. We find entries such as that for Hilborough (167b), where we are told that there were four demesne teams both in 1066 and 1086, but nothing about the intermediate period, and while ten villagers' teams of 1066 became seven later, we are given no quantity for 1086. Again, at Occold (410b) there had been two slaves. DB mentions none for 1086, and we might suspect an omission. However, the *Inquisitio Eliensis* (ms. A, fol. 60b2) tells us 'now, none'.

One of the major problems is to decide how to treat the frequent use of *semper*. Does it mean just what it would seem to imply, that there had been no change between 1066 and 1086, or were the suppliers of the information ignorant or careless of differences in quantities? We may think that if the position in King Edward's day had not been altered by the time of the Inquest, it may well not have changed in the meantime, but some phrases engender doubts. Of Whatfield (440) the clerk wrote *semper valuit vi solidos, modo xx*. Unless *semper* is here a shorter means of conveying *tunc et post*, the statement is absurd. When we are informed that at Moze (59) there were 'always' 14 villeins, but now 13 bordars, while slaves have diminished from 13 to three, are we to presume that the number of recorded inhabitants rose from 27 to 30 and that most of the slaves had been freed or were dead? Or does 'always' here too imply merely 'then and afterwards' and that 27 persons had become 16? At Higham (78b) there were 'always' two demesne and four villagers' teams, yet when its new owner received it 'he found only one ox'. It is difficult to believe, too, that at no time in twenty years did the number of demesne sheep, 381, change at Ormesby (115b).

The clerks used *semper* so frequently that calculations including or ignoring it must often differ widely. In Essex alone it is employed about the quantities of nearly 1,900 teams. This figure is so greatly in excess of the number where figures are given for both *tunc* and *post* or *quando recepit* that using only the latter entries would give a fall of $17\frac{1}{4}$ per cent, but one of only $3\frac{1}{2}$ per cent if those saying *semper* were reckoned. Even in a comparison of totals for *tunc* and *modo*, where *semper* occurs in less than half the relevant entries, it would be dangerous to exclude these. It has to be assumed that if *semper* is used, this covers all quantities where no change is mentioned. There are plenty of instances where no alteration whatever in the statistics for teams or population is recorded and *semper* is not used, though sometimes the value of the holding is said to have changed. It did not do so at the manor of Harlow (19b) as it was constituted in 1066, yet on the three hides added to the manor since the Conquest the value rose though teams and population remained unaltered. Perhaps the rent of the five free men had been raised. Sometimes the quantities show no change, but *semper* is not used; occasionally the phrase is *modo similiter*, e.g. at Abberton (28).

It is not easy, too, to decide what meaning *semper* might have when it occurs in an entry stating that certain teams could be 'restored' or employed. At Drayton (229) there was 'always' one team in demesne and three of the men, yet one team could be restored; there are several exact parallels, e.g. Raveningham (267b). The phraseology is sometimes ambiguous. On a Mileham holding (136b) there were two teams in 1086 as in 1066, yet one could be 'restored'. Perhaps when at Lakenham (140b) we are told that three teams could be restored, though two demesne teams had become one and three of the men two, this means that the men's teams could with profit be made up to three.

The problem of dealing with the statistics is intensified by the frequent impossibility of determining whether information has been duplicated or not. Sometimes the position is quite clear, e.g. the hide of the manor of Writtle (5) which became the bishop of Hereford's (26) appears twice.

But we cannot tell whether the free men of the manor of Witham (1b) whose lands had been appropriated by various lay barons are concealed within entries for their fiefs.

Moreover, there is a very large number of entries in which we are given the quantity of a category of inhabitants present in 1086, but nothing is said about how many, if any, there had been earlier. On the sokemen's land at Castle Hedingham (76b) there were three more villeins than there had been, but four less slaves; in addition, we are told that 'now' there are 22 bordars. Were there none in 1066 or later, or was their number omitted? On much fewer occasions we are given figures for 1066, but not for 1086.

The provision of statistics was here no more consistently achieved than for the counties of vol. i. We are given an altogether inadequate quantity of instances of figures for *post* or *quando recepit*, and far too many entries where we have information for 1086 only. This feature is commoner for valuations than it is for plough-teams or population. For example, values for both 1066 and 1086 are given in 38 entries for the Suffolk fief of Roger Bigot, but for 1086 only in 151: it is true that most of the latter are unimportant holdings. Also, the number of entries in which no sum is mentioned, but the value of the holding is said to be included in that of the manor of which it was a part, is in all large fiefs considerable. But sometimes, in such entries, the value *is* given, and consequently must be deducted from that of the manor as a whole when comparing Inquest values with those of an earlier date. Often the text is not straightforward, and makes it difficult to decide to what section of it a figure applies. Five free men had 26 acres 'in the king's soke' at Thurlston (352b) for which no value is given; the next entry, also for Thurlston, records eighty with the same number of acres, and then comes a valuation. But does this cover only the 80 acres or the 80+26? Probably the former, since it would make the 80 acres to be worth 2*d*. each. St Edmund's holdings at Thrandeston (371) consisted of two carucates in a tenant's hands and 42 acres shared between thirteen free men. Are these 42 acres included in the two carucates or not? Such entries, of either type, are extremely common.

It would be exceptionally difficult to arrive at an altogether satisfactory estimate of the distribution of decline in value. Odo of Bayeux had eight holdings at Helmingham (375b, 376). For one of these we have no 1066 value; four increased in value, two fell, and one remained constant. The apparent value per acre ranges from almost 2*d*. to 6*d*., with those properties showing an increase producing the highest valuation figures. Obviously it is unlikely that any external factor had occasionally reduced values in this vill, but it is also noticeable that four of the holdings had been at farm for considerably more than the value set on them at the Inquest.

Valuations, it will subsequently be demonstrated, are in some respects easier to handle than statistics for plough-teams and population, and yield more manageable results. But they too induce difficulties additional to those already mentioned. Even though a policy of demanding unreasonable rents and extending manorial territory by acquiring the land of semi-independent free men and sokemen seems here to be dominant, many appreciations in value are so huge as to cause a search for other supplementary factors. The value of land was rising steadily, but, as Davis has explained, socage dues remained fixed.[1] Thus an increment had to be added to these dues to obtain the full value of the land. This may sometimes be indicated by mention of the payment of a *gersuma*, a term which covers any form of extraordinary payment; it may have been required, though not so mentioned, in numerous instances of large increases in value. Also, when men were 'added to a manor', their customary dues and fines may have been abstracted from the Hundred and transferred to the manor, which again would increase its value. This might account for occasional mention of Hundred-dues. Great Yarmouth (118) was valued 'with two parts of the soke of three Hundreds'; men at Winfarthing (129b) were 'all free with soke' when the manor was received. The value of Thrigby (135) was 'in the outsoke of Walsham Hundred'; Diss (282) included the soke of a Hundred-and-a-half; Kettleburgh (293b) went up from £5 for the *caput manerii* to £23 11s. *cum tota soca*.[2]

In view of these uncertainties, how far is it safe to rely on the results of statistical analysis? So long as deductions are confined to broad principles, they probably are not too far from the truth. The entries in which comparable figures are given are so numerous that incorrect interpretation of the doubtful passages probably does not appreciably affect the results. At any rate, these are such as we might be expecting.

Essex was far more thoroughly manorialised than was East Anglia, and thus presents the fewest problems. Though Essex had many free men and sokemen, a high proportion of whose individual properties must have been very small, many manors were substantial ones. It is in East Anglia that we find a multitude of holdings of 30 or 15 acres or still less, and it is here that the valuation of a property in accordance with its rating is most

---

[1] R. H. C. Davis (ed.): *The Kalendar of Abbot Samson* (Camden Soc. Pubns., 3rd series, lxxxiv, 1954).
[2] Though Ely Abbey had soke over 5½ Hundreds, other men seem also to have possessed sokeright in parts of them, attached to their manors, see fols. 285, 297, 314b, 316, 338b, 413, 433, 442.

apparent. It is significant that in the coastal Hundreds of East and West Flegg almost three-quarters of the recorded population were free men or sokemen. In the west these formed at most 50 per cent of the inhabitants.

Thus we can never be unconscious of these difficulties when attempting to convert the statistics into maps. As a rule we have no means of allotting a proportion of a figure to the component of a large complex manor. It must be borne in mind, also, that the land of many a manor was widely dispersed, frequently in more than one Hundred, and distributed among a number of vills whose limits were rarely contiguous. Quite often the land was probably not in the vill named, for the reference is most likely to that which was *caput manerii*, and not to the place in which the holding lay. The complications include

(a) the frequent use of *semper*, the accuracy of which is often doubtful, which may affect certain areas, especially those in which St Edmund's manors were numerous
(b) the high number of entries which give figures for only 1086 or 1066, or for *post* and one of these, or refer to unidentifiable places, and which consequently cannot be plotted
(c) the considerable number of vills divided into numerous holdings for which the information provided is inconsistent in character
(d) the absence of figures for some vills and holdings
(e) the impossibility of allotting, e.g., the South Elmham entries among the seven present parishes.

As an illustration we may consider Stonham Aspall. For this 'vill' there are fourteen groups of entries, covering 41 holdings, nine of which represent the glebe of at least two churches. Just where these 41 pieces of land were we of course do not know. The situation is complicated by the fact that the land of one holding was partly in Stonham and partly in Coddenham, and that two holdings belonged to the manor of Mendlesham, which was in Hartismere Hundred, not that of Bosmere in which Stonham lay. In 26 entries only are we given information about teams, two of which give quantities for 1066 but not for 1086, while four do so for 1086 but not for 1066. On the remainder, where there had been 53 teams, there were in 1086 only 38. Three large manors had improved their worth (350b, 351), as had four smaller holdings (374b *ter*, 438). The remainder all fell in value (374b, 375, 375b *ter*, 422 *ter*). In all the change was from £29 12s. 4d. to £28 7s. 4d. It is, of course, unlikely that all these holdings were in the modern village; some would be detached farms.

All we can say is that throughout East Anglia we have sufficient comparable figures to make deductions drawn from a plotted map probably not too far from the truth. It is perhaps comforting to note that in six of the Stonham holdings in which the teams were fewer, values had also declined. The number of entries is so large that even such unsatisfactory maps may tell us something. Study of them discloses that nowhere is there violent contrast in the intensity of fallen values or diminished beasts of the plough. But to reduce the information to symbolic form is difficult. A decline from £8 to £4 is in the same proportion as one from 10s. to 5s., but the effects on two such holdings may have been totally dissimilar.

A factor which might be expected to have an effect on the statistics is the reduction after the Conquest in the extent of the woodland. This is considered to be the result, not of assarting, but of cutting the timber.[1] Only 122 entries record it, and some Hundreds furnish no instances of it, or only very few. Consequently it is unprofitable further to consider the possibilities.

Whether it is legitimate to relate rent to stated acreage is problematical. We cannot be sure that the text is giving us either assessment or an indication of the extent of the holding. But the very considerable quantity of entries in which value divided by acreage produces an integral number of pence or a proper fraction is suggestive. Where we find, as at Stoke by Clare (390b) 37 acres worth 74*d*., and 1 carucate 68 acres at 31*s*. 4*d*., or half a carucate plus six acres valued at 11*s*. (Shelfanger, 211), or 73 acres at 73*d*. (two churches of Shouldham, 250b), we may well suspect a real relationship.

Calculations would of course be vitiated if the acreages given were largely unrealistic. Fortunately it does not look as if beneficial assessment had been extensive in East Anglia. Instances in which the acre seems to have an exceptionally high value are rare, though fiscal and agrarian coincidence may indeed have been uncommon. But the considerable number of instances of proximity to the obvious assessments, e.g. 15, 30, 60, 120 acres, suggest that often changes in the amount of land in a holding are reflected in the acreage recorded, e.g. at Filby (180), 118 acres valued at 5*s*., where two acres of a holding formerly rated at one carucate were perhaps unlet or uncultivated.

But the difficulties induced by the acre/value relationship are many. At Oby (174) a free man held 30 acres; under him were six free men also with 30 acres. Does the value of 4*s*. refer to only one of the 30-acre holdings or to both? It is only rarely that the text gives clarity. There was a carucate at Rudham (169b), and 18 sokemen belonged to the manor; fortunately here we are told that these sokemen are 'on the same carucate'. In three places a few free men, some of whom were concerned with more than one holding, had either 60 or 65 acres (Surlingham, etc., 176b). We may think

[1] R. Lennard: 'The Destruction of Woodland in the Eastern Counties under William the Conqueror' (*Econ. Hist. Rev.*, xv, p. 39, 1945).

that the value of 10s. applies to the whole, but we cannot be sure of this, nor can we say that each of three 20-acre holdings was worth the same amount.

A predominance of acres apparently valued at 1d. or 2d. or between these sums is apparent. There are, too, a considerable number of entries where the result comes very near an integral quantity. We find 15-acre holdings valued at the *ora* of 16d., e.g. at Flordon (188b) and Sco (201), or 32d. (Bexwell, 276), or 30 acres at 3 *orae* (1½d.: Beeston St Lawrence, 219b). At Wyverstone (408) 18 acres had a value of 53d.; at *Vltuna* (409) half a carucate and 13 acres were worth 144d. But naturally there are many entries which produce ugly fractions, e.g. Morning Thorpe (150b), 33 acres worth 48d. (very close to 1½d. per acre), or Mautby (180), 20½ acres worth 8d. Sometimes it looks as if entries should be combined. At Irmingland and Corpusty (158b) 8 and 14 acres were each worth 11d., giving 22 acres at 22d.

Many entries producing non-integral acre-values, especially when the value is uneven, e.g. Middleton (222), one carucate valued at 24s. 8d., probably represent the sum of rents. Some round-figure amounts which produce improper fractions probably indicate, not the actual rents received, but the sum the holder hoped to get from tenants. Thus in estimating the total quantity of acre-values of 1d. or 2d. it would be a wise precaution to omit the more substantial organisations. It is true that there are a very large number of instances in which estates of a single carucate are rated at 10s. or £1, and those of 1½ or 2 carucates often produce an average value per acre of 1d., 1½d., or 2d.

On occasion the acre seems to be producing a good deal less than one penny. At Sturston (183) a free man's 60 acres were worth only 8d., and at Burnham Thorpe (183b) the land of two free men with half a carucate was valued at no more than 1s. But some figures are large ones. Five acres at Attlebridge (241b) are said to be worth 10s., and thirty at Crownthorpe (227b) were worth the same number of shillings. But the possibility of error must not be excluded; 'shillings' may have been inscribed where 'pence' would have been correct, e.g. at Wramplingham (145). Here twenty pence seems a more likely value for 15 acres than 20s. When it is said that four Winterton free men with nine acres were worth 24s., the value presumably refers to the sokeman's 100 acres 'under' whom these free men were. It is difficult to credit that 80 acres, shared by as many as 40 free men, were worth 90s. (Bacton, 426b). Something more than the value of the land must be involved. Equally 55 acres worth only 2s. (Gedding, 363) seems to be an abnormally low value. We should, perhaps, sometimes rely on the figures of IE rather than those of DB. An Ashfield holding (384) was valued at 8*d*.; IE's four acres might be preferred to DB's three, for they would give acres worth 2*d*. each.

About many of the figures there seems to be an element of make-believe. Of four consecutive entries on fols. 420, 420b, each for a 30-acre holding, three are valued at 3*s*. 6*d*. and one at 3*s*. 6½*d*., though the equipment of the estates was not identical, nor were their previous values. We find Hintlesham and Bramford (289) as each having been worth £10, and increasing to £22 by 1086, though they had varying quantities of teams and inhabitants. There are many instances of a 120-acre carucate being valued at 240 pence, and similar relationships producing integral values per acre. But it would be unsafe to assume that in such holdings every acre was worth one penny or threeha'pence or twopence. There must have been much variety of profitability in the larger estates, and the values must represent round-figure totals.

Essex

The very detailed information for this county permits the production of figures which we may feel are not too far distant from the truth. We are, however, deprived of a number of quantities which would enable us to come closer to completeness. We are given no values for sixteen holdings, and out of 1,033 for which valuations are given, we are unable to compare an earlier figure with that of 1086 for as many as 325. But most of these relate to small components of manors; less than half are of £1 or more.[1] It is always helpful to keep separate the royal manors, which are best treated individually. Their temporary omission leaves us 692 holdings yielding comparative figures, of which 113 make use of *semper*, representing about 16 per cent of the total values also. Thus the appearance of *semper* produces fewer problems than elsewhere, and it seems safe to include the entries in which it is used, but with certain reservations. Sometimes, indeed, there is doubt whether it is to be interpreted literally. Amberden (73b) was 'always' worth £12, yet for three years Ralf Peverel had drawn £18 a year from it; a similar situation had obtained at Moreton (88b).

In only 221 entries have we figures for *post* or *quando recepit*.[2] They show only a small total fall, from £1,715 1*s*. 4*d*. to £1,694 7*s*. 4*d*. But comparison is complicated by the fact that, including the entries which use

---

[1] Values of components said to be *in eodem pretio*, i.e. the value of the manor as a whole, have of course been ignored.
[2] For Gestingthorpe (98) the value is for 'when the king gave it to Otto'; for a holding in Lexden Hundred (99) when it was 'invaded' by Robert de Montbegon.

THE DETAILS OF DOMESDAY BOOK

semper, 268 out of 334 show no change in value. More than half the falls in value are in the coastal Hundreds. If such figures have validity, it looks as if Essex was not greatly affected by the Conquest in the years immediately following 1066.

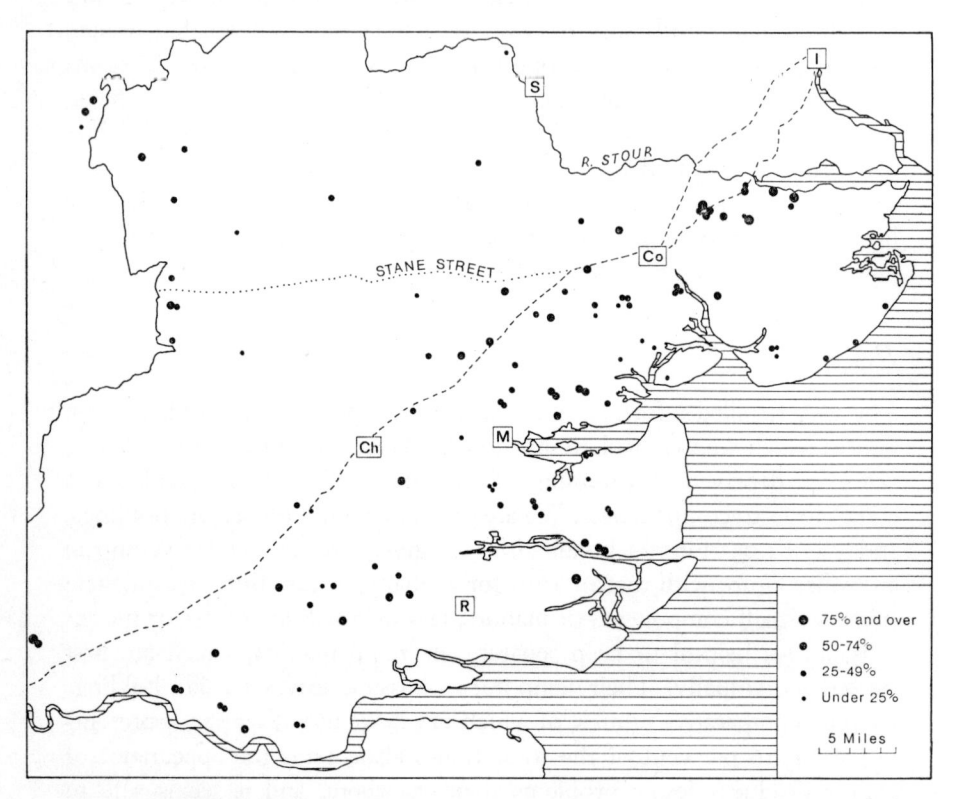

Fig. 30 Domesday Essex
Fall in value 1066–86
– – – London–Chelmsford–Colchester–Ipswich road
Ch—Chelmsford Co—Colchester I—Ipswich
M—Maldon R—Rayleigh S—Sudbury

After his coronation, and while the fortifications of London were being strengthened, King William sojourned at Barking, and is said thence to have proceeded into East Anglia, where the threat of invasion from Scandinavia was ever-present. He went as far as *Guenta*, which may be Norwich, where a castle was built, and in which he installed William fitzOsbern with the duty of governing the country towards the north, preparatory to the royal return to Normandy in March of 1067.[1] While his troops must have lived off the land as they moved, it is doubtful if a decline in values in the eastern counties can be attributed primarily to this progress.

But it might be that there was some decline in prosperity and that the new lords demanded pre-Conquest rents and services from a less wealthy, and perhaps less numerous, tenantry. It is not easy to see why Felsted (21b) should have improved in value from £20 to £30, Ridgwell (28) from £18 to £24, and Claret Hall (28b) from £18 to £22, unless the appreciation was due to the inclusion of the land of sokemen in the manor. But we are not told in these entries of recent enlargements of the manors.

Values *tunc* and *modo* improved from £3,246 11s. 11d. to £3,913 9s. 8d., or by over 20 per cent. But the figures for the Hundreds display no uniformity. Many of the coastal Hundreds show a decline. The exception is Rochford, which was largely in the hands of Sweyn the former sheriff. He seems throughout to have kept his manors in a high state of profitability (teams fell in number hardly at all), and if the decline elsewhere was in part due to piratical or Danish raids, the district protected by his castle of Rayleigh may have been avoided by an enemy. A contributory factor could have been the royal order to leave the anticipated Danish invasion of 1085 inadequate means of subsistence where raiders might land. The actions of the fleet of 1070 are another possibility. A fourteenth-century MS. in the Colchester archives is alone in reporting that in 1071 the town was burnt by Danish pirates.

The improvement derives largely from the Hundreds nearest London, which appreciated by 26 per cent. The growing demands of the capital may have strengthened the local economy. The central Hundreds improved by under 20 per cent, and the north of the shire by almost 25 per cent. Here one reason for the increase could be the absorption into former manors of the lands of the sokemen numerous in this district.

Some of the falls in value are considerable, especially on or near the coast. Clacton (11) and a St Osyth manor (11) fell in value from £40 to £26 and £18 to £12 respectively; the Clacton of 1086 had only half the teams at work in 1066. But elsewhere there were enormous increases in value, though some figures may be deceptive. Weeley (51) was valued at £8 in 1066, £19 and an ounce of gold in 1086, but though the text says *totum simul*, the £8 might not include the sokemen's land. Teams are

---

[1] So William of Poitiers (cap. 36, p. 238), and, copying him, Orderic (ii, 166; p. 194). *Guenta* is said to be *millia passuum quatuordecim* from the sea, so that it could rapidly receive assistance from the Danes; this would apply equally to Winchester, which some commentators consider should be equated with *Guenta*.

unmentioned; the recorded population remained almost constant. But some of the greatest appreciations, e.g. at Walthamstow (92), from £15 to £28 plus two ounces of gold, could in part be due to enlargement of the manor by bringing within its orbit men who earlier had been independent or virtually independent of it, in part to raising individual rents or the farm-rent demanded. Walthamstow's recorded population rose from 30 to 65, and its teams from 17 to 24.

Excessive rents were certainly demanded. Coggeshall (26b) and Rivenhall (27) was each producing £20, but they are said to be worth only £14 and £12, though this was well in excess of their pre-Conquest value. Thaxted (38b) was rented to an Englishman for a sum of £60, but each year payment was short by £10, not surprisingly in view of the fact that both English and foreign jurors valued it at only £50. Even this valuation was £20 more than that of 1066 or when Richard fitzGilbert was given the manor. Kelvedon (14) had a pre-Conquest valuation of £5, though by the Inquest it was reckoned to be £8. Yet the abbot of Westminster was drawing £12 from it.

Disagreements about valuations were not unknown. The English set a value of £80 on Barking (17b), but the newcomers on the local jury said that it was worth £20 more. Here, too, the number of inhabitants had increased substantially. In contrast, some Hundredmen appraised Waltham (15b) at £100, but the men of the bishop of Durham, who owned the manor, valued it at £63 5s. 4d., yet Earl Harold had received only £36 from it. Here we may see the people of Waltham giving their estimate of what they could pay without disaster to themselves. Harold may have treated leniently the place which held the church in which he was especially interested, or the extent of the manor may have been changed.

How far the figures are trustworthy is problematical. A Roding manor (52) fell in value only from £6 to £5 *post*. Yet we are told that when Roger d'Auberville received it he found only the land itself and one plough-team. Could it then have been worth as much as £5, as it was in 1086 when there were 2½ teams and eleven recorded inhabitants? Stebbing (56b) was worth £10 'then', £12 'now'. But we are told also that it was 'all the same' in King Edward's day and worth the same when Henry de Ferrières received it. Is 'the same' £10 or £12? 'Then and afterwards' Mount Bures (89) was worth £7, but £11 in 1086, 'and the same when he received it'. Are we to see a difference between *post* and *quando recepit*, which we have seen is not impossible (p. 10)? A Chadwell holding (98) was in 1086 worth twenty pence, yet Grimr is said to have given the king 30s. for it on its forfeiture by the Saxon holder. It seems an excessive sum to pay for twenty acres worth one penny each, unless the sum covered also Bures Gifford, the preceding entry. But stock and implements as well as the land may have been taken into account.

The information furnished about royal manors and holdings included under *Terra Regis* is extensive but inconsistent. Frequently we are not told what a manor was producing in the early years of the Conquest, while there is every reason to believe that many of the manors had changed in composition since 1066. Certainly there had been abstractions by numerous lay barons from several of these.[1] Four had rendered a varying number of nights' farm; Brightlingsea, Newport, and Lawford two each, Writtle ten. This suggests that they had been Crown demesne land. Though no royal manor is ascribed to King Edward, Harold Godwineson, who is credited with possessing more than a dozen, may not have acquired them all until he was elected king. Four had been Earl Ælfgar's, one the Fair Edith's. Ælfgar had held a manor (Great Baddow, 21b) which had furnished an eight-nights' farm, but this was given to Holy Trinity, Caen.

A dozen at least were being farmed, those of Harold by Peter de Valognes, the sheriff of the county, and by Rannulf brother of Ilger, Ælfgar's by Picot of Cambridge and Otto the goldsmith, and Edith's by Godric, the custodian of many East Anglian royal manors. Where we are told the farm-rent when the newcomers took them over, the sums are much higher than the values quoted for 1066. What had been worth £107 then was later producing £157, and one manor (Great Sampford, 7b) was by 1086 paying £4 more still. Four other manors increased in value between 1066 and 1086 from £20 to £37 2s.

Writtle (5) affords no basis for comparison. In addition to a ten-nights' farm it had provided £10 in 1066; in 1086 it had to find £100 and a *gersuma* of £5. Nor does Witham, for the sum it rendered in 1086 included customary dues and the profits of the Hundred-court.[2] A *gersuma* varying from £3 to £10 had to be furnished also by Witham, Hatfield Broad Oak, Havering, and Stanway. Nor was this the only additional payment required. Though Benfleet (1b) was valued at £8, its farmer had to render £12. From both Hatfield Broad Oak and Havering £80 had to be paid, though they were valued at £60 and £40 respectively. But when we say that the full details imply that the king was getting close on £600 from his Essex property, it could well be that he was in fact obtaining a

[1] e.g. from Witham (1b), Havering (2b), Shalford (3b), Wethersfield (4), and Lawford (6).
[2] Maldon (5b), a borough, rendered £13 2s. in 1066, £24 when Peter de Valognes received it. In 1086 it paid only £16 by weight, but there seems then to have been property there which was not royal, and some house-property was waste, probably because fortification occupied the site of eighteen *mansurae*. The entry on fol. 75 refers to Little Maldon (73) in Dengie Hundred.

good deal more in rents, sokeright, and customary dues, all of which make intermittent appearances on fols. 1b–7b.

Not royal manors alone were *ad firmam*. The value of Geoffrey de Manneville's manor of South Ockendon (57b) is said to be a farm of £16. Mundon (49b), worth only £17, had been *ad firmam* for £30 previously, and the proceeds of seven houses in London were in the *firma* of West Thurrock (63). Some of the uneven sums sound like the totals of rents, e.g. the £13 17s. 4d. of Halstead (37), the £63 5s. 4d. of Waltham Abbey (15b), or the £2 5s. 2d. of 63 acres in five villages (102). We are used to royal manors paying by weight of coin (e.g. Writtle, 5) or in blanched money. Four times the latter method is noted on Earl Eustace's lands (Great Tey, Boxted, 29b; Stanford Rivers, High Laver, 30b).

Rents which seem to be in terms of the *ora* of sixteenpence are common. Sums of 1s. 4d., 2s. 8d., 5s. 4d., 10s. 8d., appear, for example, on fols. 4b, 33, 98b; 5, 102b; 16; 20b. A unit of 20d., which might be derived from fractions of the mark of 13s. 4d., or from payments of 20d. for every 16d. liable to be paid, to cover potential loss from imperfect coins, e.g. 1s. 8d. and 3s. 4d., appear, among other instances, on fols. 7b, 98, 103b; 2b, 96. Sums of 6s. 8d. and 8s. 4d. (fols. 16, 38; 29b) could derive from either. It will have been noticed that two of the uneven sums mentioned above end in figures, 208 and 64 pence, which are multiples of the *ora*.

Land of differing character, or owned by different lords, naturally paid varying rents. Acres paying 3d. each occur on fols. 98b and 100b, and some at 2d. at Hutton (20b). A villein's 40 acres at Fanton (17b) were worth 3s. 4d., or one penny an acre, and the equation recurs for both a free man and a sokeman (Thorndon, 23b; *Careseia* or Northey Island, 100b).

The second volume of Domesday Book does not give us information about ploughlands, and so we have no means of knowing to what extent the county was being cultivated to capacity. In twenty-seven passages we are told that there could be more teams than were being employed in 1086. The quantity is not always that which would have made up the teams to the 1066 figure.[1] Information about the teams available *post* or *quando recepit* is too scanty to warrant a deduction that there was a general decline in the number of teams available in the early years of the Conquest. For nine Hundreds, indeed, we have no figures for the period. There are only 166 instances in which we are given the teams *post* or *quando recepit*, but those which say *semper* number nearly 850. Thus no substantial change in their quantity might be expected. Using only the figures for the intermediate period, there was a drop of 22 per cent between 1066 and

---

[1] e.g. at Fanton (14), Thaxted (38b), and South Benfleet (43).

THE EASTERN COUNTIES: ESSEX

then, and of 17 per cent between then and *modo*. But if we include the entries which use *semper*, these become 6 per cent and 14 per cent respectively.[1] We should probably get different figures, but not so far from those for 1086, if we had full information. None the less, it is plain that in some manors and in the small estates the number of oxen at work had become fewer. Two demesne teams at Alresford (32b) had disappeared; so had those at Chishall (38). Twenty villagers' teams at Lawford (6) dropped to sixteen during Baignard's custody of the manor, and to nine when Peter de Valognes received it, but this may not have occurred early, and this royal manor had lost a good deal of its land. But we have the same difficulty in interpreting phraseology as with values. At Coggeshall (26b) there were 'always' three demesne teams, yet we are told also that when Earl Eustace received the manor there was one. Some reduction in the number of teams in the county is to be presumed. There are recorded for 1086 $114\frac{1}{2}$ teams (which have not been reckoned above) for which we have no comparable statements for earlier years.

The decline is greatest in the coastal Hundreds of the north-east. In Tendring it was as much as $36\frac{1}{2}$ per cent, and 24 per cent for all these Hundreds excluding Rochford. But in the metropolitan and northern Hundreds it was only 11 per cent; in central Essex 18 per cent. The principal area of deficiency is thus to be found between London and Colchester and the coast. Villagers' teams suffered more than those of the demesnes; an 18 per cent decline for the former, but one of only $8\frac{1}{2}$ per cent for the latter. Demesne teams, including those of the free men and sokemen, were throughout in the neighbourhood of 45 per cent of the whole.

Nothing in the text suggests that the cause was a general change from an agricultural to a pastoral economy, even though slaves had fallen so considerably in number. Though the thoroughly unsatisfactory figures for demesne livestock show a 22 per cent rise in the number of sheep, these require less men to look after and use them than do oxen, and so we might expect to find a drop in the number of non-servile peasants. Yet these had increased substantially. There may have been widespread mortality from disease or by reason of military exigencies; twice we are told that the plough-oxen were less 'because of the death of the beasts' (Witham, 1b; Hatfield Broad Oak, 2).

Between the Conquest and the Inquest the number of villagers and slaves seems to have risen by $12\frac{1}{2}$ per cent. If the entries in which none of a particular category is recorded for 1066 or 1086 are included, the figure

---

[1] Some quantities given here and later will be found to differ, though not largely, from those in *Domesday Studies: The Eastern Counties*. The reason is a change of opinion about the interpretation of certain passages.

would rise to $15\frac{1}{2}$ per cent. If these are ignored, villeins decreased by $6\frac{3}{4}$ per cent, slaves by $30\frac{1}{2}$ per cent. Bordars increased by 60 per cent. In 1066 villeins had represented $39\frac{1}{2}$ per cent of the population, and slaves $23\frac{1}{2}$ per cent. By 1086 villeins amounted to 33 per cent, and slaves only to $14\frac{1}{2}$ per cent.

Yet on some manors the numbers of villeins or slaves increased. Seven villeins at Little Oakley (70b) became 17 by the time of the Inquest, five slaves at Tollesbury (18b) seven. It is of course possible that occasionally men had been transferred from one manor to another in the interests of more efficient operation. Equally men formerly free may have been reduced to villein status, and peasants obliged to pass into servitude.

The decrease in the number of villeins and slaves is intelligible enough. Though, if the former had to face increased rents, some may have fallen in status, we have to remember that some of those who made the returns may have seen as villeins what their fellows would have classed as bordars. On well over one hundred holdings the slaves had altogether disappeared, and if we had fuller information, this number would probably rise. This could be the result of a shift from an agricultural to a pastoral economy, necessitating fewer slaves to operate the demesne teams, but it is doubtful whether this factor could be of more than limited application, since the decline in the number of demesne teams is far less than for the villagers' teams. It is rather more likely that a number of slaves may have been freed to avoid uneconomic maintenance and classified as bordars. While *coliberti* do not appear in DB vol. ii, we might have found them to be fairly numerous had they been so differentiated. It might be suggested that only the senior male of a slave family had been counted, but all adult males when freed, but this is very doubtful.

But even if we assume these disappearing villeins and slaves are to be reclassified as bordars, we still have to explain the presence of over 2,000 bordars more than there had been in 1066. It seems to be too many to be attributed to an increase in the birth or survival rate. For if we included the bordars of 1086 mentioned on holdings where there had been none earlier, according to the text, or no fall in the number of villeins or slaves, we find 2,741 more than there had been formerly. It might be that large numbers of free men and sokemen had lost their independence, but if so we should expect to find them with villein status. A free man at Benfleet (1b) 'had been made one of the villeins'; the same thing may have happened to the three former free men at Chignal (58b), while a former free man at Abberton (46b) may be the bordar there of 1086. But the text does not suggest that this was of frequent occurrence. We cannot estimate how many free men there may have been in 1086. Many who are recorded

THE EASTERN COUNTIES: ESSEX

for 1066 may still have been newcomers' tenants in 1086 though unmentioned for that year. Englishmen or Anglo-Danes appear by name in more than forty entries as tenants in 1086, in addition to the few who held in chief, while the number of unnamed other free men recorded for that year is close on 500. About 600 sokemen are also noted, and probably the number was greater than this. More than a dozen entries in, e.g., the fief of Richard fitzGilbert mention the presence of sokemen. It seems reasonable to suppose that some or all of those who appear for 1066 in the other entries, for this and other fiefs, were still there. Free men and sokemen may indeed have been substantially fewer in 1086 than in 1066. But we can hardly suppose that over 2,000 had died, left the country, or been reduced in status. Free men and sokemen can hardly have been only about one thousand fewer in number than the villeins in 1066. Some, it is true, had disappeared from the scene by 1086, e.g. the four free men of Steeple (4b): 'now they are not there'.

Sokemen, and some free men also, may have gone virtually unrecorded in some Hundreds. We should expect to find them most numerous where the East Saxon land joins that of the East Angles, and so we do. The five relevant Hundreds contribute about 80 per cent of the sokemen recorded for 1086, and over 40 per cent of the free men. But sokemen do occur in all the other Hundreds, but are so few in a large Hundred such as Chelmsford that we cannot think we have record of them all. Many, it is true, were landholders in a very small way. One at Bendish (34) had only one acre and one rood, and two at Sible Hedingham (83) a mere three acres between them. But there were also those like the Beaumont sokeman (77b) who held $1\frac{7}{8}$ hides. Many a sokeman held far more land than some of the minor free men, some of whom had as little as five acres.[1] But then there is no clear differentiation between the freemen and sokemen of DB. To the manor of Fobbing (26) 22 free men had been added, but a few lines lower down their land is described as that of the sokemen. Two sokemen belonging to the manor of Belchamp Otton (28b) were free men when Ingelric added them to his manor. This does not necessarily imply a decline in status, but probably that in 1066 they had not been attached to any manor, unlike those at Great Tey (29b) 'who could not withdraw themselves from this manor'. Quite often a man who in DB is a sokeman is a free man in IE. Sometimes the Domesday clerk drew a distinction between them; a Finchingfield holding (35b) had been held by two sokemen and one free man. Sokemen had possessed what the Norman clerks thought of as manors in 1066; they also could 'go with their land where they would' (Writtle, 5), or sell it (Abbess Roding, 50b). Sometimes they are named

[1] Boreham (31b), Prested (75), Heydon (97).

(South Weald, 16b, 66b). Thus it is not surprising to read of sokemen with bordars 'under them', and some had villeins and slaves working on their land, e.g. at Waltham (15b), Roding (19), Thaxted (38b), and frequently on Wihtgar's former estates (39–41). So it may well be that many of the bordars who appear in 1086 but not earlier may be those working on the lands of free men and sokemen which by the time of the Inquest had been absorbed into manors of which they had formerly been independent. Such lands are as a rule only sketchily described in DB, in contrast to the original portions of the manors of 1086, and so the clerks may often have failed to note how many bordars or slaves there had been earlier. At the time of the Inquest, none the less, we find many a sokeman and free man who, so far as we know, had none but his family, and perhaps unrecorded relatives, to help him cultivate his land.

Commentators have been puzzled by the apparent lack of relation between changes in the population and in manorial values. Sometimes the details seem logical enough. At East and West Ham (64 *bis*) teams increased from 19 to 36, recorded inhabitants from 107 to 187, and the value of the manors from £26 to £42. Yet at one of the Frinton manors (32b), teams diminished by 50 per cent, inhabitants decreased from eleven to five, yet it increased in value by 50 per cent. In view of what looks like a general decline in prosperity in this part of the Essex coast, the value might be merely a potential one, for its only other major asset is pasture, perhaps rentable pasture, for 60 sheep. Such apparent discord between equipment and value is frequent, yet we may take comfort from study of the picture as a whole.

Tendring is a Hundred much of which seems to have suffered since the Conquest. Teams were fewer by about $36\frac{1}{2}$ per cent, population up by only $2\frac{1}{4}$ per cent, and total value almost unaltered. In most of the coastal Hundreds the number of teams was appreciably fewer, but not in Sweyn's Hundred of Rochford, falling but little in those near London, where demand for agricultural produce may have increased. The same is true for figures for recorded population.

The holdings of villeins are sometimes noted. On the royal manor of Stanway (4b) one had half a hide, worth 10s. At *Estolleia* near Latchingdon (3), a royal manor, one had a virgate, and another half a virgate. But on the manor of Hatfield Broad Oak (2) there was one with a single acre, worth 4d. There were immense differences in the capacity of the individual villein. The 40 acres of one at Fanton (17b) and the 20 acres of another at Little Hallingbury (60) compare favourably with many holdings credited to free men and sokemen. The holding of a single bordar is only once mentioned; at Langford (68b) one had three acres.

Owing to the enormous preponderance of bordars over villeins and the fact that if there were villeins on a manor there were usually bordars also, it is impossible to obtain satisfactory figures for the possible number of oxen possessed by either. As usual, there are plenty of instances where none is recorded (e.g. Tendring, 11b; Little Bromley, 40b). Only in eight entries where there were villeins but no bordars are oxen mentioned. In these 30 villeins had 9½ teams, averaging under three oxen each. In 49 entries where there were bordars but no villeins 360 had 51 teams, or about one ox per man. We find a villein who may have had half a team (Fanton, 17b), but such quantities obviously do not produce useful deductions. So often we are dealing with very small properties in which the sole inhabitant is a teamless bordar (e.g. Abberton, 46b; Purleigh, 64b) that we can have no clear idea of the extent to which the soil of Essex was tilled. Moreover, a few entries suggest that teams and/or inhabitants have been omitted.

Suffolk

The information provided by DB for this county is appreciably fuller than that for Essex, and consequently engenders even more difficulties. In all, allowing for duplicate and doubtful entries, and excluding *Terra Regis*, 929 entries afford an opportunity of comparing valuations in 1066 and 1086. Of these 209 make use of *semper*. There is occasional doubt as to whether this is to be taken literally. Rattlesden (381b) is said 'always' to have been worth £10. But IE (ms. A, fol. 61ai) states that it was worth £8 *tunc*. For an enormous number of holdings, usually the smaller ones, we have only the 1086 value. Quite often we are told that the value is included in that of the manor to which the holding was attached, but over and over again suspicion is aroused that when the sum is stated it is covered by the value of the manor as a whole even though DB does not say so. There are indeed over 1,200 instances of 1086 values only. Frequent disagreement between the statistics of DB and IE causes us to be uncertain which is the more likely to be correct. DB (386b) gives eightpence as the value of five acres at Bucklesham. The IE figure (65ai) of tenpence is possibly to be preferred because each acre would then be worth the common sum of twopence. For Grundisburgh and Hasketon (386) DB has 1*s*. and 4*s*., IE (65ai) 3*s*. and 2*s*., each making 5*s*. in all.

Suffolk fiefs were either so enormous or so comparatively small that we may well concentrate on the largest ones, both lay and ecclesiastical. The lands of the abbey of St Edmund occupy 31 folios, and represent 222 specified holdings exclusive of those attached to churches. Where comparison is possible, they had improved in value by over 30 per cent, from

£344 5s. to £452 12s. 7d. In addition, values where we have a 1086 figure only amount to £39 7s. 8d.[1] Only four entries show a fall in value. Comparison is possible in 123, of which 48 use *semper*. We may feel that here we are not far from the truth.

The vast estates of Robert Malet comprised 511 holdings, the land of 56 churches and shares of varying extent in others, and interests in two boroughs. They had increased in value by only 13½ per cent, from £293 13s. 6d. to £333 5s. 2d. For 270 holdings worth £90 6s. 5d. we have only a 1086 figure. Large increases are rare. Leiston (311) may have appreciated from £16 to £28 because the land of 56 free men, though said 'always' to have been worth £6 10s., may not have been reckoned in the £16; it may have been added to the manor after the Conquest. Moreover, on folios well separated from that for Leiston, certain holdings are said to be 'in the value' of Leiston: Carlton, styled a manor, and Aldringham (310), Fordley (314), and Thorpe (316b). Hollesley (317) went up from £5 to £13, because a number of holdings said to be 'in the value of Hollesley' were very probably not included in the 1066 figure. In addition to six on fol. 317, Wilford (325), and Woodbridge (327b) were 'of the demesne and in the value of Hollesley'. Yet for two of the manor's berewicks, Culesley and Bawdsey (317b), values for both 1066 and 1086 are given. The first remained constant at £3, the second rose from 25s. to 40s.

No other fief approaches these in volume. The other large fiefs all show substantial appreciations in value.

	tunc	modo	*appreciation*
	£ s. d.	£ s. d.	%
Richard fitzGilbert	165 3 1	204 0 8	23½
Ely Abbey	149 9 6	189 15 0	27
Earl Alan	62 12 0	103 14 8	66
Roger Bigot	74 6 0	103 12 0	39½
Earl Hugh	73 16 8	101 2 8	38½

Two entries from the above merit mention. The increase for the manor of Framlingham (302b), from £16 to £36, could have been caused by factors suggested above, though few free men whose lands may have been post-Conquest additions to it are mentioned. There had, however, been a substantial increase in recorded population (50 per cent) on the original manor, though teams were fewer by 24 per cent. Roger Bigot, who held the manor of Hugh, may have been increasing rents and services. A

---

[1] The values of churches, where given independently, have been omitted. Often the value of the church was included in that of the manor as a whole. Beccles (369b) and Southwold (371b) rendered huge quantities of herrings, but their value is not given.

phenomenal appreciation is to be noted at Kelsale (330b), which went up from £5 to £24. But this higher value is said to be 'with the free men'. At Kelsale itself there had been 36 of these, and land at Fordley and Stickland (334b), *Becclinga* (338b), Saxmundham (339), and Gedgrave (343b) were 'in the value of' Kelsale or 'in its demesne'.[1]

One large fief shows a decline in value, that of Roger of Poitou. What had been worth £111 18s. 4d. was now worth £90 2s. 3d., with no comparison possible for values amounting to £12 12s. 11d. Some of the falls in value are considerable. Between them Otley (347), Wickham Skeith and Ingham (348), and Risby (349b) declined from £17 to £8. In all teams show a heavy fall in numbers. This could be connected with some unrecorded occasion of his falling into disfavour with the king during the period of the Inquest. In Norfolk lands are titled as those 'which were Roger of Poitou's'. In Derbyshire and some other counties his estates are said to be currently *in manu regis*, though his fief is entered normally for Essex and several other shires. The estates of Odo of Bayeux had declined slightly in value, and so had the pre-Conquest estates of the bishop of Thetford.

We should expect falls in value to appear chiefly on the smaller holdings and where numerous free men or sokemen shared a comparatively small number of acres. Entries of this character are indeed frequent, e.g. the 1½-acre holding at Hemingstone (352b) or where 25 free men held 108 acres between them (Snape, 316). But less than half the falls are on estates valued in 1066 at £1 or less, though nearly three-quarters are of £2 and under. Some really large manors, however, declined in value. Edric of Laxfield's two at Laxfield itself and Badingham (328b) fell from £15 each to £18 between them, and in each about one-third of the teams were gone. So they were at Hoxne (379) and Barham (383b), but the former may have declined considerably because of competition from Eye with its new market.

It is noticeable throughout East Anglia that where a vill included several holdings only one or two, as a rule, declined in worth. These were usually small ones. But the occasional vill seems to have suffered general loss, as was seen in the instance of Stonham Aspall (p. 246). Of the five Clopton estates (346b, 406b, 417b, 431, 431b) one remained constant in value and four declined; on balance, £9 14s. became £7 3s. 8d., but for two small holdings (315b, 431) comparison is impossible.

With so few appropriate entries relative to the whole, we could not expect the picture presented by falls in value to be a clear one. There

[1] *Carahalla*, the Domesday place-name, is only doubtfully 'Kelsale'. It had a market, which had probably improved its value.

THE DETAILS OF DOMESDAY BOOK

remain, however, suggestions of movement by Earl Ralf's men or their assailants from east Cambridgeshire and Exning through Thetford to Norwich. The marked concentration around Ipswich and across the Stour in north-east Essex (Fig. 31) could be connected with the same rising, but

Fig. 31 East Anglia
    Holdings with fall in value 1066–86
    – – – Main strategic roads
    B—Bury St Edmunds   Cl—Clare   Co—Colchester   E—Eye
    I—Ipswich   N—Norwich   S—Sudbury   T—Thetford   W—Wymondham

suggests also seaborne raids, perhaps by the Danish fleet on its way to the Northumbrian campaigns, penetrating up the estuaries and into their hinterlands.

Excluding *Terra Regis*, the rise in value is a comparatively modest one, from £2,237 3s. 8d. to £2,697 14s. 2½d., or about 20½ per cent. In view of what has been said above, it is then somewhat surprising that as many as 206 of these holdings show falls in value. A very high proportion of these are concentrated between Ipswich and Eye and north-east of Ipswich, and also south of Ipswich along the Stour estuary. West Suffolk and the coastal Hundreds show few falls. The concentration is to a large extent, but by no means exclusively, in the area in which free men of small substance abound, and in which many values and rents are low ones. But since there is a marked line of falls between Sudbury and Clare and the Ipswich—Eye roads the decline might possibly be connected with a movement of the troops of the king's adherents towards Norwich during the campaign of 1075, or of Earl Ralf's supporters towards his ultimate base.

It is throughout the lands of the greater lords which display the highest increases; Eudes fitzHerbert's of about 57 per cent, Earl Eustace's and Ralf Peverel's by over 50 per cent and nearly 40 per cent respectively. But there were not infrequent falls in value. Barton Mills (435b) fell from £8 to 30s., after declining earlier to £6: population and teams were both substantially less. Willingham (407), worth £3 in 1066, was valued at 32s. 6d. in 1086, but 3,000 herrings had also to be provided.

Some appreciations were even more startling. Selecting only a few instances, Eriswell and its berewick of *Coclesworda* (402b), Aldham (419), Wittlesham (427b), and Cavendish (428) increased in value from £38 to £77. In only the last were teams more numerous, and in none did the number of inhabitants increase. Equally puzzling is the rise for the land held by 35 free men at Akenham (422b). Seven teams had become half a team, yet the value is said to have increased from 40s. to 109s.

It is always difficult to estimate the extent to which renders in kind, which probably were not always mentioned, may have affected valuations. The *breve* for Hugh de Montfort (405b–10b) makes frequent mention of herring-renders, but it is doubtful if an apparent fall in value between 1066 and 1086 is compensated by such an amenity. For, if so, the *Beketuna* render would make 1,500 herrings worth 704d., whereas at Willingham double this quantity would be worth only 320d. The rise in value at both *Wimundahala* and Kirkley is in each case one shilling. This could hardly be accounted for by a render of 500 herrings at the first, but only 200 at the second.

Some of these changes may have been caused by vastly increased rents and services, though of the former we are told only intermittently. Elmham (356) is said to have been 'worth' 7s., but to 'render' 20s. The increase can hardly have been caused solely by the possible acquisition of two free men with only five acres and half a team. Bildeston (426) was worth £10, but it had to render £12. Similar information appears for Rushmere (316b).

Sometimes we are told that the rents imposed were too high. Assington (416) had a 'value' in 1086 of £20; it must have been the rent demanded, for 'it could not render it by £5'.[1] Pettaugh (440b) had been worth 60s., and in 1086 was valued at 40s.; however, it had been at farm for 75s., but the men who farmed it were in consequence ruined, and the jurors revalued it at 45s. Charsfield (343b) had been rendering 30s., but the free men were unable to pay so much, and it was valued at only 20s. Drinkstone (381b) had been at farm for 100s., but the lessee could not pay this sum, and indeed it was valued at only 60s. Thorney (350b), where there was a single ox of the plough where formerly there had been first a whole and then half a team, had been worth 10s., but in 1086 could 'scarcely render' 5s. Thorpe (409), formerly worth 30s., was at the Inquest 'hardly worth' 10s. Of two of Robert of Mortain's manors it is said that they could scarcely render the sums demanded, each much in excess of the 1066 values. The free men of Combs (291) were being asked to pay £31 for what had been worth £16; no wonder that 'they could not suffer it without ruin' (fol. 291).

Of the putting out of manors at a farm-rent we have further occasional mention. Six of Odo of Bayeux's (367–8) had been at farm for £11 13s. in all, but they were valued at only £6 11s. 6d. Hoxne (379) had fallen in value from £28 to £20, perhaps because of the damage to its market caused by the rival which William Malet had instituted at Eye, but while Bishop Herfast had the Suffolk see it had brought him in £30. A tenant of Richard fitzGilbert's gave Ringsett (393b) at farm for 70s., but he could obtain only 60s. from it, and a reeve had had Desning (390) for £65, though it was worth only £40. Farm-rents had obviously been pitched too high, as at Framsden (298b), Ousden (303), Westleton (313b), Weston (335b), Saxmundham (338b), Boxted (349b), and Higham (436b). Kembrook (343) had been and was still rendering £6, but the Hundred-jury said it was worth no more than 48s. The new lords, avid for profit, had been trying to exploit their lands to the full, but to ruin their tenants and peasantry would defeat their object.

It does not look as if there was either appreciable improvement or

[1] It had been worth £10, and later £12. Most of the holdings here considered show appreciation on figures for both *tunc* and *post*.

decline in the value of manors immediately after the Conquest. Entries giving a figure for *post* are comparatively few, and out of 78 only six show a rise in value and sixteen a fall. The total fall for these is less than 14 per cent, while by 1086 they were worth 20 per cent more than in 1066. But it is clear that some statements refer to a period fairly soon after the Conquest, others to a later period.

The king's estates are more difficult to evaluate than those in Essex. There are the complications encountered elsewhere induced by renders in kind, payments *ad numerum* and *ad pensum*, blanch payments, sums which may or may not be covered by manorial valuations, the imposition of *gersumae*, Hundred-soke, manor-soke, and possible textual errors.[1]

So far as can be determined, a revenue in 1066 of £311 7s. 6d., much of it from land then not royal, had become one of £456 5s. 2d., an improvement of 47 per cent. Whether much of this was due to the incorporation of free men's lands in manors to which they had not previously been attached is uncertain. Some of the increases are enormous. Though 33 out of 40 sokemen had been lost from Thorney (281b), a payment of £15 in counted coin had become one of £40 blanch, and this was £5 more than it had been when Roger Bigot began to administer it. Mildenhall and its berewick Icklingham (288b) went up from £40 to £70; both Hintelsham and Bramford (289) from £10 to £22.

We are not, however, told that such sums were considered to be excessive, or that they could not be produced. To challenge the authority of the royal *ministri*, except in desperation, might indeed have been deemed unwise. But the instance of East Bergholt and its components (287) shows that some payments demanded were far too high. It had lost nearly half its 210 sokemen, but when Robert Malet administered it renders of £33 had been increased to £60. In King Edward's day the sokemen had been paying 4d. each, but Roger Bigot, during one of his turns of office as sheriff, ordered his officials to require £15, and Robert Malet increased this to £20.

The royal property is classified according to the farmer or custodian, eight in all, who exploited it.[2] Roger Bigot's share was worth the most, though that of William de Noyers was not much less; in third place came the former lands of Earl Ralf which Godric administered. It is curious that

---

[1] e.g. the free men of various vills had been rendering 13s. 6d.; in 1086 they are said to render £30. 30s. seems a more reasonable figure.
[2] There is no mention of Hugh of Houdain, who at the time of the Inquest was the king's prisoner (Bricett, 448b), but he is mentioned on fol. 284b in connection with free men who in 1066 had been rendering 20s. *ad firmam*. Ælfric the reeve, Ælfric 'Wanz', a royal official, raised this to 100s. 'In the time of Hugh', it was reported, this became the incredible amount of £50.

sometimes payments *ad firmam* are less than the valuation recorded, e.g. on fol. 288.

Though many of the sums appearing must represent rents in terms of the *ora*, 16, 32, and 64 pence being prevalent, it is only twice mentioned by name (fols. 281b, 360). Even more strongly marked is the large number of instances in which the number of acres credited to a holding gives a value of whole numbers of pence from one to six. Acres valued at 2*d*. each appear most frequently. They are to be found a score of times on *Terra Regis*, and in thirteen out of twenty entries for the king's *vavassores* (446–7b).[1] The Ely lands furnish nearly forty examples, and it must be remembered that a carucate worth £1, or multiples thereof, which occur frequently, makes each acre worth 2*d*. Sometimes the acres are not even whole numbers. Coddenham church (338) had 12½ acres, and was worth 25*d*. There are a great many valuations of multiples of 20*d*., and one cannot help wondering whether they represent payments of twenty pence for each sixteen of liability. The silver mark of 13*s*. 4*d*. is mentioned only once by name (Thorington, 412b), but this sum and 6*s*. 8*d*. recur. The mark of gold of £6 enters into the Bergholt payments (287).

Finally, a few oddities may not be without significance. Chickering (330) had been mortgaged for 60*s*., but the two holdings were worth only 16*s*. The value of stock, implements, and buildings presumably entered into the mortgage price as well as that of the land itself. Perhaps that is why early in the reign the abbot of Bury paid the king's legates 100*s*. for Ixworth Thorpe (367b), which in 1086 was worth only 30*s*.

Three times the curious sum of 11*s*. 5*d*. appears on fol. 395. There was a half-team on each holding, but they were of 60, 60, and 30 acres, and the last had no recorded population. One had been worth twice as much as the others. Stoke by Nayland, Withermarsh, and Polstead (401) had all been worth £10 and in 1086 were valued at £12. The population of the first declined by over 30 per cent, of the last two by 16 per cent. But whereas the teams of these declined by 36 per cent, those of Stoke were only 28½ per cent fewer. The figures seem to even themselves out.

The plough-teams at work in 1086 were fewer than those of King Edward's day. As in Essex, they decreased less on the demesnes than they did on the villagers' land. The decline is at times very considerable. At Weybread (329b) a single ox was all that remained of 2½ teams; there was half a team on the lands of the Akenham free men (422b) where there had been seven full teams. The value of Barkestone (425b) fell from 20*s*. to 12*s*., and where there had been one demesne team and seven others there

---

[1] Correction of possible clerical errors would give us more; e.g. 6½ acres worth 14*d*. (Claydon, 446b) is very close to an acre of 2*d*.

THE EASTERN COUNTIES: SUFFOLK

were now none at all. A falling-off in the number of teams often goes with a lessening of the value and/or a diminished population.

In 26 entries we are told that there could be more teams than there were at work, or that they could be 'restored', which shows that witnesses and clerks were conscious of the deficiencies. This information, however, is never reported in some Hundreds, though that does not imply that it could not have been. Some of the details lack clarity. 'Then and afterwards' there was a demesne team at Thorney (281b), in 1086 none. But there could have been two in King Edward's day, and the use of *tunc* suggests that the deficiency was pre-Conquest. Here, too, seven sokemen had 'always' had a half-team, but here *semper* can hardly include 1066, for *tempore regis Edwardi* four of them had had a whole team.[1]

It is impossible to say how intense the decline may have been. Sometimes we are told of teams operating at the time of the Conquest, but are given no figure for 1086, and the reverse is of far greater frequency. The first may not have entirely disappeared; the second may have been fewer than in 1086. All we can say is that the fall was probably within the limits 15–25 per cent, and probably nearer the lower figure. But it is much heavier than average in an area with Ipswich as centre and some thirty miles broad by twenty long, as were valuations also. Here it was at least 30 per cent. The heaviest falls seem to occur in the eastern and southern Hundreds, perhaps because these contained large numbers of free men who may have been unable to maintain pre-Conquest conditions, or whose oxen had become unnecessary where the holdings had been absorbed into a complex manor. Many fiefs, e.g. those of Sweyn of Essex or Geoffrey de Manneville, show a fall of about 30 per cent of the number of teams, which could be the result of a possible shift to a more pastoral and less agricultural economy. But on the Ely lands numbers fell nearly as much, probably because Ely had been robbed of so many of her estates. On the other hand, St Edmund's holdings show only a small decline, though it is true that *semper* is here frequently used.

Clarity as regards changes in the numbers of any category of the population is inevitably lacking. In 1,243 instances it is possible to compare the quantities of villeins, bordars, and slaves recorded for 1066 and 1086. But in over half as many instances, 626 in all, we are given quantities in 1066 or 1086, usually the latter, but no means of comparison.

If we use only the figures affording the opportunity of comparison, the result suggests that the total decline in the villager and servile population was very small, only about 1 per cent. Villeins were fewer by just over

---

[1] See also Stradbroke (328b), where 'restored to twelve teams' must be meant, not that twelve could be restored, and Shotley (287), Bridge (331), and Wrentham (399).

10 per cent, slaves by just under 25 per cent, while bordars increased by nearly 12 per cent. These are figures such as we might expect. But while the remaining instances make little difference to the figures for villeins and slaves, they bring the increase in bordars to almost 35 per cent, and produce one of 17 per cent for the three categories combined.

	Comparison of total percentage possible:		*Including those in which comparison is not possible*	
	1066	*1086*	*1066*	*1086*
Villeins	39	35	38	30
Bordars	49	56	46	61½
Slaves	12	9	16	8½

Somewhere between these limits the truth must lie. It must however be remembered that these figures take no account of the free men, sokemen, and others, and that it is highly unlikely that where we have only a quantity for 1086 there were always none of that category in 1066.

The general trend is as it was in Essex. In the south-east, the district in which there was a multiplicity of the small holdings of free men, slaves represented only 3¼ per cent of the recorded population. By 1086 there were in all not much more than 300 holdings on which there were slaves. Some of those who had disappeared since the Conquest are no doubt represented among the bordars, and so may some of the former villeins be. But such cancellation still leaves us with about 1,600 bordars apparently unrepresented in 1066, and these cannot all have been former free men or sokemen. But they may have been their helpers.

There are occasional suggestions of the extent of the holdings of villeins and bordars. Those of twenty or thirty acres (Raydon, 411, 411b) were doubtless above the average for a Suffolk villein. The Hemley bordar (431) who had five acres is paralleled by many entries in the eastern midlands. But there must have been large differences between the standards of either villeins or bordars, and the material for estimating how many oxen either may have possessed on average is lacking.

Norfolk

Out of 1,604 passages in which the value of a holding is given, only a little over a half, 879 in all, afford the opportunity of comparison with earlier values. Of these, almost 200 make use of *semper*. An intermediate value appears in 246 entries, but it is unlikely that these refer to even a short space of time. Some relate to a period when Earl Ralf possessed the manors (e.g. Burnham, 128) or when Robert Blond farmed or administered them (Eaton, 135), or when Robert the crossbowman held Roger of Poitou's properties in Tunstead and elsewhere *in manu regis* (244). It is accordingly impossible to say whether a general rise or fall in values is apparent during the first decade of the Conquest.

Only half a dozen Norfolk fiefs were really large ones. Each shows substantial appreciation where comparable figures are available.

	tunc	modo	*appreciation*
	£ s. d.	£ s. d.	%
Bishop of Thetford	224 3 10	337 12 4	51
William of Warenne	177 12 6	253 19 4	42½
Roger Bigot	167 17 2	245 0 3½	46
Earl Alan	94 1 0	152 12 0	62
Ralf Bainard	104 3 0	147 0 8	30
Odo of Bayeux	59 2 6	100 2 6	69

For the entire county, omitting *Terra Regis*, the increase was 38 per cent, from £1,670 7s. to £2,306 17s. 11½d. Some fiefs seem to show only small improvement, e.g. those of Hermer de Ferrières (5 per cent) and Rainald fitzIvo (5¼ per cent), while St Benedict of Ramsey's fell by 14 per cent, and this had indeed lost many of its former customary tenants and sokemen.

Some increases are so great that changes in the composition of the manors are to be presumed. Odo's holdings attached to Snettisham (142) went up from £50 to £85, but we are none the less told that it was 'the whole' which was worth £50 in 1066. Hickling and some other holdings (148) appreciated from £2 to £9, but perhaps the 25 free men at Ludham Stalham, and Ingham had been added since 1066. Sometimes rents and payments seem to have been increased. Litcham (207) had been worth 40s. In 1086 it was worth 50s., 'and 10s. above that'.[1]

A decline in value is also frequently considerable. Hunstanton (183) fell from 16s. to 4s., but nothing except proximity to the coast and the disappearance of six out of eight oxen suggests why this should be so. Rushford (214) had only a single ox where there had been 2½ teams, and its value had fallen by 60 per cent. Flitcham (173), however, probably did not drop from £2 to 1s., for the 1086 figure is surely a mistake for £1. Except for an almost total disappearance of 180 sheep on the demesne, the figures show general improvement.

In this county, however, falls in value are comparatively infrequent.

---

[1] The manor had a quarter-share in a market. If this was a novelty, it would improve the value.

THE DETAILS OF DOMESDAY BOOK

Nowhere is there even a small concentration of these which might suggest a reason for local decline. But occasional entries furnish clues. The values of Croxton (136b) and Hilgay (215) probably lessened because 17 sokemen had been detached from the former manor and eight customary tenants from the latter. At Bodney (237) six teams had been reduced by 75 per cent and the demesne livestock had decreased from 121 to 28; the £5-manor was in 1086 worth only £3. At North Tuddenham (214b) the mill was 'waste', and the holding was valued at 8s. less than in 1066. It is, not surprisingly, on the smaller holdings that we usually find reduced values. Two-thirds of the instances come from properties valued in 1066 at £1 or less.

Static values or only slight falls could be deceptive. Billingford (254) is given a constant value of £4, though six sokemen had been abstracted from the manor. Since teams were less by $36\frac{1}{2}$ per cent it looks as if Ralf Peverel was obtaining more from less, and such a situation is not uncommon, e.g. at Tatterford (262b). Falls in value are widespread, but only the western Hundreds, especially in the Fenland and the Breckland, show frequent declines, and these holdings number in all fewer than 100, less than half as many as in Suffolk.

Some rents were deemed to be excessive. Sculthorpe with Toft Trees (168), worth £6 in 1066, was in 1086 valued at £10; it had been at farm for £15, but 'could not pay it'. Mundham (176b) had always been worth 5s., but Earl Alan's men had had 10s. from it for the previous four years. Aldborough (185), worth 30s., double its pre-Conquest value, had been *ad firmam* for 40s., but also 'could not pay it'. Rainham and its associated holdings (237b), whose value fell from £8 to £3 after the Conquest, could now produce £8 10s. only 'with great difficulty'. Manors had been 'given to farm' by Earl Ralf at twice the value set on them at the Inquest, e.g. Swanton Morley (226b) and Deopham (227).[1] It is probable that a good many sums represent farm-rents though the fact is not stated.

Quite often the value of the manor and of the land of the free men incorporated in it are given separately (e.g. Castle Acre, 160b), and sometimes the value of the demesne (e.g. West Rudham, 169b) is stated. In a few entries we are given only the 1066 value, e.g. at Holme next the Sea (126) and Fundenhall (152b), while in a few others the value is not given, e.g. at Ludham (150) or Watlingsete (114).

Occasionally we are given the value of manorial attributes. Four acres

---

[1] Other instances of exorbitant demands include Shropham (152), Runton (184b), Whimpwell (220), Stokesby (225), Wereham, Upwell (230b), Stanford (238b), Merton (252), Dersingham (256), Ingoldisthorpe (256b), and probably entries such as Bradenham (276b) and Sutton (179b). It is likely that there were many more instances which did not happen to be recorded.

of woodland and one of meadow are valued at 12*d.* (Yaxham, 232b), six acres of meadow at the same number of pence (Melton, 254b). In addition to the 260 Halvergate demesne sheep (128b), there were 700 which 'rendered 100*s.*' (? a rent for their pasturage); the value of extensive pasture at Well Hall (221b) was reckoned with that of the whole manor. The more irregular values probably represent the sum of rents, e.g. £1 3*s.* 7*d.* for Swanton (181b), or £15 5*s.* 5½*d.* for East Carleton and its contributories (187b). The mark, and then a gold one, appears by name only once (Rackheath, 217b).

The king's estates were numerous. Three men had their custody; Godric, whose share was the largest one, William de Noyers, and one who is unnamed but was probably the sheriff, Roger Bigot. Apart from renders in kind, largely of honey, and over a score of instances of a *gersuma*, they had increased in value by 77 per cent, from £579 11*s.* to £1,020 5*s.* 8*d.* But much of this increase would seem to be the result of enlargement of the manors. Fakenham (111) could hardly have improved in value from £8 to £43 unless the holdings of free men and sokemen had been added to it and were not included in the 1066 reckoning.[1] Earsham (138b) rose in value from £11 to £40 'with all that belongs to it'. This may have included the profits of the Hundred-soke, for many a holding 'rendered soke in Earsham', while on fols. 138b–41 numerous properties are said to be 'valued in Earsham'. Free men 'used to render £4', but Richard Poignant 'caused them to pay rent in Earsham' (139), and in 1086 they were paying £16, a substantial proportion of the £29 difference between the values given for 1066 and 1086.[2] Holt (111b) had been worth £20 plus £5 of customary dues and a honey render, while in 1086 it was worth £50. But on fol. 112b we read of 'the whole of Holt' as paying £66. The difference might originate in the addition of land to the former manor. The contribution of the free men, conveying the suggestion that they had been added to the manor, is frequently recorded (e.g. Eaton, 135), and though sometimes this is distinct from the manorial value (e.g. at Mautby, 134b), often it must have been included in the single sum given.

The *ora*, as we might expect, is of frequent occurrence. It is specifically named in seven entries.[3] Rents which were surely based upon it also appear in some quantity. There are nearly sixty instances of 16*d.*, and more than two dozen of 32*d.* Sums of 8*d.*, 5*s.* 4*d.*, 10*s.* 8*d.*, 8*s.*, 16*s.*, 32*s.* occur

---

[1] There are equally striking examples, e.g. Southmere (109b), Buckenham (126b), and Mileham (136b).
[2] Free men later attached to Shotesham (124) *non erant ad censum*, but the royal *minister* Robert Blond had 'put them to rent' (*adcensavit*); see also Redenhall (125b).
[3] Stody (112), Morston (128), Shotesham (185b, 243), Chedgrave (253), Holkham (258), Somerton (277b).

THE DETAILS OF DOMESDAY BOOK

frequently. At Caston (163b) and Creake (168b), and several other places, 17s. 4d., 13 *orae*, appears, as does 45s. 4d., or 34 *orae* (Crostwick, 229). Probably many more instances are concealed where only the sum of rents is given. It would not be surprising to find that the value of Garvestone (207b), £2 15s. 4d., was really 50s. plus three *orae*; a similar division might account for some of the copious instances of 6s. 8d. and 13s. 4d. The figure of £1 6s. 8d. recurs, but the final figures may not represent ten *orae* or 80d., but one-third of a pound; 13s. 4d., the value of the silver mark, is also common.[1] Though there may be no connection, it is noticeable how often the quantity of 16 acres appears.[2] Two-fifteenths is not an obvious fraction of the carucate. There is an instance of a rent of 16d. becoming one of 20d. (Billockby, 272b), as though the free men here were paying *de xx denariis in ora*. Certainly amounts of 20d., 40d., 60d. are extremely common. It is not impossible that when, as often happens, 15 acres are given a value of the same number of pence, 1s. 3d. was really 1s. 4d., reduced to produce an even working. It may be, too, that 15 acres, the eighth of the carucate, were sometimes treated as 16 to blend with rents in terms of the *ora*.

In Norfolk acres valued at 1d. are of far more frequent occurrence than those of 2d. There are three areas in which the 1d. acre is especially conspicuous. One is the western portion of Clackclose Hundred, where densities of population and of teams per square mile were low, another occupies much of Clavering Hundred near Yarmouth. But the most obvious one occupies the coastal Hundreds of East and West Flegg and Happing and persists until the country south of Norwich is reached. This was a district in which the usually small holdings of free men were numerous. The vill of Waxham near the coast was composed of the holdings shown on the opposite page.

A general fall in the number of teams at work is apparent. In over one hundred entries we are told that there could be more teams than there are available, or that teams could be 'restored'. The appearance of such statements is probably accidental, for they never appear in one-third of the Hundreds, while 40 per cent of the instances come from those of Launditch and Guiltcross. But there are some fifty entries in which the teams of 1086 are more numerous than they had been earlier. This could often be because the extent of the manor had been enlarged by the incorporation of previously independent holdings, resulting also in an increase in the population. The teams on the royal manor of Foulsham (114) were in 1086

---

[1] e.g. Marham (159b), Burlingham (199), and three successive entries on fol. 216b, suggesting equal division of £4; Tichwell (183).
[2] e.g. Framingham (143), Matlask (146, 146b).

more numerous by 15 per cent, and the recorded inhabitants had increased from 68 to 77.[1]

fol. WAXHAM:	Holder T.R.E.	acres	value	pence per acre
			£ s. d.	
148b	2 free men ⎫	161 ⎫	1 15 0	2½ approx.
,,	4 ,, ⎭	10 ⎭	1 4	
,,	church glebe	20	1 4	⅘
149	Edric, a free man	80	10 0	1½
,,	church glebe	18	1 6	1
,,	2 sokemen	3½	6	1¾ approx.
,,	8 free men	80	5 0	¾
187	half a free man	7	valued in Palling	
220	St Benedict of Holme	248	4 0 0 ⎫	6 approx.
,,	25½ sokemen	160	⎭	
,,	2 free men	20	2 10	1¾
272b	3 free men	10	1 4	1½
			average 2 approx.	

Teams appear to have been reduced in quantity more between *tunc* and *post* than between 1066 and 1086. The number of teams recorded for *post* is only about three-quarters of what it had been in 1066, but it must be remembered that figures are given in comparatively few entries. By the time of the Inquest the decline was only 17 per cent. Demesne teams decreased, as we might expect, only to about one-third the extent to which villagers' teams did.

Out of 740 'vills' 333 had fewer teams than in 1066, while 279 show no change. For 62 we have no comparable figures; in all there were less than 100 teams in 1066 for which we have no 1086 figures, and nearly 400 in 1086 on holdings for which no 1066 quantity is given. The losses are fairly evenly distributed over the whole county, though they are at their lowest in the Fenland, the Breckland, and the district now occupied by the Broads. In such areas teams and recorded population per square mile are below average. Here manorialisation, inducing an economy requiring the employment of fewer teams than previously, may not have proceeded as extensively as elsewhere, nor demesne land have been largely increased. There are also a number of instances of few teams round about Norwich and near the roads leading there from Suffolk. In all the teams at Wymondham (137b, 166b) fell by nearly 50 per cent, and in one of the entries we are told that 'this destruction (*confusio*) was made by Ralf'. This and other

[1] Here, though six out of thirty sokemen had been appropriated by Walter Gifford, the teams of 1066 did not diminish, nor did the half-team on land added to the manor.

losses may then have been caused by the rebellion of Earl Ralf in 1075.

Only the roughest estimate of the extent of changes in the population is possible. If we use only the entries in which figures are given for both 1066 and 1086, we obtain the improbable result that it fell after the Conquest by 4 per cent. If we use all the figures available, it would seem to rise by $12\frac{1}{2}$ per cent. Neither system is satisfactory. Using only comparable quantities, the increase in Docking Hundred was 2 per cent. If all the entries are used, this becomes 150 per cent. This is because (and this applies throughout the county) we have no 1066 quantities for some holdings, e.g. Brancaster (215b), which had a recorded population of 46. Equally there are problems such as that posed by the Swanton Morley entry (226b), where the numbers of villeins and slaves remained constant but that of the bordars rose from 38 to 54, or by that for Flockthorpe (122), where there were in 1086 a dozen bordars where none is mentioned for 1066, while the quantity of villeins remained unchanged and of slaves fell from six to three.

But that there was some increase in the village population is certain. While the number of slaves fell, apparently by $23\frac{1}{2}$ per cent, and villeins were fewer by about 3 per cent, there were in 1086 over 2,000 more bordars than are noted for 1066. The servile population, the figures suggest, never represented more than 7–10 per cent of the total. In 1086 six eastern Hundreds, where free men and sokemen were numerous, could muster only 40 in all. Such men would neither need nor be able to afford slaves. Throughout the shire slaves seem to have disappeared on a great many holdings; the figures suggest that often they had been emancipated and were now classified as bordars. It is not uncommon to find no change, or only a slight one, in the total recorded population, e.g. at Hempstead (248b), but quite considerable variations in the proportion of villeins, bordars, and slaves at the two dates specified. At Kerdiston (247b) 30 villeins became 16, but 14 bordars appear where none is mentioned for 1066, while two slaves had become one.

In over thirty entries there is a suggestion that we are being given the extent of the holdings of villeins and bordars. Those of villeins rarely exceed 15 acres, though at Acre (120) one had half a carucate and a whole team, while at Corpusty (225) another had 40 acres. A Plumstead bordar had nine acres (228b), but most entries suggest only very small holdings for this category. At Hilgay (213) four bordars had only two acres, and in the same place (209) two had a single acre.

It is impossible to determine, too, how far the numbers of free men and of sokemen may have changed, since we do not know whether, when they are mentioned for 1066, they were still there later, nor how many individuals appear in more than one entry. There is indeed no suggestion of a heavy fall in their numbers. At Bintree (269b) there were 'then as now' two sokemen, at Swannington (147b) 'then' eight, 'afterwards' and 'now' five. But at Hockering (227b) three had become seven, and at Welburne (166) ten had become a score. Some of the pre-Conquest holdings were so small that it would not be surprising to learn that many had become villeins or bordars after the Conquest. Ten free men in Stibbard and elsewhere (111) had only three acres between them; one at Colney (204b) half an acre, and one at Hindringham (198b) a single acre. A sokeman at Saxlingham (125) also had only an acre; by contrast, one at Roydon (142b) had a whole carucate. A Postwick entry (279b) suggests that free men had been newly obliged to perform labour service. Formerly their land was worth 5s.; 'now they render 2s. with service'.

9
The South-West

In this circuit the Inquest authorities did not cause triple valuations to be even fairly regularly recorded, and unfortunately they do not seem to have troubled to collect information about the state of things in 1066 except in so far as tenancies and conditions of tenure were concerned. While this is true of many of the circuits, for most counties we at least have manorial values for both 1066 and 1086 in the majority of entries. But here we seem to be given valuations for 1066 only rarely. Collation of the Exchequer text with that of the *Liber Exoniensis* suggests that the *valuit* or *olim* of the former implies *quando recepit*. Since we do not know when the tenants-in-chief of 1086 may have received their manors, and these are not always the men to whom a grant was initially made, we have no means of estimating the extent and calibre of changes in manorial values in the preceding score of years. Nor can we try to discover whether after initial decline in the early years of the Conquest there had been partial or substantial recovery.

It is of course possible that for *olim* or *quando recepit* are given figures which were little, or not at all, different from those of 1066. This might well be true if the south-west did not greatly suffer from the advent of Norman forces. But we have to consider also the possibility that, as in other shires, they represent a general decline in manorial values induced by the arrival of the foreigners and the military campaigns in connection with the post-Conquest revolts. Perhaps the impression gained from the texts is that values, generally speaking, had not fallen substantially since King Edward's day.

Indeed, figures can here only be given with marked reservations. The

Liber Exoniensis shows us how frequently the composition of manors had changed, and some of the passages suggest that the earlier of two values is that of the manor as it was when received, while that for *modo* is based on the manor as it was composed at the time of the Inquest. Thus apparent appreciations in value could be highly misleading. All that can be said is that on the whole values in Wiltshire seem to have increased fairly substantially, but in Dorset very little. Somerset and Devon give results similar to that for Wiltshire. In Cornwall many falls in value are recorded, and what increases there are appear largely in the demesne manors of Robert of Mortain and in those of the see of Exeter. A deficiency of teams against ploughlands increases from east to west, but there is a good deal of artificiality about many of the quantities for the latter. As we might expect, Cornish villagers possessed fewer plough-oxen than those in the other shires.

Wiltshire

We have only a solitary Exeter Domesday entry for Wiltshire, and from the Exchequer text we can learn little about the shire in King Edward's day except as regards landholders and tenancies. It is, however, apparent that much of the extensive ecclesiastical property was leased and that the number of minor thegns who had small estates was a very large one.

Unfortunately we are given no information for this county about values earlier than those of 1086 for 40 per cent of the holdings, representing about 30 per cent of the total values if *Terra Regis* is excluded. Where comparative figures are available, these show an average rise of 18 per cent. Only thrice are values in 1066 given.[1]

Only 32 holdings display a fall in value, but we might well find more if we had comparative figures for 88 properties still held by king's thegns. So few instances furnish small scope for diagnosing potential causes of diminished values. A quantity of the falls in value are to be found in the east of the county, which might suggest that the holdings had not wholly recovered from the possible passage in 1066 of a detachment of the invaders moving from west Hampshire through the Collingbournes to Marlborough and then by way of the Swindon area to Highworth. In 1086 a number of places about the line of this possible movement were deficient in plough-teams in relation to ploughlands (Fig. 9).

Increases in value seem to depend on the tenant-in-chief rather than

---

[1] Coombe Bissett, 65a2; Damerham, 66bi; Castle Eaton, 68b2. Brixton Deverill (68bi), in 1086 worth £12, had been worth £15 when Queen Matilda, who gave the manor to St Mary of Bec, was alive.

situation, though we are handicapped by having few comparative figures for several large fiefs, e.g. that of the local bishop. Of the religious houses only Glastonbury shows a substantial increase (70 per cent) and the appreciation on the sheriff's manors (40 per cent) is above anything the other large lay fiefs can show. Those on the holdings of Robert fitzGerold, Gilbert de Bretteville, Arnulf de Hesdin, and Osbern Gifford range from 23–32 per cent. Some increases are indeed considerable. Downton (65bi) was worth £60 when the bishop of Winchester received it, perhaps on Stigand's dismissal in 1070; in 1086 the demesne was valued at £80 and the manor church and the tenancies brought in £26 more, even though four hides were in the king's Forest. It is no rarity to find a small manor which had doubled in value, e.g. Swindon (66a2), Draycot Fitzpaine (66a2), Baycliff (69bi), and Langley Burrell (69b2). Rises of 50 per cent and more are also common. The nunnery of Wilton's manor of Stanton St Bernard (67b2) had appreciated from £16 to £24; of St Mary of Winchester's two holdings (68a2), Urchfont had at least doubled in value, while that of All Cannings was 50 per cent more than it had been.

Some increases may have been due to changes in the composition of a manor, others to increased rents. Four royal manors paid by weight what the English had set as the value by tale (65ai). Glastonbury's manor of Damerham (66bi) was paying £61, with thegnland worth an additional £7 15s., against a 1066 value of £36. But the English claimed it was worth only £45, partly because of the state of the manor (*confusio* could imply either 'ruin' or doubt as to the legal implications of tenancy), partly because the rent was too high. Newton Tony (70a2), which had been worth £10, was said to be worth £8 more in 1086, but the English valued it at only £2 more. Apparently they agreed that the value had appreciated; they may have accepted that under their new masters rents would be raised.

Waste land figures but little in the text, though it makes rare appearances in the geld accounts for the shire. There is also far less reference to Forest than we might expect. Only five entries, and three passages in the geld accounts, specifically mention it, but there are also a few oblique indications of its existence, e.g. to *silva Milcheti* or Melchet Forest (68ai,2), 'the wood called Chute' (65a2), and wood *in manu regis* (Britford, 65ai) which contributed to the royal *firma*. But the unmentioned existence, or proximity, of Forest land could well be associated with low values and a paucity of teams in the relevant areas.

Interest is consequently largely confined to the royal manors (64b2–5bi). Six of these were under the obligation of furnishing one night's farm. We cannot be certain that this had been commuted and discharged by a payment of money instead of provender. Chippenham is said to be worth £110 and Tilshead £100, both in counted coin, but while the *firma* in adjacent counties was usually worth in the neighbourhood of £100, we should not assume that this was universal. There is considerable variation in the recorded population and teams of these six manors, but then at Tilshead, for example, pastoral was of far greater importance than arable. Possibly Westbury and Melksham had also provided a night's farm, for the first is said to be worth £100 in counted coin, and the second had paid over £100.

The remaining fifteen manors fall into two groups, for nine of which we are given undated values for a time earlier than 1086. Eight of these were at the Inquest bringing in almost one-quarter more than previously. Six had to pay in weighed, not counted, coin. We are not told the previous liabilities of Britford and Compton Chamberlayne, but Coombe Bissett, which had paid £24, would now have to find about £30. Of three the English jurors said they were overvalued and paying too much. Aldbourne they valued at £60 in counted coin; it must have been paying much nearer £90: Corsham at £31, whereas it probably had to produce nearly £40. To Melksham they gave the precise value of £111 11s.; it was liable for for this sum in counted coin, and must have had to find about £140. In all the royal manors were producing somewhere in the neighbourhood of £1,350. The owner of the next most valuable fief in the county, the bishop of Salisbury, was receiving about £300.

Not that this was all King William was receiving from Wiltshire. Fol. 64bi tells us what he was getting out of the borough of Malmesbury; 42s. 6d. in house rents, 10s. from a mill, £5 from the mint (presumably for the privilege of coining money), £14 in all for the 'third penny', which included the profits of the pleas of two Hundreds. The third penny of three other Wiltshire boroughs brought in £15, and the royal share of the borough of Wilton £50, an increase of £28 on its former payment.

The county as a whole, together with royal manors and borough proceeds, seems to have been farmed by the sheriff, who paid a premium of £60 by weight, possibly £75 in counted coin, in addition to whatever sum the above, and perhaps receipts of which we are not told, represents.[1]

The sheriff, by virtue of his office, received a valuable payment in kind which included bacon-pigs, various forms of grain, honey, hens and their eggs, lambs, and cheeses. This passage (69ai) includes a statement which suggests that his profit from farming the shire was normally £80, but that

---

[1] The churches on the royal demesne (65bi) can hardly have been valueless to the king. We are told also that he had from the shire £10 in lieu of a falcon, 20s. for a pack-horse, and more than £5 for fodder.

in a bad year he had to make up the difference between the sum he had contracted to pay his royal master and the shortfall from the king's property.[1]

Thus it looks as if the only farmer of royal manors was the sheriff, in contrast to the system current in neighbouring shires. The only mentions of a farm-rent are at Cholderton (70ai) and at Chedglow (70a2), where a thegn had of his own accord become the man of Arnulf of Hesdin, and was paying 40*d. de firma* for what had been worth 15*s*. The wording and the fall in value suggests that the thegn was less prosperous than he had been. 40*d.* occurs in three other entries, and the use of *reddit*, not *valet*, in only six.[2]

The number of ploughlands is usually furnished for the larger fiefs, and in all we are lacking them for only 16 per cent of the entries. Only on very few occasions do the ploughlands exceed the teams (about 8 per cent); the reverse is true in $36\frac{1}{2}$ per cent of the entries.

But the high number of instances of correspondence may be largely deceptive. The number of occasions on which there is a large quantity of ploughlands, but not a round number, and an equal number of teams, is high. We find, for example, Calne (64b2), 21+8; Bedwyn (64b2), 12+67; Rushall (65ai), 12+14+$1\frac{1}{2}$; Westbury (65a2), 7+40; Netheravon (65a2), 6+16; Bishop's Cannings (66ai), 5+28+8+4; Ramsbury (66ai), 8+29+11+6; showing this equivalence. It is impossible to avoid a suspicion that the number of ploughlands was arrived at by adding together the teams. But the result might still be the truth or very near it.

The large number of instances with high round figures equally provokes doubt. Thirteen royal manors out of nineteen have ploughlands numbering 100, 50, 45, 40, 30, 25, 20, 15, or 10, and of the remaining six five are in the category described above. On other large fiefs we find 60, 40, 30, 25, or 20 ploughlands, e.g. at Potterne (66ai) and Tisbury (67bi). Yet decimal quantities of ploughlands are less frequent than duodecimal ones. The former represent 16 per cent of the total number of instances, the latter 34 per cent. But there is no obvious correlation between ploughlands and assessments. Where there were in 1086 eight ploughlands, the assessment ranges from 27 hides (Elcombe, 70a2) to 5 hides (e.g. Poulton, 68b2). Duodecimal quantities are at their most frequent in the northern half of the shire, nearest Mercia.

A deficiency of teams is more marked in the northern half of the shire than in the south, and the same distribution is apparent for the holdings for which no teams are mentioned. Widely scattered though the instances

---

[1] Did Edward of Salisbury have this note included because 1086 had been a year of bad weather?   [2] Fols. 73b2, 74bi,2; 71b2, 72ai,2bi, 73ai, 74ai,b2.

of both are, there are three concentrations. The first runs from the junction with Hampshire at a point where a lack of teams and decline in values in that county is marked, splits at the Kennet valley, and then passes up both Winterbourne and Ogbourne to lead into Berkshire at a point where team-deficiency and falls in values are also markedly apparent. This might reflect a continuation of the march of foreign troops between the battle of Hastings and the surrender of London. The second is between the Cotswolds and the Bristol Avon; the third in the south-east. Here, as elsewhere, the cause might be the proximity or extension of the royal Forests. Districts bordering on the Forests display many total absences of teams.

A frequent absence of villagers' teams is a feature. We cannot be sure that when we are told, following the extent of the demesne land, that so many are 'there', and none is specifically allotted to the villagers, that all were in fact demesne teams. But on 71 out of 447 holdings there were only demesne teams, and the inclusion of teams implied to be demesne ones would bring the figure up to 132, or 30 per cent. No teams are mentioned in 85 entries, in few of which villeins appear, and in 35 of these no peasantry or slaves appear either.

Wiltshire is a county in which the less prosperous element in the population was numerous. Just over half the recorded peasant population were bordars, cottars, coscets (treated as a single class in the Glastonbury Summary, *527b*), or coliberts. Slaves furnished a fairly high proportion of the whole, 15·9 per cent, and made up as much as one-quarter of the personnel of the royal manors. The impression gained from the text as a whole is of a general down-grading, both of landholders and peasantry.

The instances in which a single category of the peasantry have teams are far too few to allow deduction, and some information may be misleading; e.g. the presence of only bordars on the Ramsbury tenancies (66ai) seems improbable. Only 23 entries give us such information, and work out at 2·6 oxen per villein, 1·4 for bordars, 1·0 for coscets, and 0·9 for cottars. Villeins held (rented?) $2\frac{7}{8}$ hides at Swallowcliffe (73bi), worth 30*s*., and four cottars half a hide at Durrington (69ai), but these entries are unlikely to be representative ones. *Terra villanorum* had sometimes become a tenancy, as at Bromham (65a2) and on some estates of Malmesbury Abbey (67ai,2), but there is no suggestion that villeins had regularly lost land, and some changes may have been because villeins who might have tilled it were no longer there.

The list of king's thegns is a long one, amounting to one hundred entries. Many of the holdings of the surviving Englishmen or their heirs were indeed only small ones, though nearly a score were of five hides or more, and nearly 40 per cent appear in the geld accounts as including exempt fiscal demesne. In over fifty entries Englishmen, named and anonymous, appear as sub-tenants, and for all we know others were still holding their former land from a newcomer. So substantial a native element in 1086, in a shire in which ecclesiastical influence was so strong, argues that here the settlement had proceeded without general opposition. But the number of English tenants was surely small in relation to the number of thegns of 1066.

Dorset

Though we have here the advantage, but for twelve fiefs only, of the text of the Exeter Domesday, the material as a whole does not enable us to form judgments as definite as we should like them to be. We are not given individual accounts of a number of the larger royal manors; instead, the details are combined for the constituents of each of the groups which had to provide the whole or a half of a *firma unius noctis*. As many as 209 entries give us values for 1086 only, and these represent almost one-third of the total sum of the manorial values provided. Earlier values, save for three entries, are entirely absent from the Abbotsbury and Milton Abbey fiefs and that of the bishop of Salisbury. A dozen times we are not told the number of the ploughlands. There are a few additional entries where these are not mentioned at all, but since no teams are recorded either, these may not be omissions. The quantity of holdings without teams, even though many of these were very small, is striking. There are 105 of them, and on 48 no inhabitants other than the tenant or owner appear. Since on these the numbers of both villeins and slaves are few, we have to visualise a high proportion of isolated and unrewarding small properties.[1]

The number of entries which give us a valuation for a date other than 1086 is 296, so that for about 40 per cent of all the entries we cannot compare changes. Nor can we say that the date of the earlier valuation is necessarily that of 1066. Indeed, in a number of entries we are told that it is not. For many royal manors it is said to be when it was taken over at a farm-rent, and this, in view of King William's lust for gold, may well have been higher than the value or rent of King Edward's day, especially as many manors were paying in 1086 a sum identical with that of the occasion of their being accepted by the farmers. But the farm-rents of some did change. Cranborne (29) had been worth £24 when Queen Matilda was alive; since November, 1083, it had been compelled to render £30. The previous entry, for Little Frome, displays an advance from £12 to £18,

[1] Villeins occur in only sixteen of these, and slaves in only one more.

THE SOUTH-WEST: DORSET

but does not say when this took place. Of three manors which had been administered by the former sheriff, Hugh fitzGrip, one was producing a little more and two rather less.[1]

The expressions used, *reddebat, valuit, valebat, quando recepit*, tell us little or nothing. We do not know when Ida, countess of Boulogne, may have obtained her manors (*33*), or when William *de Monasterio* became Cerne Abbey's tenant at Little Puddle (*36*). Worth Matravers (*51b*) had been a royal manor; it does not appear under *Terra Regis*, but in Roger Arundel's *breve*. We cannot be sure that £6 7s. 6d., which suggests a farm-rent, had been the value before he received it. The Exeter Domesday for the county almost always uses *quando recepit*, but when the Exchequer clerk made his version, he usually altered this to *valuit*. The implication must be that though the value may have been unchanged since 1066, the Dorset authorities were thinking in terms of the date at which a manor changed hands. The Exeter clerk gave the value of Littlebredy as when the former abbot of Cerne was alive.

Nor can we be sure that *valere* and *reddere* should be interpreted differently. It is quite common for *reddit* to be used of the 1086 sum, *valebat* of the earlier one. Several times a clerk struck through *valet* and substituted *reddit*, e.g. in the Cerne Abbey *breve* (*36–38b*), and for the royal manor of Child Okeford (*25*). He would hardly have done this unless it seemed of importance to someone that it should be made clear that it was a rent which was in question.

Once only are we given a triple valuation. Chaldon Herring (*59b*) had been worth £10 when sheriff Hugh received it. During his lifetime it had rendered £1 more, but now a tenant was holding it of his widow it was producing £2 less.

The renting of properties occurs in the Dorset text with unusual frequency. It is hardly to be supposed that the use of *reddit* was applicable only to royal manors, those of Cerne Abbey, and to Broadway (*55*), an anonymous holding, probably Stokeford (*56b*), and a Blandford St Mary holding (79bi). There are a quantity of entries where the sums suggest the rent being charged, e.g. the £3 15s. 8d. at Crichel (83ai), or the 9s. 2d. of Rushton on the same folio. Some of the statements are indeed quite definite ones. Four villeins had three hides at Wraxall (*51*), and paid £3 *de gablo* for them. At Allington (80bi) nine *censores* were paying 11s.; at Askerswell two paid 15s. (78bi); on Exeter fol. 42 they are *gablatores*. Fishermen and saltmakers were renting the sources of their livelihood; rents in kind, of honey, appear; and even two bordars were paying 20d.,

[1] Tarrant Gunville, Shitterton (*Scetra, 31b*), Tarrant Rushton (*32*). Exeter Domesday folio references are italicised.

presumably for their land.[1] Six men held Ringstead (84bi) *ad firmam*, and paid 25s. for their holding; two at Galton (85ai) 12s. 4d. Some, if not all, of the land attached to churches was rented (? by the incumbents). The three holdings of the abbey of St Wandrille (*28*) produced £7, three of Bollo the priest on the same folio 57s. 6d.

But it is with the royal manors which were not liable for the *firma unius noctis* that we hear most of the renting, or rather of the farming, of manors. We are told the names of four of the farmers: Fulcred, Aiulf the sheriff, Roger (probably Roger Arundel), and Schelin, though only twice is a manor said to be *ad firmam*.[2] Only the Isle of Portland (*26*) had been King Edward's; the rest had belonged to the Godwine family, to Ælfric the former sheriff, to Beorhtric Ælfgarson, the queen's predecessor, and to a miscellany of thegns. Unfortunately we are very rarely told of any change in the amount paid for the privilege of farming the manors, and never what they had been worth in 1066.

Whatever the dates implied by *quando recepit*, there had since then been a slight appreciation, but of only about $3\frac{1}{2}$ per cent, from £1,699 17s. 6d. to £1,761 18s. 10d. There are, it is true, some entries which show values much higher in 1086 than earlier. A small estate at Hethfelton (83ai) is said to have gone up from 5s. to £2, but the feeling cannot be avoided that 40s. should be 40d. Another at Moulham (85ai) increased from five to thirty shillings, and one at Crawford Bridge (84a2) from 2s. 6d. to £2, though £2 could well be an error, and really 2s. The manorial appurtenances listed do not suggest that such huge increases were reasonable. But we should expect the officials of some landowners to extract more from their charges. All but one of the Shaftesbury Abbey manors increased in value, and in all they appreciated by about one-third. Edward the sheriff of Wiltshire, whom we have seen improving the value of his Wiltshire estates, was obtaining £70 from his two manors which earlier had been worth £50. Some manors of Aiulf, the local sheriff, were worth considerably more than they had been: Wootton Fitzpaine (83ai) had doubled its former value of £10. Another baron whose property was now worth more was William of Eu.

But against these appreciations there were some gigantic declines in value. Gussage, mistakenly entered in the Wiltshire Domesday (69ai), fell from £40 to £10. It had been the property of Aubrey de Coucy, and had become royal when he forfeited his fief. Sturminster Marshall (80a2), which had been Archbishop Stigand's, went down from £66 to £55, Silton (82ai) from £11 to £6, Iwerne Courtenay (81a2) from £15 to £10.

[1] Lyme Regis (75b2), Bridge Lane (83ai, 84bi); Ower (*44b*); Holworth (*44b*), Rushworth (82a2); Lewell (84b2).   [2] Child Okeford (*25*), Loders (*26b*).

We cannot tell what local difficulties caused such figures, but we do know that the Cerne Abbey manors of Bloxworth and Affpuddle (*36b*) rendered only £15 in place of £19 10*s*. because they had been plundered (*depredati*) by Hugh fitzGrip. Possibly the avaricious Stigand had been demanding more than was reasonable.

With so few entries giving comparable values at our disposal, it would be unwise to deduce where and in what manner the county was principally affected in the early years of the Conquest. The most one can say is that there is a string of diminished values along the line Salisbury—Dorchester. This could be connected with the rebellion of 1069, when the bishop of Coutances found it necessary to employ troops from London, Winchester, and Salisbury to suppress it. The rising is said to have been directed against Robert of Mortain's new castle of Montacute west of Sherborne; probably fortifications had been raised in the Dorset boroughs also, where DB tells us of the destruction of large numbers of houses. If such information as we have *is* connected with the effects of this revolt, it suggests further troop movements from Dorchester in the direction of Montacute, in the neighbourhood of which some rebel forces would presumably concentrate. Of this we shall find suggestion when Somerset is considered. The accounts of the boroughs unfortunately tell us nothing of the royal receipts therefrom, only their assessments and the liability of the moneyers.

Of waste land we hear very little. A Hurpston holding (*60b*) was 'altogether waste', yet it had a potential value of 12*s*. 6*d*., and one at Nyland (79a2) was also waste. The latter might have been included in Gillingham Forest, but the only reference to Forest is that which complains that the king had the two best hides of the capital manor of Horton Abbey 'in his Forest of Wimborne' (78bi). But, though DB does not say so, some diminutions of value in appropriate places could have been caused by land being taken into royal Forest. The text and the geld accounts contain many references to huntsmen, and probably there was far more Forest land than that mentioned.

The great majority of the entries furnish the number of ploughlands, but those which do not mention teams, whether correctly or not, is high. It seems probable that these holdings, mostly very small ones, were teamless. It could be said that 28 show more teams than there were ploughlands, 178 parity, and 184 deficiency, but from these last we ought perhaps to deduct those in which teams are not mentioned. If we do, we find an overall deficiency of about $14\frac{1}{2}$ per cent; if we do not, of about $19\frac{1}{4}$ per cent. The deficiencies are greatest in the neighbourhood of what may have been Forest land, e.g. near Gillingham, the later Holt and Bere Forests, and in the thinly-populated and unrewarding south-east. But quite a number of large deficiencies are to be found on royal manors. On the first two groups which furnished a night's farm (*27*) there is one of 38 per cent; Loders (*26b*) had only half as many teams as ploughlands. Surpluses are only rarely considerable ones; 21 teams for 16 ploughlands at Abbotsbury (*39*), 22 for 16 at Stockland (*44b*).[1]

Ten entries mention carucates of land which would seem all to be additional to the ploughlands mentioned. On some of these the existence of teams is recorded, and for all we know there may thus have been in all more teams than can be included in the count.

In only 17 entries can we isolate the teams of various categories of peasants, which is far too few for reasonable deduction. However, they produce estimates of 3·1 oxen for each villein and 1·3 for each bordar. At Winterborne Kingston (79bi) seven coscets had half a team.

The number of holdings of the king's thegns is fairly large, 66. Naturally, few are of much magnitude, though half of them were worth £1 or more. In addition there are 35 sub-tenancies held by Englishmen, none of which was a large one. But despite the number of survivors, there would seem to have been far fewer thegns than there had been in 1066. Some may have been reduced to villein status, though this is not necessarily implied where there happen to be the same number of villeins as of pre-Conquest thegns who are unmentioned for 1086.[2] Certainly the two bordars on an anonymous holding (84b2) seem to have lost their status; in 1066 they had held freely. The fact that bordars, cottars, and coscets well outnumber villeins suggests that the Dorset peasantry might not have been of average affluence. They, like the small thegns, may well have suffered in consequence of the revolt.

Somerset

Most of this county should not, so far as we know, have been seriously affected by clashes between newcomer and native. The two raids of the sons of Harold Godwineson, in 1068 and 1069, cannot have had much effect beyond local and temporary destruction; the only major irruption would seem to have been the revolt of the men of the county in company with those of Dorset in the latter year.[3] We might expect, then, a general increase in manorial values, partly because after 1069 there seems to have been peace in the district, partly on account of probable increases in rents

[1] The possibility of an artificial basis for the Dorset ploughlands is being investigated by Dr C. E. Hart.

[2] e.g. at Poorton and Higher Kingcombe (80bi).

[3] G. H. Fowler: *Bedfordshire in 1066*, p. 80, states that 'Somerset was punished', but gives no evidence for his statement.

and services following the installation of new lords and the combination of minor estates into manors more economically administered and exploited.

Preliminary inspection of the figures might suggest that on the whole the value of holdings had improved appreciably, but totals may in fact be somewhat deceptive. It is fortunate that in over 80 per cent of the entries a figure is given both for 1086 and, as a rule, for the date when the holder acquired it. In all we have

	instances	%
Increase	286	30½
No change	337	36
Decrease	131	14
1086 value only	182	19½

and from this might expect to find a substantial total increase. But the figures (to the nearest £) are £2,696 in 1086, £2,386 earlier, a rise of only 11½ per cent. But, as will be considered later, the increased liabilities of the royal manors might enlarge this difference. Also, the 13 out of 20 demesne manors of Glastonbury Abbey for which we are given comparative figures had increased in value from £94 to £205.[1]

As in Dorset, the royal demesne manors had been grouped so that each group was liable for a *firma unius noctis*. The sums of money for which this had been commuted are given. Two groups each produced £106 0s. 10d., one £105 16s. 5½d., and two £100 10s. 9½d. each. All the sums are said to be *de xx denariis in ora*. Now whether these are the sums to be produced in counted coin or not we are not told. They seem too close to £100 to represent the additional payments demanded to compensate the king for receiving coins of imperfect substance. Most of these manors had had land added to or taken away from them, but the value of this can hardly represent the differences, especially as the components of the groups were liable for proper fractions of the varying totals. We are not told if they were farmed, but the sheriff, William de Mohun, paid £12 as the value of Wedmore, which the bishop of Wells had for long held as part of the royal manor of Cheddar.

The fifteen comital manors formerly held by Earl Godwine's family probably all paid multiples of 23s., though some of the figures as they stand do not suggest this unit, and of white silver, that is, blanched and assayed coin.[2] All were farmed by the sheriff. Possibly 3s. in the £ was in

[1] The Summary (*173, 528*) says that the demesne is valued at £288 4s. (DB figures £293 4s.), but seems to include land not treated as demesne in DB. Glastonbury's Somerset estates are said to have improved in value under Abbot Thurstan by £128. One possible factor is suggested later (p. 288).

[2] Not mentioned for Langford Budville (*104b*), but it is unlikely this was exempt.

this group reckoned to be adequate compensation for sub-standard coin, and instead of £235 the actual render was over £300. Queen Edith's former manors were all producing more than they had done formerly, assuming that Martock, for which no earlier value is given, had also had its liability increased. The other three, paying *ad numerum*, were responsible for almost exactly 50 per cent more than they had been in the former queen's lifetime. But the sums given might be deceptive.

Of these Keynsham (*111b*) is said to have been worth £80 when Walter *hosatus* received it *ad firmam*, but £108 in 1086. It may be that the five tenancies, which included villages some distance from Keynsham, are included in the latter figure but not in the former. For three of these we are told of increases in value amounting to £2 on £11, while in all they were worth £14 5s. Keynsham itself, then, may have appreciated only from £80 to £93 15s. Finally, a few properties of the late Wulfweard 'White' are listed, but the values of these had not increased.

The other royal interest in the county was in the boroughs. From Bath and the contributory manors the king was obtaining £60 *ad numerum* and a mark of gold, £5 from the mint, nearly £8 in house dues, and £11 from the 'third penny'. The third penny of six lesser boroughs brought in £8 15s.

Taunton (*173b*) may be an instance of deceptive information similar to that of Keynsham. It had rendered £50, but in 1086 it was rendering a little over £104. We are told of sub-tenancies valued in 1086 at £43 18s., and if these were not included in the pre-Inquest figure, the increase would be only from £50 to just over £60. Alternatively, such a manor may well have been enlarged, as so many Somerset manors had been, since the Conquest, by incorporating within it holdings which in 1066, and perhaps later, had been independent of it, though all were the bishop of Winchester's. Many a village known to have been a component of Taunton at a later date goes unmentioned in DB.

Some of the sums given for the Glastonbury manors, too, may reflect a similar procedure. Brent (*170b*) rose from £15 to £50, Walton (*163b*) from £5 to £15, Butleigh (*165b*) from £3 to £8. Such increases seem too large to be credible if each refers to a single estate. Some of the Glastonbury increases could well be due to the draining of the marshland and its partial conversion into arable or pasture. It is noticeable that several of the largest appreciations in value are within the area.[1] Both Exeter Domesday and *Terrae Occupatae* frequently record major alterations in the structure of manors. $4\frac{1}{2}$ hides had been added to Cameley (*150b, 522b*).

[1] The point is discussed in W. G. Hoskins: *Fieldwork in Local History* (London, 1967), pp. 166–7.

These had been worth £3, and in 1086 were valued at £4 10s., but if we had not been told of the extension of the manor we could easily have thought that the vill of Cameley had increased in value from £4 to £10, whereas in fact the figures are £7 and £10, as on fol. 89ai.

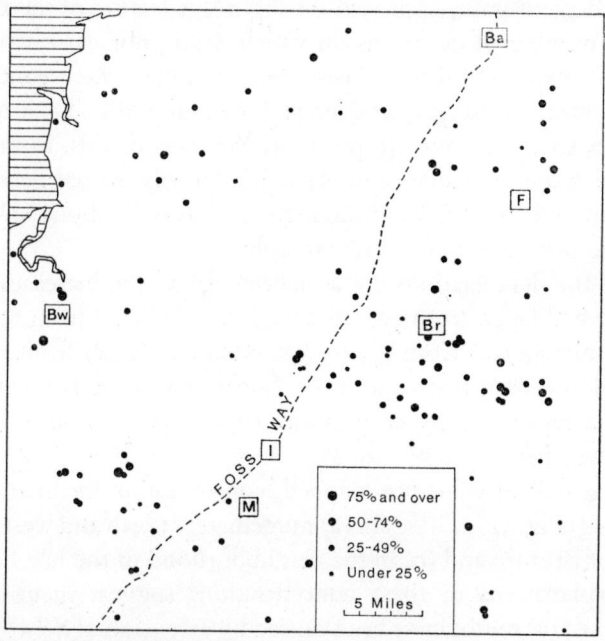

Fig. 32 Section of Domesday Somerset
Holdings with fall in value *olim–modo*
Ba—Bath Br—Bruton Bw—Bridgwater F—Frome
I—Ilchester M—Montacute

Manors other than the above, however, also show vast increases in values. Combe Hay (*492b*) appreciated by 300 per cent from £1, Charlcombe (*186*) from £2 10s. to £6, a holding at Long Ashton (*143b*) by 400 per cent, one at Bratton (*360*) from 5s. to 30s., another at Midgell (*151b*) from 4s. to £1, Compton Durville (*265b*) from 10s. to £3. On the whole, the marked increases do not seem to depend upon the holder, or on being demesne manors, or from their situation in a prosperous area. The Bath Abbey demesne manors did indeed appreciate by nearly 20 per cent and William of Mohun's by nearly 25 per cent; Osbern Gifford's three demesne manors increased in value from £6 to £8. The figures for sub-tenants, however, also show increases. The numerous holdings from the bishop of Coutances by Azelin appreciated by 13 per cent and those held of him by William de Monceaux by 15 per cent. The lands of Robert of Mortain's tenants, too, mostly show increases; Alfred's by as much as 50 per cent. An exception here is Mauger of Cartrai, whose lands declined in value from £40 10s. to £28, and the geld accounts show that he had been owing geld; perhaps there was a connection between these facts. The value of the manor held of William of Mohun by Durand had doubled in value, and Roger's gains approach this figure. A feature of the Exeter text is the high number of occasions on which *reddit*, not *valet*, is used.

We might expect land to increase most in value where conditions for agriculture were most favourable, and certainly the Taunton district increased its worth by over 30 per cent. Yet west of this, in the lands in and around Exmoor, values appreciated by nearly 20 per cent, whereas around Bath and south thereof the increase was only about $11\frac{1}{2}$ per cent, which is the possible county average figure.

Some of the depreciations are as spectacular as the increases. Standerwick (*434*) had fallen from 50s. to 20s., Porlock (*315*) from 80s. to 25s., Timberscombe (*442b*) from £5 to £2, Honibere (*478*) from 20s. to 5s., North Bradon (*268b*) from £4 to 10s. Some may possibly be attributable to local disaster caused by crop failure or animal murrain or prolonged inclement weather.

But if the falls in value are mapped, concentration in three districts is most marked (Fig. 32). These are (a) immediately north and west of Frome, (b) south of Bruton, and (c) in the neighbourhood of the Isle River. Two possible explanations of these concentrations suggest themselves. The eastern part of (a) might have been caused by extension of Selwood Forest, though such a cause is not recorded in DB; there are also some falls in (b) close to the south of Selwood and to Gillingham Forest. The rising in 1069 against Montacute castle may have been the origin of (b), and perhaps of (c) also. Forces moving from the direction of Malmesbury and Salisbury, and perhaps from Taunton, or the rebels themselves, may have damaged local economy. A further weak line of falls north of Mendip towards Frome might reflect movement from a district largely under the control of the bishop of Coutances to join troops in the Frome neighbourhood. Alternatively, the line of some falls in value trends in the direction of Honiton and so to Exeter, and might be connected with one of the post-Conquest south-western campaigns.

Manors which had earlier been waste, with few exceptions, had apparently been colonised.[1] Almsworthy in Exmoor (*430*) was 'altogether waste' when received, but at the Inquest there were four teams on its six ploughlands, a recorded population of 17, and it was worth 25s. On the

[1] Treborough (*463b*), worth only 7s., 'for it is waste', had not improved in value, and Stone (*431b*) was waste both when received and in 1086.

other hand, one cannot help being somewhat suspicious of this entry. Almsworthy is well isolated from other Domesday place-names, and it may be that lonely farms which had gone out of occupation had been resettled, and that not the whole area known to DB as 'Almsworthy' had been waste. Recovery elsewhere from waste is certainly less spectacular. Downscombe (*430*) was in 1086 worth only 2*s*., Pitney Wearne (*479b*) 15*s*., the addition to Capland (*491b*) 6*s*. At Downscombe there was only one bordar and four oxen, and the same, plus a slave, at Pitney Wearne.

The deficiency of teams against ploughlands is so considerable (almost 20 per cent) that there is small point in considering individual inadequacies in detail. Moreover, something like 40 per cent of the ploughland figures are decimal quantities of ten or more, and some of these are obviously artificial. Three manors are indeed said to possess one hundred ploughlands each.[1] Another three have sixty, six fifty, and seven forty.

When we read that Winsford (*104b*) had land for 60 teams, but only 15 teams available, this may well mean that the manor included land which would occupy 60 teams, but that only a portion of this was indeed being cultivated. Much of the land of such manors may have been only periodically ploughed and sown, and after harvesting was left fallow for a year or more to recover from crop-bearing. The deficiency, as we might expect, is at its maximum in the western Hundreds (36½ per cent) and in the central marshland area which was almost entirely Glastonbury's (30 per cent). Yet an excess of teams over ploughlands is no rarity; it is to be found on 80 holdings. But here as elsewhere such a relationship seems to have suggested an anomaly to the Exchequer clerk, for on seven occasions he wrote *Terra est* n *carucis. Tamen sunt ibi* n+ *carucae*. Some of the figures for ploughlands may have been arrived at by giving the total of teams in the manor. The main account of Wraxall (*144b*) gives 26 of each, while Portbury (*143b*), Drayton Fivehead (*188b*) and Barrow Gurney (*143*) had 18, 15, and 14 respectively.

The apparent deficiency is probably greater than it should be. For nearly 70 holdings, with over 100 ploughlands between them, no teams at all are recorded. There would naturally be none at Stone (*431b*), which was waste, or at the Exford holding (*359b*) which 'lay in pasture', but we cannot help having doubts about entries such as those for Lydeard and Leigh (*175*) or East Bower (*371b*). The first two had a recorded population of 16, and the second of 17, and a total absence of teams seems unlikely. But though Porlock (*315*) had a recorded population of 15, there may well in 1086 have been no teams for its dozen ploughlands, since its value had

---

[1] The triple manor of Williton, Cannington, and Carhampton (*89*), Keynsham (*113b*), and Taunton (*174*).

for an unstated reason (perhaps a piratical raid) dropped from 80s. to 25s. Sutton Bingham (*444*), too, had fallen in value from 100s. to 30s., and its six bordars and four cottars may have had no teams. Again, a suspicion that the clerks omitted some teams is inevitable. There are plenty of instances such as those of Woodspring (*369b*), where, though $3\frac{3}{4}$ of the $6\frac{1}{4}$ hides were in manorial demesne, no demesne teams are mentioned, while the peasantry had six teams and there were 12 ploughlands, or Aldwick (*452b*), where for five ploughlands there was a demesne team, but the four villeins and a bordar are not credited with any oxen. In only about a dozen entries are the ploughlands omitted.

It is, however, not always easy to decide how many ploughlands should be reckoned for some of the complex manors. Are we intended to include the *carucatae nunquam geldantes*? I think we are, for we are told that at Shapwick (*161b*) and Pilton (*165b*) the villeins' teams are 'on the land which never gelded', and the wording of the Taunton entry (*173b*) suggests similar treatment. At Henstridge (*107*) there were 21 teams, 16 ploughlands, and 'land for eight teams which never gelded'; unless there was a considerable superfluity of teams, we must reckon 24 ploughlands in all for the 21 teams. Often we are given a single figure for ploughlands, but the number of demesne teams, those of the villeins, and those of the sub-tenants are given as separate figures. In most entries the ploughlands probably cover those exploited by the sub-tenants; e.g. Brent (*170b*) had 30 ploughlands; there were eight demesne teams, and 16 villeins' teams. On the four sub-tenancies there were four demesne and three villeins' teams. It seems more likely that there was one team more than there were ploughlands, for the 30 may be an arbitrary round figure, than that additional ploughlands should have been recorded for the sub-tenancies. But there are also difficult entries such as that for Winscombe (*161*): 30 ploughlands, two demesne teams, nine villeins' teams, and five teams on the sub-tenancies. Since the deficiency is so considerable, it is unlikely that the five ploughlands independently recorded for the sub-tenancies should be added to the 30. Moreover, the bishop of Coutances had one hide of this manor, which is separately described as his manor of Winterhead (*140*), where there were two ploughlands and two teams. Thirty ploughlands and 16 teams seem figures more probable than 37 ploughlands and 18 teams. Equally Keynsham's 100 ploughlands probably cover the 17 recorded for the detached sub-tenancies at Belluton, Stanton Drew, Burnett, and elsewhere. If so, we have 90 teams, not 73.[1]

If cottars and coscets are equated with bordars, as in the Glastonbury

[1] Belluton is also the subject of a separate entry, fol. *282b*.

and other Summaries, the number of these three classes is almost equal to that of the villeins. There may, especially in the west, have been many a settlement which bore small resemblance to the true village, where, on the fringe of the uplands and woodland, peasants of humble status and scant wealth cultivated a little land on isolated holdings but were more concerned with pastoral activities than with agriculture, and most of the land was in demesne. Some 45 per cent of the Exmoor Hundred of Carhampton was in fact manorial demesne. Such peasants may well have been classed for the most part as bordars rather than villeins.

But the Somerset bordar was not necessarily poverty-stricken. One at Weacombe (*428b*) could pay 7*s*. 6*d*. for the virgate he held; at Fivehead Langford (*431b*) four held a virgate, and at Isle Abbots (*188b*) three held 15 acres. The acres mentioned may be geld-acres, and in four instances the bordars' holdings averaged 5 acres.[1] There are fifteen entries in which, save for the occasional slave, bordars represent the entire recorded population. These 75 bordars had in all 14 teams, giving them on an average $1\frac{1}{2}$ oxen each. The non-demesne land averages only a ferling and a half, or $11\frac{1}{4}$ geld-acres, but the inhabitants may, of course, have held more arable acres. At Earnshill (*431b*) three had two ferlings, and at Compton Martin (*453b*) two a single ferling.

On thirty-two occasions it is clear that the teams are those of villeins only. These, numbering 49, were held by 109 villeins, giving them an average of over $3\frac{1}{2}$ oxen apiece. A villein at Eleigh (*426b*) seems to have possessed an entire team; so did one at Beechenstoke (*452b*), and on ten holdings the villeins average half a team apiece or more. Two Ashwick villeins could pay 42*d*. a year for a half-hide holding, though they are not said to have any oxen (*186b*); one of the seven at Alford (*277b*) rendered eight blooms of iron, though on what account is not stated. Possibly, when we are told that the land 'rendered' so much, it is villeins who were renting it, but it happens that on the smaller of these holdings no peasantry are mentioned. Sometimes we are given the extent of villein holdings: at East Pennard (*166b*) four had a hide, while at Avill (*359*) one held 12 geld-acres and at Swang (*425b*) one had 10 acres. We find villeins at Aller in Sampford Brett (*286b*) and at Combe Sydenham (*362b*) with a ferling apiece, though the seven at Bratton Seymour (*352*) and North Barrow (*353*) averaged a virgate each or almost as much, and nine at Milton Clevedon (*450*) seem to have had five hides between them.

Equally we find a number of passages where the peasantry had no land; e.g. at Nether Stowey (*373b*), once a manor of Earl Harold's, where there were four villeins, three bordars, and a slave, but all the land was in

[1] Drayton Fivehead (*188b bis*), *Terra Alwini* (*424*), Pillock (*425*).

demesne, or at Crandon (*465b*), where there were no villeins, merely four bordars and a slave, and no oxen, and which was worth only 5s.

We might expect to find slaves most numerous either where demesnes were extensive or a pastoral economy employed slaves as herdsmen and shepherds. But there do not seem to be obvious geographical fluctuations. The percentage of slaves to the appropriate recorded population is 16½ per cent; the figures in the triple eastern Hundred of Frome are, for Wellow 26½ per cent, Kilmersdon 22½ per cent, Frome 9½ per cent. In the extreme western Hundreds which include Exmoor 14 per cent of the population was servile. The Bath Abbey demesnes had 28 per cent as slaves, but those of Glastonbury only 13¾ per cent. On the lands of the Glastonbury *milites* the proportion was higher, 17½ per cent. The *coliberti*, presumably fairly recently enfranchised slaves, amount to 9 per cent of the total slaves and coliberts recorded.[1] It looks, then, as if slavery was declining, but that the proportion of the slave element depended largely on the economic policy of the landlord and his administrators.

The number of Englishmen holding lands in 1086 is quite considerable. King's thegns and sergeants were holding over 80 hides valued at almost £70, and few of their manors were really small ones. Sub-tenants held well over a further hundred hides, valued at almost £100, which included some of the Glastonbury and Wells thegnlands. Some of their properties, too, were substantial holdings. Ansford (*352b*) and Norton Malreward (*140b*) were 5-hide manors; Withycombe (*139*) was valued at £6 and Blackford (*163b*) at £5.

These figures, too, may well not give all the facts. Sæwine, reeve to Arnulf of Hesdin, does not appear in DB, but the Bath Hundred geld account (*76*) shows him as holding a virgate. There may have been many sub-tenancies held by Englishmen not mentioned in DB. Also, a man with a foreign name may still have been English, and, as in other counties, some of those styled *milites* may have been natives. If neighbouring shires are a guide, Selwood Forest may have necessitated the employment of men who had long known its characteristics, and so may the haunts of the Exmoor deer. Roger of Courseulles had a number of English tenants in this area.

Devonshire

So large a county, with such great variation in the character of the terrain and the soils, made up of a mixture of manors which covered wide areas,

[1] Slaves on royal manors were only about 10 per cent of the recorded population, in contrast to those of Wiltshire, but the figures would be 18 per cent if the coliberts were added.

THE SOUTH-WEST: DEVONSHIRE

though often less substantial than those of its more easterly neighbours, small villages, and isolated hamlets and farmsteads, is not easy to treat as an unity. While the mass of Dartmoor, the Exmoor region, and much of the west, supported only a scanty population, there were also areas around Exeter, east of Totnes, and in the lower basin of the Torridge and the Taw, which were as prosperous as most of Dorset or Wiltshire.

We have comparative values for about four-fifths of the entries. Of these about 16 per cent show a fall in value, and 47 per cent a rise. On balance the improvement in values is about 15 per cent, but it is most unevenly distributed, and if royal manors are excluded, the figure becomes 19 per cent. On the whole the southern and eastern Hundreds, as we might expect, display the greatest increases, while many areas in the west declined. It is, however, noticeable that if the recorded population and teams to the square mile yield high figures, the value of the manors is, as we should expect, also high. But ploughlands with an average value of 5s. 3d. do not argue a very high standard of prosperity, but we shall see that possibly the average ploughland tilled in any one year might give a figure considerably larger than this. Though such a calculation would make a ploughland in North Molton worth 9s., it would make those at West Putford (*399*) worth only 1s. 10½d. But the value of land in a county such as Devon would vary enormously. Appreciation in the Taw and Torridge lowlands is far less than we might have expected it to be. But again we do not know just what period the difference covers, for the phrase normally used by the *Liber Exoniensis* is *quando recepit*, which the Exchequer text reproduces as *olim* or *valuit*, though often it gives no information for dates prior to 1086. The solitary value given for 1066 is that of Werrington (*98*), probably because of late years it had not been lawfully possessed by the abbot of Tavistock.

Spectacular falls in value are not numerous, though Yarnscombe (*407*) went down from £5 to £1, and Tamarland (*411b*) from £2 to 10s. There are, however, some incredible increases, of 300–650 per cent; indeed, well over 200 manors had doubled or even further increased their values. Rockbeare's value (*216*) rose from 1s. to 7s. 6d., Whipton's (*404b*) from £1 to £6.[1] The bishop of Exeter's manor of Paignton (*119*) went up from £13 to £50. Are we here reading of a manor which had remained identical in composition? It may well have changed in extent. For Gappah (*341b*) would seem to have improved its value from 5s. to 30s., but *Terrae Occupatae* (*502b*) shows that the former manor had increased only from 5s. to 6s. The remaining 24s. was the value of the land of four thegns which

---

[1] In entries such as that for Rockbeare, one cannot help wondering if 12 pence was not a mistake for 12 shillings, and that the manor had fallen in value.

had been added to the manor. Additions to manors are very frequently noted, and in some instances the sums mentioned may be as deceptive as those of Gappah.

The figures give us no clue to diminution of resources which might be the result of the revolt which culminated in the siege of Exeter in 1068 or the subsequent rebellion of the following year, or of the raids of Harold Godwineson's children. We are, however, told that nine manors in the extreme south had been devastated by Irishmen. Seven of these were in 1086 worth less than they had been.[1] It could be that similar piracy, including that of Harold's sons, had occurred elsewhere. There are clusters of falls in value between the lower course of the Avon and the Tamar, and near Barnstaple. A further concentration along the line Launceston—Lydford—Okehampton might be connected with the king's Cornish campaign and the foundation of castles in these places (Fig. 33).

Yet holdings said to be waste in 1086 number only eight, and two of these are given values, actual or potential. Five more had been waste, but all were inhabited in 1086. The instances occur in different parts of the county, and it looks as if Devonshire as a whole had not been seriously affected by post-Conquest troubles.

Some of the values given probably represent actual rents. There are eight instances of 40*d.* and two of 50*d.*, while the 21*s.* 7*d.* of the manors added to Bratton Fleming (*212b*) looks like the sum of rents. Possibly the *ora* of sixteenpence was the occasional basis: Newton (*468*), where there was no demesne, rendered 80*d.* and Shapleigh was worth 8*s.* The sum to which the holdings added to Bridestow (*289*) had increased from 30*s.*, £3 less 20*d.*, is one we shall be frequently meeting and considering in Cornwall.

The royal manors in the county were numerous. King Edward had owned about a score, and the children of Earl Godwine over thirty. Sixteen which King William had acquired by 1086 had been the property of Beorhtric Ælfgarson and others. Though there had been some losses of land, there had also been some additions to the manors of 1066. King Edward's manor of Bampton had been exchanged with Walter of Douai for Ermington and Blackawton, apparently to the royal profit.

The phraseology of the entries for these is irregular, but probably all were being farmed, and only those not King Edward's or the House of Godwine's were paying *ad numerum*.[2] In only a few entries are manors definitely said to be *ad firmam*, but on fol. *97b* what three of the farmers were paying is stated, Reginald (de Vautort) was paying £24 for Ordulf's

[1] See *Dom. Geog.*, v, p. 274.
[2] Totnes, which had been royal but was now a borough in Juhel's hands, had paid £3 'weighed and burnt', but in 1086 £8 'by number'.

THE SOUTH-WEST: DEVONSHIRE

former land; Broad Clyst (*95*), the manor concerned, was worth that sum in 1086. Jocelin, brother of the royal official Walter de Claville, paid £108 for Queen Edith's property; this is the sum her four manors were worth. He is mentioned as the farmer of the late Queen Matilda's manors, once Beorhtric's, but fol. *97b* does not say what he was paying for them. Their total value was over £170. The sheriff, Baldwin de Meules, the brother of Richard fitzGilbert, is most frequently mentioned. He is said to be paying £375 *de terris comitis*. This probably represents the estates of Earls Harold and Leofwine and of their mother Gytha, which had a value of £373. He also farmed or had the custody of King Edward's demesne, which was worth £224 10*s*.

The previous values of thirty royal manors is given. Only seven show dues increased since they had been 'received', or before Baldwin took them over; all, except Broad Clyst, were in Baldwin's hands. The extra payments are about 45 per cent of the previous values; Hartland's went up from £23 to £48. But the total increase is only a little over 10 per cent. Over thirty of the renders demanded are multiples of £3; possibly others also display this basis, e.g. Diptford, Farley, and West Alvington, £15 between them. In the great majority of Baldwin's manors payment is said to be 'by weight' or 'by weight and burning', while Queen Edith's manor of Wonford paid in 'pence of twenty to the ounce'; Axmouth had to find a silver mark as well as its £8 render. Some of the apparent increases may represent the difference between payment at face value and payment demanding twenty pence for each sixteen due. There is no indication whether this was an innovation or not.[1]

One royal manor shows a fall in value. But this, Werrington (*98*), though it had been Gytha's, had been unlawfully transferred to Tavistock Abbey, and some of its Cornish components had been acquired by Robert of Mortain. Sutton-on-Plym, King's Tamerton, and Maker (*86b, 87*) had been appendages of Walkhampton, and these had furnished a night's farm. But Maker (in Cornwall) had also been appropriated by Robert.

Still, the royal manors and burghal property were worth not far short of a thousand pounds, probably more, for some manors (e.g. Axminster, *84b*) should have received dues from other holdings, and the king had the third penny of some Hundred-dues, and pasturage dues (*95, 96b*). No other manors are specifically said to be farmed, but an unusually frequent use of *reddit*, 63 instances outside *Terra Regis*, suggests that many were. The values of the two manors of St Mary of Rouen are given in 'Rouen pence', worth only half the English coin.

[1] But what was possibly an addition to Teignbridge paid 10*s. ad numerum* besides £14 *ad pensum*.

The accounts of the royal boroughs are very meagre, and the towns were lightly assessed. Exeter (*88*) seems to have been farmed, and the farmers received £18 from it. Barnstaple produced only £2 for the king, and Lydford £3, both by weight (*87b*).

Over a score of rural properties are said to be rented by Englishmen, villeins, or bordars, at sums ranging from 10s. to 2s. 6d.; the higher amount (*in Colum*, *470*) was for a virgate. The number of entries in which only villeins or bordars occur is large. In 153 entries 684 villeins had $313\frac{1}{8}$ teams, or over $3\frac{1}{2}$ oxen apiece, while several had a whole team, e.g. at Stoodleigh (*129b*), Bradford (*367*), and Heavitree (*343b*). In 21 entries 96 bordars possessed $21\frac{5}{8}$ teams, or over $1\frac{3}{4}$ oxen apiece on average. Those at East Buckland (*131*) seem to have had half a team each. Many a Devonshire villein may have been a former small thegn unable to maintain his status, or a well-to-do farmer not of thegnly rank. The holding of some of the pre-Conquest thegns had been small. Six with manors afterwards added to Bridestow (*289*) held land worth only 30s., and fifteen at Bovey Tracey (*93*) had only seven teams between them. Many of the king's thegns of 1086 held land worth only 5s.; Twynyeo (*488b*) was worth only twenty pence. But the entries for the king's thegns number nearly sixty, and if, as the rearrangement of the Exchequer text suggests, the occurrence of a name reflects the individual, some must have been fairly influential persons. 'Colvin' might be the Colsweyn who farmed royal property; however, his eight manors were very small ones. A Godwine had eleven, including one worth £7 (Chittlehampton, *484*).

Many of the ploughland figures are probably artificial ones. Well over a hundred instances have a decimal quantity above five. Bishop's Tawton (*118*) is said to have land for 150 teams, North Molton (*94b*) for 100. Crediton (*117*) had 185 teams and 185 ploughlands, Paignton (*119*) 60 and Bishopsteignton (*117*) 55 of each. Here we must suspect that the number of the ploughlands was arrived at by adding up the numbers of the teams. Artificiality, or the recording of the potential ploughlands, not those actually tilled in a given year, is to be suspected in instances such as those of Hartland (*93b*), with 45 teams for 110 ploughlands; or King's Nympton (*98*) with 19 for 50. Though in a very few entries the teams outnumber the ploughlands, the deficiency is more than one-quarter the number of ploughlands recorded (26 per cent). Many a manor, especially a large manor, was probably unable to till all its potential arable, or acquire sufficient teams to do so, and in the small manors oxen would have to be used on more holdings than that of their owner. There are copious instances of these where less than a full team is recorded. Four villeins and the same number of bordars had only a single ox at Thorne (*122*), and even with the demesne team the three ploughlands, if all were simultaneously in use, could not have been tilled without outside help. In Lifton Hundred, Nigel, the man of Juhel of Totnes, had but $19\frac{3}{8}$ teams, while there was land for 45 in his holdings.

Cornwall

Despite the deficiencies and *lacunae* of the Cornish Domesdays, which give imperfect or no information whatever about a number of holdings of the abbey of St Petrock, and in which parallel passages furnish statistical inconsistencies, a very fair picture of post-Conquest Cornwall may thence be obtained.[1] In much of the county the Domesday place-names are so dispersed that there must have been numerous settlements and solitary farmhouses which are concealed under the name of the manor to which they belonged. Even the few surviving Cornish charters tell us of places unmentioned in DB, but which probably existed and were inhabited in 1086.[2]

Almost all pre-Inquest values are given for the moment when the owner in 1086 acquired it. Osbern became bishop of Exeter in 1072, Geoffrey abbot of Tavistock ten years later. Robert of Mortain may have succeeded Brian of Brittany in 1075, if Brian disappeared from England on the occasion of the revolt in which so many Bretons were implicated. If values refer to when the 1086 holder succeeded, manorial values fell heavily during the second decade of the Conquest, whereas we should have expected a decline to result from the events of 1067–8 and after. But the clerks may have implied by *quando recepit* William's earliest grants and confirmations in 1067–8.

The most prosperous parts of the shire were the extreme north, the eastern parishes bordering the Tamar valley, and the eastern half of the south coast. The districts largely occupied by moor and upland, around Bodmin Moor, Hensbarrow, and the St Breock Downs, for example, naturally show very low figures for teams and density of population.

Cornwall's consistent poverty is demonstrated first by its low assessment of approximately 400 hides and secondly by the enormous exemptions from geld, conferred possibly because of inability to endure the assessments. Only about one-third of the land paid geld, and the number of manors which had obtained no exemption is very small. At times we

[1] On fol. *101* Poundstock and St Gennys are said to have 12 ploughlands between them, but on fols. *238, 238b*, 16. There are also discrepancies about the values of the holdings which had formed the manor of Winnianton.
[2] See H. P. R. Finberg: *The Early Charters of Devon and Cornwall* (Leicester Univ. Press, 1954).

may suspect the existence of beneficial hidation, since St Petrock's 30 hides had never gelded, and over three-quarters of the bishop of Exeter's hides paid no geld.[1] But exemption seems on the whole to have depended on the local economic standard. Both the royal manors and those which became the Mortain demesne manors, among the wealthiest and best-stocked in the shire, had received reductions rather below the average, 46 per cent on those which Earl Harold possessed in 1066, 58 per cent on the Mortain demesne manors.

But while Cornwall not unexpectedly shows itself to be thinly populated and meagrely cultivated, manorial values suggest that by 1086 many manors were far more impoverished than they had been earlier. Four manors of the bishopric of Exeter had, however, improved in value from £28 to £58. Thirteen demesne manors of Robert of Mortain appreciated from £122 to £239 3s. 4d. Otherwise an appreciation in value is very rarely found, though just over fifty manors show no change in value. If the manors of the bishop and of the count referred to above are ignored, the decline in value is 44 per cent, from £392 18s. to £217 5s. 11d. But if these are included the fall is only some $2\frac{1}{4}$ per cent, from £540 16s. to £528 17s. 7d. The addition of holdings where no comparative value is given would bring the total up to £658 4s. 4d.

Some of the decreases in value are spectacular, and in the region of 90 per cent. Penhole (*261b*) fell in value from 10s. to fifteenpence, the lost 'Hagland' (*262*) from £1 to 2s. Around the Helford River Treworder (*100*) fell from £2 to 3s., Tregoose (*99b*) from £2 to 2s. 6d., Tucoyes (*225*) from £3 to 5s. The manor of the Canons of St Stephens by Launceston (*206b*) was worth only half what it had been, while the value of *Dunhevet* or Launceston (*264b*) had dropped from £20 to £4. This, though we are not told so, might be on account of the destruction of houses and the clearing of land to make room for the castle there. The other place with a castle (Trematon, *256*) fell in value from £10 to £8. It is suggestive that in apparently undisturbed north Cornwall values declined by only 29 per cent. Many of the depreciations in value are on the smaller manors, and those which earlier had been worth only £1 or less. On the whole, the higher the value, the less the proportionate fall.

The highest value recorded for a Cornish manor is only £35 18s. 4d. Seven are valued at as low a figure as 1s., and indeed only some 30 per cent of the manors have values of £1 and over. The great majority of the values are multiples or sub-multiples of 5s. Sometimes we are told that

---

[1] But while the landowner would profit, this would not necessarily improve the peasant economy, for St Petrock received the geld due from his manors (*72b*), the bishop that of Lanisley (*200b*), and St Michael that of Truthwall (*258b*).

the sum is the rent paid (e.g. Trebeigh, *262*), and occasional odd sums, e.g. the 3*s*. 4*d*. at Trewen (*240b*), suggest the actual rent paid.

When analysed, the figures do, however, suggest a realistic basis. As the value increases, so do the number of ploughlands, oxen, and inhabitants in a manor, the numbers of demesne livestock, and the number of *villani*.[1] In the 56 manors with a value of 4*s*. or less, only 15 are said to have any plough-oxen, and only thrice is there a full team between those of the lord and his villeins. There are villeins in only 14, and never more than two in any manor. Of the 48 manors valued at 5*s*., only two have more than one full team, and only 25 have *villani*, while three alone have

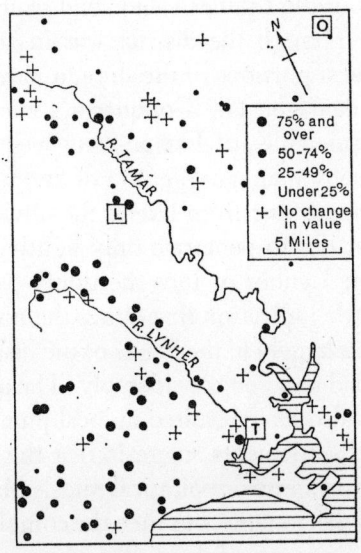

Fig. 33 East Cornwall and West Devon
        Holdings with fall in value *olim–modo*
        L—Launceston   O—Okehampton   T—Trematon

three or more, but there is reason to suspect that 5*s*. is not the correct value of these three. Of the first group, 31 possess no manorial demesne, and none more than 20 acres of woodland. The extent of pasture obviously has no real meaning, for there could be extensive pasture-land and yet few beasts to use it. Of all this there must be some explanation. One reason for general decline would be crop failure; another, heavy mortality among men and livestock, from disease or military disturbance or both. Or perhaps, finding in the aggregate an unsatisfactory economy of so many

[1] Demesne livestock may not be a good guide if valuations represent rents paid to the lord: still, stock went with the lease.

small, impoverished, and isolated holdings, landowners had been moving men and equipment into manors more favourably situated, even though a number of those concerned are obviously not sited in nucleated villages but are complexes of an unknown number of separate settlements.[1] Perhaps this is why we find 43 villeins at Caradon (*102*)—over 50 per cent of the recorded population—a figure approached by very few of the relevant manors, which average only 25 villeins. Why, too, do we find 50 slaves at Trematon (*256*), when the average number in this group of manors is but 15? Had they been brought from outlying settlements to labour on the new castle and its defences?

Fig. 33 furnishes one further suggestion. It displays a concentration of heavy falls in and about the Lynher valley, and from its southern portion to the river Fowey. Though the district was in 1086 among the best-populated and wealthiest portions of the shire, it may be that it had indeed suffered appreciable damage. The Conqueror's march into Cornwall in 1068, following the surrender of Exeter, may well have resulted in the impoverishment of many manors. We do not know William's route, but it is reasonable to suppose that from Exeter the obvious procedure would be to cross the Tamar but to penetrate only lightly, if at all, beyond the broader reaches of the Lynher or into the thinly-peopled areas of West Cornwall. There is little indication that either the north of the county, or the extreme south-east, largely in the hands of the bishop of Exeter and the abbot of Tavistock, had suffered considerably. The attack on Exeter from the west in 1069 may also have resulted in local punishment.

A map of recorded settlements suggests that the pattern was to some extent determined by danger from piratical raids.[2] Many Cornish parishes include no Domesday place-name, but then the complex composite manors must have occupied all or parts of these. But we can see several apparently unpopulated areas where manorial components, if in existence, must have been very small. Among these are the mouth of the Tamar, the country about Carrick Roads and the Fal estuary, Mounts Bay, St Ives Bay, and Padstow Bay. The information for the district south of the Helford River might reflect fairly recent trouble from this source. It includes the only two manors said to be waste, Skewes (*225b*) and Trembraze (*226*); twelve manors out of twenty-four have no teams and six no inhabitants recorded, though there may have been tenants and their families. The proportion of teams to ploughlands is only 27 per cent, and the total value declined from

---

[1] This is what, it has been suggested, happened in Yorkshire after the ravaging of 1069–70 (T. A. M. Bishop, 'The Norman Settlement of Yorkshire' in *Studies in Medieval History presented to Frederick Maurice Powicke*, pp. 1–14, Oxford, 1948).
[2] See Fig. 69 in *Dom. Geog.*, v, p. 469.

£25 3s. to £8 3s. 6d.[1] North of the river values had dropped by 85 per cent.

It is unfortunate that we are given only the 1086 values of the sixteen royal manors. Obviously they were being farmed; in all they produced a farm rent of £115, and a 60s. unit seems to enter into nine of the quantities, as in much of Devon. The geld accounts show that two of the custodians were Baldwin the Devonshire sheriff and Walter de Claville; possibly Aiulf (? the Dorset sheriff) farmed Carworgie (*112*).

Adopting and supplementing Dr Salzman's figures for the Mortain demesne manors (*VCH: Cornwall*, i, 8, p. 52), it may be that these were having to find almost twice as much as before. The '£30' of Stratton (*237*) and Rillaton (*264*) might really be '30 marks' or £20, just as Tybesta's £12 (*247*), in Dr Salzman's opinion, should be 12 marks or £8, and the former value of Helstone (*237*) also £8. Probably Fawton (*228*) should have a value not of £16 18s. 4d. but, as in four other manors, of £15 18s. 4d. Tywarnhale (*202b*) was held by Robert of St Petrock; its value of £13 18s. 4d. suggests that he had dealt with it as for his demesne manors, and that the previous value, like nine of these, had been £8. If they had been enlarged by the consolidation of many small properties, these increases might be intelligible. As it is, it seems sheer exploitation.

Nine of the Mortain manors and one owned by St Petrock are said to render sums ranging from £9 to £35, plus the odd sum of 18s. 4d. Maker (*87*), appropriated by Robert of Mortain from the Devonshire royal manor of Walkhampton, was valued at £6 less 30d. If *xxx* was an error, and should have been *xx*, 18s. 4d. recurs here. To this sum the Rillaton entry (*264*) may possibly furnish a clue. This manor rendered £15 and a mark of silver and 5s., which together make 18s. 4d.; it may be that this is the basis of the other figures which include this amount. Whether they represent a premium for a lease, or a *gersuma*, we cannot tell. An alternative would be the deduction of 20 pence from integral quantities of pounds. Obviously the fixing of renders, if inequitable, had been systematic.

Here is an oddity. 18s. 4d. is 220 pence; if this sum is increased by one-quarter, or the difference between the *ora* of 16d. and the 20d. so often actually said to be paid, the result is 275 pence, or one penny less than the 23s. unit of the Somerset comital manors. There may here be no connection, but it is curious that there should be an apparent relationship between two units far from self-explanatory.

The number of ploughlands is given for almost every entry, and only twice is this less than one. Decimal figures are of frequent occurrence:

[1] We have no pre-Inquest figure for Winnianton (*99*).

60 ploughlands		5 instances
50 „		1 instance
40 „		6 instances
30 „		10 „
20 „		9 „
15 „		7 „
10 „		12 „

We cannot assume the accuracy of such figures. But, while many can be no more than approximations, they may not be without their use. Where comparison is possible, the teams amount to almost 50 per cent of the ploughlands. The suggestion is that in any one year only about half the available land is in use.[1] If so, the mysterious Ludgvan entry (*260*) which tells us that 'there is land for 30 or 15 teams' is, though unique, explicable. There is arable land which would occupy 30 teams, but half of the poor soil lies fallow each year to recover from crop-bearing, and on the 15 ploughlands used in 1086 there are in fact only 12 teams at work.

A 2:1 relationship between ploughlands and teams is of course only an average figure. In the more prosperous areas, especially those of north and east Cornwall, we find teams amounting to 70 per cent or little less of the ploughlands, while the figure falls to only about one team per four ploughlands around Winnianton. Over fifty holdings seem to have had no oxen at all, but then the pastoral as opposed to the agricultural element must frequently have been very marked, and the available oxen must often have been used co-operatively. Many a holding cannot show a full team of eight: Thorne (*233*) and Westcott (*239b*), for example, had only two oxen apiece, and Tremar (*234*) a single ox. There was a full team at Buttsbear (*244*) and half a team at Whitstone (*255b*), but the sole recorded inhabitant is in each case a slave. In most of the entries, the presence of very few inhabitants is coupled with only a small number of oxen.

Quite a high proportion of manors (almost one-quarter) have no manorial demesne recorded, and about the same quantity no demesne livestock. But such a figure is probably inaccurate, for we find demesne oxen and/or livestock where no manorial demesne is recorded, e.g. at Penfound (*242*), Tremar (*234*), or Trelowia (*234b*). Nearly one-third of the oxen belong to the demesnes, and there are almost fifty holdings where the only oxen are demesne oxen. The inhabitants of many a Cornish manor must have been very poor indeed. The relationship between recorded teams and ploughlands is inevitably open to suspicion of inaccuracy. We must at times feel that we are not given all the facts; e.g. Bodardle (*249b*) had eight ploughlands and four teams, none of which is

---
[1] So Maitland: *DBB*, p. 425 (490), thought.

—: *The Norman Conquest* (London, 1965).
Lyon, B. D. and Verhulst, A. D.: *Medieval Finance* (Bruges and Providence, 1967).
Maitland, F. W.: *Domesday Book and Beyond* (Cambridge, 1897).
Margary, I. D.: *Roman Roads in Britain* (revised edn., London, 1967).
Matthew, D. J. A.: *The Norman Conquest* (London, 1966).
Miller, E.: *The Abbey and Bishopric of Ely* (Cambridge, 1951).
Mitchell, S. K.: *Taxation in Medieval England* (ed. S. Painter; New Haven, 1951).
Prentout, H.: *Guillaume le Conquérant* (Caen, 1936).
Ramsay, J. H.: *A History of the Revenues of the Kings of England* (Oxford, 1925).
Rennell of Rodd, Lord: *Valley on the March* (Oxford, 1952).
Round, J. H.: *Feudal England* (London, 1895).
Stenton, D. M.: *English Society in the Earlier Middle Ages: 1066–1307* (London, 1952).
Stenton, F. M.: *Anglo-Saxon England* (Oxford, 1943).
—: *William the Conqueror and the Rule of the Normans* (London, 2nd edn., 1925).
Taylor, C. S.: *An Analysis of the Domesday Survey of Gloucestershire* (Bristol, 1889).
Tait, J.: *The Domesday Survey of Cheshire* (Chetham Soc., Manchester, 1916).
Victoria County History of the Counties of England (London, 1900–).
Vinogradoff, P.: *English Society in the Eleventh Century* (Oxford, 1908).
—: *Villainage in England* (Oxford, 1892).
White, L., Jr.: *Medieval Technology and Social Change* (Oxford, 1962).
Whitelock, D.: *The Beginnings of English Society* (London, 1952).
Wolter, H.: *Ordericus Vitalis: ein Beitrag zur kluniazensischen Geschichtsschreibung* (Wiesbaden, 1955).

Articles, etc. (place of publication London unless otherwise stated)

Ballard, A.: 'The Sussex coastline' (*Sussex Archaeol. Collns.*, liii, Lewes, 1910).
Baring, F. H.: 'Domesday and some Twelfth Century Surveys' (*EHR* xii, 1897).
—: 'Oxfordshire traces of the northern insurgents of 1065' (*EHR*, xiii, 1898).
—: 'The Conqueror's Footprints in Domesday' (*EHR*, xiii, 1898).
—: 'The Hidation of Northamptonshire in 1086' (*EHR*, xvii, 1902).
—: 'The pre-Domesday Hidation of Northamptonshire (*EHR*, xvii, 1902).

Baring, F. H.: 'William the Conqueror's March through Hampshire in 1066' (*Papers and Proceedings Hants Field Club*, vii, Southampton, 1915).
Beeler, J.: 'Castles and strategy in Norman and Early Angevin England' (*Speculum*, xxxi, Cambridge, Mass., 1956).
Darlington, R. R.: 'Anglo-Norman Historians' (Inaugural Lecture, 1947).
—: 'The Norman Conquest' (Creighton Lecture for 1962: University of London, 1963).
Davis, R. H. C.: 'The Norman Conquest' (*History*, li, 1966).
Davison, B. K.: 'The Origins of the Castle in England' (*Archaeological Journal*, cxxiv, 1967).
Demarest, E. B.: 'The Hundred-Pennies' (*EHR*, xxxiii, 1918).
—: 'The *Firma Unius Noctis*' (*EHR*, xxxv, 1920).
Douglas, D. C.: 'The Norman Conquest and British Historians' (David Murray Lecture for 1946, Glasgow, 1946).
Edwards, J. G.: 'The Normans and the Welsh March' (*Proc. Brit. Acad.*, xlii, 1956).
Finberg, H. P. R.: 'The Domesday Plough-team' (*EHR*, lxvi, 1951).
Finn, R. W.: 'The *Inquisitio Eliensis* Reconsidered' (*EHR*, lxxv, 1960).
—: 'The Teamland of the Domesday Inquest' (*EHR*, lxxxiii, 1968).
Fowler, G. H.: 'The Devastation of Bedfordshire and and the neighbouring counties in 1065 and 1066' (*Archaeologia*, lxxii, 1922).
Gaut, R. C.: 'A History of Worcestershire Agriculture and Rural Evolution' (Worcester, 1939: chapter 3).
Glover, R.: 'English Warfare in 1066' (*EHR*, lxvii, 1952).
Hart, C. E.: 'The Hidation of Huntingdonshire' (*Proc. Camb. Ant. Soc.*, lxi, Cambridge, 1968).
Harvey, S.: 'Royal revenue and Domesday terminology' (*Econ. Hist. Rev.*, xx, 1967).
Holly, D.: 'The Domesday Geography of Leicestershire' (*Trans. Leics. Arch. Soc.*, xx, Leicester, 1939).
Hoyt, R. S.: 'The Farm of the Manor and Community of the Vill in Domesday Book' (*Speculum*, xxx, 1955).
Lennard, R.: 'The Destruction of Woodland in the Eastern Counties under William the Conqueror' (*Econ. Hist. Rev.*, xv, 1945).
—: 'The Economic Position of the Domesday Villani' (*Econ. Journ.*, lvi, 1946).
—: 'The Economic Position of the Bordars and Cottars of Domesday Book' (*Econ. Journ.*, lxi, 1951).
—: 'The Economic Position of the Domesday Sokeman' (*Econ. Journ.*, lvii, 1947).

—: 'Domesday plough-teams: the south-western evidence' (*EHR*, lx, 1945).
—: 'The composition of the Domesday *caruca*' (*EHR*, lxxxi, 1966).
Mason, J. F. A.: 'Roger of Montgomery and his Sons: 1067–1102' (*Trans. Royal Hist. Soc.*, 5th ser., xiii, 1963).
—: 'The Rapes of Sussex and the Norman Conquest' (*Sussex Archaeol. Collns.*, cii, 1964).
Moore, J. S.: 'The Domesday Teamland: A Reconsideration' (*Trans. Royal Hist. Soc.*, 5th ser., xiv, 1964).
Prestwich, J. O.: 'War and Finance in the Anglo-Norman State' (*Trans. Royal Hist. Soc.*, 5th ser., iv, 1954).
Ritchie, R. L. G.: 'The Normans in England before the Norman Conquest' (Inaugural Lecture, Exeter, 1948).
Round, J. H.: '*Carucata Terrae*' (*EHR*, vii, 1892).
—: 'The Hidation of Northants' (*EHR*, xv, 1900).
—: 'The Castles of the Conquest' (*Archaeologia*, lviii, 1902).
—: 'The Domesday *Ora*' (*EHR*, xxiii, 1908).
Salzman, L. F.: 'The Rapes of Sussex' (*Sussex Archaeol. Collns.*, lxxii, 1931).
Sawyer, P. H.: 'The Wealth of England in the Eleventh Century' (*Trans. Royal Hist. Soc.*, 5th ser., xv, 1965).
Slack, W. J.: 'The Shropshire Ploughmen of Domesday Book' (*Trans. Shrops. Archaeol. and Nat. Hist. Soc.*, l, Shrewsbury, 1939).
Stenton, F. M.: 'Norman London' (Historical Association, London, 1934).
—: 'Sokemen and the Village Waste' (*EHR*, xxxiii, 1918).
—: 'The Road System in Medieval England' (*Econ. Hist. Rev.*, 1st ser., vii, 1936).
Stephenson, C.: 'The *Firma Unius Noctis* and the Custom of the Hundred' (*EHR*, xxxix, 1924).
Sylvester, D.: 'Rural Settlement in Domesday Shropshire' (*Sociological Review*, xxv, 1933).
—: 'Rural Settlement in Cheshire' (*Trans. Hist. Soc. Lancs. and Cheshire*, ci, Liverpool, 1950).
Tait, J.: 'Flintshire in Domesday Book' (*Flintshire Hist. Soc. Pubns.*, xi, Prestatyn, 1925).
Taylor, I.: 'The Ploughland and the Plough' (in *Domesday Studies*, ed. P. E. Dove, i, 1888).
Wightman, W. E.: 'The Palatine Earldom of William fitzOsbern in Gloucestershire and Worcestershire' (*EHR*, lxxvii, 1962).
Wilkinson, B.: 'Northumbrian Separatism in 1065 and 1066' (*Bull. John Rylands Lib.*, xxiii, Manchester, 1939).

Index

Since references to the principal towns of Anglo-Norman England mostly occur in the section for the shire in which they are situated, very few of these have been indexed, nor have villages and persons only incidentally mentioned. Names of laymen will for the most part be found under the places from which their owners derived their style; e.g. for Walter d'Aincourt, *see* Aincourt, but where there is no particular association with a place, *see* under the personal name, e.g. Ælfgar.

Abingdon Abbey, 10, 78, 79, 82, 83
Acres, geld, 293
—, values of, 106, 209, 244, 247–9, 254, 259, 266, 272
Ælfgar, earl of Mercia, 89, 140, 151, 165, 180, 253
Ælfgarson, Beorhtric, 284, 296, 297
Agricultural services of peasantry, 189, 275
Aincourt, Walter d', 183, 190, 216
Aiulf, sheriff of Dorset, 274, 284, 303
Alan, Earl *see* Richmond
Alselin, Geoffrey, 183
Almsmen, 96
Amounderness, 210
Angli, holdings and teams of, 180
Anglo-Saxon Chronicle, 5, 27
animalia, as render, 164
Ansculf, Ghilo fitz, 82
—, William fitz, 82, 177, 179
Arable, conversion of pasture to, 29
Archenfield, 140, 142, 143, 151
Assarts, 29, 147, 247
Assaying of coins, 52, 89, 101, 105, 287 and *see* blanched money
Assessments (*see also* geld)
—, beneficial, 100, 179, 191, 247
—, duodecimal *see* ploughlands
—, reduction of, 73, 100, 239
—, relation to ploughlands of, 18

Atiscros Hundred, 168, 171, 172
Auberville, Roger d', 252
Aubrey, Earl *see* Coucy
Avranches, Hugh d' *see* Chester, earl of
Axholme, Isle of, 188, 213, 214

Baderon, William fitz, 149
Bailleul, Rainald of, 165
Bainard, Ralf, 269
Baldric, Hugh fitz, 199, 203, 204, 210
Baldwin *see* Meules
Balliol MS. 350, 144
BARING, F. H., 19, 117, 240
Bath Abbey, 137, 289, 294
Battle Abbey, 43
Bayeux, Odo, bp. of, 4, 42, 43, 45, 46, 47, 55, 89, 100, 121, 212, 231, 238, 244, 261, 264, 269
'Beneficial hidation', 18, 132, 226, and *see* geld, exemption from
Berewicks of manors, 8, 56, 129, 133, 152, 153, 154, 168, 174, 180, 183, 184, 186, 187, 188, 193, 194, 195, 196, 199, 200, 202, 204, 205, 206, 208, 211, 240
Berkhamsted, Great, 17, 20, 106
—, Little, 17, 20
Bernay, Ralf de, 143
Beverley, St John of, 206
Bigot, Roger, 244, 260, 265, 269, 271
BISHOP, T. A. M., 27, 190, 302

313

INDEX

Blanched money, 76, 89, 101, 105, 137, 149, 183, 240, 254, 265, 287
Blanch farm, 76
Bleddyn ap Meredydd, 141
Blond, Robert, 114, 269, 271
'Blooms' of iron, 11, 293
bordarii
—, holdings of, 102, 106, 113–14, 258, 267, 274, 293
—, rents of, 24, 69, 71, 114, 132, 173, 177, 178
—, teams of, 31, 50, 64, 70, 74, 77, 81, 82, 91, 96, 102, 106, 114, 122, 126–7, 132, 139, 150, 161–2, 173, 180, 184, 185, 192, 202–3, 210, 220, 226, 232, 259, 281, 286, 293, 298, 305
Boroughs, 5, 23, 24, 40, 90, 94, 122, 173, 177, 178, 200, 253, 279, 285, 288, 296, 298
bovarii, 31
Braiose, William de, 56
Bretteville, Gilbert de, 119, 278
breves, 11, 145, 193–4, 210, 263
Brian, *see* Penthièvre
BROOKS, F. W., 205
Buci, Robert de, 228
Bully, Roger de, 190
burgenses, 96, 200, 205
—, rents of, 162
buri, 82
'Burnt money', 105, 137, 296, and *see* assaying of coins
Burton Abbey, 179
Bury St Edmunds Abbey, 238, 244, 245, 259, 266, 267

Caerleon, 143
CAMPBELL, E. M. J., 94
Canterbury, abp. and abpric. of, 41–2, 53, 109
caput manerii, *see* manors
Carrying-service, 105
carucae or *carucatae nunquam geldantes*, 29, 292
Carucates, 29, 95, 179, 185, 191, 196, 220, 223, 248, 266, 286, and *see* ploughlands
castellariae, 47, 143, 146, 150, 151, 164
Castles, 123, 136, 140, 156, 170, 177, 183, 237, 250, 251, 285, 290, 296, 300, 301, 302
censores or *censarii*, 55, 179, 184, 185, 195, 203, 204, 210, 218, 283
Cerne Abbey, 283, 285
Changes in population, 243–4, 255–8, 267–8, 274–5, and *see* slaves
Charnwood Forest, 229
Chase, rights of, 120
Chertsey Abbey, 51, 53, 55
Chester, bp. & bpric. of, 172, 178
—, Earl Hugh of, 26, 170, 172, 173, 174, 216, 228, 233, 260
Churches, value of, 42, 69, 201, 208, 237, 260, 266, 279, 284
'Circuits' of Domesday Inquest, 23, 84, 116
clamores, 193, 194, 198, 212, 223–4
Clare, Richard fitzGilbert of, 47, 51, 52, 55, 100, 252, 257, 260, 264, 297
Claville, Walter de, 297, 303
Clifford, 142, 143, 151
coceti, 281, 286, 292
Coinage, 3
coliberti, 70, 82, 256, 281, 294
—, rents of, 71, 149
Comital manors, 24, 287, 303
Commendation, 55
consuetudines, *see* customary dues
cotarii, 49, 62, 64, 107, 281, 292
—, holdings of, 102, 106, 112, 114
—, rents of, 114
—, teams of, 82, 106
Coucy, Earl Aubrey de, 124, 238, 284
'Counted coin', *see numerum, ad*
County Hidage, 167
Courseulles, Roger de, 294
Coutances, Geoffrey, bp. of, 11, 100, 285, 289, 290, 292
Cows, as render, 164
Craven, 199, 210
Crowland Abbey, 212
Customary dues, 48, 61, 95, 101, 148, 149, 151

DARBY, H. C., xii, 112
DARLINGTON, R. R., 10
Dates of valuations of manors, 8, 10–11, 122

314

INDEX

DAVIS, R. H. C., 245
Dean Forest, 138
defensio, 147
Deficiencies of Domesday Book:
  anonymous holdings, 32
  arbitrary figures for ploughlands, *see* ploughlands
  illogical composition of circuits, 23, 117, 122, 127
  incorrect quantities, 9, 46, 97, 102, 104, 113, 118, 265, 295
  interpretation, difficulties of, 10–11, 138
  lack of information regarding complex manors, 32
  omission of holdings, 41, 186
— information, 7, 245
Delamere Forest, 170, 174
Demesne, 9–10, 103, 110, 120, 156, 161, 162, 164
—, fiscal, 13, 74, 166
— livestock, 96, 243, 255, 269, 270, 271, 301
—, manorial, 29, 151, 292, 293, 304
— ploughlands, 28, 120
  — plough-oxen, 76–7, 114, 119, 185, 211
—, royal, 24, 47, 147, 224
Denbighshire, 172
descriptio, 137
Domesday Geography of England, xii, 25, 90, 107, 108, 112, 116, 120, 148, 150, 158, 171, 186, 189, 191, 193, 204, 206, 208, 214, 218, 233, 302
Domesday Monachorum, 41–3, 47–9, 53, 61–2
domus defensabilis, 147
Dore, River (Golden Valley), 144
Douai, Walter de, 296
Dues, *see* customary dues and individual substance to berendered
Duodecimal assessments, *see* ploughlands
'Duplicate' or parallel entries, 11, 122, 129, 144, 181, 197, 200, 240, 299
Durham, bp. of, 194

Eadgifu, 133
Earl's third penny, 152–3

Edith, Queen, 52, 55, 68, 164, 165, 288, 297
—, sister of Earl Odda, 151
— the Fair, 98, 253
Edmund, King, 142
Edric of Laxfield, 262
  Streona, 141, 165
  'the Wild', 141–2, 146, 152, 156, 165, 168
Edward the Confessor, King, 24, 53, 61, 137, 151, 153, 159, 164, 224, 235, 253, 284, 296
Edwine, Earl, 95, 122, 129, 141, 159, 164, 165, 168, 172, 173, 174, 180, 196, 209, 229, 235
Eel-renders, 63, 239
elemosina, holdings in, 96, 114
Elmham, bp. of, 264
Ely Abbey, 97–8, 105, 260, 266, 267
Englefield, 168, 172
Englishmen and Anglo-Danes surviving the Conquest, 55, 71, 75, 91, 96, 121, 126, 133, 138, 165–6, 174–5, 179, 198–9, 220, 227, 257, 281, 286, 294
Ermine Street, 16, 101, 104, 135, 213, 215, 225
Ermin Way, 135
Escalers, Hardwin d', 97
Eu, Robert d', 57, 59, 61, 63
—, William d', 134
Eudes fitzHerbert, *see* Ryes
Eustace II of Boulogne, Count, 42, 46, 102, 254, 255, 263
'Evesham A', 127–8, 165
Evesham Abbey, 127–8, 165
— Chronicle, 188
Ewias Harold, 142, 143, 146, 150
Excerpta, 41
Exestan, 168, 171
Exeter, bp. and bpric. of, 58, 137, 277, 295, 299, 300
— Domesday, 8, 10, 30, 277, 282, 288

Falcons, as dues, *see* hawks
Farm (*firma*)
—, night's, *see firma unius noctis*
— of boroughs, 122
  salt-wiches, 179
  shire, 24

315

INDEX

Farm-rents of manors, 24, 46–8, 52–3, 61–2, 69, 75, 80, 90, 101–2, 105, 112, 119, 122, 125, 129, 136, 152, 153, 162–3, 171, 218, 231, 240, 254, 264–5, 270, 280, 282, 296–7, 303
— -rent in excess of value of manor, 46–7, 52–3, 61, 68–9, 72, 73, 75–6, 79, 90, 92, 123, 134, 136, 137, 149, 184, 218, 245, 248, 252, 253, 264–5, 270, 278, 280
Farringdon, Ælfsige of, 119, 136, 138
feorm, see farm
Ferrières, Henry de, 79, 80, 124, 228, 252
FINBERG, H. P. R., 299
firma unius noctis, 69, 95, 136, 149, 253, 278, 282, 284, 285, 287, 297
Fisheries, 24, 61, 69, 89, 90
—, dues from, 48
—, rents of, 13, 63, 161, 218
Flintshire, 172
Florence of Worcester, see Worcester
Food-renders, 24, 101, 136
Forest, 25, 26–7, 34, 52, 63, 68, 69, 70, 71–3, 79, 89, 111, 125, 128, 130, 138, 146–7, 164, 167, 169, 170–1, 174, 178–9, 183, 187, 188, 189, 202, 224, 237–8, 278, 281, 285, and see names of Forests
—, equation of 'park' with, 63, 68
—, equation of 'waste' with, 26–7, 125
—, extension of, 52, 68, 118, 125, 130, 146, 224
—, land taken into royal, 25
—, lowered value through inclusion in, 26–7, 68, 138, 178
—, poor soil of, 70
Foresters, 55, 147, 173, 174
Formulae of Domesday Book, 10–11, 52
Foss Way, 123, 135, 188, 213, 229, 230, 231, 236, 289
FOWLER, G. H., 19, 21, 94, 117, 286
francigenae, 62, 111, 150
—, teams of, 139, 150, 173
free men, see *liberi homines*
Furness with Cartmel, 210

gablatores, 283
gablum, 48, 49, 50, 53, 55, 283

gafol, 48, 55
GALBRAITH, V. H., 7, 97, 101, 144, 240
'gardens' (*orti*), 186
Geld accounts, 13, 282, 285, 294
—, assessment to, 167–8, 233
— -carucates, 29
—, effects of, 12–13
—, exemption from, 13, 95, 100, 111, 125, 132–3, 147, 150, 151, 165–6, 220, 225, 299, and see assessments, beneficial
— levy, 13
— liability, 12–13, 100, 111, 112
gersuma, 47, 48, 129, 245, 253, 265, 271, 303
Ghent, Gilbert of, 216
Gherbod of St Bertin, Flanders, 173
Gifford, Osbern, 278
—, Walter, 273
Gillingham Forest, 285, 290
Glastonbury Abbey, 11, 277, 287, 288, 291, 294
Godgifu, Countess, 124, 165, 180
Godric *minister*, 101, 253, 265, 271
Godwine, Earl, 24, 58, 66, 74
— family, 284, 287, 296, and see Edith, Gytha, Harold, Leofwine, Tostig
Gold mark, see mark
—, ounce of, 62, 79, 95, 101, 105, 149, 231, 251, 252
Grain-rents, 95, 101, 149, 279
Grentmaisnil, Hugh de, 233
Grifin ap Meredydd, 152
Gruffydd ap Llewelyn, 140–1, 172
Gwynedd, 140
Gytha, widow of Earl Godwine, 297

haiae (deer-hays), 147, 159
Hardraada, Harald, 141, 205
Harold Godwineson, Earl, 55, 66, 74, 105, 115, 117, 140, 141, 151, 159, 165, 168, 180, 196, 206, 224, 252, 253, 293, 297, 300
— sons of, 286, 296
HART, C., 84, 225, 239, 286
HARVEY, S., 15
Hastings, Battle of, 20, 44, 55, 227, 281
Hawks, dues of, 24, 53, 149–50, 164, 279
Hay, sale of, 90

INDEX

Hen-rents, 12, 279
Hereford, bp. and bpric. of, 137, 145, 243
—, Earl Ralf of, 140, 151
—, Earl Roger of, 75, 101, 125, 127, 128, 143, 144, 145, 146
Herefordshire Domesday 1160/70, 144
Hereward's rebellion, 100, 225
Herring-renders, 260, 263
Hesdin, Arnulf of, 11, 64, 134, 278, 280, 294
Hidation, beneficial, 18, 226
Hide, 226
—, in relation to peasant holdings, 112
—, value in relation to ploughland, 18
Holy Trinity, Rouen, 109
homines, 31, 113, 226
—, rents of, 125, 129, 163, 185
—, teams of, 150, 161, 180, 219
Honey-renders, 95, 101, 130, 146, 150, 271, 279, 283
Horwood Forest, 138
HOSKINS, W. G., 288
hospites, 146, 147, 158, 161, 163, 170
Hounds (dogs), dues of, 150
—, payments for, 95
Housecarls, 115
House-dues, 279, 288
Hundred
—, evidence of, 8, 12, 60, 279
—, land in no, 151
—, profits of pleas of, 136, 152-3, 164, 170, 245, 253, 265, 271
—, third penny of, 152-3, 297
Hunting and hunting rights, 130, 147, 159, 164, 173, 183, 197, 285
Huntingdon, Eustace of, 222-4, 225
Huntsmen, 55, 71

Icknield Way, 87-8, 101, 107, 120
Inland, 120, 193
Inquisitio Comitatus Cantabrigiensis, 96-8, 101-2
Inquisitio Eliensis, xi, 28, 96-8, 101-2, 226-7, 242, 248-9, 257, 259
Interpretation of valuation figures, 10-11
Iron, renders of, 11, 90, 150
Ironworks, 238

Ivry, Robert d', 134, 136

Judith, Countess, 102, 103, 233
Juries, Hundred, 103, 178, 233, 238, 252, 264
—, Shire, 133, 224

Kind, renders in, *see* under substance rendered
King's Forest, *see* Forest
Kingswood Forest, 138
Knights, *see milites*

Lacy (Lassi), Ilbert de, 194, 198
—, Roger de, 146
—, Walter de, 143
Lead-mining, 42
Leeming Lane, 267
legati regis, 137, 266
LEMMON, C. H., 19, 44-5, 79, 94
LENNARD, R. W., 31, 48, 114, 131, 134, 247
Leofric, Earl, 24, 165
Leofwine Godwineson, Earl, 107, 297
Liber Eliensis, 4, 6
Liber Exoniensis, 275, 276, 295
liberi homines, 29, 31, 55, 103, 113, 132, 163, 175, 176, 247, 257, 261, 264, 275
—, holdings of, 132, 138, 180
—, rents of, 265
—, teams of, 139, 150, 161-2
Lincoln, bpric. of, 119-20, 191, 216, 224, 238
Llewelyn, *see* Gruffydd
London, 3, 5, 20, 21, 45, 54, 79, 85, 89, 94, 101, 104, 107, 251, 254, 255, 281
—, bpric. of, 109, 112
Lonsdale, 210
LOYN, H. R., 4

Madoc, 152
MAITLAND, F. W., 7-8, 12, 103, 112, 113, 191, 228, 232, 233, 240, 304
Malet, Robert, 260, 265
—, William, 264
Malmesbury Abbey, 279

INDEX

Malvern Forest, 128, 130
Manneville, Geoffrey de, 113, 267
Manors
—, addition of land and men to, 245, 251, 257, 265, 271
—, appropriations from royal, 92, 105, 137, 143, 278
—, *caput* of, 25, 69, 129, 178, 180, 184, 187, 188, 193, 194, 196, 227, 246
—, changes in composition of, 56, 60, 65, 68, 79, 92, 97, 105, 136, 137, 143, 149, 164, 174, 223, 251, 269, 271, 278, 287, 288, 295–6
—, comital, 24, 287, 303
—, components of, 8, 137, 152, 153, 164, 171, 177, 180, 187, 188
—, composite and complex, 41, 158, 181, 184, 246
—, consolidation of former, 29, 143, 146, 157, 177, 196, 212
—, dispersion of Yorkshire, 246
—, potential additions to, 134, 204
—, rents of, *see* farm
—, royal, *see* Terra Regis
 with 'appendages', 177, 180, 297
mansiones, 184
— *de regno*, 121
Marches of Wales, *see* Wales
Markets, 12, 261, 269
Mark, gold, 58, 62, 71, 266, 271, 268
—, *ora-*, 171, 190
—, silver, 53, 148, 190, 202, 218, 232, 239, 254, 266, 272, 297, 303
Marlborough, Alfred of, 151
Marshland, 3, 28, 288, 291
MASON, J. F. A., 57
Matilda, Queen, 55, 88, 89, 137, 277, 282, 297
Meadow, 7, 77, 186, 220
—, rent of, 107
 recorded in terms of oxen, 84
 in New Forest, 72
—, value of, 130, 271
Melchet Forest, 278
Mellent, Count of, 233
Meredydd, 150, 152
Meules, Baldwin de, 297, 303
milites, 46, 111, 115, 161, 207, 294

—, holdings of, 164
—, rents of, 163, 164
—, teams of, 139, 173, 180
Mill-rents and values, 11, 13, 63, 90, 136, 163, 202, 218, 239, 279
Mills, 77, 149, 171, 184, 186, 237, 270
ministri, 47, 101, 105, 137, 265
Mint-dues, 24, 287, 289, 290
Mohun, William de, 287, 289, 290
Montfort, Hugh de, 263
Montgomery, Earl Roger of, 51, 56, 63, 68, 122, 153, 156, 158, 159, 161, 164
Monmouth, 143
Monnow, River, 140
Morkere, Earl, 93, 159, 164, 165, 168, 173, 174, 180, 196, 206, 209, 229, 235
Mortain, Count Robert of, 11, 56, 57, 59, 61, 105, 194, 238, 264, 277, 285, 290, 297, 299, 300, 303, 305
Mortemer, Ralf de, 133, 164
Moustières, Lisois de, 97

New Forest, *see* Forest
Norman, William fitz, 143, 147
Northamptonshire Geld Roll, 235, 239
Northumbrian revolt of 1065, 93, 118, 183, 188, 221, 225, 228, 229, 235, 237, 240
Noyers, William de, 265, 271
numerum, ad, 53, 105, 265, 282, 288, 296, 297

Odda, Earl, 151
Offa's Dyke, 171
ora, 13–14, 90, 96, 98, 102, 106, 107, 125, 136, 147, 148, 163, 171, 184–5, 190, 197, 202, 206, 209, 211, 217–18, 232, 239, 248, 254, 266, 271–2, 296, 303
—, *de xx in*, 14, 53, 76, 129, 137, 148–9, 179, 184–5, 190, 272, 287, 297
Orderic Vitalis, ix, 4, 141, 142, 251
Osbern, William fitz, 4, 71, 75, 116, 119, 129, 132, 136, 137, 141, 142, 143, 144, 151, 156, 250
Oxen, plough—*see* teams and classes of inhabitants
Oyly, Robert d', 137

INDEX

Pannage, 147, 201
Parks, 63, 68, 159
Pasture, 7, 90, 220, 258, 288, 301
—, conversion of arable to, 29
—, rent and value of, 11–12, 63, 90, 107, 149, 170, 297
   taken into Forest, 72
Pence, ounce of, 163
—, pounds of, 164
'Penny, Third', see 'Third Penny'
pensum, ad, see weight, payment by
Penthièvre, Brian de, 11, 141, 299
Perci, William de, 194
Pershore Abbey, 137
Peterborough Abbey, 220, 223, 270
Peverel, Ralf, 249, 263, 270
—, William, 233
Picot of Cambridge, 97–8, 253
Pigs, see swine
Piratical raids, 15, 25, 27, 135, 251, 292, 296, 305
Pleas of Hundred and shire, 122
Ploughlands, 7, 14, 16–17, 28–31, 53–5, 63–4, 73, 74, 76, 81, 90, 95–6, 102, 106, 110, 118, 119, 120, 125–6, 131, 138, 148, 152, 160–1, 170, 171, 173, 179, 185, 190, 191, 211, 219, 225–6, 227, 232–3, 239–40, 241, 254, 280, 282, 285, 291–2, 295, 298–9, 303–4
—, approximation of quantities of, 28, 280, 304
—, artificiality of figures for, 28, 40, 49–50, 54, 70, 81, 110, 176, 185, 191, 219, 225–6, 233, 241, 280, 291, 298
—, blank for quantities of, 40, 49, 63, 70, 74, 76, 81
—, demesne, 28, 120, 225
—, duodecimal quantities of, 28, 84–5, 121, 125–6, 171, 179, 280
—, excess of, 54
—, formulae for, 73, 74, 160
—, relation of assessments to, 17, 18, 223
—, relation of teams to, 15, 39–40, 50
   tilled with teams of different manor, 29, and see teams, syndicated
   unmentioned for sub-tenancies, 28, 30, 50, 54, 70, 76

Ploughshares, renders of, 90
Poignant, Richard, 271
Poitiers, William of, ix, 46, 100, 251
Poitou, Roger of, 190, 210, 211, 216, 261, 269
Powys, 140
Premiums for leases, 79, 149, 303, (see also *gersuma*)
Priests
—, holdings of, 106, 132
—, payments of, 49, 146
—, teams of, 150, 161, 173, 180, 203, 207

Radmen
—, holdings of, 132, 138
—, rents of, 163, 164
—, teams of, 129, 132, 139, 150, 161–2, 173
Raimbeaucourt, Guy de, 233
Ralf II, Earl of East Anglia, 100, 101, 262, 263, 265, 269, 270, 273, 274
—, Earl of Hereford, 140, 151
Ramsey Abbey, 95, 227, 238, 269
Rapes, Sussex, 56–7, 60
Reeveland, 143
Reeves, 45, 61, 96, 103, 106, 137, 150, 183, 233, 264, 265, 294
—, Welsh, 134
Renders in kind, see under substance rendered
Rents, see under Farm and classes of inhabitants, e.g. villeins
Revolts against Norman government, 27, 100, 141–2, 156, 168, 214, 225, 228, 237, 285, 286, 290, 296, 302
Rhiwallon, 141
'Ribble & Mersey, Between', 211
Richard, Osbern fitz, 131, 147, 151, 190
Richard's Castle, 143, 144
Richmond, Earl Alan of, 193, 198, 199, 207, 208, 212, 216, 260, 269, 270
Rhuddlan, 141, 172, 173
—, Robert of, 172, 173, 174
Robert *latinarius*, 47
Rochester, bpric. of, 43
Rockingham Forest, 237
Romney, 44
'Rouen money', 297

319

INDEX

ROUND, J. H., 69, 101, 235, 238, 240
Ryes, Eudes fitzHerbert de, 64, 97, 103, 238, 263

St Albans Abbey, 105
    Augustine's, Canterbury, 41, 46, 49
    Denis, Paris, 133
    Mary's, Cormeilles, 132
    Mary's, Lire, 77
    —, Rouen, 297
    —, Winchester, 278
    Paul's, London, 109, 112
    Peter's, Gloucester, 133
    Petrock's, 299, 300, 303
Salisbury, bp. & bpric. of, 279, 282
—, Edward of, 54, 137, 280, 284
Salmon, renders of, 150
Salt, 130–1, 170, 283
—, wood for producing, 129–31, 148
Saltpans, 12, 13, 63, 171
SALZMAN, L. F., 57, 101, 303
SAWYER, P. H., 3, 127
Scrob, Richard fitz, 141, 151
Selwood Forest, 290, 294
semper, use of, 10, 51, 242–3, 246, 249, 254–5, 259–60, 267, 268
servientes, 152, 161
Severn, River, 154, 155, 156, 159
Shaftesbury Abbey, 284
Sheep, renders of, 150, 279
Sheriffs (and *see* under names of sheriffs), 74, 75, 101, 105, 122, 124, 151, 240, 265, 271, 283
—, appropriations by, 92, 97, 100, 137, 143, 278
    as farmers of manors, 34, 47, 127, 129–130, 287, 297, 303
—, farm of, 34, 55, 127, 129–30
—, payments of, 129, 130, 136
—, receipts of, 52, 53, 95
Sherwood Forest, 187, 188, 189
Shires, pleas of, 122
Silver, *see* mark of, white
—, payments of pure, 183
sine censu, 11
Siward *dives*, 165
—, Earl, 196, 209

Slaves, 162, 185
—, absence in Hunts. of, xi
—, high local figures for, 76–7, 294, 302
—, low local figures for, 112
—, possible emancipation of, 82–3, 256
—, reduction of quantity of, 6, 243, 244, 255, 256, 267–8, 274, 294
—, unexpected absences from text of, 40–1, 63, 74, 81, 176, 185, 191, 219, 226–7, 241
Smiths, 55
Socage dues, 149, 216, 245
Sokeland, 176, 180, 186, 187, 188, 193, 194, 195, 196, 197, 202, 204, 205, 206, 208, 211
Sokemen, 29, 31, 55, 96, 98, 176, 185, 191, 195, 197, 202, 204, 205, 206, 207, 210, 219, 220, 225, 226, 232, 239, 240, 244, 247, 248, 256–8, 265, 267, 268, 270, 274–5
—, holdings of, 91, 101, 103, 105, 113, 247, 257, 275
—, rents of, 101, 184, 190, 204, 239
—, teams of, 90, 185, 192, 203, 204, 207, 208, 210, 219, 226, 232, 267
Sokeright, 224, 254, 265, 271
SOUTHERN, R. W., 24
Stane Street, 250
STENTON, F. M., 191, 216, 219–20, 222–3, 226, 228
STEVENSON, W. H., 199
Stigand, abp., 43, 47, 68, 79, 95, 101, 137, 278, 284, 285
Stur, William fitz, 75
Summaries, Domesday, 97, 193–4, 210, 287, 293
Sweyn, sheriff of Essex, 251, 258, 267
Swine-rents, 48, 63, 146, 147, 279

tailla, 189, 200, 216–17, 220
Taillebois, Ivo, 95, 212, 216
—, Ralf, 92
TAIT, J., 153, 156, 164, 165, 167
Tale, payment by, 89, 90, 278, 279
Tavistock Abbey, 295, 297, 299, 302
TAYLOR, C. S., 138

320

INDEX

Teams (plough-)
   as basis for quantity of ploughlands, 28–31, 41
—, deficiency or surplus of, 17, 29, 53–5, 63–4, 70, 74, 76–7, 81–2, 90, 131–2, 135, 138, 148, 152, 153, 160–1, 162, 170, 172, 177, 179, 185, 191, 219, 226, 229, 233, 241, 266, 272–3, 277, 280, 285 291, 298, 304–5
—, demesne, 172
—, hiring of, 28, 81
—, meadow for, 84
—, number of oxen composing, 50–1
—, possibility of employing additional, 90, 120, 138, 146, 148, 160–1, 241, 243, 254, 267
—, potential omission of, 41
—, syndicated, 29, 54, 77, 148, 203, 219, 220
terra villanorum, 49, 50, 55, 62, 162, 164
Terrae Occupatae, 288, 295
Terrae Regis, 196, 206, 210, 222, 223, 224, 228, 233, 238, 249, 277, 287—8
— —, appropriations from, 79–80, 136, 137, 143, 224, 253, 296–7, 303
— —, exclusion of from calculations, 24, 35, 228
— —, in New Forest, 73–4
— —, possible early compilation of DB for, 194
— —, values of manors on, 24, 34, 52, 73–4, 75, 79, 95, 101, 105, 119, 128–9, 134, 137–8, 149–50, 178, 180, 183, 186–7, 208, 212, 215–16, 223, 231, 253–4, 265–6, 271
Textus Roffensis, 41
Thegnland, 143, 176, 180, 278, 294
Thegns, 55, 105, 126, 137, 179, 211, 226, 227, 280, 284, 295
   connected with hunting, 164
—, decline in number of, 96, 103
—, earls', 115, 151
   equated with free men, 175
—, holdings of, 163, 298
—, king's, 75, 114, 115, 138, 194, 198, 210, 227, 277, 281, 286, 294, 298
—, possible reduction to villeinage of, 91, 185

—, teams of, 173
Thetford, bp. of, 261, 269
'Third penny', 152, 279, 281, 288, 297
Thoret, 165, 174
Thorkill, *see* Warwick
Tison, Gilbert, 203
Tolls, 12, 89
Tonbridge, Richard fitzGilbert of, *see* Clare
Tosny, Ralf de, 127
Tostig Godwineson, Earl, 74, 105, 141, 196, 206, 209, 211, 235
Turbary, 218

Usk, River, 123

Valognes, Peter de, 105, 253, 255
Valuations, artificial, 196, 206, 209
Veci, Robert de, 212
Villeins, 81
—, holdings of, 102, 106, 112–13, 132, 197, 258, 267, 274, 281, 293
—, rents of, 49, 62, 71, 77, 113, 132, 145, 149, 159, 161, 163, 185, 197, 202, 206, 281, 283, 293
—, royal, 13
—, teams of, 30–1, 50, 55, 64, 70–1, 74, 77, 81, 82, 91, 96, 102, 106, 113, 114, 121–2, 126, 132, 139, 148, 150, 161–2, 173, 180, 184, 185, 192, 202, 206, 209–210, 218, 219, 226, 232, 241, 259, 281, 286, 293, 298, 305
VINOGRADOFF, P., 4, 112

Wales, 14, 26–7, 116, 135, 140–7, 151, 156, 168, 171–3
—, Marches of, 140–2, 151
Waltheof, Earl, 97, 101
Warenne, William de, 56, 57, 61, 100, 224, 269
Warren of hares, 12
Warwick, Thorkill of, 124
Waste, 25–8, 33–4, 72, 89, 95, 124, 126–7, 129–30, 131, 144–8, 152, 154, 156, 157–8, 168, 169, 177, 179–80, 183–4, 188–9, 196, 197, 204–6, 208–9, 210, 211, 218–19, 224, 229, 235, 237–8, 278, 285, 290–1, 296, 302

321

INDEX

caused by inclusion in the Forest, 26, 34, 72, 125
—, interpretation of formulae for, 26–7
Waste, partial, 26, 33–4, 143, 145, 154, 157, 158, 189, 197, 204, 218, 220, 237
—, resulting from military activity south of the Trent, 27, 124, 127
—, resulting from piracy, 25, 296
—, resulting from possible transference of people, 27, 156, 169, 170, 178, 179, 183, 190, 214
    with potential value, 25, 89, 129, 145, 147, 158, 187, 189, 197, 208, 218
    with rent or value stated, 25, 95, 149, 157, 163, 169, 170, 189, 195, 197, 200, 208, 296
Watling Street, 21, 86, 87, 88, 92, 104, 105, 109
Wat's Dyke, 171
Weight, payment by, 52, 68, 76, 89, 101, 105, 137, 253, 254, 265, 278, 296, 279
Wells, bp. and bpric. of, 287, 294
Welshmen, 140–2
—, rents of, 158, 163, 164
—, teams of, 150, 161–2

Westminster Abbey, 51, 54, 109, 112, 128, 133, 252
'White silver', 137, and *see* blanched money
Wiches, salt-, 168, 169, 170
Wigmore, 143, 146
Wilton Nunnery, 278
Wimborne Forest, 285
Winchcombe Abbey, 135, 138
Winchester, bp. and bpric. of, 69, 75
Wirce, Geoffrey de, 124, 238
Woodland, 7, 12, 77, 89, 90, 107, 111, 125, 130, 173
—, hunting rights in, 130, 147
—, importance to sheriffs of, 130–1
—, pasturable, 202
    reckoned in terms of swine-pasture, 84
—, renting of, 12, 90, 107, 125, 130, 149
—, value of, 271
Worcester, bp. and bpric. of, 116, 123, 130, 131, 133, 138, 165
—, Florence of, 100, 141
Wye, River, 133, 140, 144
Wymarc, Robert fitz, 151

York, abp. and abpric. of, 134, 196, 200, 206, 216
—, St Peter's, 198, 208